Uva Berry
1500 Catherine St. Apt. Q
Walla Walla, WA 99362

AFTER ETAN

AFTER ETAN

THE MISSING CHILD CASE THAT HELD AMERICA CAPTIVE

LISA R. COHEN

GRAND CENTRAL
PUBLISHING

NEW YORK   BOSTON

Grand Central Publishing
Hachette Book Group
237 Park Avenue
New York, NY 10017

Visit our Web site at www.HachetteBookGroup.com.

Printed in the United States of America

First Edition: May 2009
10 9 8 7 6 5 4 3 2 1

Grand Central Publishing is a division of Hachette Book Group, Inc.
The Grand Central Publishing name and logo is a trademark of
Hachette Book Group, Inc.

Library of Congress Cataloging-in-Publication Data

Cohen, Lisa R.
    After Etan : the missing child case that held America captive / Lisa R. Cohen. — 1st ed.
    p. cm.
    Includes index.
    Summary: "The full story of Etan Patz—his family's long search for him, the
extraordinary efforts to bring his abductor to justice, and the investigation that solved a
decades-long mystery."—Provided by the publisher.
    ISBN 978-0-446-58251-3
    1. Patz, Etan Kalil, 1972–1979.   2. Missing children—New York (State)—
New York.   3. Kidnapping victims—New York (State)—New York.
4. Kidnapping—New York (State)—New York.   I. Title.
    HV6762.U5C65 2009
    364.15'4092—dc22
                                                                        2008053713

*To my three beloved teammates. And to my co-captain, Mike,
who let me run with the ball . . . no matter where it led.*

Contents

Prologue

In 1981 I interviewed a couple named Stanley and Julie Patz.... This was before pictures on milk cartons, or AMBER Alerts, or even the National Center for Missing & Exploited Children, which Etan's disappearance helped create. Stan Patz is a photographer, and a picture he had taken of his son, bright eyes, long bangs, became iconic overnight. Etan Patz: the most famous missing child since the Lindbergh baby.
   —*Anna Quindlen,* Newsweek, *April 19, 2004*

"I've been thinking about letting my nine-year-old ride the city bus to school on his own come September. I think it's really important for his sense of independence."
   "I have just two words for you... Etan Patz."
   —*two New York moms overheard in Central Park, summer 2004*

Etan Patz. Those two words are code. To many Americans and to an entire generation of New Yorkers, the two words are synonymous with the terror of suddenly, mysteriously losing a child forever.

On May 25, 1979, six-year-old Etan Patz vanished sometime between 8 and 8:10 a.m., somewhere between his home and the school bus stop. He was walking the two short blocks solo for the very first time. His smiling face on the posters, billboards, and tabloid front pages that took his place tugged at America's heartstrings in a singular way. Like another iconic New York tragedy—Kitty Genovese's brutal stabbing death in 1964 as neighbors turned a deaf ear to her anguished cries for help—the Patz case didn't touch most of us personally, yet it somehow went beyond the purely shocking, to fundamentally alter our collective perceptions. And like events of more historical significance—the Kennedy assassination or September 11—Etan Patz's disappearance off his own street in broad daylight is a moment frozen in time, a bridge leading us away from a more innocent world, where such horror couldn't possibly happen, to a darker one, where it did.

Today our president doesn't travel unprotected in an open car like John F. Kennedy did in 1963. Americans stand acceptingly in long lines at the airport and uneasily scrutinize the faces around us; and when a scream is heard outside our window in the early morning hours, we think twice about ignoring it. Thirty years after Etan vanished, his case has also changed our cultural landscape in ways that we take for granted: about our children's safety, their independence, our peace of mind.

Today some of the children missing in 1979 would be found more readily, with the help of resources like the National Center for Missing and Exploited Children, and AMBER Alerts. Today, our children learn about "good touch, bad touch," family security passwords, and, for better or worse, they're intensely aware of stranger danger. So are the parents, the ones who don't let their kids walk alone to school these days; schedule them to the hilt with supervised playdates; and shake their heads sadly because those same children live in fear of the world outside their backyards. For most of those parents, the Patz case seems like a mythic, cautionary tale, an artifact of a past era. But quite a few of them remember the Patz case vividly. One mother recently told me, with tears in her eyes, "It changed everything."

Whenever I mention my years of reporting on the case to one of those parents, I get that immediate jolt of recognition, like a current of electricity, followed by a rush of questions. "Didn't the parents split up?" "Wasn't the boy in Israel?" "I heard they caught the kidnapper and he's serving life." The answers that I give surprise people and inevitably lead to more questions. Until this account, the first book ever written on the case, no one has unraveled the details of this decades-long mystery.

So little is known publicly about the case itself. It has remained an ongoing investigation for the past thirty years, which means that a curt, official "No comment" by authorities has always precluded a full account. But bit by bit, as over the last two decades I produced television reports on the story for both ABC and CBS News, then spent four years researching this book, I've been able to piece together a narrative that continues to amaze me. I found a mix of detective story, human drama, and a thousand other twists and turns as I traced the case from its origin in 1979 to its conclusion—of sorts—twenty-five years later.

I started reporting this story in the fall of 1990, when as a fledgling ABC News producer at the network's start-up magazine *PrimeTime Live*, I was handed a newspaper article literally "ripped from the tabloids." The *New*

York Daily News's Joanne Wasserman had followed a New York federal prosecutor to Pennsylvania, in his own pursuit of a prime suspect in the Etan Patz case. KEY TO THE PATZ PUZZLE? read the bold headline running over a photo taken from high above a man sitting at his desk. A poster of Etan Patz emblazoned with the words STILL MISSING was prominent among the stacks of case files surrounding it. Assistant U.S. Attorney Stuart GraBois looked straight into the camera, radiating determination and purpose. That impression was confirmed as I scanned the article, about an extraordinary move on GraBois's part, to be sworn in as a deputy prosecutor in Pennsylvania in order to go after the man he believed had kidnapped Etan Patz, by prosecuting him on a completely different case.

"Check out this story," my boss, senior producer Betsy West, said, thrusting the article at me. "If it's something for us, and you can get it, we'd let you produce it yourself." It would be my first producer credit on the show, and I was out the door. My first trip was shorter than the *Daily News*'s Wasserman's, a subway ride downtown to catch GraBois in the U.S. Attorney's Office a few blocks from City Hall. I came away intrigued by his passion and force, even more pronounced in person. And so I joined the ranks of other journalists, like Wasserman, but also former WNBC crime reporter John Miller, and a coterie of stalwarts for whom this little boy's story had burrowed irretrievably under the skin. I eventually went to Pennsylvania too, and many other places, tracking this remarkable tale.

Crime stories are the bread and butter of television magazine shows, but they had never particularly appealed to me. I preferred the subjects of my stories to be alive, and often the only living figure in a crime drama is the bad guy. I also preferred my subjects to be the good guys, the ones who showed viewers their humanity. So what initially drew me to this story wasn't the crime part. I had no children, so I couldn't relate as a parent. In 1979 I didn't live in New York City, didn't live through the power this case held over its inhabitants. In 1990, what tugged at me was the unlikely intersection the Patz case had with the one in Pennsylvania, where another small victim, shoved aside by the system, had now been championed. And the way that fate, resolve, and exemplary detective work had combined against the odds to see justice served.

When my report finally aired on *PrimeTime Live* more than a year later, it featured a chilling appearance by GraBois's prime suspect, Jose Ramos, his first and only television interview ever. But his bad juju was overshadowed by an unlikely group of natural opponents who had overcome their differ-ences to join forces against him. I got to tell my story about the good guys, and I was hooked—on both a career and this particular story. Along the way I'd developed an admiration for the prosecutor Stuart GraBois and his tenacious pursuit of the case.

"You can't just say it's over," he said at the end of the story, "because it's not over."

It wasn't. Ten years later I was at CBS News and produced a follow-up for *60 Minutes II* with the first interview in over a decade of Etan's father, Stan-ley Patz. He had turned me down—politely—for the earlier piece at ABC, but for reasons that will become clear as this story unfolds, in 2000 he felt such a pressing need to come forward that he overcame his natural reserve. And I found someone else who inspired me with his grace and strength.

By the time I sat down with him, Stan Patz knew what had happened to his son. But he talked vividly about the nights he'd lain awake, trying to imagine an explanation that would make sense. It wouldn't ease the pain of losing Etan, but the not knowing was, for the Patzes, worse. Should his son's death be mourned? Should his family try to move forward with their lives? Should Etan's toys be thrown away? Or was he not dead at all, but out there, somewhere, trying to get home? The need for answers drove Stan as much as anything else, and in turn it drove those around him who wanted desper-ately to help. Stan and Julie Patz are two "everymen"—a childcare worker and a commercial photographer—whose lives would almost certainly have gone unchronicled except that they lived through what is always referred to as a parent's worst nightmare. And then they lived through its aftermath, and an unfathomable mystery, and they endured. They are both wise, kind, empathetic people. Their wryly humorous take on life and basic faith in others has seen them through not just a tragic moment, but also the years that followed while they, and so many others, searched to find answers.

While reporting the story, I have interviewed more than two hundred people, including the Patzes themselves and their extended family, friends and neighbors, reporters, bystanders, and policy experts. I've also spent end-less hours talking to a long list of former investigators. They were the cops, FBI agents, attorneys, and others in law enforcement who threw themselves into the search like they were looking for their own child. One of them said the following to me, and it bears repeating: It is always easier to inves-tigate a crime going backward in time. Likewise, making judgments with the benefit of hindsight serves no purpose. This book is not an attempt to find fault and lay blame. Rather, it fills in the gaps, clarifies, and sets several records straight about the trail of this case up to the current day.

A few notes about methodology: First and foremost, I could not have written this book without my primary collaborator and consultant, Stuart GraBois, who joined forces with me to ensure a faithful retelling of the story. Throughout this process, I turned to him to corroborate, to hash through conflicting accounts, and to point me toward other sources when either he didn't have information or because of legal constraints, couldn't give it to me. He also read multiple versions of this book and corrected my language and occasional misperceptions.

Beyond the hundreds of interviews I conducted, scores with Stuart Gra-Bois and Stan Patz alone, I also pored over every available article on the case, and spoke with many of the reporters who wrote them. The Patzes were gracious enough to offer me unfettered access to their copious files of news clips, personal correspondence, and documents. This included twenty-five years' worth of phone logbooks in which they recorded virtually every call and which ultimately became almost a faithfully kept family diary. From those first days in 1979, the police taught them to record their every activity, and in the interest of cracking this case Stan and Julie Patz were vigilant. The vast files served me well as primary source material in a story so distant in time to everyone I interviewed and so traumatic to some that memories could hardly be my only resource. I also spoke to Julie Patz on several occasions, although much less often than her husband, and I relied more heavily on lengthy early interviews she gave to the media, as well as her personal writings over the years. The Patzes asked for one caveat, to which I readily acceded. Their eldest child, wishing to guard her privacy, asked not to be included in the book, and I agreed, beyond a few important early scene-setting mentions.

But what the Patz family gave me was just one small part of my extensive body of research. I immersed myself in court transcripts and documents; investigative reports; videotape archives; and actualities from the time. Citing the case's ongoing status, neither the New York Police Department nor the District Attorney's Office of the County of New York would make official comment. Jose Ramos also declined several requests to be interviewed for this book, but I was able to dip back into primary source material for conversations with him from my TV days. A self-avowed pack rat, I had held on to all my notes and original material since I first undertook the research and reporting of this case in the early 1990s. I also found that to be true of many of the subjects I interviewed—it was astonishing to see how many reporters and investigators still kept their files on this case, buried in an attic or hidden beneath their current work in a desk or cabinet nearby.

When at all possible, dialogue in this book has been taken faithfully from transcripts, but by the very nature of this far-reaching story, many of the conversations have been reconstructed based on historical records and interviews with at least one—and often more than one—of the parties present. In a very few instances, particularly those involving victims of sexual abuse or their family members, I have changed names. In addition, there are two notable sources whose lives could be endangered behind prison walls by my identifying them publicly, and I have changed their names as well. In those two cases, I have seen timely corroborating documentation and interviewed other credible sources that back up the two men's lengthy conversations with me over several years.

Finally, all of the accounts I read and people I spoke to, whether they were searchers or survivors, inspired and moved me forward in the long pursuit of this story. Although what follows in these pages was triggered by a terrible tragedy, what it's really about, and what has always resonated for me, is what happened to the men, women, and children whose lives were touched by one little boy *after* he vanished. Through twenty-five years of this unfolding mystery, life went on—agonizing, suspenseful, frustrating, even comedic, since that is what real life can be at the worst of times. Much of what followed that one day was not tragic.

The search to solve the mystery of Etan Patz's disappearance is a heartbreaking story, but it's not just a true crime story. Yes, what happened to Etan Patz on May 25, 1979, was a truly unthinkable crime. What happened afterwards is a story of true heroes.

AFTER ETAN

CHAPTER 1

May 25, 1979

Police hypnotist: About what time is it?
Julie: About 7:00 a.m.
Hypnotist: What do you do?
Julie: Get out of bed.
—*Julie Patz hypnosis transcript, August 7, 1979*

I n August of 1979, nine weeks after Etan Patz disappeared, his mother, Julie, was hypnotized by police to recall the events of Friday, May 25. She was nervous but eager to do anything to add to the shortage of clues. She began to retrace her steps that day, minute by minute. After a stoic ten minutes, the NYPD hypnotist stopped her and told her she was doing a wonderful job, but that she had to start all over again from the beginning. And this time, he said, she needed to stay completely in the present tense, as if every minute were just happening now. He thought it would help her to recall the day more easily. He actually used the word "easily." Julie started again. "The alarm clock is ringing," she said. "Stan is shutting it off."

———

Her husband turns over and goes back to sleep. He had worked late the night before. Julie pulls herself out of bed, unwillingly, but she has a lot to do. Their across-the-street neighbors, Larry and Karen Altman, have invited them to their country place for the weekend. The weather is changeable this time of year—lots to pack. Julie's in-home daycare group will be arriving soon, bringing their daily chaotic mess of arts-and-crafts supplies, spilled Cheerios, and sweet cacophony. The other wild card this morning is Ari,

1

her two-year-old. A playmate of his had slept over the night before, the toddlers snuggled under blankets on the floor in the front room that doubled as the daycare center. This means an extra wiggly body to keep track of. And when Julie peeks in, sure enough they are awake already, "reading" their books amid the bedclothes.

As usual, when Julie wakes Etan, he hops right out of bed. Eight-year-old Shira is a different story. Once awake, Shira might lie in bed imagining ways to get out of having to go to school. Today is really part of the long weekend, she might argue, and then it's almost the end of the term, and it isn't like anyone's learning anything this late in the year anyway. Julie has already decided she isn't going to push her daughter too hard.

She goes to her room to throw on a long blue-and-yellow peasant dress with white flowers and pull her shoulder-length brown hair back in its usual casual ponytail. Then she checks on Etan, who is putting on his blue pants and a T-shirt. While Julie goes to the kitchen, he laces up his racing sneakers, the light blue ones with the fluorescent green lightning stripe on the side. His best friend Jeff has just grown out of a blue, wide-wale corduroy jacket and Etan is now its proud owner, even though the name sewn inside hasn't been changed. He already has on his favorite hat, the Future Flight Captain pilot's cap he bought for a dime at a garage sale and sometimes slept in, as he comes into the kitchen where his mother is making lunches.

Julie watches as, unbidden, he takes the milk out and pours himself a glass. With a naturally contrary older sister and a typically terrible-twoish younger brother, Etan is an easy middle child. There are the usual qualifications, of course. He actively tries to please, a refreshing change of pace after Shira, but he knows the secret ways to provoke his sister as only a sibling can. He is fiercely protective of baby brother Ari, but equally jealous. He is sunny and sweet, but has a stubborn, moody streak. He is fanciful and full of stories, planning trips to far-off lands with his imaginary playmate Johnny France-America. For a while, he felt like he could walk on water as Jesus had, if only he practiced hard enough, so he spent hours walking flat-footed around the house.

He is on the slight side, but not undersized. His smile reaches up his whole face and through his blue, blue eyes to light up a room. He looks a lot like his mother. She encourages his self-sufficiency, and every morning he fixes his own breakfast of toast and chocolate milk. Now he quickly finishes up both, picks up his cloth lunch bag, the blue one with the white elephants, and heads into the front room to position himself by the door.

Etan has a reason for being one step ahead of his mom. This is a big day. The school bus stop is two short blocks away, down Prince Street, then a quick right onto West Broadway, in front of the corner bodega. All year he has been begging his mother to let him walk it on his own. A lot of the other kids are allowed, why not me, Etan would say, with classic six-year-old logic. Now first grade is almost over, and he has only a few more weeks to carry out his mission.

Stan and Julie were of mixed minds about this walk to the bus stop thing, but Etan's pleadings wore them down. It wasn't as if there had been one moment when they decided, yes, this was the day. It just sort of happened. His parents also thought it would be a good confidence builder for him—they were concerned about the tentative streak that coexisted with his thirst for adventure. Etan was particularly fearful of being lost. Once, when he was five, he and his mother rode an elevator, and when the door opened, she made it off but he didn't. She turned as the door closed and would never forget the expression on his face. She could hear him screaming all the way to the top and back down safely to her.

But this morning he is so pleased with himself, acting so grown-up, and at the last minute he even remembers to bring the dollar he "earned" the day before. On his way home Etan had run into the neighborhood handyman who'd pretended to need the boy's help in some small task. Now Julie tells her son to put the dollar in his pocket, but he wants to hold it in his hand as he walks. He plans to stop at the bodega before getting on the bus, to spend his pay on a soda for lunch.

Just before eight, Julie calculates it's time to go. Etan walks ahead of his mother down the three flights to the front door. He isn't tall enough to reach the lock himself, and has to wait while she opens the door. Julie looks up the street. It's a gray day, and at the moment the sun is behind her back, hiding around the corner. She feels it rather than sees it, struggling to come out.

The detective poised taking notes beside Julie in the hypnosis session had never sat through one of these. He was skeptical and suddenly confused. May 25 had been a drizzly day; how could Julie see the sun? Later, after she'd gone home, she called him. She'd just realized that the time sensor on a streetlamp behind her that morning had been defective and it had flickered on and off. That must have been what I felt as sunshine, she explained.

Looking up the street, Julie hopes the weather will be better for the next few days, since they plan to spend most of it outdoors, on this holiday weekend in the country. She sees the familiar figures of other parents and their children beginning to congregate near the bus stop, which is just barely out of sight around the corner. Mother and son stand in front of their door, heads together, talking briefly about afterschool plans. Come home quickly, she tells him, you have to help pack for the trip. She kisses Etan goodbye.

He smiled and waved, turned around and walked away. She watched him, head down, as though he were counting his steps. She waited until he crossed the first of the two streets that stood between their home and the bus stop. If she was wavering at all, well, there were the babies upstairs, unsupervised. She turned and went inside, back upstairs to contain whatever toddler havoc Ari and his friend had wrought in the few minutes she'd been gone.

As Julie relived those few last moments to the hypnotist, she slipped unaware from present tense to past. Living in that exact moment again seemed to be just too hard.

> Julie: I'm kissing him and I give him a hug. I say so long, tell him to have a good day. I watched him for a little while and I went in the door and flipped the lock and closed it, I ran upstairs. (LONG PAUSE)
> Hypnotist: Let me just wipe those away.
> Julie: No, that's alright. They feel good. There haven't been enough.
> Hypnotist: Well, you can have all you want here.
> —hypnosis transcript, August 7, 1979

The account contradicted one important detail widely reported in the days following May 25. When Julie Patz first told police about her movements that morning, she remembered coming back inside and going out on the balcony fire escape that fronted Prince Street, to watch her son reach West Broadway and turn the corner.

But under hypnosis, she discovered her mind had played a trick on her. Perhaps her unconscious wanted her to have gone out on the balcony so badly, it had given her the false memory. In reality, back upstairs, she eyed the toddlers, then went off to take a quick shower and get ready for work. The rest of "her" kids would be showing up soon, as well as her staff. Julie's in-home daycare made good use of their space. Five days a week eight kids and two assistants filled the rooms with snack time, rest, and play.

Showered and ready, Julie tidied up, packed Shira off to school after all, and began gathering the weekend belongings before the daycare kids arrived. Karen Altman would be picking up Etan along with her own daughter Chelsea at the bus stop after school, as she often did, so at least Julie would have a little extra time to prepare. But soon, her chattering, riotous group was spilling in, pushing at every molecule in the room, and bouncing back off them, and Julie was immersed in her day job.

———

By 3:30 p.m. Etan was still not home, and Julie was a little concerned. A lengthy school bus strike had just ended. This was the drivers' first week back, so maybe the bus had been delayed. Julie kept sticking her head out the wide expanse of windows in the front, where she was always able to see her children approaching from well up the block. Finally she phoned Karen Altman, whose own windows looked in on the Patz loft from directly across the street. "Is Etan over there with you?" Julie asked. "No," said Karen. She'd assumed that when Etan hadn't gotten off the bus he had gone to another friend's, as he often did, for a semi-regular playdate. With Julie on the line, she asked Chelsea if she knew where Etan had gone after school.

"Etan wasn't in school today," Chelsea said.

Julie tried to contain her panic, but her voice, one of her most revealing features, betrayed her with a tight shake, and she immediately ended the call.

At ten minutes to four on Friday afternoon, at the start of a holiday weekend that would shut the city down for three days, Julie Patz phoned the First Precinct to report her son missing. The officer who answered asked Julie if she and her husband were having marital troubles—maybe a custody dispute? No, said Julie. Maybe he ran away? No, Julie insisted, her voice rising. The officer promised to send someone over.

Julie hung up and called her husband, Stan, a photographer who was working at a friend's photo studio uptown. By this time she was frantic. Stan, in a moment of pure denial, finished the soggy cheeseburger that was his late lunch, then jumped on the subway downtown.

At the loft, a group of preschoolers were being shepherded into the lobby, Julie's assistants handing off children to their moms, trying not to frighten any of the youngsters. The contained, tense faces of the adults gathering outside shook Stan and a sense of urgency overtook him. He ignored the elevator, running up the back stairs to the third floor. It was almost 4:30. Stan took one look at Julie and knew nothing good had happened during the time he had been on the subway. She was ashen. Stan's fantasy as he sat on the R train rattling down Broadway, that he would arrive to learn the whole thing was a big misunderstanding, was just that—a fantasy. In between calls to neighbors and friends, his wife had been dialing local emergency rooms, and wondering where the hell the cops were.

> Time—16:25. No cops yet. Julie was very nervous. She had called every-body for a clue. I called 1st Pct to find out where the cops were. Minutes later two patrolmen were in our place, asked basic questions (marriage, friends, family) and jumped in their car to go down to PS 3 Annex.
> —*Stan Patz's account of May 25, 1979 (written June 1979)*

The police told Stan and Julie they needed to confirm that Etan really wasn't in school that day, but on the Friday evening of Memorial Day weekend, there was no one at the school to call. When one of the officers realized he knew the custodian there, they headed over.

Stan went into his home darkroom. He had no photos of Etan lying around, but remembered that back in March he'd done a lengthy photo shoot of the boy and there were proof sheets—thirty-six miniature headshots on each page. He grabbed a few of them and ran down the stairs, heading out onto Prince Street to show them to shopkeepers, brushing past his downstairs neighbors on the landing coming in. Peggy Spina had just picked up her seven-year-old daughter Vanessa from afterschool art class. Vanessa was one of Etan's constant companions, but Stan didn't even notice the girl, let alone question her. He tossed back one sentence to Peggy as he bolted past. "I think we've lost Etan." Then he was up the street, leaving a bewildered mother ushering her own child in the front door of their apartment.

"Lost Etan," Peggy thought. "How do you 'lose' a kid? And how could he be lost in the middle of the afternoon?" Her older daughter, ten-year-old Paula, was home, having shamelessly faked sick that morning to skip school. Julie had just called down, she told her mother, to ask if anyone had seen Etan. Still, Peggy assumed this was a simple mixup.

Stan took his proof sheets to the health food store, the bodega, the M&O Market, and the Eva Deli, then to the Houston Street playground. No, everyone said, shaking their heads as they looked at the tiny pictures, they hadn't seen Etan.

Sometime that afternoon Sandy Harmon, a woman who sometimes worked for the Patzes, arrived at the loft. She had come to pick up the keys from Julie. The place had once been burglarized in their absence, and Julie had asked Sandy to housesit while the family was away for the weekend. Sandy, of course, now learned she would not be staying in the loft that weekend after all; instead she helped Julie look for phone numbers to nearby hospitals, sitting awkwardly in the front room, trying to think of other places to call. After a brief stay she left, to pick up her own son, who himself was in daycare nearby.

At the P.S. 3 Annex school, a police officer went through the school records to confirm Etan's absence, before he finally called back to headquarters to ask for backup. Ten long hours after Etan was last seen, a full-on search for him began.

At 5:15, Detective Bill Butler got the radio call. He and his partner immediately drove to Prince Street, where by 5:30 they were joined by three other detectives from the First Precinct. Stan showed them pictures of Etan, while Julie repeated the day's events as she knew them. She would recite them again and again countless times in the days to come.

"He's a very friendly boy," she said. "Very loving, trusting and warm."

By 6 p.m., as if to compensate for the first hour of inactivity, radio patrol cars began to roll up, and through the night some three hundred police officers descended on Prince Street. A temporary police headquarters was set up in the Patz loft. Up and down the block squad cars were left standing in the middle of the street. As the light grew dim, the car doors were propped open and high beams left on to illuminate the evening air. An area diagram was drawn, to divide up and designate the different buildings. Uniformed cops patrolled on foot, moving door-to-door in the streets around Prince, knocking to gain access, to shine their flashlights into dark basements and onto rooftops. Helicopters with floodlights swooped back and forth. Walkie-talkies crackled as false leads and rumors flew.

Peggy Spina answered her door to find a policeman politely asking to come in. She examined the card he handed her, ushered him into her home, and told him everything she knew, which was almost nothing. She was shocked to find herself following him as he began methodically opening all her closed doors, rummaging behind the clothes in her closets. She wasn't outraged at this invasion, but sickened by the realization that the cops had to think this way in such cases—had to assume a small child might be secreted away in the downstairs neighbors' closet. It must actually happen like that sometimes, she thought, horrified. The experience was so disorienting that afterwards she couldn't remember the man's last name, but spent weeks thinking his first name was "Det," until someone pointed out that he most certainly was of detective rank.

Upstairs Julie Patz sat in the loft surrounded by officers. She felt almost incapable of functioning, although the only outward signs besides the tears were the trembling tic in her jaw and the occasional stumble as she got up to answer phones or to walk across the loft, to forage for Etan's toys and other items potentially laden with his fingerprints. His stuffed hippo, Biggie, or his Star Wars X-wing fighter. But inside she quelled the overwhelming urge to vomit and the uncontrollable flood of guilt: Why had she let her son walk to the bus stop alone? As night fell, the guilty feelings were supplanted by more damaging fears of the horrors he might be living through, or whether he was even alive.

For Stan Patz, who spent hours conferring with police from the front of his loft turned temporary staging area, the rest of the day and night were as lost to him as his son. It was as if it had all never happened, as if he had never experienced it in the first place. Or maybe, in the way that Julie imagined the balcony scene, remembering was just not permitted.

Karen Altman had already come and gone, taking Shira and little Ari back across the street, where she made everyone soup. There would be no more talk about the trip upstate. Instead, two-year-old Ari Patz watched the goings-on from the Altmans' front window. This was turning into his second sleepover in a row and his first away from home, but he didn't cry. When Shira and Chelsea stopped playing cards in the other room and drifted off to sleep, Ari stayed at the front window. His face pressed up against the panes of glass that stretched the length of the Altman loft, he watched his mother and father, moving from the street below to the Patz front room across the way, and back again. The Patzes' tall windows showcased the blur of activity. From her vantage point over Ari's shoulder, Karen Altman watched Stan too, as his wiry frame paced the length of sidewalk in front of the building, the floodlights illuminating his thin, now pinched face. Karen could see just by the way Stan was holding himself and by the expressions on his face that he was enraged. Not at the cops, not at his wife, but at the gods, she thought. She half expected him to start shaking his fist at the skies.

The gods seemed to be piling on when, shortly before midnight, they began spitting on the searchers in a slow, steady drizzle. By 1:15 a.m., when authorities requested bloodhounds to be brought in from upstate, any traces of Etan—his prints or a scent the dogs could follow—were in the process of being washed away.

"Wouldn't it be awful," whispered Karen's husband, Larry, from behind her and just out of Ari's earshot, "if they never found Etan, and they never found out what happened?"

CHAPTER 2

Twenty-four Hours and Counting

LOST CHILD
Etan Patz

113 Prince Street
Missing Since Friday May 25th, 1979, Last
Seen 8 a.m., at Prince St. & West B'way.

Description:
Date of Birth: October 9, 1972   Male, White, 6 yrs.
Height: 40 inches   Weight: 50 lbs.
Blond Hair, Blue Eyes, Wearing Black Pilot Type Cap,
Blue Corduroy Jacket, Blue Pants, Blue Sneakers with
Fluorescent Stripes, Carrying Blue Cloth Bag with
Elephants Imprinted.
  —1979 missing flyer, posted with Etan's
    picture throughout New York City

Subject: initial investigation

Initial investigation on 5/25/79 in the vicinity of the residence of the subject of this investigation was conducted as follows:
1. A temporary Headquarters was set up at 1800 hrs. in the subject's loft....
2. Emergency Service responded with lights and assisted....
3. An in-depth canvas and search of buildings, rooftops, basements
    and elevators shafts backyards and alleys was conducted....This
    met with negative results.
4. Investigation continuing—CASE ACTIVE
    —NYPD Police Report, 5/26/79 (DD5)
      Bill Butler re: Lost Child #687

At the First Precinct, ten blocks southeast of 113 Prince Street, NYPD detective Bill Butler finished typing up his one-page sheet. His sleep-deprived brain was still alert enough to recognize it would be the first of many such reports. Butler had stayed on the scene until sometime around 4 a.m., then headed home for a quick shower and a few hours of sleep. He then made a quick stop at the station in search of a typewriter to at least start the paperwork.

"Investigation continuing." Twenty-four hours had passed since Etan set off for the bus stop, and Butler couldn't shake the feeling that was knotting his gut more than the dozen-odd cups of bad coffee he'd drunk through the night. Arriving in the first wave of detectives the day before, he'd at first thought it was no big deal. He saw this all the time, although he could understand the mother being distraught. A kid doesn't come home from school at the right time, he's probably playing hooky, lost track of time hanging out at the park. A classmate's mom with her own house full of kids makes dinner and just sees one more mouth to feed, forgetting to call. In most of these cases, after a few hours the child pops up. But once the school had confirmed Etan had indeed been marked absent, it looked like more than just a simple mistake or miscommunication.

As long as there'd been hours still left in the first day, though, hope had remained that Etan had run away, was hiding out with a friend, was en route home. But even as police helicopters made use of the dawn's light to comb rooftops, as launches from the NYPD Harbor Unit searched the water around the Hudson River's retaining walls in a swath from Greenwich Village south to the tip of Manhattan, Butler had lost the previous day's optimism. In law enforcement, there are a whole slew of hour markers to choose from—the first nine, the first twelve, the first forty-eight—beyond which chances for recovery drop precipitously. But for a child this young, once a night had passed, it marked the beginning of the end of denial.

Bill Butler was a twenty-four-year veteran of the New York Police Department. He was a bluff block of a man. His many years of moderate drinking to drown out memories from his job hadn't marked his face with clear signs of dissipation, except perhaps for the watery blue eyes now concealed behind square-framed brown tortoiseshell glasses. Eyes lined by all those memories, by the squint of unapologetic chain-smoking, and ready laughter.

But for Butler, like most cops, missing children were the cases you couldn't tough out. Butler had six of his own, all old enough to fend for themselves. Two were in the Police Academy, another planned to enter. They were past the age that engendered this kind of panic. Once a parent, though, you're forever in tune with it.

Butler reread the single page of his DD5—Detective Division Form Number 5, "Report of Ongoing Investigation." Cops called them "the fives," and were supposed to write up a new one after each new development. Butler was among the few who scrupulously did. It could make him feel he had something to show for himself, especially when that was *all* he had to show. This was one of those times. His single page didn't do much to convey the man-hours hundreds of officers had poured into the previous twelve.

There were rougher parts of the city than this one where kids disappeared regularly, to turn up again soon afterwards. There weren't a lot of children living in this downtown section of Manhattan. The First Precinct was a weekday precinct, covering not just SoHo but the Wall Street area. Off hours, the Financial District rolled up so tight, it looked like the aftermath of a neutron bomb. Add the empty streets of the holiday weekend and the First could focus all its resources into the hunt for a missing six-year-old.

Butler rubbed his grainy, half-slitted eyes one more time and put away his reading glasses. He grabbed his detective's standard-issue trench coat to insulate him from the drizzle and headed back up to the Patz loft. When he arrived there, he learned he'd just missed the dogs.

Sometime after 8 a.m. on Saturday a state police truck had pulled onto Prince Street and wedged itself between the cop cars lining the block. Two large bloodhounds were led out the back of the caged half of the van. Julie offered up Etan's size six pajamas, which the dogs eagerly inhaled. Then, one at a time, each set off at a run down the street. But with twenty-four hours and light rain separating the trail from Etan's last sighting, police weren't counting on a lingering scent.

The animals *looked* productive, racing up the block between the bus stop and the Patz loft, only to race back. This prompted the first in an infinite number of theories that could never be proved—that Etan had missed the bus and walked back to his home; too short to reach the buzzer, he had wandered off again. Then the dogs crisscrossed the surrounding blocks, traversing a good portion of SoHo; in and out of nearby Eva Deli, the Bruno Bakery, and the local fruit stand. They stopped outside Gem Lumber on

Spring Street, one block south and a few blocks west of Etan's Prince Street home, entered and went to the counter, exited, then later came back. The state police handler was confident—Gem was part of the boy's route.

Butler made notes on the dogs' path and checked in with Stan and Julie, who looked as though they hadn't left the front room in the intervening hours. They were clearly dazed, two smallish, slim figures unmoving in the harsh morning daylight streaming in through the windows above them. Stan's angular face was unshaven, stubble now picking up where his long sideburns left off, covering faint acne scars. Julie's face was more expressive than her impassive husband's; the small twitch by the right side of her mouth was more pronounced than Butler remembered it from the evening before. The parents sat side by side on a worn couch, its brown and white polka dots covered by a yellow sheet, placed there to take the abuse of muddy prints from tiny sneakers and grubby hands. It was now littered with phone books and scribbled pages of notes—names of people called, still to be called. The two talked quietly before Stan went back to take his place with the uniformed officers at the table by the door, to answer more questions.

During the night, the makeshift command post had drifted across the hall to the next-door neighbor's apartment. Fred Cohn, an iconoclastic defense lawyer, lived there with his wife, Suzanne, but they were away and the apartment had clearly been annexed, thanks to the passkey Stan Patz possessed as de facto super of the co-op.

Looking in the door and already anticipating another long day into night, Butler wondered whether the couch in Cohn's apartment would accommodate his six-foot-two-inch frame. One officer was on the phone in there too, and another was finishing a makeshift breakfast.

Butler had heard some of the other cops wondering out loud where Cohn was this weekend, and he too was curious about just when the couple had left town. Was it before or after Etan disappeared? The eight-hour gap between when the boy left home and when the alarm was raised made alibis so much easier.

Fred Cohn had spent his career representing anti–Vietnam War protesters and other high-profile radical left clients. His antiestablishment bent didn't automatically make him suspicious, but it caused speculation. The detectives planned to track down the lawyer today, because during the school bus strike, Cohn had frequently dropped off Etan at school on the way to his nearby law office. The cops hoped his route could provide a clue to the direction Etan would have headed on foot if he'd missed the bus. Plus, the theory went, a rabble-rousing lefty lawyer who was often alone with a six-year-old and was conveniently out of town was someone to talk to. Just on principle.

Back at the Patz loft, the officers sitting with Stan continued to add to the lists of friends, acquaintances, anyone who might have had a connection to the family. Maps of the neighborhood, both commercial and hand-drawn, were laid out on the work table near the phone, which rang continuously. Access to much of the area's real estate was going to be especially tough because of the holiday weekend and the shuttered commercial spaces. In the meantime, authorities were focusing on the people who lived and worked in those buildings, particularly those who knew Etan and his parents.

———

Etan." Stan Patz mechanically corrected another officer yet again. "Sounds like A, Y, T, A, H, N." There were many different ways to say his son's name, but even taking into account the hint of New England accent that still permeated Stan's broad vowels, there was no misinterpreting the pronunciation of his family name. "Not Patz, like 'cats'; Patz, like 'hates.'"

The last word was stuck in his brain. Throughout the long night, cops had been asking if anyone hated his family. "Any enemies? Someone who might want to hurt you?" It was a perfectly logical question, and Stan was *trying* to focus, but he had never even thought about it. "No," he kept repeating, over and over, even as he considered it anew each time they asked. There was no one.

The other questions—about himself, about Julie—they weren't pointed, really, not yet. But any moment now he expected a high-wattage lamp to be shined in his face. He doubted such a light would even register, though. He felt an overwhelming numbness for which he was vaguely thankful, because it protected him from all other sensations. Certainly hunger—he had no idea when he'd last eaten, probably the hamburger that had delayed his arrival at the loft the day before.

Julie hadn't eaten either. She'd tried to, aware that she needed her strength so she could help. But it was no use. Even if she went through the motions of chewing the food, she couldn't swallow it. She was also having trouble walking, her legs shaking so much they threatened to give way. Her mind was racing, and as the police asked their questions, she fought to reach back into her memory, to make sense of any detail that might provide a clue. But all she could think of was what her son might be going through.

———

Three blocks away, Jack Lembeck sat and watched his son Jeff's face and waited for the boy to wake up. Jeff was Etan's best friend. His was the name sewn into the back of the jacket Etan had been wearing the previous morning. Jeff and Etan swapped clothes regularly, and it was not lost on Jack that the two six-year-olds were interchangeable in most ways. Except that Jeff was sleeping peacefully just inches away.

Finally, Jeff opened his eyes. Jack didn't want to tell him what had happened, didn't want to allow those kinds of fears to enter into his son's head, let alone be the one to put them there. But maybe Jeff could offer a clue, and Jack couldn't just sit still anymore, he needed to do something. So after a few minutes, he quietly told Jeff that Etan hadn't come home the night before. Jeff got a small, scared look on his face, and Jack said, "We're going to go look for him now." The six-year-old was motionless for a moment, then jumped up and headed for the kitchen. He said, "We have to bring him some food and water. He'll be hungry."

Jack and Jeff gathered supplies, foraging around the loft, a 4,000-square-foot open space that was once a cardboard-box warehouse. They wrapped up some crackers, poured Juicy Juice into a bottle, and packed it all into a backpack. Then they wheeled their bikes into the elevator, down six flights to Broome Street, two blocks south and one block east of the Patz loft, and set off. Jack gave Jeff strict instructions to ride only one bicycle length ahead of his dad. With one eye glued to the small figure poised on his stubby yellow banana-seat bike, Jack searched for a glimpse of another blond head.

Jack let his son guide him through the streets as they pedaled around to the boys' familiar haunts. They headed toward West Broadway, then wound back east, working their way south. This was SoHo—the thirty-seven-block neighborhood "SOuth of HOuston." Dotted with warehouses and galleries, parts of SoHo were not yet legally zoned for folks to raise their families. The days were just about over when shades were drawn at sundown to hide signs of life after regular business hours. But this was still a fairly makeshift community, where a greeting shouted from the street would be followed by sock-wrapped keys hurled from an upper floor, then a ride up a freight elevator.

SoHo was the bastion of a new generation of New York artists and poets.

Jack's good friend, the unorthodox portrait artist Chuck Close, lived a block west of the Patzes, jazz great Ornette Coleman a block east. Composer Philip Glass had a child in Julie's playgroup.

Jack himself was a painter-slash-messenger, although of late he'd been lucky enough to support himself with his art. Now his messenger days, learning the nooks and far corners of lower Manhattan, served him well as he and Jeff pedaled south.

As they rode, the news was spreading to other residents of SoHo, the ones staying home for the long weekend, who began to mobilize on a larger scale. The SoHo Cooperative Playgroup, another neighborhood preschool, was scheduled to hold its annual picnic that afternoon and instead transformed into the Etan Patz Action Committee. Independent of the police search, some twenty people had organized themselves, and without access to Stan Patz's photography files or any random prints of Etan, they tapped the skills of their artsy members to produce a flyer with Etan's drawn likeness. They photocopied thousands of sheets, then split up to post them around town. Volunteers took stacks and stood on the street, handing them out to passersby.

———

Sometime early in the day, the Patzes' upstairs neighbors Barry Ensminger and his wife, Sylvia Law, arrived from upstate, turned around less than a day into their Memorial Day weekend getaway. Barry and Sylvia's two-year old son Ben was Ari Patz's close friend, as close as toddlers in parallel-play could be. The boys easily wandered up and down the back stairs from one apartment to the other—sometimes it felt like they all lived in one big house. Ben was in Julie's daycare, one of those children sent home early the day before when Etan was discovered missing.

Sylvia and Barry had left New York on Friday, soon after they had picked up Ben, to spend their long weekend at a friend's country home. They had driven off still debating whether they should leave town at all. But Etan was surely just at a friend's house, or, they thought, pretending to run away. We can always come back if we're needed. Early Saturday morning, they got a call from Sylvia's sister Judy, who often housesat at the Prince Street loft. "Come back. They haven't found him." Sylvia and Barry packed Ben back up and drove home.

Now the couple walked down the stairs to the third floor and found

Stan crouched over the front room desk, flanked by two officers and pages of lists. Julie sat immobile on the balcony, chain-smoking. Her gaze never left the street below.

Stan and Julie were both so distracted that they didn't register their neighbors' return, but there was a quick exchange of hugs and tears. "I can't believe this," said Sylvia. "I must have walked right past Etan and Julie yesterday morning, on the street, on my way to work."

"Any news?" Barry asked Stan, although he already knew the answer from Stan's face. Barry quickly moved on. "What can we do?" Stan's slight shrug and look of mute helplessness prompted Barry to speak, despite his misgivings. Both he and Sylvia were lawyers—Sylvia a professor at New York University's law school, Barry an adviser to Carol Bellamy, then New York City Council president. In the car on the way down from Woodstock they had come up with the one offering they could make.

"Have you thought about press?" Barry probed gently. "I know a lot of the guys in Room 9." Room 9 was the notorious City Hall press office, filled with hard-charging, modern-day Hildy Johnsons and Lois Lanes.

Both Stan and Julie looked alarmed. "Oh God," said Stan. "This place has already been invaded. I don't know if I can handle a crush of reporters." Both he and Julie looked as though one light touch in the wrong direction would topple them.

"It's a trade-off," replied Barry. "You give them something they need—access to a human interest story, putting a bit of your lives out there. Which will be awful, agreed. But you also give them a photo of Etan, and a reason for New Yorkers to help look for him. It's not an easy choice." He paused, letting the idea sink in. "But I don't think you can say no. I can get to a bunch of these guys, talk them through this, and you can limit what you let out there."

Stan looked at Julie. He couldn't think straight. Bringing in the press would be an irrevocable acknowledgment that this was a crisis. He turned to Detective Butler, now standing beside him. Stan hadn't yet grasped that Butler was going to be a mainstay on the case; for now he was just another large, blurry shape in a dark suit who exuded authority.

"I think you should do it," Butler said. "I don't usually want the press involved. But this is one of those times where you can let them work for you. Especially if he knows people personally, you may be able to hold on to a little control."

"Do it," said Stan. "Just ask them to be careful with Julie." Barry moved to go back to his fourth-floor rear apartment and a clear phone line. "I'll come with you," said Stan, and the two walked together on the stairs. "If you're going to get the press in, I think I have to call Massachusetts. I've been hoping I wouldn't have to, but I don't want my mother to hear this on the news."

Stan Patz and his two brothers had left the Boston area decades earlier, but it was still home, where Stan's parents and extended family lived within a few miles of each other.

He dialed the number to his parents' Hyde Park house, steeling himself to hear his mother's voice. She was the one who always picked up the phone.

"Mother, it's Sim." Sim was what Stan's grandmother had always called him, the name he went by to those who knew him best. "You better sit down," he said.

It wasn't until Stan Patz hung up the phone that he finally felt a wave sweep over him that almost knocked him to the floor. Reporting the news, saying the words "Etan is missing" to his parents had done the same thing as agreeing to call in the press. When he had to say it aloud to someone outside the insular Prince Street, it finally became true. He realized that's why he had put off the call as much as anything else. But this new truth was fleeting, thank God, as he willed away reality and headed back downstairs. Julie couldn't see this. He couldn't afford to feel it. Barry Ensminger lifted the phone and started his round of press calls.

Even before Ensminger had broached the prospect of the press, those wheels were already in motion, and sometime in the afternoon the TV crew trucks began to pull up, one local station after another. In a story like this one, you didn't really need to go looking for media attention, it quickly found you. By early morning, the previous night's police detectives had typed up an "unusual"—a brief on any out-of-the-ordinary incident that might attract the public interest. The report was sitting on the chief of detectives' desk when he came in, and he passed it on to the office of the deputy commissioner for public information.

"Whadyagot?" asked New York Channel 5 weekend crime reporter John Miller when he checked with the news editor as he did every Saturday and Sunday morning.

"This came over the teletype from DCPI. Missing kid, they've set up a command post at his home."

"Where's he missing from?" Miller asked. Even if it hadn't been a quiet holiday weekend, Miller knew the story was a no-brainer as soon as he heard that a white kid from a seemingly intact family in a gentrifying neighborhood hadn't been seen in twenty-four hours. If a black kid from the projects were missing, he wouldn't have automatically disqualified it as news, but the cold hard fact was that the more unusual the details, the newsier it got. He told the camera crew he'd meet them downtown and took off in his own car.

John Miller looked more like a college sophomore reporting for his student paper than a jaded New York street reporter. That's because the twenty-one-year-old *was* a college sophomore, commuting down from Emerson College every weekend for the last couple of years to cover the gritty New York crime beat. His father was a well-connected national gossip columnist in the tradition of Walter Winchell, and the younger Miller had been kind of a child prodigy news junkie. He unconsciously affected a tough, old-school street reporter's manner, and his competitors liked to joke that he'd show up someday in a fedora with a press card tucked into his frizzy blond 'fro. But the crusty style, along with his droll charm, worked for him by disarming the news gatekeepers, and he often got the last laugh, and the scoop.

This time, all the television crews seemed to arrive simultaneously, reporters in an assembly line of microphones and notepads as the press breached the loft. Miller pulled up behind a bakery truck, one of many now sharing the crowded curb with cop cars and TV production vans. Usually the delivery trucks owned the streets, as all night and day they moved breads and rolls out of the R&K Bakery diagonally across the street from 113 Prince, delivering wholesale to a tri-state clientele. This was not one of Miller's usual neighborhood haunts. He surveyed the makeshift residential real estate where the commercial space was clearly being overtaken by New Yorkers desperate for affordable housing, and wondered who the people making their homes here were. Then he walked up the stairs into the apartment and took his turn to interview Stan and Julie Patz.

The loft was crawling with cops, and Miller waited patiently for the parents to disengage from an exchange with one of them before getting their comments. He'd reported on his share of grieving parents, and these two did not seem like media grandstanders, primping before their shot or speaking in hollow platitudes. He was impressed with Julie's teeth-gritting eloquence and grateful she was willing to oblige the crew by posing on the balcony. He wondered if that's where she had spent most of her time in the last twenty-four hours anyway.

Spreading the word, it soon became clear, had its drawbacks. Sometime in the afternoon, even before the local news segments and the sensational headlines, Stan Patz had his first taste of life without filters to screen the rest of the world. A fleshy white woman of indeterminate age climbed the stairs, accompanied by a man Stan assumed was her husband. "I have important information that I can share only with the parents," she announced importantly to the cops. They didn't know what to make of her. The police had an understandably tough time differentiating between concerned neighbors and the mystical seers, curiosity-seekers, and just plain kooks who were beginning to show up. The problem was, anyone might present a viable clue, so in the first days no one was discounted. Soon afterwards, a "cops only" policy was instituted in the loft, but when this woman announced she had "information," she could have been E. F. Hutton. She was the first of countless psychics, and as the first, the cops gave her a free pass.

Stan led the woman next door to the Cohns' and sat with her on the couch. Her husband said nothing. She appeared to marshal her forces, then intoned dramatically, "I see a hand." Then a long pause. "I see water." She didn't say much more, just shook her head, sighed, and looked profoundly sad. It didn't sound good, or particularly helpful. Stan politely said goodbye, frustrated, angry at the vagueness of her "information," and no more informed. But he was so desperate for something constructive to do, he knew he wouldn't turn away the next fruitcake with a vision.

Back in the loft, Bill Butler was cursing the holiday weekend, with its tightly shuttered storefronts. Then a call came in, the first real spark of hope. One of the few businesses open was the hardware store, with the lumber yard the bloodhounds had liked. Now manager Howard Belasco had been questioned, and yes, he remembered seeing two boys playing in the lumber yard around 4:30 or 5 o'clock the previous afternoon. This could close an eight-hour gap, and Butler rushed to question Belasco, showing him Etan's photograph on the newly created cards Stan had made him from four-by-five prints. Butler carried them everywhere with him now. The two boys had been playing in a dumpster, Belasco told Butler, and then had bought a few boxes of nails. He looked at Etan's photo and was sure it was one of the boys. Butler was elated. Someone else identified the other child, and he was tracked down. But Belasco was wrong. The boys had bought the nails to build a stall for the upcoming St. Anthony's festival, and then they had gone home. The manager was very apologetic, but Butler thanked him for his help.

As the day waned, Jack and Jeff Lembeck turned home too, abandoning the futile search. Nearing their apartment, Jack began to see the posters more frequently on streetlamps, parking meters, and storefronts. He heard the voices, amplified by megaphone, of other searchers.

"We're trying to locate a lost child by the name of Etan Patz," one man's voice boomed. "He's only six years old. Blond hair and blue eyes. He was last seen wearing a black cap, blue pants, blue sneakers, and blue jacket."

Jeff's jacket, thought Jack Lembeck. It so easily could have been Jeff. Stopped at one corner, Jack was aware of a couple staring, then pointing at his son. "He looks just like the picture," Jack heard the man say. As Jack rode past the next poster, he focused on Etan's image. Seeing the boy's face was like lightning striking the roof next door.

CHAPTER 3

∽

The Occupation

Reporter: If you could speak with the persons who may . . . have your son,
   what would you say?
Julie: I would simply say we hold no malice towards them, all we want
   is our boy back. We have no intention of prosecuting, we just hope
   that they treat him nicely and get him back to us somehow, anyhow.
   If they want to walk right up here, they can walk back out as far as I'm
   concerned. Right now we have absolutely no clues—nothing to go on.
   —*Julie Patz, May 27, 1979, interviewed in her apartment*
      by Channel 5 WNEW

From pulpits around lower Manhattan on Sunday morning, parishioners heard about Etan in earnest appeals and prayer. Folks who may have skipped church got the word on the street, when police on loudspeakers trumpeted a detailed description of the boy. The NYPD had also notified transit authorities, who broadcast Etan's description over their radio frequencies every half hour.

New Yorkers who were out of earshot or who hadn't tuned in to local TV news the night before read the first newspaper accounts on Sunday morning, either in the tabloids or the hefty Sunday edition of the *New York Times*, which carried a brief account buried among the full-page Memorial Day weekend blowout furniture sale ads.

Stan's sister-in-law Naomi Patz was at home in suburban northern New Jersey when she learned the news leafing through her Sunday paper. Stan had left a message for his brother, Rabbi Norman Patz, after calling their parents the day before, but no one had picked up the message yet.

Naomi immediately called the synagogue, and her husband rushed into the city.

At the apartment, neighbors were moving quietly through the front room with food offerings: home-baked bread and fruit. Stan sat with detectives at the table or listlessly on the couch, puffing mechanically on a pipe. Julie intermittently couldn't seem to move, then couldn't seem to sit, pacing the room, arms wrapped around herself. She would burst into tears, then pull herself together, trying to ignore reality so she could continue to function. Both parents had had next to no sleep since Friday morning, and now as they waited, the hours stretched on unendurably. Stan had lost the ability to distinguish between one minute and the next, to logically feel time passing. Each minute took forever, and like a grade-schooler waiting for the three o'clock bell, he agonized through each one, never sure if he'd still have his sanity sixty seconds later.

Taking Barry Ensminger's advice, Stan managed to find respite, as he always had, in the darkroom. There he'd begun making actual prints from his proof sheets. He and Julie handed these out to the TV crews and reporters, and when the supply ran low, Stan simply stepped into the darkroom he'd built adjacent to the front room to print out a hundred more. And what pictures.

As a commercial photographer, Stan Patz conducted some of his photo shoots right in the loft, with the kids hanging around. Off-hours, he turned his 105 Nikkor lens on the family, so there was a trove of captured moments in his darkroom files. Most were of Etan.

Etan relished posing for the camera, and the camera loved him back. Even in his work, Stan would save hours and money by using Etan to light the room before a real model arrived. Toddler Ari wouldn't sit still, and Shira was old enough to be jaded and bored. But Etan was just the right age, had the best temperament to stand in, and loved to mug.

There he was, a toothy grin close up into the lens, the rest of his face hidden under winter layers, his knit cap weighed down by clumps of melting snow from the great blizzard of '78. There, with wads of stuffing peeking out of his shirt for the great "indoor" blizzard of '79, created by Julie, who'd spent several long days patiently ripping up pounds of old newspaper into "snow." Etan cavorting in an open fire hydrant with family friends. Etan with Grandpa at the World Trade Center.

Shira, who was learning to share her father's love for the medium on a cheap, refurbished Argus camera, had snapped one of the standouts. In that timeless image, taken at his Halloween-themed sixth birthday party in October 1978, Etan sits in Julie's lap surrounded by cardboard witches and black-cat party favors. Their arms enfold each other, and their eyes are closed; Etan's small face, bearing an openmouthed smile and a rapt expression, rests on his mother's neck. Julie's smile is more enigmatic—a classic Madonna with child.

The cops and neighbors joining in the search were now well supplied with Stan's handiwork. In any missing child case, a photograph is the surrogate for the real boy or girl, giving the public a compelling reason to remember him, to keep the search alive. Most missing kids' pictures are indiscernible, blurry photo-booth snaps, or two-year-old class portraits that no longer bear a resemblance to the child, and maybe never did. Not Etan Patz. Grinning out from his father's portraits, each strand of his hair finely rendered in the sharp focus of Stan's professional cameras, you could literally see the sparkle in Etan's eyes. These pictures brought him to life more tangibly than most other missing children.

By the end of the weekend, Stan's evocative photos were on new posters going up all over New York. Eventually there were versions in five languages: English, Spanish, Italian, Yiddish, and Chinese. When one of Etan's neighbors told police he wouldn't recognize the boy without his favorite hat—the one he'd worn when he'd left home on Friday—an NYPD helicopter was dispatched from the Eastern Airlines terminal at JFK with a duplicate Future Flight Captain cap. Bill Butler crumpled up the stiff new black hat, then a police artist graphically added it to one of Stan's most recent photographs and lengthened Etan's hair for the next round of posters.

On one of those first nights Sandy Harmon was watching a breathless news report when her boyfriend, Michael, joined her. Sandy, who'd been hired by Julie, Karen Altman, and one other mother to walk their three children home during the six-week school bus strike, may have watched with the strange sense that comes when you see a bit of your own life unfold on the screen. She told Michael how terrible she felt for the boy she had safeguarded every afternoon for six weeks.

Her own four-year-old son, Bennett, was safe, hopefully fast asleep in the tiny room at the back of her cramped apartment on East 13th Street, a mile or so northeast of the Patz loft. While her connection to the Patz family was tenuous—the strike had ended the week before, and with it her employment with them—it had been one of Sandy's few paying jobs during the hard-luck period since she'd brought Bennett to New York from her home in Augusta, Maine. For that brief stretch, Sandy had been drawn into the warm climate of 113 Prince Street. She and Julie had talked about Sandy's staying on, helping out at Julie's daycare center, maybe as a trial run that could lead to something permanent. Now while half the city was out looking for the boy, there was no way to know how it would end, and how all this mess would affect Sandy's chances. She and Michael listened in silence as the broadcast detailed the extensive search.

"Where are you going?" Sandy asked the man as he stood up and walked to the door. "Out to help look for that little boy," Michael answered, and he was gone.

As the Memorial Day weekend ended, neighborhood residents made their way back into town to learn the news, and the search party swelled again. Neighbors now recovered from their initial reluctance to interfere congregated on the street below 113 Prince and canvassed passersby, stopping friends and strangers alike. At this point, it wasn't just about Etan. The first settlers of this urban frontier already shared a sense of community born of close-knit, shared hardship, of watching out for each other's unconventional backs. SoHo residents now felt like they were banding together to beat back an unseen enemy invasion, with the dawning knowledge that something sinister may have happened to one of their own.

The people here lived their life organically, and in the same way, the search for Etan moved block by block, spreading and growing. The police eventually went down to City Hall's archives to pull out the blueprints for every building in the area, and the search became more organized, although its obstacles also became more evident. These were hundred-year-old buildings, many former factories that had never been designed for family living. Their labyrinthine architecture precluded a methodical sweep.

Up in the loft, even though Julie and Stan Patz had both lost their sense of time, they were acutely aware of the urgency of the massive manhunt blanketing the city for their little boy. Every day, every minute that passed decreased the likelihood of Etan's safe return. He could be hurt, lying wet and shivering in the bottom of a construction site or huddled in the basement of an abandoned building; the possibilities were too numerous and disturbing to dwell on any one scenario. On the outside, their shock was evident, but they maintained a veneer of calm, even good cheer. It was a survival tactic, the alternative to total hysteria.

"I have to keep going," Julie told a group of neighbors meeting to organize their search effort, "or else I'm not going to get through it."

Stan Patz, always more the commanding officer to his wife's efficient
master sergeant, now alternated between short periods of formulating strategy and much longer moments of paralysis, which in turn fomented a brew
of impotent rage. When Julie wasn't providing information, describing
Etan's identifying characteristics—the baby teeth all still intact, including the one in the back that wore a stainless steel crown; the mole on his
back just above the buttocks; the place on his forehead where he might still
have scar tissue from a long-ago automobile accident—she plunged into
self-distracting tasks. She had always been a doer, a coordinator; it came
naturally to this eldest of nine children, who had grown up the mother hen
corralling her brood of younger brothers and sisters. It was the way she ran
her daycare, and the way she related to the uniformed troops now camped
out in her front room. As shock bled into abject denial, she rushed around in
a diminutive blur, providing an extra notebook, maps, directions; it was like
navigating tourists through her family's world.

"Is there anything I can do?" Karen Altman would ask her, wanting to
help share the load, yet aware she was posing the most clichéd and useless of
questions. But Julie would always have an answer.

"Yes, go down to the bodega and get everyone a soda." She would wave
her hand at the cops bent over the maps. Move things forward. Take action,
no matter how inconsequential. Julie herself couldn't leave to fetch her own
beverages—she and Stan were virtually under house arrest, needed by the
phone, answering an onslaught of questions, questions that were becoming
increasingly insistent. The longer Etan was gone, the less likely it seemed
he had merely wandered off or been hurt. The police were now looking at a
darker scenario, and they were looking specifically at Stan and Julie. They
were separated from each other by the wary watchers, even assigned their
own personal detectives, who followed them outside the apartment on the
rare occasion either parent did leave.

Of course we're suspects, Julie told herself over and over. They're playing
the percentages. Parents kill their children. That's how most of these cases
end. I was the last known person to see Etan alive. With no other evidence,
we both have to be suspects. It was by far the least of their problems, and she
didn't take it out on her minders.

"You have to eat," she'd say to the officers, even as concerned friends were saying the same to her; even as she herself was eating nothing. Other close neighbors—Jack and Mary Lembeck, Peggy Spina, and a handful of others—hovered around, clearing and replacing food, doling out large homemade platters and casseroles that kept arriving from other neighbors pitching in from home.

One woman who lived below the Altmans in the building across the street had a similar view to Larry and Karen's into the Patzes' front windows. She sent over a huge Thanksgiving-size feast—her way of giving thanks—and later told Julie she just hadn't been able to stand the way the men were eating anymore. "I can see them—they're all going to die, eating nothing but junk. And all that smoking!"

Stan wasn't conscious of much, but he was a creature of habit—healthy habit—and it disoriented him even more than he already was to see cops sitting in his living room, munching potato chips and swilling soda. All those caffeinated, carbonated, sugary beverages, he found himself thinking, and anything that came in a bag you could rip open and jam your hand into. How could these guys subsist? How could this be his home? As he looked around his loft, it felt like an occupying army of foreigners with strange, alien ways had moved in. His personal landscape had become empty junk food wrappers as far as the eye could see, and big men with guns.

Adding to the chaos was the shrill sound of the phone trilling nonstop. Next to Stan's pastel blue office phone, whose number was now published in every New York newspaper, the police had installed a dark red handset with the phone number that was printed on the bottom of Etan's missing poster. As soon as it was replaced on its cradle, it rang again. There were no typewriters—just notepads—but each call was logged with a two- or three-line description. Rather than disregard the clearly crazy ones, the police had to scrupulously track them, since, in the upside-down logic of child abductions, only a crazy person would kidnap a six-year-old.

There was always the chance one of these would be the magic ransom call. But the majority of the approximately five hundred calls a day were useless—"I saw a blond kid with a woman," or "I saw a boy with an older black man." Then there were sightings that accurately described Etan coming from everywhere in the city and then beyond, placing him in fifty different places at the same time. There were the awkward solace calls as well, and the occasional vindictive frame jobs to falsely accuse an enemy.

At first Stan and Julie jumped to answer every one, but after the first day or so that was no longer allowed. This was partly because some cops increasingly viewed the parents as suspects, and because the sheer volume required shifts. But mostly, Stan and Julie were made to sit out the calls because no parent in their place should be subjected to the false hopes many of these strangers inflicted, or the vicious intent of others. Indeed, Stan picked up one call to hear a boy's voice—clearly not Etan's—yelling, "Daddy, Daddy, help me, help me."

To keep from scaring away the real perpetrator, male and female officers took shifts, assigned to play the telephone voices of Stan and Julie. On top of all the other confusion in the loft, listening to a pair of faux parents was so perplexing to two-year-old Ari that he believed the cops when they told callers they were his mommy and daddy. After all, his own parents were acting so strangely, and the police kept taking them away from him to talk to them alone.

The holiday weekend over, anxious adults lined Prince Street, and a human chain ran down to the bus stop, like a bucket brigade handing off water to put out a fire. As neighborhood children got on the bus and went back to school, mothers, and some fathers, were firmly fixed at the corner of Prince and West Broadway, sentinels now, guarding the bus stop.

Julie was back at the apartment surrounded by police officers plotting out search areas. In rare solitary moments, she could be seen outside walking the length of the fire escape, smoking her Mores and peering the length of the street, in her own hellish version of a widow's walk. Her daycare center would have started back up that Tuesday, but it was gone. May 25 was its last day of operation. Julie could not keep it going anyway, but it was a moot point. What parent, she could understand, would ever entrust their child to a woman who had lost her own?

Her other children weren't even in her care. Neither she nor Stan had spent any time with Ari and Shira the whole weekend, and the days to come were no better. The two siblings were being shunted off to neighbors and friends, as Stan and Julie answered more questions. "Do you know this guy?" "Did Etan know him?" "Could this have happened?"

The Patzes were told to make lists of everyone they knew, or even came in contact with, as potential suspects. As they attempted this impossible task—looking at their friends, their relatives, their business associates with fear and mistrust—it skewed every one of their well-grounded beliefs. Already, authorities were eyeing so many: from next-door neighbor Fred Cohn, who turned out to have been safely packed off to a college reunion in Ohio by the time Etan disappeared; to the free-spirited longtime family friends who had taken Etan on a camping trip at what his parents now learned was a nudist camp; to the Jamaican handyman who had given Etan his dollar wage the evening before. Othneil Miller had just laid a cement basement a few doors down from the Patz loft, and there was talk of jackhammering it in search of a body.

"You want to break it up," Miller said wearily, "you go right ahead. But someone's going to have to pay for it." He himself was stunned by the loss of his little friend. The idea was ultimately abandoned, but Miller's name remained on the growing list of friends, family, and acquaintances who were under suspicion. Miller's basement office operated out of the same building as the city's first gay erotic art gallery, whose owners were also questioned with some intensity. The area's flourishing gay community was targeted in general, by old-school investigators to whom the words "gay" and "pedophile" were, if not synonymous, then largely overlapping.

Some of those investigators even wondered if Stan Patz was connected to that scene. The same morning that Etan's classmates returned to school to be greeted by plainclothes detectives who interviewed them, as well as the teacher and the bus drivers, the New York Post published a full-column, front-page photo Stan had taken of Etan. Straddling the top of a ladder, one arm bent on his knee, Etan gazed directly into the camera with a look of pure pleasure. He wore a pair of blue jeans, but no shirt. To anyone familiar with such things, it was a classic pedophile's pin-up.

What wasn't in evidence was that the photo was taken in Etan's own home, where just prior to the shot he'd been running around playing with his brother, and the idea of wearing or not wearing a shirt had seemed inconsequential. He'd been helping his father prepare for a much taller adult model, so the ladder had been brought in to approximate the right height. Besides, Stan wasn't responsible for the pose; Etan had scrambled up and goofed around in a variety of stances, sticking out his tongue, waving his arms.

In the same way that disseminating Etan's personal family photos got the word out, publishing this photo under the headline "Dad's Portrait" got a different word floating in the air. Even before the picture was made public, a number of cops and press moving in and out of the loft had been uncomfortable with Stan's cool manner. Unlike Julie, he'd displayed no outward signs of distress—the tears and emotion you'd expect. He was calm and seemingly unaffected, other than the skin stretched taut over the cheekbones now protruding from his gaunt face. And he was almost clinical in the way he'd unearthed his collection of photos and discussed their merits in helping the search.

"If it were *my* kid, I'd be a basket case," was the start of more than one conversation among observers. So this half-naked, perched-suggestively-on-a-ladder series of photographs—and there was an entire proof sheet of them—caused an even bigger stir.

As the week passed, Stan and Julie were taken out of their home to be interviewed over several days at more than one police precinct. This immediately felt different, and not just because they were on the cops' turf. Homicide detectives at the 13th Precinct were brought in at the end of the first week, since by that point the missing child case was starting to look like something even worse. The detectives' curt demeanor hit the Patzes as coldly as the word "homicide" on the door of their squad room. At first the detectives asked all the same questions that elicited the portrait Stan and Julie had already painted numerous times of Etan, as a sunny, well-adjusted first grader, an average, healthy child. Yes, he knew his own address and phone number. His mother feared he was trusting enough that he might conceivably get into a car with a friendly stranger. He might balk, she said, at taking the subway, which he had always disliked, clinging to her until they were back aboveground. No, he'd never tried to run away, but Julie recounted his newfound desire for independence, how he'd taken to walking ahead of her instead of staying at her side, how he chafed at holding her hand. He negotiated for free run of Washington Square Park, the concrete-and-grass landmark six blocks from their home, known as much for its bohemian flavor as for the seventy-seven-foot version of the Arc de Triomphe that marked its northern entrance. Julie often took the children there to play among the folk musicians, chess players, and street vendors who sold Italian ices in summer, fragrant roasted chestnuts in the chill air, and sinsemilla year-round. She resisted Etan's demands for more freedom, but he just pushed harder.

Juile told police that the evening before he'd disappeared, Etan and his little neighbor Vanessa had skidded their matching Big Wheels through the rain puddles on the sidewalk outside their building. Etan loved racing his plastic quasi-tricycle, customized with Shira's handpainted hearts and a big "I love you, Etan" on the seat. His boundaries were Wooster and Green streets, at either end of the block, but Julie had ducked off the fire escape at one point to tend to Ari and came back to find only Vanessa.

"Where is he?" she'd yelled down, and Vanessa had explained that he was taking a turn around the block, overstepping his bounds. He'd bristled at the stern reprimand he'd gotten when he'd reappeared, but obeyed when Julie admonished him not to go out of sight again.

The detectives noted these memories, but also asked the Patzes a probing series of questions about their own history, and made note of their empty savings account and modest annual income—under $20,000. As the story took hold of the city, theories abounded as to why this one case deserved so much attention, and some attributed it to the rich, white, privileged Patz family background, which would have made Stan and Julie laugh, if they'd been able to laugh. Instead, they gave the detectives a truer picture.

Stan Patz's father, they explained, had put three sons through college driving a cab in downtown Boston, until he'd sold his taxi medallion and retired young on careful investments in the late sixties. Stan and his two brothers had grown up in Mattapan, a section of Boston that was largely home to immigrant Jews. He'd arrived in New York in 1963, after graduating from the University of Massachusetts with a degree in sociology, although he'd spent less time taking classes and more time taking pictures for the school newspaper. That's where he'd met Julie. Growing up in rural Sudbury, Massachusetts, only half an hour west of Boston but a world apart, Julie often talked about raiding the local watermelon fields in summer, to cut open the sun-warmed fruit and eat her fill on the spot. Folks there, especially women, were born, married, raised children, and lived out their entire lives without ever venturing elsewhere. Not Julia Place. As a schoolgirl, she'd been bused into Boston to appear on a local "Whiz Kid" radio show, and later she'd left home to go to college, one of only two in her large band of siblings ever to do so.

For Stan it was classic "love at first sight," or at least "love at first date." He fell hard for the attractive, spirited woman who was so good with children. So what if she wasn't Jewish—that kind of thing barely registered on his radar.

They began dating in her junior year, but Julie, needed at home to attend the other children when her mother gave birth again, left school soon afterwards. She got a job back in Sudbury and thought only in vague terms about a future with her boyfriend, until the next year when Stan coaxed her to join him. "You can come marry me," he cajoled, "or you can stay home and raise your mother's children." Julie arrived in New York a few weeks before the wedding, and after converting to Judaism in deference to her mother-in-law-to-be, she and Stan were married by Stan's brother, the rabbi. The honeymoon was on West 85th Street, a night in.

They eked out a meager living, as young newlyweds do in New York. Soon after Julie gave birth to Shira, the Patzes started looking for more room. One day in 1971 Stan brought some photo equipment down to his boss shooting an assignment on Prince Street and discovered SoHo. Serendipitously, the shoot was for a local real estate developer, and not three days later, Stan had found a new home, in a building attached to two others that together comprised a residential co-operative. Previously, the space had housed a range of concerns: a leather finishing company was on the farthest west third floor; ladies' undergarments were sewn on the second floor; and the Patz apartment itself, one floor up, was reborn from a hand luggage manufacturer, where Stan imagined underpaid seamstresses jabbing thousands of pins into the oak woodwork on the front windows, rendering it unsalvageable when he began his renovations.

The storefront ground floor of the three buildings was commercial retail space, like the label maker who left behind stacks of Davy Crockett iron-on transfers when he eventually vacated, or the artist whose "art aquarium" consisted of one small shark and assorted other tropical fish swimming in a giant wood-and-fiberglass pond. But by the time residents began moving in, the upper floors were deserted and raw. The landlord used the center second-floor area to dump the ashes from the basement coal boiler. Along two walls of an otherwise empty room, literally tons and tons of ashes were piled halfway to the ceiling.

The upper floors, as Stan liked to say, were a bum's paradise. Most of the individual front doors were broken open, and an assortment of street people had taken up residence. One wild-eyed soul, nicknamed "Hemingway" for his looks by incoming neighbors, made a rat's-nest-like haven out of knee-deep newspapers in what later became the Patzes' living room. He could often be seen around the neighborhood, railing about the Supreme Court, and ultimately about the people who'd shooed him from his home to make it theirs.

The Patzes' new homestead was typical of the neighborhood—the proverbial loft that Stan built. He and Julie paid $7,500 for twenty-one hundred square feet, and that's all they got for their money—square feet. It was the rawest of raw spaces: no electricity, no plumbing, no heat, no running water. While renovating, Stan washed in the fire hydrant out front and his toilet was a paint can. When they finally got indoor fixtures…then they really needed walls. Stan raised them himself, carving one room at a time. He built a raised sleeping area along one eight-foot brick wall, eventually adding handmade bunk beds. Etan slept on the top, contained by guardrails made of iron plumbing pipe. Stan laid the floors too, pulling maple strips off of a truckload ordered from a neighborhood flooring distributor. He liked to joke that when Shira was one year old, her play space grew plank by plank every day.

Julie filled that play space with the fruits of her own creative labor, improvising with industrial castoffs that were found treasure on the streets three floors below. The Patz loft was a focal point for neighborhood art projects. A nearby paper factory threw away its mill ends, twenty-foot rolls that didn't make it into a customer's order, and now they served as canvas for the apartment's colorfully painted murals. Sometimes the children would simply coat themselves in washable finger paints and body surf on the giant sheets. There were strips of tinselized paper to bend into fantastical shapes for an imaginary circus. Once, the kids themselves gathered giant cardboard boxes, added a plastic tarp lining, and attempted to fill it with the hose to make a swimming pool in the family room. They were caught before leaping in, and the whole messy venture had to be carefully drained out the front window.

Now the detectives were talking about examining the murals for leads. When Etan drew his fanciful trip around the world with superhero Johnny France-America, did he leave any clues as to his destination in the real world? Are you sure he never talked about running away? Are you sure you never gave him a *reason* to run away?

Suddenly Stan and Julie weren't sure of the answers to any of these questions. Their whole reality, their sense of self and of each other, was being called into question. Etan was so young and tentative in so many ways, but maybe he *had* run away. Had they missed the signs? They had encouraged his open, trusting nature. Had they failed to prepare him for the danger he might now be facing? Could either of them in fact be in some way culpable? It was a small step from the crushing guilt they already bore to outright blame and suspicion.

If the session at Homicide had left them drained and disconsolate, both Stan and Julie were relieved when Bill Butler tentatively approached them with the idea of a polygraph.

"We thought you'd never ask," they said, wanting desperately to get it over with, to clear themselves and focus attention on the real culprit, whoever it might be. That was before they knew what the polygraph actually entailed, or how it could interpret the data.

"Don't call them lie detector tests," Stan would later insist. "They measure three things—perspiration, respiration, and pulse. Not the truth." If you were a sociopath, you could sail right through, as long as you believed your own lies. Used only as a guide, they were never admitted as evidence in court. Julie passed with flying colors, but Stan did not immediately exonerate himself.

When he walked into the room, the officer in charge pointed to what looked like an old electric chair, silhouetted by harsh fluorescent lights overhead. The walls crumbled in places, as though someone had tried to escape through them, with footprints plastered all over their scarred surface. Broken tiles lay scattered on the floor. They sat him down and strapped him in. After asking a series of test questions the officer got down to business.

"Did you take part, in any way, in the abduction of Etan?"

"No."

Just hearing Etan's name made him feel like he was being gouged with a knife. Stan couldn't concentrate. Not just from the emotional pressure, but from physical discomfort. He could not stand having something around his arm. When Etan had disappeared, Stan was already a stick—five foot eight, 140 pounds. He'd lost more weight; within days he was down another fifteen pounds. When they put a strap around his biceps to press the sensor against an artery, his arm went numb. The pins and needles creeping up from his fingertips made Stan itch to bolt from the chair.

"To the best of your knowledge, have you had any contact with Etan since he disappeared on 5/25/79?"

"No."

He could hardly think of anything except getting the tourniquet off. As he struggled to answer the questions, he certainly *looked* guilty. During the thousands of calls in the last week, and the countless trips through the streets, to the parks and ball fields, Stan had talked to hundreds of kids. Many had sounded or looked like Etan. He'd had glimpses—he'd thought, he'd hoped—of his son at every bodega, on every street corner within a five-mile radius of his home. He didn't really know the right answer to that question. And indeed the test showed "signs of deception."

The day of Stan Patz's tortured polygraph was the one-week mark. The media thrives on anniversaries, and the next day John Miller was back to update his reporting of the previous weekend. He checked in with the new mobile command post, two vans parked on Prince Street in front of the building, after it was finally decided to cede their home back to the Patz family. Seven days was an eternity in the city's news cycle, but Miller could understand why this case was still playing in heavy rotation. The press rarely covered a missing child case while the child was still missing, only once he was found, or the body recovered. And if they did, there was usually no eloquent spokesperson, no citywide mobilization, no meticulously shot pictures. By now, Stan Patz had mounted a series of his photographs to make it as easy as possible for the camera crews. It was drive-through TV production.

This was a beautiful boy, a white child—and there could be no denying that it was a factor in the level of both predominately white public and press interest. He lived in a neighborhood where criminal acts were uncommon. And no one yet knew where this story was going to end. Both of the Patzes were likable and articulate, speaking in perfect soundbites with a high tolerance for the endless loop of boundaryless questions. And Julie, at least, wore her heartbreaking emotions openly.

Most reporters were respectful, kind, and did their job. But by definition, in a story this sensitive almost any question risked crossing the line to inflict pain. What were Etan's likes and dislikes? Do you miss him? What does your gut tell you happened to your son? And the ubiquitous "How do you feel?" One tabloid photographer didn't even bother with a pretense of civility. He just went straight for the bottom-feeders line. "Would you mind working up a few tears for me now," he asked Julie, adding words she would never forget, "so I don't have to come back and bother you again when they find the body?"

Reporters were confined to the front room, but they infiltrated the private back area, even finding their way into Stan and Julie's bed one morning, when their private line rang sometime around 6 a.m., waking them up from a rare moment of the sleep that largely eluded them. Stan's heart immediately went into his throat at the thought someone was calling with news that couldn't wait for a decent hour. Fumbling for the phone, he managed a groggy hello. A cheery voice answered, identifying himself from an unfamiliar radio station, "...and we're live on the air. We want to know how you're holding up?" Stan went from shock to rage in an instant, and glanced over at his wife's drawn face. "Are you recording?" he asked the DJ. "Yes, we are," was the reply. "Well, then record this," he said, and let loose with a few choice words of his own before hanging up.

Stan vented to the station manager later that day. "Just because we're a news story doesn't mean we should have no privacy." The man, dutifully apologetic, agreed, but those words were to become a mantra in the Patzes' lives. During moments like these, they regretted opening the Pandora's box of press coverage. But there was no turning back. For all the lunatics and the invaded privacy and the sudden need to "manage" a public persona—not too morose, but God forbid, no laughter, not even nervous laughter—the trade-off of Etan's face in every local press outlet, reaching millions of readers and viewers, had to be worth it.

Except on those days when the press coverage completely defeated their efforts. In its one-week anniversary coverage, the *New York Post* published a story whose explosive headline alone threatened to derail the search. IS MISSING SOHO BOY WITH KIN IN BOSTON? it asked. "According to sources close to the investigation," the article read, "detectives have received information that Etan is safe and staying in Massachusetts. The tip, which police sources describe as 'strong,' came from a resident of SoHo."

In fact, the same tipster had also contacted other papers, including the *SoHo Weekly News*, which had offered a $1,000 reward for information leading to Etan's recovery. The man asked if he could collect the reward even though he'd already given his story to the *Post* reporter.

Within hours of the article's appearance on newsstands, Stan Patz had seen one area resident ripping down a missing poster. Throughout the next days more posters were struck, and many people abandoned the hunt. Rumors circulated that the boy's Jewish grandparents, unhappy with his secular upbringing, had taken him, or that his parents had orchestrated a stunt, perhaps a deliberate attempt to further Etan's imagined "modeling career." But while the "tip" had no basis in fact whatsoever, the rest of the article construed what factual information it did contain to hint that the Patz family was under a cloud of suspicion: "Julie Patz, Etan's mother, underwent a lie detector test yesterday. The results were kept confidential.... Police have been re-interviewing the parents separately."

The police immediately issued a statement denying the Massachusetts part, but couldn't say the same about the separate interviews. Of course they were being questioned separately. That was standard procedure.

Not long afterwards, a few of the detectives with whom Stan had grown marginally comfortable invited him for a tour of their station house. Over the previous days, he'd talked shop with them some, yearning for a sense of affiliation to the investigation, and he was eager to stay occupied, so he went down to the First Precinct, "to see where they worked." It was after hours, few personnel were on duty, and the gritty second-floor squad room where they sat was empty. The conversation started off in neutral, but devolved quickly from "Who do you think could have done it?" to "Did you ever hit your son?"

"I don't think I ever did," Stan answered. "He never needed it. The others, yes, but him? Never."

The line of questioning continued and sharpened. "Did you ever get so angry at Etan that you *wanted* to hit him?" "Did you have any reason to hurt him?" "Did you beat Julie?" It went on and on, with an intensity he'd yet to experience. Most were not new questions, but this time it was relentless and repetitive. "Did you fight with your wife?" "Do you have a lover, problems in the marriage?" "Are you the real father?" "How badly did the family need money?" Sitting in the empty, sterile squad room, Stan Patz felt his steely reserve crack.

He was mortified to realize he was crying. He had never thought it was proper for a man to cry in public. But now he was bawling like a baby, the tears pouring out like blood from a severed artery, draining from such a large open wound that it threatened exsanguination.

In all the time since his son had disappeared, he'd presented his detached stoicism. But inside, he'd been silently going mad from the terror, the guilt, and the muscle-clenching helplessness. Talking to the press and sorting and handing out photos had given him a concrete task, one that even felt marginally productive, and helped override the internal voice screaming in self-condemnation, "DO SOMETHING! FIX THIS! WHAT ARE YOU WAITING FOR?"

Now, aloud, he pleaded to the detectives that they were wasting their time. "Look somewhere else," he said. "I don't care what you're doing to me, but you're taking up precious hours, and I promise you it's fruitless."

In one way it wasn't fruitless. As the detectives watched Stan display the emotion they expected from an innocent, grief-stricken father, they finally began to suspect him less. Not enough to take him or Julie off the list, but enough to convince them to widen their focus.

The problem was, despite the massive police investigation, there was nothing to focus on. For all their looking, the police had actually seen nothing that gave them a clue about what had happened after Etan crossed Wooster Street.

And now that the first, second, and third round of combing all thirty-seven blocks of SoHo had been completed unsuccessfully, the police occupation began to decamp, to move on to someone else's battlefield. As cacophonous and disorienting and outrageous as the whole invasion into their lives had been over the last few weeks, for Julie and Stan, this evacuation was worse.

~

CHAPTER 4

A Year for the Books

Missing Persons Unit Case #8367: As of June 4: 688 manhours on telephone...2,760 manhours on 345 search assignments...880 manhours
on 110 investigations, not including emergency service, harbor unit,
aviation unit and missing persons....Daily aviation unit aerial searches
since May 26th....Over 500 DD5 [detective interview forms] have been
filed, 10,000 circulars have been distributed.
  —*June 4, 1979, NYPD Status Report on its two-week emergency
  response to the disappearance of Etan Patz*

B y the start of week three, with still no sign of Etan, the emergency
response phase was called off. The centralized Missing Persons
Unit would take over the case.

On the eleventh floor at Police Headquarters, the twenty-detective MPU
oversaw some thirty-thousand new reports each year; people of all ages
who'd disappeared in New York City, and whose descriptions were cata-
loged in drawer after drawer of four-by-six-inch cards. A specially created
five-person task force would exclusively investigate Case #8367, Missing
Person Etan Patz. Detective Bill Butler was "taken off the chart" for any
other cases at the First Precinct and loaned indefinitely to Missing Persons.

The phones at the Patz apartment were still ringing in tandem on the
table in the front room, but soon there would be no team of cops, pretending to be Stan and Julie, to answer them. Instead, a yellow legal pad and pen
sat next to Stan's powder blue phone.

"When you take a call," Butler instructed Stan and Julie, "you need to
mark it in the book. We need a date at the top of each page, and a time
stamp next to each entry. Friends, heavy breathers, hang-ups, psychics. If it

looks like something, you contact us and we'll follow up immediately. But every single person who calls should go down in the books."

The succession of notepads and then spiral notebooks—once the pads were found to shred their pages all over the loft—would go on to track not just the case, but the Patz family's life. In the beginning, the overwhelming majority of callers were cranks, and one departing detective suggested maybe it was time to change their phone number. Stan and Julie found that inconceivable. They had taught Etan those seven digits—although, they regretted, not his area code—and they would never cut off his one sure avenue of contact. If he were out there trying to reach them, they wanted to be as reachable as possible. In the meantime, from the late-night caller who was sure Etan's attacker had just tried to kidnap her own son, to the overwrought, misinformed folks who thought they'd found the quickest way to get in touch with the cops when they dialed the number on Etan's missing poster, Stan and Julie took turns noting the times and taking down the messages. Julie wrote in a neat, rounded, clearly legible hand, and the dots over her i's sometimes formed a perfect circle. Stan's words were more crabbed and hasty, the letters often slurred together.

> 2:30 a.m. Mrs. Widholm [from a NJ number]; she was at Yankee Stadium—someone tried to grab her blond 10 year old—[she] has description
>
> 2:51 p.m. Jan [NY number]—Call Life Institute; re: Dr. Massy—psychic— he spoke last nite, and feels he can help us
>
> 4:21 p.m. Sel Raab, NY Times
>
> 4:39 p.m. $10,000? No money? No talk? Hispanic male—Info on your son
>
> 5:06 p.m. got a big fire in the project—get the police, please.
> —Patz logbook, June 21, 1979

A few days after the crush of regulation blue had cleared out, Stan and Julie dared a first family outing to the nearby annual Feast of St. Anthony street fair a few blocks away. It felt terribly strange and inappropriate to be going somewhere so festive, and they were all too aware of the irony that St. Anthony was the patron saint of lost objects. But neither Stan nor Julie had spent any time in the last frantic weeks with their two other children. They felt a strong need to at least pretend normalcy, for Shira and Ari's sake. The festival was an annual event and the kids always looked forward to it. For days now the aroma of Italian sausage and peppers had been drifting into the front room from the balcony windows, beckoning them out of doors. Julie strapped Ari into the fold-up stroller, and they set off.

As the family walked four blocks west on Prince Street to Sullivan, they passed the new round of Etan's posters replacing ones that had been mistakenly torn down. Earlier in the week, Stan had bought ink pads to hand-stamp them with the urgent red message "Still Missing," hoping to dispel the misperception that Etan was back home.

On this sunny early summer day, the three blocks of Sullivan Street south from Houston Street—where St. Anthony's Church was—down to Broome Street were blocked off. Vendors wheeled their carts through the streets and hawked marzipan, pistachios, and torrone, the chewy Italian nougat and nut confection. Doughy balls of zeppole bubbled in huge vats of oil. Once fried to a crisp brown, they were swirled in powdered sugar and sold six to a bag. Squealing neighborhood children played water-pistol games for cheap polyester-stuffed animals, or rode the creaky Tilt-a-Whirl. One of the big annual draws was the three-story Ferris wheel that towered over Houston Street, its colored lights twinkling in the dusk.

As Stan and Julie carefully eyed their children, they became aware that they too were being watched, as though *they* were the fair's new attraction. Some in the crowd had never met the Patzes but recognized them from the press coverage, which had conferred on them a macabre celebrity. Stan and Julie were equally nonplussed to recognize some of their neighbors, and then receive no return acknowledgment. It suddenly felt as though people they knew were shrinking from them. They felt badly to disappoint Shira and Ari, but it wasn't long before the Patzes fled back to the relative safety of their loft. They felt branded as neglectful parents or, worse, suspected murderers.

If nothing else, many of their neighbors had been struck dumb by the understandable fear of saying the wrong thing. But until that moment, the Patzes had been cocooned by friends who'd wanted to show them nothing but humanity to counter their despair.

The newly created Etan Patz Action Committee, spearheaded by Sally Gran, a neighbor with a seemingly infinite amount of energy and organizational skills, would eventually swell to 170 members. Each had delegated tasks. There were poster "depots" sprinkled around SoHo where volunteers could pick up flyers to distribute. There was a message center, a media coordinator, even someone in charge of vehicles for transportation. Teams solicited donations from local businesses to keep the search going. A few neighbors even turned detective, seeking out the hidden sweatshop workers who might have seen something but would be reluctant to come forward to the cops.

Many of the Patzes' friends were fellow freelancers, who took extended time off from work to devote themselves to the search. There were volunteer cooks and housekeepers, a babysitting network, and a team that brought groceries. People considered canceling summer vacations, and the Patzes began to feel like the neighborhood quicksand pit. "It's a trap," Julie told a reporter several months later. "You get caught up in it and you can't get out."

Julie sometimes wondered how much the parents who were helping her and her family were glad to be distracted from new fears about their own children's safety. But when a neighbor's nine-year-old daughter who'd been left in charge of her siblings called the loft one day, Julie became aware of some of the collateral damage their crisis had generated.

"Can you please let my mother come home for a while?" the girl asked plaintively. So some six weeks in, Julie called her friends together and sent them home. "Your own children need you," she told them, "and we need to take care of ourselves."

Both Ari and Shira had been left to struggle with their fears, nightmares, and confusion at a time when their parents were least able to help them. Their brother was suddenly gone, their parents were like strangers, and a rotating cast of caregivers couldn't answer their questions. Assurances felt hollow, because they were. As uncomfortable as their own parents were about saying the wrong thing, Shira's friends either shunned her or, too young to feel the discomfort, said the wrong thing.

"Your brother's not coming back," they'd blurt out, in the blunt way of children. "He's probably dead." Some who only knew Shira because of the newfound attention were jealous. "I wish my brother would disappear so I could get on television," she was told.

Ari took to wearing Etan's clothes, and, not yet three, he toilet trained himself almost overnight. He slept in the bottom bunk, below the empty one, and worried about playing with Etan's toys. When Shira went up to

Massachusetts to spend time with Julie's family, Ari was terrified that she too would never come back. It was a logical conclusion. One of his well-intentioned minders had told him in the earliest days of the search that everyone was busy looking for Etan, who was "lost," and he didn't understand why his parents, who always found his lost toys and stuffed animals, couldn't just do the same with Etan. Young children need the security of believing their parents are all-powerful, and it was devastating for both Shira and Ari to plainly see that their parents were completely powerless instead.

Ari seemed to pin his hopes on Bill Butler, the most familiar face, who stayed on the case when the larger police presence ended. At first, the revolver tucked into Butler's ankle holster at toddler-eye level had frightened Ari, who thought his parents were about to be arrested—or that he was. But eventually, he grew convinced that if Stan and Julie had failed in their parental responsibilities, then the kindly hulking detective would bring his brother home. He would call "Policeman Bill" on his plastic play phone every day for an imaginary update.

Butler called the family for real every day too, and several times a week he could be seen walking the blocks surrounding Prince Street. He would start his canvass at 7:30 a.m., in hopes of meeting someone whose regular route would have crossed Etan's path at that hour. In those first months, Butler worked the case seven days a week. He and his wife had long-standing plans to attend a wedding out of town over the summer, but his wife boarded the plane alone.

As the days wore on, Bill Butler became Stan and Julie's touchstone. He never raised an eyebrow or betrayed irritation no matter how far-fetched the "leads" they passed along from wacky tipsters and the ever-present psychics.

> 9:09 a.m.   Jim X Kansas City Mo.—wife psychic—picture boy—brown hair—city sidewalk…boy alone—emotionally deprived—streetwise—undernourished,…man on 2nd floor 60's—maybe alcoholic—sad and angry—E. calls him "Red" but his name is Paul

> ??? Gloria X: alive—Sexual abuse—held for long time unharmed—abductors now running scared…2 people involved: 1 tall, 1 med—Etan knew person very well—will be all over by 5/15/80—1st news by April

15:40 [Julie's] return call to Zora X—psychic—Etan alive in a province of
    Italy,—boat trip: Bermuda, S.A. then Italy. "a relative," maybe distant
    knows more than telling—someone is watching our pain + won't tell
    (vindictive)
    —*Patz logbook, various psychic calls, 1979–80*

Over the first months an astounding three hundred psychics weighed
in, with no two scenarios alike. The only thing any of them could agree on
was the recurrent phrase that Etan was "near water." Nonbelievers from the
start, Stan and Julie realized how useless that particular spiritual guidance
was—what *wasn't* near water? Are we talking river? A lake? What about a
bathtub? Stan would shake his head in disgust. But one after the other, the
Patzes welcomed these psychics to their home... just in case.

Jack Lembeck, the father of Etan's best friend Jeff, had been a steady,
calming face in the loft throughout the initial onslaught. Tall and quietly
commanding, he'd unknowingly passed himself off as some enigmatic FBI
agent, and his presence was never questioned. As the real cops had drawn
back, Lembeck had stayed on, finding himself an unofficial liaison to this
growing legion of psychics. He drove them around the city so they could
soak up their "impressions," took notes, and reported back. It was the most
productive thing he could think to do.

12:30—Julie call to Dorothy Allison.—4 people know what happened
    that morning and are not coming forward.—1 or 2 people took [Etan]
    out of love.
    —*Patz logbook, August 17, 1979*

Lembeck spent most of his time with Dorothy Allison. The fifty-four-year-
old mother of four was by far the most renowned of her profession, and she
was quasi-legitimized by her reported past success. In her trademark overalls
and red sneakers, she walked into the Patz loft and started the usual way, by
running her hands over Etan's toys and stuffed animals. Some in law enforcement revered her skills, but Allison was scorned by others as a classic psychic
"retrofitter," tailoring her history after the fact to appear more credible. But
she came with a track record, genuine or not, and the Patzes jumped at the
chance for a breakthrough. Jack Lembeck repeatedly drove her around the
five boroughs. She kept Stan and Julie—mostly Julie—immersed in following up on her cryptic visions. When Allison saw the name "Scott," it sent
Julie to the phone book for days, making pages of lists; every Scott in the

city; first name Scott, last name Scott—perhaps Scotty's Bar was the key, or maybe Dr. John Scotti.

Julie would compile hundreds of "Scott" entries, with accompanying addresses, maps, and overlays throughout the city, and hand them over to the detectives for further pursuit, just in time for Allison to see the name "Ralph," or "Gonzalez," and Julie would start again. In one way, she didn't mind—it kept both her and Stan occupied. They were also grateful for Allison's telling them she thought Etan was alive. The reason she was having such difficulty, she said, was that her gift was communing with the dead.

In between servicing the psychics and passing along leads now coming in from around the country, Julie's goal was to establish a routine and stick to it. She knew such routine was critical, and it soothed her. The home day-care center was gone, but she took back her household duties from friends, the cooking and mopping, dusting and laundry; all the rote work that put her body through the comfortingly familiar motions she could salvage from her life pre–May 25.

Stan had a harder time. He couldn't concentrate, and work was scarce. His freelance assignments had dried up, clients going elsewhere while he was consumed by the initial search. Now there was nothing in the pipeline and the personal contacts that had fueled his business were shying away. His routine was different from Julie's. Every day he'd hold fast to sobriety until six o'clock, then check out in a haze of marijuana smoke.

When he began counting down the minutes until the hour hand hit six, he knew it was time to stop. Both he and Julie realized neither one could afford to lose their health—it would be too much to bear this alone. Besides, Shira couldn't stand the smell of the tobacco pipe and wouldn't sit next to him when he puffed on it. Sometime in late summer he quit both pot and tobacco on the same day, struggling more with the latter.

Instead, Stan spent a hundred dollars on a used three-speed bike, deliberately choosing one with peeling black paint, dilapidated-looking enough to deter thieves. In the days before bicycle safety was an issue, he fashioned helmets out of cast-off hard hats and, buckling Ari into the child seat behind him, Stan rode the length of the empty, under-repair West Side Highway with Shira. The exercise calmed Stan and gave Julie some downtime. They'd strap on their cameras—Shira had continued with her hand-me-down Argus and Ari toted a toy with plastic lenses that nevertheless took real pictures. Once, pedaling around Battery Park, they rode past members of the task force, and everyone exchanged waves. If I'm still under suspicion, Stan thought, this Father Goose and his goslings scene might sway them in my favor.

But often, when he biked alone, Stan would go for miles at top speed, and to distract or punish himself, he'd ride in the highest gear, deliberately making his muscles scream. Like a self-flagellating monk, he welcomed the physical pain. He was angry at the person responsible for his son's disappearance, at the world, at himself, and he couldn't vent on Julie or the kids. So he took out his fury in rants on unsuspecting pedestrians and cyclists who crossed his path.

Both Stan and Julie worked hard not to blame themselves for what had happened, and they never blamed each other. There was enough of that coming from outside the loft, especially toward Julie. Did she murder her own child, went the nasty gossip, or did she just somehow manage to lose him? And if she dared be seen in public—at the park or playground—with a smile or a laugh for the two children she was still trying to mother, she was the woman who didn't *care* that she'd lost her son. She chuckled at some little joke one of the kids told, and strangers walked over to interrupt. They told her if she was so unfeeling about her missing son, maybe he was better off missing.

Stan and Julie weren't imagining the widespread speculation that had been there from the beginning among their own community, even among their friends. For every awkward, heartfelt offer of help, there was a hushed whisper or unspoken thought about neglect or irresponsible parenting. Some of the parents who were saying, "There but for the grace of God go I" were simultaneously thinking, "It could never happen to me—I would never let Johnny walk by himself." It was a common enough phenomenon, this mental trick designed to provide insulation from the tragedy of others. Recognized in psychology and even law enforcement as the "just world" theory, it was one reason prosecutors sometimes struck women from rape juries. If the world was just, so the theory went, you got what you deserved. If you can find any way to blame the victim, you yourself will feel less vulnerable.

So a neighbor who'd brought food over to the Patzes allowed herself to voice her thought to her husband—"How could she be so stupid?"—before feeling instantly ashamed at the words coming out of her mouth. And one June morning during the last few weeks of school, Karen Altman had been incensed as she waited with her daughter Chelsea at the bus stop, to hear another mother disparage an absent Julie for letting Etan walk alone. This was a woman whom, like most of the parents standing there, Karen had never seen at that bus stop before May 25.

Once, Julie took Shira and Ari to Little Italy and a group of mamas approached, tongues clucking, to offer their condolences. "How terrible you must feel," one said, "especially since it was all your fault."

"It's almost like we have a communicable disease," Stan told a reporter. "Like we've been touched by something very ugly and if people get close, it will rub off." But, in fact, no isolating quarantine could keep this epidemic from spreading. Everyone had been touched.

Life had changed irrevocably not only for the Patzes, but for every neighborhood family. Etan's face, in the posters that now hung on every SoHo storefront, lamppost, and blank wall space, was an ever-present, unavoidable reminder of the new reality. Fear was the prevailing emotion, as parents accompanied their children to the school bus stop, or better yet all the way to the schoolhouse door. Seven-year-old Vanessa Spina's mother had been promising to let her walk to the corner bodega by herself for weeks. Soon, she'd said, soon. Soon was unforeseeable now. A young boy from a few blocks over, Etan's age and also blond, rang the Patz buzzer one morning and tearfully begged Julie to tell police to stop pulling him aside for questioning.

Parents worked to shield their children and talked over their heads, with unsettling glances that were arguably worse. As a result the kids were often either confused or blissfully unaware. But the parents themselves were in panic mode. No one could say that the person who took Etan wasn't still out there, an unknown, real-life bogeyman, poised to strike again. A few weeks before the end of school, a simple misunderstanding led Etan's friend Jeff Lembeck to stay on the school bus past his stop. In the brief moments before all was well again, his terror-stricken parents felt the blood draining to their toes.

Even as the local media blitz was subsiding, national magazines and television had picked up the story and Etan's image was reaching outside New York City. A U.S. representative from New York, Peter Peyser, read the story into the *Congressional Record* at the end of July. "I am asking all Members to do an act of kindness for a family in New York.... It is now assumed that Etan may have been taken away from the New York area and is somewhere in the United States. A poster is being delivered today to each Member's office.... Perhaps someone, somewhere, has seen this young man and can help bring him back to his family." A SoHo travel agency volunteered to send the poster to sixty foreign countries.

While at a standstill in New York, the investigation was also extending beyond the city. In July, a Missing Persons detective went to Rabbi Patz's New Jersey synagogue for an unannounced visit and discovered from his secretary that the rabbi was on his annual six-week trip to Israel, leading a group of American schoolchildren to summer camp. The news raised eyebrows among investigators, who knew that in kidnapping cases, statistics showed a family member was the most likely culprit. The speculation was fueled by the unfounded rumors about religious differences in the family. Had Etan been spirited far away to a more religious environment?

The NYPD turned to Israeli authorities, who told them forty-one children had passed Israeli frontier control. All forty-one children were vetted, and every one of them returned to the United States six weeks after they'd left.

The FBI was tapped to interview Stan's parents as well as Julie's sizable family in Massachusetts, and they were ruled out as suspects. There was talk of a reward, but Stan and Julie worried the prospect of money might encourage copycats. The police adamantly advised against it. Already overwhelmed by false leads, they felt a reward would just elicit more crazies, offering information tainted by profit motive.

The summer ended and other children went back to school, including Shira and Ari. The little boy started part-time at a preschool in a church basement near Washington Square Park, where Julie then took to volunteering. It gave her an outlet for her natural affinity for children, and the little ones welcomed her unreservedly. It also gave her a sentry post from which to guard Ari.

> Ari at bedtime: "I don't like my bed anymore 'cuz Etan won't come sleep with me." Crying.
> —*Patz logbook, October 8, 1979*

With the change of season, even the most stalwart civilian foot soldiers were overtaken by battle fatigue. Jack Lembeck turned to his wife, Mary, one morning and told her he just couldn't do it anymore. Until then, he'd been propelled by the notion that he and his neighbors were no different than the Patzes. His mantra throughout the summer—it could have been our son—propelled him to drive the streets, answer calls, and search playgrounds. It could have been Jeff wearing his jacket instead of Etan who walked out the door into nothingness. But Lembeck had begun to realize his family differed from Stan and Julie's in one critical way. He and his wife woke up every morning, and their child was still safe with them. The Patzes did not. At the risk of his family's health, he and his wife decided they had to acknowledge that difference and move on. Mary Lembeck took her son out of state to stay with relatives for a few months.

Etan's seventh birthday, October 9, came and went, bringing a spike in press calls and ensuing wackos. Police released the one and only sketch of a possible suspect, to another flurry of press, but this portrait was based on the flimsiest of connections, more a mark of the authorities' desperation than anything else. A woman had seen a strange-looking man talking to a little boy near the Patz apartment on the morning Etan had disappeared. She'd come forward the very next day with a description. She had no idea if the boy was Etan—he'd had his back to her. She didn't know if the man was doing anything nefarious. She wasn't even sure her sighting was from the right day. But in the four-month interim she'd been questioned repeatedly, and finally hypnotized to provide a vague picture of the man's features. Now his crude sketch was in every New York newspaper as a potential suspect. Nothing came of it, except for the predictable burst of false leads.

> 18:49 Ina X: [The first name of the man in sketch] has "D" and "V"; David Divine, etc.... [The man is a] surrogate who took Etan to someone else.
>
> 19:34 Pathmark, Bronx—looks like our kid—distressed w/a man who mishandled him.
>
> 16:16 You need a psychic witch—can break evil spells—their whole family has evil spell and cannot succeed.
> —*Patz logbook, various, October 1979*

Tips trickled in on the answering machine now attached to the phone or in letters from all over the world, along with well-wishes and prayers. Stan Patz, who had always disdained organized religion, was deeply touched if not slightly bemused at the thought of strangers uttering his son's name in their churches and synagogues. Then there were the fervent believers who *blamed* the Patzes, who, they rationalized, must have lost their child because they'd lost their faith.

If there is a God who punishes me this way for not believing, Stan thought when he read those letters, what kind of a stupid, jerky God would he be? It seemed specious logic to Stan, who felt God must have far more important things to deal with than one inconsequential nonbeliever. He wrote back to a few of the correspondents, but he never responded to those condemnatory notes.

There was even a religious/con artist combo variation: a man who guaranteed their son's recovery if they slaughtered a sheep in their living room, after having a "good Muslim woman" clean and prepare it first. "You have to eat some of it," he called back to say later. He would supply the sacrificial lamb for just $125, but he required an additional $2,000 after Etan was safely returned. The cops, who had begun to feel protective of this family battered on all sides by the press and the prying public, hated the idea of anyone taking advantage of their charges and instructed the Patzes to call the man back and set up a meeting. Then the detectives, who'd been hiding in the apartment, emerged with guns drawn and led him away. Julie felt a little sorry for him.

> 1:28 female, 20's (?)—heavy N.Y. accent—well-wisher (at 1:28 a.m.!!)
>
> 23:20 Man—rang bell—on drugs?—came about Etan—had seen him once in Wash Sq—very emotional—had tattoo on left forearm
> —*Patz logbook, September 8, 1979*

The preponderance of log entries were of angry or lonely or disturbed individuals who took advantage of their easy access to the Patzes. The most obsessive ones called repeatedly. Stan and Julie recognized they might be the only people these callers talked to. Sometimes the police were able to track down their therapists or counselors and Julie would get on the phone with them, to try to mediate a cease-fire of sorts. She didn't just want to leave such a troubled sympathizer hanging. Once, a man actually appeared in their home, beaming at Stan and Julie.

"You are not going to believe me," he said, in the only believable part of his remarks, "but I have become your son and I have come home for dinner." Who, they would shake their heads in amazement, would leave the angry message "I fucked and killed your son"? But as dreadful as those were, perhaps the toughest were the ones Stan and Julie came to call the "look-likes."

15:43 p.m.—anonymous, boy, blonde, pilot's cap in courtyard behind
Lex Ave everyday—not noticed before Etan reported missing—never
leaves yard.

23:25 Anthony, on 5/31/79 . . . NY upstate . . . picked up boy and 21 yr old
w/girl hitching . . . almost positive was Etan . . . exit 113 dropped off 3
people.

2:05 Lisa from VA . . . female—approx 50 years old . . . boy looks like Etan
and not belong to woman. [Woman is] nut—from Greenwich Village . . . boy was in 1st grade in public school system, . . .—boy called
"Erin"—boy beautiful.
—Patz logbook, various, 1979–80

The intricate stories took up pages and pages in the Patz logbooks but
never panned out. They exacted the biggest emotional cost, riding Stan and
Julie on a steep vertical incline up the tracks, to plunge straight back down
to hell every time.

They almost never talked to each other about the toll that it all took. The
subject was too raw to think of inflicting it on one another, and besides, they
had to stay strong. In self-defense, they began to see themselves as investigators, as though they were looking for someone else's child.

The whole family was in counseling, off and on, and Julie found it enormously helpful, giving her a place to unload some of her grief. Stan was less
enthusiastic. His New England upper lip was usually stiffened resolutely
into a "No." He kept his feelings in—where they belonged—but he was sure
that within his body they'd rerouted into the excruciating, chronic back and
leg pain that had only begun after Etan had vanished.

He and Julie took their small comfort from the task force's reassuring,
unflappable presence. The initial mutual wariness soon faded, as on one side
the cops grew to understand the defense mechanisms behind Stan's gruff
manner and biting wit. On the other side, Julie acknowledged and rejected
her unconscious biases toward police—"the man"—as some kind of faceless
paramilitary force. She had grown to see them as humans—humans who
made mistakes like everyone else, but who had the best of intentions to help.
They worked overlong hours and came in on their days off, sometimes bringing their own kids to hang out in the loft and play with the Patz children.

With his benevolent smile and dry humor, Detective Bill Butler was
lovingly dubbed a "second father," cruising the neighborhood in his bat-

tered yellow car, prowling Prince Street with a stash of photo cards of Etan tucked into his pocket, scratching down new leads with an endless supply of patience. But the case clearly haunted him, and he took it home at night. He would jolt awake sometimes in his bed wondering, "Did I do that? Did I remember this?"

Butler was convinced that if Etan had been murdered, there would be a body to show for it. So he maintained a positive outlook.

"I know we're going to get our boy back," he'd say to Stan and Julie. "It's just a matter of time."

But Julie felt trapped between true believers on the police force like Butler and the shopkeepers who'd quietly begun to take down Etan's posters, convinced there was no longer a need to look for him. If she believed, as they now did, that her son was dead, it might break her heart irreparably. But it would also allow her to begin to mourn. She herself had begun to tentatively feel out the heretical possibility he was not coming back, but she felt she could never say it—that would be a betrayal to the cheery optimism that met her every time a member of the task force came to the door. Despite her affection and gratitude for their efforts, she sometimes resented the cops' blind conviction.

At Christmas the Patzes made the semiannual pilgrimage to Julie's family in Massachusetts, where they would also see Stan's parents. Along with Julie's eight siblings and their families, the New York contingent would converge on Sudbury, to the modest house that never changed, not its faux clapboard aluminum siding outside to ward off the harsh New England winters nor its striped, flowered wallpaper inside. The Patzes would stay in the cozy upstairs bedrooms, once shared by all the siblings and still occupied by the two youngest ones. In the summer visits they spent the days dispersed outdoors, but at Christmas the house swarmed with children, babies passed from shoulder to shoulder, cousins playing with their parents' old toys on the large enclosed front porch, teens swapping a year's worth of tall tales. Most of Julie's brothers and sisters had settled in the area, the only exceptions a sister who'd moved to nearby Connecticut and, of course, Julie.

When Etan had disappeared, Julie had called her parents soon after Stan had called his, but she'd forbidden her family from coming to New York. She'd been adamant. She hadn't even wanted them to call, knowing she would fall apart in the face of their own sadness. The Patzes had missed the Fourth of July reunion, and so this marked the first time they had all been together since the previous winter. Remarkably, no one spoke of Etan or his absence. It was Christmas, Julie's parents thought. He's gone, and everyone knows it. It'll just make things worse, when we should all just try to enjoy the holidays.

Back in New York, the new year brought not a single spark of light to shine on the dark hole that had swallowed Etan. How could a six-year-old boy have made it to seven on his own? How could Etan still be alive? How long could they sustain the fantasy of Etan alive and healthy, being cared for by strangers? In the real world, that just never happened.

> 5:38—WQXR—Bob Lewis, Merced, Calif. [Teenager] (14 yrs old—
> missing 6 years) found walking st. 200 m. N of home w/5 yr old kid-
> napped boy.
> —Patz logbook, March 2, 1980

Almost ten months into a year that seemed to hold no hope, a small boy peered into the windows of a Ukiah, California, police station and was spotted by an officer, who followed him outside. On the street the boy was talking to a teenager.

"What's going on?" the cop asked the two. "We're just trying to find this kid's home," the older boy said.

The "kid" was five-year-old Timmy White. Missing for two weeks, he'd been the subject of an intense local search. The other boy, a fourteen-year-old named Steven, wasn't sure of his full name. But authorities were astonished to discover he was Steven Stayner, abducted from Merced, California, seven years earlier by a forty-year-old man named Kenneth Eugene Parnell. Parnell had enticed the then seven-year-old into his car by asking if he wanted to contribute to a charity and then telling him they'd go ask his mother for permission. For almost seven years, Steven Stayner had lived two hundred miles from his home, with the man he'd come to call Dad. He had escaped only after being forced to recruit a new boy for Parnell. At the time of Stayner's stunning reappearance, no one knew what horrors he'd endured. For a few weeks at least, the news was simply painted as the miracle it was. But soon, reports of his sexual abuse surfaced, changing the tone of the story.

For Stan and Julie Patz, Steven Stayner's return to his parents opened the door to a whole new range of conflicting emotions. Was Etan out there thinking they weren't looking for him? Despite an extensive search, that's what Steven Stayner had believed. Your parents don't want you, Parnell had told him, saying he'd legally adopted the boy from his parents.

If their own son were alive, Stan and Julie wondered, did he even want to come home? The thought was disturbing, although far better than an alternative that saw Etan abused and hurt. While the Patzes rejoiced at the news that the teenage Stayner had come home, his return also meant that unless they found their son, or his body, there would never be a date after which they could assume the worst. Not one year, not two, not seven, or even more. And after hearing some of what Stayner had gone through, they were no longer sure what "worst" meant.

> 12:43 p.m.—Harold—25 yr old girl w/hypo glycemia disappeared in
>   middle of night almost a year ago—no clue.
>   —Patz logbook, March 21, 1980

Scattered among the look-likes and the lunatics in the pages of the log-books were messages from bewildered parents of other missing children, who would call or write begging for Stan and Julie's help. It was ludicrous, Stan and Julie thought, that they were considered experts and sought out for advice. But they had now spent the last several months learning as much as anyone else about what to do—and not to do—when your child goes missing.

Since her daycare center had closed, Julie had been unable to find work. Her skills and interest lay with childcare, but she still suffered from the stigma of "losing her child." ("We didn't 'lose him,'" Stan would bite out angrily every time it was phrased that way. "He was taken from us.") Finally, one administrator at a school where Julie had applied revealed that he feared the parents there would object to her hiring. After she was interviewed at another school, the director was approached by a group of parents who actively opposed her employment. Since no one yet knew what had happened to her son, they were uncomfortable having their own children in her care. The Patz family was slipping into debt, but there wasn't much they could do to shovel out.

As Stan slowly returned to his photography, Julie's full-time, nonpaying job was the search for Etan. But as the months passed it had gradually become about more than just her son. As she met other parents of missing children and heard their heartwrenching stories, as they shared the frustration of nowhere to turn for help, Julie saw a gap that demanded to be filled.

09:45 Gus Engelman WABC—Radio, telephone taped interview

14:32 Gene Ruffini, NY Post, sorry about the bad rewrite job....

16:10 Rich Lamb, WCBS—Radio, coming here now for interview

15:00 Carl Gottlieb? Ch 11 w/c/b for appt later in week

10:22 Pamela Roderick—WINS Radio

11:00 Jane White/AP

12:09 Richard Higgins Boston Globe 10 AM Thursday

17:04 Ch 2. News to be here 6:15 pm

12:00 60 MINS Allan Maraynes Mike Wallace/Producer

15:48 Peggy Stockton WNEW radio will come for interview

16:13 Jim Unchester WNBC-TV will call Sunday for interview

11:30 Mark Kresing (sp) Ch 11 re: interview today

11:55 Sylvia Pahy (?) photog will be here for NYT mag Sunday 5/25 at 11

15:13 Jerry Schmetterer Daily News article Sunday

08:00 approx WMCA Radio—I declined telephone intvw—woke me up.

    —Patz logbook, various entries, week of one-year anniversary, May 1980

A few days before May 25, Stan looked around the front room at the circle of reporters and cameras gathered to prepare their stories.

"Thank you for coming here on this very sad anniversary. I hope you don't mind me saying that next year I'd prefer not to be seeing you all again."

In the weeks of press leading up to the one-year mark, both Stan and Julie had decided the media message deserved to be something beyond "Have you seen my son?"

"There are lots of failings in the system of locating missing children," Julie said to the *SoHo Weekly News*. "No one even knows exactly how many children disappear each year. There is no effective nationwide system."

They wanted to talk about a whole list of ideas for making change going forward, but the weight of the past year was also never far from their thoughts.

"It's not getting easier, it's getting harder," Julie told the *New York Times*'s Anna Quindlen. "We thought that any minute it would be over," she said.

"You can always come to grips with a set of circumstances—I mean the finality of death," Stan continued his wife's thought. "This is a psychological wound that will never heal, never close up, without a resolution of one kind or another."

He shook his head sadly, his mouth tight. "We're sitting here with as many questions as we had the first day."

"More," Julie said. As they talked, Julie's feet perched on the couch next to her husband, Quindlen saw two profoundly broken people who seemed to each have their hands full holding the other together. She marveled at a marriage staying intact under such conditions.

An AP reporter whose anniversary feature appeared in Baton Rouge, Minneapolis, Fargo, Honolulu, and dozens more papers around the country wrote a stirring account that highlighted the couple's determination and the efforts so many were continuing to make on their behalf.

"Sometimes I think the worst thing that could happen would be never knowing what happened to Etan," Julie told the reporter. "It is something we live with every day."

There were few personal calls noted in the logbook in the days leading up to or just after May 25. Even on that Sunday itself the phone was relatively quiet. But a few days later, Stan took the kids on another photo expedition and spotted a local tribute to Etan on a cast-iron column around the corner from the loft. In uneven block letters, the paint trickling down from the I and the M, someone had spray-painted the words I MISS ETAN P.

CHAPTER 5

The Bigger Picture

11:27 Diana, let her know on 4 city talk-show by end of week. (Boston, Phil, Baltimore, Pittsburgh)

15:00 Bob Morton, would like to have Julie 6/17 on Tom Snyder "Tomorrow" tape from 6 to 7 pm, runs from 1 to 2 am, same night. Interview just Tom and Julie. . . . NBC 30 Rock Plaza, Studio 3K, 5:30 Be there!
    —*Patz logbook, June 1980*

I know where thousands of missing kids are," Stan Patz said, even if he didn't know where his was. His voice had that characteristic trace of irony and sarcasm that put some people off, until they considered his circumstances, and then they usually found his manner perfectly reasonable. "They're in schools. Many are enrolled in schools in other states. Maybe just one state away from where their families are."

The reporter perched on their living room couch was taking notes on his yellow legal pad as fast as he could. Richard Rein was a freelance journalist, who wrote for *People* magazine and other general-interest magazines, and he had come by one day in September 1980 as the new school year was getting under way. Shira herself was in class; Ari had just turned four and was bouncing in and out of the room as the adults talked.

Rein had contacted the Patzes for an interview because he was thinking about writing a book, not about their case, but about the bigger phenomenon of missing children, a topic of growing national interest. He'd come to meet the most renowned example, to hear their story and their thoughts on what needed to be done. Stan and Julie were glad to hear that this wasn't just about their sad plight. Yes, they wanted to use the coverage to look for their son, but they had learned so much more about what needed to be fixed, and they were eager to pass it on. "We have something to say," Stan told Rein, "other than that we're waiting for Etan to come back."

As strange as it seemed, they knew they'd been lucky, at least compared with the parents of other missing children they were hearing from. Their local law enforcement had been the NYPD, not a small-town sheriff with few resources and little reach outside his county. Unlike local authorities in many other parts of the country, the New York police hadn't been hamstrung by twenty-four- or forty-eight-hour waiting periods before beginning their search. Some police departments required seventy-two hours—three days and nights—to allow a child to return home on his own before getting involved. The Patz case had garnered phenomenal publicity, and as much as they hated cameras being thrust in their faces, Stan and Julie knew what a gift they'd been given. They felt that they needed to use their platform to advocate for the less visible and to make real change.

"Even if we can't help ourselves," Stan said, "maybe at least someone else won't have to go through the ordeal we have. What we are trying to stress is the vulnerability of all children."

Stan especially wanted Rein's readers to understand just how large a role schools could play. As he talked he became less caustic and more earnest. The Patzes were particularly sensitive to the school angle and had given it a great deal of thought. They couldn't ever lose sight of the fact that Etan had left home at eight in the morning and almost another eight full hours had passed before Julie had known there was a problem. Schools, stressed Stan and Julie, needed to let parents know when their kid didn't show up. It could literally be a matter of life and death.

"It's a question of poor inventory control," Stan acidly told Rein. "Our children are our most precious possession, but any business has tighter inventory control than almost any school. Adults come to the schools, they take children out on a regular basis. Kids come in late, they don't show up in the morning. It's all very loose. People move from state to state, and take their kids with them. There's no control."

While the technology was fledgling, Stan's own brother Jerry was a software programmer, and he had developed a program several years earlier to help the Boston school system keep attendance. "We have to look at this like we're living in the '80's," said Stan, "and use technology that private businesses have been using for years."

But beyond such "inventory control," there was so much more schools could do, Stan explained. The biggest problem facing parents of missing children like them was that there was no coordinated way to search outside their hometown. Like Steven Stayner, who'd attended several schools in his home state, Etan could even be alive and well, sitting in a classroom right now as close as New Jersey, and they might never know. And if he turned up dead, his body could sit in a local morgue unidentified until it was buried in an unmarked grave. There was virtually no way to match up the missing with the dead.

Although he liked to call himself a "knee-jerk liberal," Stan Patz found himself advocating national fingerprinting programs for schoolchildren, which, with their shades of Big Brother, would have been abhorrent to him before Etan disappeared

"I now see this as just as inevitable as Social Security numbers," he wrote in a letter published in the *New York Times* on December 7, 1980. "I know that groups like the A.C.L.U. strongly oppose fingerprinting, and I agree with its concern for privacy, but since tens of millions of people have already been fingerprinted, I believe these civil libertarians should concentrate on ways to prevent abuses of this system.

"The pros and cons of national fingerprinting should be openly discussed. A person's right to privacy should be tempered by the fear of becoming an anonymous corpse." It went against Stan's long-standing convictions that he and Julie had given up their privacy, but they would have done so gladly before the fact instead of after.

The Patzes had already begun the painstaking effort to search the schools themselves, contacting school district superintendents throughout the country, asking that Etan's poster be circulated to check it against new students. They had successfully tracked down contacts for all the public school districts, but had no easy way to contend with all the private schools. The postage alone was ultimately prohibitive. Months of their own fruitless efforts underscored the weakness in a national infrastructure to look for missing children. Apparently, there wasn't one.

The closest thing was an FBI database—the National Crime Information Center—that kept a record of stolen cars, boats, and other crime statistics. It even tracked missing children, but a database is only as effective as the people who enter its data, and in this case, many in law enforcement didn't even know it existed. This was especially true when it came to kids who went missing. As of May 1981, there were almost twenty times more stolen license plates than missing children listed in the NCIC.

Even as Stan lobbied public opinion on the staid editorial pages of the *Times*, Julie was the one who more often stood in the limelight. She was willing to ride a train or take a flight to any media market, no matter how small, to do what the nonexistent national machinery should be doing—getting the word out to farmers and businessmen and housewives that her son and God only knew who else was missing.

There were no statistics, no clear definition of what "missing" even meant. Were runaways "missing"? That upped the numbers exponentially. Were children snatched by one angry parent from another in a custody dispute "missing"? Again, a whole different set of figures came into play.

So many wildly fluctuating figures were thrown around in the first years—from hundreds to thousands to an astounding 1.3 million missing children. There were no studies to cite, just anecdotal evidence and blind extrapolation. But one thing was clear. There needed to be a number—without it Julie or Stan or any missing children's advocate got stuck on the first question. How can you talk about a problem that doesn't exist?

In the early 1980s people began writing about the subject, and for the most part they simply quoted each other's statistics. In early 1981 a journalist named Kristin Cole Brown wrote a lengthy feature on missing children for the *New York Daily News Sunday Magazine*, and cited another article in the *American Bar Association Journal* on parental abductions, saying that one hundred thousand custodial spouses snatched their children annually. She hoped it was a good figure.

Kitty, as her friends called her, was a mother of two young children herself, and she'd become profoundly interested in the subject, but as she'd researched the article she'd realized that the only real experts out there seemed to be the parents themselves. She was uncomfortable asking such sensitive questions, of compounding the grief of these mothers and fathers. She had called Julie Patz with her heart in her throat, cringing inwardly at the sense of intrusion. But Julie quickly put her at ease, giving her implicit permission to ask the most sensitive of questions.

By this point, Julie had had so much experience telling her story and appealing for help that she'd become resigned to the draining effort it took. If Etan had become the poster child for missing children overnight, Julie had gradually become the poster mother. Parents from every part of the country facing the same terror knew who to contact and learn from, as they too suffered the agonizing wait and pressed for help. The horrific Atlanta child murders were occurring over this period of time, twenty-nine black children and young adults killed over a two-year period, their families ultimately uniting to decry the lack of attention their cases received. When Atlanta mother Camille Bell began to speak out about her nine-year-old son Yusef's death, the only other name she'd ever heard connected to missing children was Julie's.

Julie was in touch with grassroots shoestring organizations around the country—from the Bergen County Missing Persons Bureau to California's Stolen Child Information Exchange. From sea to shining sea there were parents of missing children who, in trying to find their children, found each other. And they all seemed to converge at Julie Patz's door.

So a few months later, Kitty Brown called Julie again, to ask her about appearing together on a Philadelphia talk show. By then, Kitty was doing volunteer work for an upstate New York group, Child Find. Founded by a woman whose ex-husband had gone into hiding with their daughter, Child Find focused on parental abductions, getting missing children's photos distributed as widely as possible, and serving as a point of contact for runaways as well. If for whatever reason a child didn't want his parents to know his whereabouts, Child Find could work as a third party to mediate or get messages through. Like other fledgling advocates, the group was feeling its way, but as the issue of missing children got more exposure, Kitty, the newly named information director, was being asked to make media appearances.

The Philadelphia show was *Whitney & Co*, hosted by local TV personality Jane Whitney. It would be a one-hour live telecast, and Kitty's maiden voyage. Would Julie train down with her and add her expert input? Julie agreed. They caught the Amtrak together, and en route, Kitty confided her stage fright. She felt the burden of speaking for her organization as the panel's "expert" without the chops to back it up. Every time she'd spoken to the show's producers to prepare, she'd gotten a sense of vertigo that had almost knocked her off her feet. She told Julie she was petrified she'd open her mouth and choke.

"What if I sit there, struck dumb, on live television?" she worried.

"Oh, that used to happen to me," Julie replied reassuringly. "It still does sometimes, but I've got a trick. When you can't squeeze a word out, just put your hand up to your mouth and pretend you're coughing." She illustrated. "Works like a charm every time."

Kitty tried it a few times, but she was skeptical. Her heart began to pound the minute she and Julie walked into the studio the next day, getting worse as she sat to be thoroughly powdered and primped. Julie, the veteran, disregarded the fuss, didn't glance twice at a mirror, and spent the moments leading up to airtime reviewing her notes. She seemed oblivious to all the hoopla that stood out in Kitty's first-timer consciousness.

"Aren't you nervous?" Kitty asked her as they sat on the set and waited for the countdown to go live.

Julie smiled. "I'm not nervous," she replied. "I'm excited, because this is another chance." When the cameras rolled, Julie retold with quiet composure the story of the day Etan walked off for school alone, the terrible days that followed, and the uncertainty they still faced. She talked about their search and the futility of trying to reach every small town where her son might be, not knowing his family wanted him back.

"The police have been wonderful, but they're limited," she said. "There's no way for them to get into every school in the country, where Etan might be at this very minute. If a child is taken, unless it's a crime of passion, the chances are they're taken elsewhere, to a different city, state, or country, but most importantly a different police jurisdiction." And if he had been killed, there was the horrible possibility he was one of the thousands of unidentified bodies there was no system in place to identify.

"We don't know that our son is dead," she stated calmly, as she had so many other times. "We hope he's alive, although we realize he could be dead. But mostly we need to know so we can put our lives back into order."

Kitty knew from their conversations that Julie was a reluctant spokesperson, but you couldn't tell that from her public persona. As the younger woman listened and took in Julie's understated but SoHo chic wardrobe, the sleek chignon she often wore to keep her hair out of her eyes, and her dignified bearing, Kitty couldn't help but be grateful that Julie was willing to tell her story over and over to help other families and other children. You couldn't watch her face on a television screen and say, "That could never happen to me."

When it was Kitty's turn to speak, and her legs got numb, her mouth so dry she couldn't swallow, she thought of Julie's advice. She put her hand up to her mouth, coughed discreetly, and the words flowed, conveying her natural, unstilted passion.

"We envision a computer bank in every state," she said, "tied into a nationwide database." Perhaps a federal agency would oversee it, she continued, to collect and distribute the names and faces of the missing, along with descriptions, medical records, all the critical information that might bring a boy like Etan back.

"It may take a federal agency to make it happen," Kitty said. "The odds are slim, but we will fight for it and it will happen because it is important."

"See?" Julie said after the camera lights shut off. "You did fine!"

———

By the time the Patzes marked the second year of Etan's disappearance, Julie was working not just to get the word out, but to turn words into action. She'd been employed part-time at an art gallery in the neighborhood, Gallery 345, run by artist and fiery political activist Karen DiGia. In advance of that anniversary the gallery mounted an exhibit called "Weeping in the Playtime of Others," after a book of the same name by Ken Wooden, a journalist who had written extensively about missing and sexually abused children.

Over the next week there would be workshops on the sexual exploitation of children and child snatching by a noncustodial parent. Julie had helped Child Find put together information packets, which included tips and practical strategies for how to protect your own kids: Don't write your children's names on the outsides of their clothing or their bags; don't inadvertently give strangers help in gaining your children's trust. Teach your kids their phone numbers—with area codes. Come up with a family password that a stranger must know before your child will go with them willingly. When Julie Patz gave that advice, parents always took it more seriously.

The stark white walls of the airy East Village space were covered with framed articles on the subject and school photos of children known to have been missing or abused. The cheery portraits in the context of such a disturbing topic were difficult for some to take, but Julie urged people not to put their heads in the sand. Child abuse and molestation existed, and wishing it away did nothing to help fight it.

"Kids have become big business and big pleasure," she told a reporter at the show's opening, "and something has to be done about this."

The opening-night reception was a strange affair, wine and cheese surrounded by the haunting faces of these lost children. Swedish actress Liv Ullmann provided star wattage, moving among the small collection of locals, parents, and Village art scenesters. The clinking glasses and hum of small talk provided a contrasting soundtrack to the show's theme of missing and exploited children. A few of the art critiques were especially difficult for Julie to hear. One section of the display was devoted to pictures of Etan, those beautiful portraits taken by his father.

"What's *he* doing up there," she overheard one woman, referring to Etan's picture, "when everyone knows he's dead."

In fact, a new development in the case suggested otherwise. Julie came alone to the event, her usually pale face flushed and animated. "Why isn't Stan here?" Kitty asked.

"Can you believe it, we have a lead," Julie replied. "He's been talking to the police all day."

Stan arrived sometime later, and hugged Julie.

"No apparent news," he said with a grimace, although he filled her in later.

Stan had picked up the phone the evening before and spoken at length with a man who called himself "Marlowe" but who had immediately admitted the name was fictitious.

"I know this lady in New Jersey who has Etan," Marlowe told Stan. "She did me a solid once, and now I want to return the favor. She goes back and forth about contacting you, and it's taken her eighteen months to even go this far. I told her I'd act as a go-between to confirm your telephone number."

Stan had learned not to say much to these kinds of callers, but he was taking copious notes. The man sounded young, but it wasn't clear.

"Where are you now?" he asked. "Can we meet?" From the noises in the background, Stan presumed he was in a private residence. There was the sound of a televised ball game in the background, which at some point switched to pop music.

"No," said Marlowe, he was wanted by New York cops. He explained that this woman couldn't care for the child properly anymore. He said that the woman was older, and that she knew the Patzes. He hadn't met the child himself, he said, but Marlowe had seen a picture of him, one processed by a well-known lab, over the weekend. It was dated two months earlier, March 1981.

"I just had a baby recently myself." The man seemed to be trying to relate. "So I understand how you feel...I'll try to talk to her, and now that I know I have the right number, I'll call you back again soon." Marlowe hung up.

The call had lasted eight minutes. Stan wasn't sure if he should get excited or not. Both he and Julie had learned to steel themselves against cruel hoaxes and rip-offs. Still, "Marlowe" had had a lot to say.

The next day as Julie was busy getting ready for the gallery opening, Stan called Bill Butler and filled him in.

"Do not pick up the phone," Butler admonished. "Let the machine get it."

Less than two hours later, Marlowe called back. This time, the background noise suggested a bar or party, with both male and female voices blending together. The tape recorder spooled as he said he was waiting for the woman to call him. Etan was fine, he assured, and he'd been in private school for the last two years. Marlowe spoke with the smooth confidence that suggested he'd made a career out of such conversations. Initially dubious, Stan's bullshit meter was going off the charts.

Stan immediately called the cops back. We're working on a plan, they told him. Just keep recording the calls and we'll get back to you. Over the next hours Marlowe called repeatedly, obviously hoping to get Stan himself on the phone. Finally on Wednesday, Marlowe left the instructions on the tape. Stan must take the Long Island Railroad to the West Hempstead stop. Next to the train station, he should check into the Hotel Hempstead Motor Inn. Bring $2,500.

The man was firm. "This is not a ransom. It's a loan. She's going to pay you back." He promised to call Stan in the hotel at 2 p.m.

Butler and the other detectives went into action. Stan would go along with the instructions, surrounded by undercover officers and wired for sound. He was waiting outside his apartment when an oversized yellow Checker cab pulled up. The back door flew open.

"Get in," said the driver. Stan did, and realized there was a man sitting on the floor in the back, concealing himself. They might be under observation, the man indicated, better not to take chances. The cab drove to Sixth Avenue, and when it turned north toward Penn Station, the man sat up to wire Stan.

"Pull up your shirt." When Stan did, the cop was dismayed to see he had nothing on underneath the long-sleeved pullover.

"You should have worn a T-shirt," the detective complained.

"No one told me. It's summertime." The detective had no choice but to wire Stan without it, plastering the microphone with heavy electrician's tape to his bare chest. Stan recognized the absurdity of speeding uptown, half naked and half lying on the backseat as a man worked over him. Is this whole thing really necessary? he asked himself. He didn't dare ask the cop.

"Now, don't worry. Our guys are going to be all around you, watching and ready to move, but you won't know who they are." The man left him at the entrance to the train station.

Stan rode the train, easily picking out his team. When he checked into the hotel, another undercover duo posing as man and wife came up to the desk next to him. This place probably has never seen this much action, he thought. Up in the room, Stan opened the door to a sharp knock and was given an envelope, the handoff, with the $2,500. But when he looked inside, it was filled with torn newspaper.

"You've got to be kidding," he said. "You couldn't come up with the real $2,500? This is not big business here, this is retail." For the first time this didn't seem like a game. "I would have coughed up the money myself somehow, if I'd known I was going to be stuck in a hotel room with a criminal, handing him this." He had no interest in getting roughed up for a wad of newspaper.

After the detective left, Stan walked to the window and drew the curtains. Directly below him a man stood in the parking lot and Stan made a few nervous remarks into his chest about sending out for pizza for everyone, thinking the man looking up at him might hear. He later learned that no one had heard—the mikes had died almost immediately after being taped to Stan's bare skin.

But the cops did catch their perp—in the very same parking lot. He was calling it off anyway, he told police, because he'd mistaken the husband-and-wife team in the lobby for the Patzes themselves and was angry that Stan had disobeyed him by bringing Julie. Marlowe turned out to be a thirty-two-year-old con artist named James Slaughter, whose previous criminal career involved stealing people's pets and holding them for ransom. He was charged with attempted grand larceny and aggravated harassment. And as much as Stan Patz had grumbled about how silly the whole exercise had seemed, using him as bait, he wouldn't have begrudged the cops any request, no matter how outlandish or inconvenient. For their part, the task force detectives had long since overcome their own initial suspicions of Stan and his cool, even sarcastic façade.

"Stan was instrumental in making the extortionist's arrest," one detective later told a reporter. "The Patzes have been terrific. They'll do anything you ask."

A month after the gallery exhibit, Kitty Brown brought her children to the city to meet Shira and Ari and accompany them to a neighborhood fair. "There's a big street festival a few blocks away. It's my kids' favorite," Julie had told her. "You can stay over."

It was the annual festival of the Feast of St. Anthony. Kitty's children were in wonderland—they had never seen anything like it, with the lights, the noise of the music and the throngs of people, and all those rides. They'd been to their local county fair, but this was so compressed, souvenir booths and homemade stands displaying icons of the saints, all sandwiched between the city buildings. Kitty held the kids' hands and they navigated the crowded streets. She strained to hear Julie say something over her shoulder about the last time they'd been to this fair, just after Etan disappeared. The four-year-olds wanted to stop and play all the games; Ari loved the tommy gun that shot BB pellets at a target. Everyone rode the Tilt-a-Whirl, which threatened stomachs full of fried dough and cotton candy.

This is overwhelming, Kitty thought, of the chaos and the din. She spent her days talking about missing children and knew how easy it was for a child to suddenly vanish in a sea of faces. Other parents can let their children run around here, how can I do that? Kitty was acutely aware of her anxiety—even, she'd admit, her paranoia. If she was so disconcerted, she wondered how Julie could deal with this scene. But she noticed the way Julie kept an eye on her children without seeming to smother them. It was subtle, just a sense that she didn't stop to look at every exhibit or spend twenty minutes trying on earrings. Instead she would intermittently skim the crowd, noting where Shira and Ari were and what they were doing. Kitty found herself modeling her behavior after the older woman's as the fair surged around them.

When her kids pleaded to go on the Ferris wheel, and Kitty just couldn't shake off her fear of heights, Julie laughed and held out her hand.

"I'll take them all," she said. Kitty stayed safely on the ground, tracking Julie and the four children riding to the top for a view of Greenwich Village and the festival spread out below them. She smiled as she watched her kids shriek with rapture, arms thrown up in the air, and she remembered one of Julie's remarks that had stuck with her from the Philadelphia morning talk show where they'd met.

"I die a thousand deaths every day before they come home," she'd said in response to a question about her two other children. "But you have to draw the line between letting them grow up and gain independence and not letting them be taken away."

Later that summer, Karen DiGia, the owner of Gallery 345, brought Julie for a picnic near Kitty's home north of the city. They talked about the recent release of *Still Missing*, a novel by the mother of one of Julie's former preschoolers, about a six-year-old boy who goes missing and what his family endures. The author, Beth Gutcheon, had spent a lot of time with Julie in the months following Etan's disappearance. She was one of the few to whom Julie had allowed herself the luxury of unloading her anguish, and although Beth had told Julie that the topic of her book was missing children, Julie hadn't expected it to mirror so closely her own family's circumstances. Now the book was all over the press, and an ad in the *New York Times* heralded a movie in the offing. It was the talk of the neighborhood, and the talk of the women's picnic. The Patzes had a mixed reaction to the book; on the one hand it might indeed raise the profile of the missing children issue. But on the other, it felt invasive to Julie, who also worried that readers would confuse the novel's fictional details—the disintegrating marriage of the boy's bereft parents, for example—with the real-life story of her family. She found that out firsthand when a local paper called asking for pictures of Etan to accompany the review of the "Etan Patz" book.

"You mean it's fiction?" the caller asked. "We all thought it was about Etan!"

Reiterating that it wasn't, Julie had refused the photo request, asking to speak personally to the reviewer, to beg him to emphasize that unlike the invented Alex Selky, Etan was still missing. At the picnic she was still circumspect about her feelings, but Kitty couldn't contain her outrage.

"I had a fit on the phone with Beth," Kitty admitted to the other women. "I told her I thought not only was it a cheap way out, but people are going to think Etan's been found, and they'll stop looking. I know she thinks it's going to help. I think I really shook her up."

The following month, in early August, life showed just how much uglier it often is than fiction. Julie got a call from Kitty one Saturday to say she'd be in the city on Monday meeting with a Florida couple whose son had disappeared two weeks earlier from a shopping mall and hadn't been seen since. Adam Walsh was six and a half, just like Etan. He'd gone with his mother to the local Sears, and while she went to look at lamps, he'd stayed in the nearby toy section to watch some older boys play with a new toy, called a video game. When his mother came back minutes later, all the kids were gone. One of the employees had kicked out the others for being too rowdy, and no one knew if Adam had been swept up with the group.

John and Revé Walsh were to appear on ABC's *Good Morning America* with David Hartman, and Kitty was going to try to meet with them. John Walsh was already championing the need for a better way to track these cases, calling the current void a national disgrace. Kitty wanted to tell him more about their own efforts and discuss joining forces. But it was, of course, a delicate thing. The parents were frantic; Revé especially was a wreck. Would Julie be around if she needed her? This was the kind of encounter that always unnerved Kitty. Again, she doubted her fledgling expertise, but people like the Walshes were turning to Child Find for help. If anything, Kitty knew more about divorced parents who abducted their own children, and she knew that Julie would be much more effective offering her shoulder. Of course, Julie assured her. Call me when you need me.

The Walshes arrived in New York on Monday, for an early Tuesday morning appearance on *Good Morning America*. At 5:30 a.m. John received a call in the room from his best friend in Florida. The man needed to get his hands on Adam's dental records. He told John that a head had been found in a canal one hundred miles north of their home, and while investigators doubted it was Adam's, they wanted to eliminate the possibility. On air a few hours later, John Walsh hinted at the possible break in the case.

"What happened last night?" David Hartman asked. "Can you tell us that?"

"They had found the remains of a young person," John said, "and at this time they are trying to identify them."

Afterwards Julie got a call from Kitty.

"It's so awful. They may have found Adam's remains in Florida," Kitty said anxiously. "Can you come to the Plaza? Revé and I are having something to eat, and I need your help." Julie could see as soon as she walked into the hotel restaurant that Revé Walsh was in bad shape, wan and fragile. The woman looked shell-shocked and had already skipped several meals. Julie and Kitty tried to talk her into eating. Between them, they convinced her to order breakfast.

The talk stayed on a light, superficial level. John's best friend had been so supportive and Revé wanted to buy him a new kind of gadget he couldn't yet find in stores back home. Julie and Kitty were trying to help her figure out where to get a "Walkman," when Revé was paged. The next minutes were complete chaos. Julie remembers a Plaza staffer bringing a phone to the table and he happened to place it in front of her. Revé, sitting next to Julie, turned even paler than she already was as Julie handed her the receiver. Revé listened, gave a cry, and dropped the phone. It was clearly bad news, and she needed to get back to the hotel, now.

Julie watched helplessly as Revé collapsed, sobbing and gasping for air. Julie and Kitty half walked, half carried her down the street to the Walshes' hotel room at the St. Moritz. Someone called the EMTs to administer first aid. Julie and Kitty sat waiting in the lobby, unsure what to do next, each numbly lost in her own thoughts. Before the Walshes left for the airport, to return to Florida, John Walsh came to say goodbye to the two women.

They hugged him, murmuring words of regret.

"This isn't over," John said fiercely. "We have to change things."

———

A little over two months later, Julie Patz and Kitty Brown were on an American Airlines flight to Chicago. It was a real nail-biter, the plane dipping and bucking all the way, and the two women finally indulged in a drink to steady their nerves. But they were also celebrating, in a sense, because the following day, along with the Walshes, Camille Bell, and an Oklahoma couple, John and Norma Pallett, whose daughter Cinda had been missing a month, they were scheduled to tape *The Phil Donahue show*.

It was a reunion of sorts, because just two weeks earlier John Walsh, Julie, and Camille Bell had sat at a rectangular table in a Dirksen Senate hearing room, testifying on behalf of S 1701, a bill introduced the day before. The bill joined a similar effort in the House by Congressman Paul Simon that would require missing children to be entered into the NCIC database and create a national tracking system for unidentified bodies. Paula Hawkins, an enthusiastic and passionate freshman senator from John Walsh's home state of Florida, had authored the Senate's draft and called for the hearing. Together in a public forum for the first time, the three parents told their stories, and a cumulative grief filled the room. Some in the audience were moved to tears as they heard about the urban child missing from a close-knit New York artists' enclave; an African American nine-year-old from the Atlanta projects found strangled in an abandoned school; and the son of a marketing executive who had vanished from a suburban Florida mall. It didn't matter who you were, the message was clear: It can happen anywhere, to anyone.

Hawkins and cosponsor Senator Ted Kennedy had listened with appropriate expressions of shock and horror to the three parents telling their stories. Yet the testimony didn't get the public's attention as the three had hoped. That night on the evening news there was no mention of the hearing or the bill. Every newscast was consumed with the day's bigger story—the assassination of Egyptian president Anwar Sadat.

But someone at the *Donahue* show had noticed. In 1981 *The Phil Donahue Show* was the hottest, most watched national talk show on television. *Donahue* was substantive, it was topical, it was the dream of any nonprofit or cause to land even a segment, and the show wanted to devote the whole hour to missing children. More than eight million viewers would hear the stories of Etan, Yusef, and Adam and their parents, and with bills pending in the House and Senate, they would be urged to take specific action.

The group stayed up late in the hotel coffee shop the night before, strategizing and assigning different points each one should be sure to hit the next day. A current of anticipation hummed through the air, with the idea that they would be able to accomplish something important. Someone might be watching who would get a child back home. Parents would learn how to keep their children safe. And new law might be made. These were the moments that in some infinitesimal way countered Julie Patz's grief.

Standing on the talk show's set was like being onstage in an actual theater. The crew was extremely professional, expertly pinning on the lapel mikes as soon as the guests sat down. For all the local broadcasts, the *AM Detroit*s and the *Midday Lives*, *Donahue* was as big as it got, and the broadcast did everything Julie and the other guests had hoped for. They showed pictures not just of Etan and Cinda Pallett, but of several other missing children. Etan sightings were coming in while they were still on the air, although Donahue cautioned about all the false leads Julie had already endured. Together, the parents and other advocates lobbied for a national clearinghouse and broadcast Child Find's 800 number several times. They personalized the bureaucratic words of the legislation, not just with their own accounts but other stories as well. One family in Texas had spent their entire life savings, $40,000, on private investigators to find their missing daughter, only to learn later that her body had sat in a nearby morgue for eighty-seven days.

"It could be your child, or anyone else's child, next," Camille Bell pleaded. "If nothing else, please write your congressmen and senators and get this bill passed."

At the end of the broadcast, Donahue paid tribute to the families sitting on the set in front of him, who were able to channel their own grief for a greater good.

"They hope, as do all of us, that their children will be found. We can't really say much that's going to make you feel any better, other than you make us feel good about human beings, just the fact that you are on your feet. You are a testimony to the human spirit."

It was a heady moment. For days the Child Find phones, which at the time consisted of two or three lines manned by a handful of volunteers, were overwhelmed with sightings and tips. Congressional offices, especially in the home states of the *Donahue* panelists, were flooded with phone calls, letters, and petitions calling for support of the Missing Children's Act. At House hearings the following month, Florida representative Clay Shaw credited the power of the media.

"I have in my office received literally thousands of names on petitions and letters," he said, "perhaps more than on any other issue than I have seen.... Much of this was caused by the good work of Phil Donahue on his nationally broadcast show."

The November hearings led to revisions on the House's draft legislation to bring it in line with the pending Senate bill, and in early December a comprehensive summit of politicians, academics, law enforcement, child advocates, and the parents of missing children themselves met in Louisville to create an agenda for the next push. It would take another full year before the legislation was finally signed into law, and two years after that for the National Center for Missing and Exploited Children to be created, but by the end of 1981, dozens of disparate, far-flung organizations were coalescing into a movement and a national dialogue had begun. Americans were now aware that the problem existed.

For Julie Patz, who knew all too well about the problem firsthand, the gains were gratifying. But her own child's case—which had gotten the attention so many others had not—wouldn't benefit from that attention. The sightings called in during the *Donahue* show had, like all the others before, led nowhere. She and Stan still had no idea what had happened to their own son. All the lobbying and new laws wouldn't change the fact that there wasn't a single clue to grasp on to and follow to its conclusion.

CHAPTER 6

⸻

The Devil in the Drainpipe

TV news anchor: It's a hauntingly familiar picture. A little six-year-old boy who vanished on a street in the SoHo section of Manhattan. That was almost three years ago. Etan Patz is still missing and no trace of him has been found yet. But an arrest in the Bronx yesterday has again revived interest in the case. A man named Jose Ramos is charged with petit larceny, a misdemeanor. Police believe Mr. Ramos may be able to provide them with leads in the case. John Miller reports.
    —studio intro to John Miller report, Channel 5 News, March 19, 1982

Car 615, responding to Van Cortlandt Park search near Gun Hill Road."
The voice crackled over his police scanner as Channel 5's John Miller drove his midnight blue Buick LeSabre south through Manhattan on his way to the newsroom. He turned his car around. It was a brisk end-of-winter Friday in March, a slow news day so far but, Miller thought, maybe no longer. In the three years since he'd interviewed Stan Patz in his SoHo loft a day after Etan vanished, Miller had solidified his credentials as a crime reporter. He usually kept his scanner tuned to the NYPD Special Operations Division frequency to monitor communications with the emergency vehicles, helicopters, and police launches; anyone that would respond to the kind of newsworthy events Miller cared about.
    Car 615, he knew, was Daniel St. John, a.k.a. "the Saint," the high-profile commanding officer of all emergency services. If St. John was heading to a routine search in the middle of nowhere, the Bronx, something was going on. Miller pointed his car north, but without an exact address he'd have to

shoot for the general direction, then go by instinct. While it sometimes got him into trouble, more often that instinct landed him the lead story on the 10 p.m. broadcast. Maybe it's a Mafia graveyard, Miller thought hopefully, or a cache of bombs. He didn't want to use his two-way radio to alert the newsdesk; the competing NBC station shared their band, so he stopped at a street-corner pay phone to call in and request that a camera crew head up to meet him. Driving up and down streets near Gun Hill Road, Miller finally spotted an emergency vehicle turning down Webster Avenue and followed. When he saw the cars lined up in front of the metal fence across from a cemetery, he stopped and rummaged around in the trunk that basically served as his mobile office to grab a flashlight from its place next to a bulletproof vest and a set of walkie-talkies. Folding his suit jacket neatly, he shrugged on a weather-worn khaki coat, then walked three hundred feet downhill from the gate, following a trail made by the cops. Pushing through the brush, Miller finally could make out his destination ahead, the entrance to a wide-mouthed drainage pipe wedged in below the Conrail tracks. There were heavy wooden planks obscuring one side of the pipe's entrance, but Miller could see cops practically crab-walking out sideways, holding armfuls of what appeared to be trash.

He quickly ran back and guided the camera and soundman in by radio. The camera crew filmed the operations outside, as Miller looked around for St. John, who seemed to have come and gone. He folded his six-foot frame and ducked into the tunnel, moving around slowly. Still daylight outside, it was full dark inside. Switching on the flashlight, he inched farther down the length of the pipe and realized that midway through someone had set up house. Whoever it was, he was a lousy housekeeper. The floors, walls, and ceiling, such as they were, were completely obscured by refuse. Indistinct piles of clothes, sheets, and blankets were strewn around like hurricane wreckage. Stacks of decaying magazines—*Hustler*, gay porn—and newspapers covered the floors, mixed with piles of old bottles and other objects, mostly unidentifiable, except for a large plastic blow-up doll. Back outside he looked around and approached one of the cops.

"John Miller, Channel 5 News." Miller always said it like it was one word, his signature greeting to any potential source. "Whaddya got?" That was NYPD parlance to ask for a quick summary. Usually it worked to signal that Miller was comfortable and accepted at crime scenes. Long after-hours sessions in countless bars, trading quips and tips, had made him "one of the boys." It did the trick here. He learned that the previous day railway police had arrested the drainpipe's inhabitant on a petit larceny charge. That wasn't worth bringing the head of emergency services up here a whole day later, he thought. Except that the victims were two young boys who'd run home to tell their parents a strange-looking man had taken their schoolbooks, then tried to entice them into the tunnel to get the books back. The story got more interesting when Miller learned what the cops had found on the perp: several photographs of young boys, some with blond hair and blue eyes.

In the three years since Etan Patz had disappeared, a lot of New York children had gone missing, but most were parental custody cases, and few remained a mystery. None of them had generated the public interest of this one blond-haired, blue-eyed boy. Miller was skeptical of such a tenuous connection, although now at least he was starting to understand why the top brass had been alerted, and why cops were still crawling all over the scene, carting out garbage.

From his years tracking the case, Miller was all too aware there had never been any real leads to follow. No witnesses, no good suspects. There wasn't even a crime scene. If there were a connection to the Patz case, it would be big news. But he wondered if a stronger connection than the photos existed.

———

The day before, Assistant District Attorney Frank Carroll had picked up his phone to hear Bronx DA Mario Merola's familiar rich baritone in his ear. "I want you to go talk to this guy they picked up in the drainpipe," his boss had said with the air of a man who was obeyed without question. "No one else, not the cops, no FBI, no one in the room but our office. Don't let anyone at him 'til you're finished."

"Hey Carroll," another ADA in the Bronx County Courthouse office joked in passing, "who's going to play you in the movie?" Clearly the word had leaked out that he was going to do the interview. Almost from the moment they'd brought the "drainpipe man" in earlier that morning, talk had been flying through the building. There were excited whispers of "We got the guy!" It was possible. After all, this office had been part of the high-profile "Son of Sam" prosecution just four years earlier. The skeptics argued, on the other hand, that this was "a bunch of bullshit, just more chasing tails." But Carroll had a lot on his plate, and he couldn't be bothered with either argument.

Frank Carroll had a few nicknames around the office. One of them was "Father Francis." Defendants had a history of confessing to him—even, on occasion, from up on the witness stand in the middle of cross-examination. There was something about his easy, nonthreatening, seemingly nonjudgmental tone and signature handlebar mustache that disarmed bad guys. Soon after Merola's call, Carroll took off the conservative bow tie he wore every day, except when he was in court or questioning a suspect, and left for the secondary courthouse nearby where the suspect was being held. The buzz met him over there too. As he sat in a side room debriefing the arresting officers, younger, overenthusiastic DAs would pop their heads in to be met with a cool, blank regard, and then duck back out. Carroll had the sense that the transit police who had actually brought the perp in were being pushed to the background, and now he listened carefully to their report. He wanted to give them their due.

The man had told the cops his name—Jose Antonio Ramos—but little else. One of the boys was clearly taking a huge risk, not by going in to retrieve his book, but by telling his parents what had happened. This boy, the cop told Carroll, was threatened by his folks with a sound thrashing if he ever went near those railroad tracks, and he'd had to rat himself out. "The kid's the hero," Carroll thought.

He looked through the photos the cops had found. Several of the faces looked well under ten years old; Ramos stood cheek by jowl in the pictures with a few of them. The towheaded faces of two different boys jumped off the paper. One, Carroll was told, had the look of, just might be, the Patz boy. The parents were going to be shown the photos soon.

It all did seem creepy, he admitted to himself, but he was not going in with preconceptions. All the talk of "breaking the case" was irresponsible. This could very well be a pathetic lost soul who had no life of his own, so he'd created a two-dimensional one out of other people's families, to surround himself as he huddled alone in his cold, damp tunnel. Carroll had seen just this kind of thing before, and it was thoroughly unprofessional to assume anything else. He needed more information. At the moment all he had at best was a petty theft charge, maybe nothing more than simple criminal trespass. Not much to hold on to someone.

At 7:20 p.m., Carroll sat down with Ramos in a fourth floor lineup

room, a desk between them, a video camera recording them. Carroll introduced himself and the audiotape technician and stenographer in the room
with him. Behind the prosecutor, a one-way glass window also hid a revolv-
ing parade of onlookers, although Ramos stared over his shoulder often, so
Carroll knew the man was aware of being watched.

He was a dark, bedraggled creature, hunched into his seat, arms akimbo.
He certainly looked the part of a vagrant living amid garbage in an abandoned drainpipe. "Rasputin" was the name that popped into Carroll's head
when he first saw the long, flowing black hair and bushy beard. Indeed,
Ramos could pass for an ancient master of the dark arts if not for his
modern-day headgear, a trademark of sorts. A flat leather newsboy-type cap
with a brim, it was nearly obscured by the buttons covering it, a collection of
pop culture found among the junk he claimed to forage for a living. There
were peace signs, a Rolling Stones tongue, photo buttons, and slogans, all
crammed against each other, with no visible space underneath.

Was he a sinister malevolent or an odd, harmless throwaway? When he
began to speak, it was even less clear. His voice was disarmingly soft, almost
sweet. At one point, the audio technician taping the proceedings asked him
to speak up. "Okay," he responded helpfully, raising his voice only slightly.
"Testing...Is that all right?"

But it was his eyes that drew Carroll. The prosecutor always liked to fix in
on his man's eyes. These were dark and flat, disturbing and furtive. Carroll
shuffled through several matchbook-sized photos, retrieved from the Gucci
wallet Ramos was carrying, as he read Ramos his rights and did a round
of routine questions. The man spelled out his name and gave Carroll his
birthdate, July 23, 1943, at a hospital in the Bronx. Did he have any other
names? Carroll asked. No, Ramos assured him. They went through his past
addresses, tenuous as they were for a frequently homeless man. Before the
tunnel there was a Manhattan address where he'd lived for a time in the late
seventies. Before that, nothing, other than the four-year Navy stint right
out of ninth grade, and the Bronx apartment he'd left at the age of fourteen.
Otherwise, he moved around a lot.

The conversation quickly turned genial, almost convivial. Ramos started
off defensive, but then seemed to relax, with the air of a colleague aiding the
investigation. He explained that he was "self-employed," reselling junk he
collected all over New York. Most of his sales were in Greenwich Village,

where he'd been based for twenty years, he said, usually from a ware-laden blanket on the street.

Carroll was struck by the complexity of this man's existence. Ramos listed a storage space in Brooklyn where he kept more junk, and where he often slept several times a week. He wasn't homeless, thought Carroll, just homeless-like. He'd set up the drainpipe with all the amenities of home, describing a bed, and night table, an assortment of Bibles and a crucifix. Ramos had even been tapping into a power source to siphon off amperage for a bedside reading lamp. This is not your typical bum sleeping on a cardboard box over a vent, thought Carroll. He's got a very viable life, and the ability to slip from place to place unnoticed. He cuts a wide swath.

The junk-selling business paid off pretty well, Ramos boasted. He'd even taken a recent trip to Europe from the proceeds—a three-week jaunt to London, France, and Morocco. "I only took a twenty-two-day vacation," he said.

"You mean there have been others?" Carroll acted impressed.

"Oh, yeah," Ramos responded to the man's feigned envy. "The first time, I went for six months…that was a booming year. I had a lot of trash that year."

"I'm in the wrong business," Carroll cracked. The two men laughed, and Ramos agreed. He told Carroll that after a short, unhappy stint in the corporate advertising world he had vowed to be his own boss for good. He was so miserable at one point, he said, that he'd "had a nervous breakdown, as a matter of fact." He went on to describe various rounds of psychiatric treatment, including an involuntary ninety-day inpatient stint, thanks to his mother. Recently, he'd been going to the clinics again, he said, to help him beat back the voices in his head. Like the voice that "would try to force me to get violent."

"Okay," said Carroll, and waited. He was rewarded for his patience.

"And I had to hold it back," Ramos continued. He spoke matter-of-factly, calm, like he was telling a charming anecdote. "I had to do a lot of really forceful holding back," he said, " 'cause I was ready to explode."

The mention of aural hallucinations exhorting violence can raise the frightening specter of a man overtaken and out of control. But Carroll wasn't buying it. Voices, he thought immediately, that's bullshit. This was not the delivery of a lunatic driven to murderous rages. This was the crazy-like-a-fox sound of an insanity defense being seeded, a common ploy for anyone who knew how to play the system. And defense to what? Carroll wondered. You don't need a psych defense for stolen property. This guy might well be into something much more. Carroll played with the photos and wondered if any of this was the truth.

Ramos rambled on. He wasn't clear about the time sequence of his violent voices, but he knew he'd had a run of them three years earlier, back in 1979. They came and went, he said, but sometimes they were with him all the time, telling him to hit people, push them. That was why he'd moved out into the woods. With no people around, the voices subsided. He'd been living in the drainpipe off and on for about six months, after he'd gotten back from his European vacation.

Ramos was looking to wind up his story. "I think you got everything down," he said, "unless you want me to sign the biography now. I wanna write a biography. 'Cause you ever heard of anybody digging garbage, and going to Europe with it?"

"No," said Frank Carroll. He never had. That was one of the reasons he wanted to keep this discussion going.

They moved on to his arrest, and Ramos explained what a big mistake it was. In his version, the two boys had discovered his drainpipe and were pilfering his inventory, stuffing jewelry in their pockets. When Ramos appeared they ran, dropping their schoolbooks. Ramos pursued them to give the books back, but they kept running, all the way to the cops. "Listen, I woke up, my hair was straggly out like that." Ramos gestured good-naturedly. "They probably got scared. That's why they ran. And here I am, trying to give them the book bags." It was all just a silly misunderstanding.

Carroll let him finish his spiel, thinking of the kid whose parents had probably walloped him good for disobeying their orders not to play near the tracks. It would have been infinitely easier for the boy to feign the loss of his book, but instead he had confessed his sin. This was no misunderstanding.

"Now, you know what *they* say?" Carroll finally countered. "They say that you stole the bags from them."

"But I have no need for children's book bags!" Ramos appeared to consider this from a business standpoint. "There's no monetary value, whatsoever, in two kids' school bags... I just left them where they had left them."

The man was indignant. "I have no need to do that," he repeated, "to do any harm to any child, whatsoever."

More than an hour into the conversation, Frank Carroll finally worked his way around to the pictures of the little boys. Carroll held each tiny paper square delicately between his thumb and forefinger. They were so small, he had trouble handling them as he passed them over, but one after the other, Ramos went through them, describing the subjects as his friends and companions; he said one boy, who looked no more than ten, was his "Dianetics instructor." Ramos himself appeared in three of the photos, an arm draped around the boy in each one. In all three cases Ramos made it clear the child had asked to have the picture taken.

Ramos talked about knowing one boy from time spent in New Orleans, but most of the boys were in New York. He described these as nurturing friendships, reaching out to needy youngsters who valued their time with him. One boy had junkie parents, he said, and several had no fathers around. He filled a void, Ramos suggested, giving them support and affection, returning one child who'd gotten lost to the arms of his grateful mother, rescuing another from a fall from his window. A self-described mentor and father figure. That kind of description was enough to raise Carroll's hackles, but then Ramos told the prosecutor he took the pictures in a Times Square movie lobby. Carroll blanched inwardly—what kind of "father" takes his kid to the movies in Times Square? In 1982, the only movies screening there were triple X. And what kind of mother was letting this man take her kids to hang around there?

When Carroll held out the next picture, Jose identified him as Bennett, the son of his former girlfriend Sandy, a woman he had met in the welfare office, had dated back in 1979, and still saw occasionally. The boy was around five years old when the picture was taken, he guessed, living with his single mom. Bennett had given him his school picture because "he considers me a good father for him," Ramos told Carroll. "We did everything together," Ramos said. "Even looking in garbage and selling together."

When Carroll had worked his way through all the photos, he finally asked the question on everyone's mind. "Did you ever know a kid named Etan Patz?"

Even though, like most people, Carroll mispronounced the unusual last name, calling him "Etan Potz," Ramos immediately knew who he was talking about. "No, no," he said quickly, and gave a funny little laugh. It was almost as though he'd been waiting for the question, like, Here we go, of course you're going to ask that. Without pausing to take a breath, Carroll moved on to ask about another name, then asked Ramos if he ever read the papers.

"Oh, yeah," said Ramos, he read the *New York Times* every day, and the *Wall Street Journal*—a well-read tunnel dweller. Then Carroll came around a minute later to try again, asking about Etan Patz.

"Yeah," Ramos responded immediately this time. "That was in the papers, in '79."

Carroll always felt that if you didn't get the answer you were looking for at first, deflect it, then circle back. And give the person a way to tell you something that doesn't incriminate him right off the bat. But none of those pictures could possibly be of Etan, Ramos made clear, because he had never met the boy, only read about him, like everyone else.

Then, moments later, Ramos offered up a connection, with no prompting, that stunned the room.

"Sandy used to take care of him," he volunteered.

Sandy, his old girlfriend. Sandy, the woman from the welfare office.

Sandy, Bennett's mom. Bennett was picture number three, the boy who Ramos had just said "did everything" with him.

"Bingo," Carroll thought. Suddenly what had been a fishing expedition transformed into a hard lead, the first in years, clearer than the blurry figures in the photo-booth squares who bore a faint resemblance to Etan. But was this link real? Frank Carroll made excuses about needing to put fresh tape in the camera and stopped the interview, to confer with detectives on the other side of the glass.

He walked out of the room. "What's this name, Sandy Harmon?" he asked the detectives congregated around the viewing area. "Is this a good name? Or is this more bullshit?" There were hurried instructions to get someone down to the Patz home with the photos. "We need a handle on this Sandy woman, too." Cops scattered, as Carroll went back into the lineup room for another round of show-and-tell.

Carroll walked back into the interview room and started again with a fresh tape, but he could tell Ramos was just about done. They went around again on the Patz questions, and Ramos tangled himself up a bit more as he pointed to one of the blondest boys. "People told me that this one looks like him—this one, Justin," he said. "But I couldn't see no resemblance."

Maybe, thought Carroll, we can go somewhere here. "What's the difference between him and Etan Patz?" he ventured.

"The smile, I think," Ramos said.

"Does he have the same color hair?" Carroll asked, thinking that newspapers don't publish color pictures. But Ramos wasn't taking the bait.

"I never saw Etan. I never met him. But, from the photographs I saw of him, in the paper..." Ramos paused and Carroll tried, "Did Etan look like this in the papers?"

"No," responded Ramos. "He had a bigger head, Etan."

"He had a bigger head?" Carroll repeated. That would be a hard thing to measure by newspaper photos.

"Yeah," said Ramos, but he'd had enough. "I never saw Etan Patz in my life... They didn't describe too much in the newspaper. I didn't pay attention to it that much."

Ten minutes and a round of terse monosyllabic answers later, Carroll ended the interview. He walked out of the room, and into the hall to a crowd of question marks.

"He's involved," Carroll pronounced. "I'm convinced of it." But this was a one-off deal, and he knew his part was over. Carroll had gone into this with a clear understanding that if he succeeded in pushing the Patz case along, it was not going to go anywhere in the Bronx. The best he could do, and had done, he felt, was to lay groundwork for the Manhattan DA's Office. Some ADA down there was going to benefit from this lead, and when they contacted him to follow up, he just hoped they'd be appreciative.

20:05 Det. Gannon—coming by with photo to be checked
—*Patz logbook, March 18, 1982*

The phone rang and Stan Patz picked it up in the studio, where he often worked late. The voice identified himself as Detective Gannon, and Stan assumed it was a "heads-up" call. Three years on, these calls came much less frequently, but every once in a while the Patzes were still dragged into the nightmarish arc of a new lead. The detectives had taken to deliberately leaving them out of the loop on most of these. Among the succession of cops cycling through this investigation, there were the occasional few who still saw the parents as suspects. Others withheld information to avoid unnecessary grief, on the theory that there was already enough to go around in the Patz house. But sometimes the media, followed quickly by the public, got involved. A heads-up call would come in, that Channel 4, or the *New York Post*, or any one of ten other local press gangs was getting ready to go with their "exclusive," to be quickly followed by the others running, pushing and shoving, in close step behind. The cops and the family had agreed that in those cases, it was kinder not to be blindsided.

Stan had never talked to Detective Gannon before, couldn't even remember his first name in the moment it took to hang up and note the call in the logbook. He wanted to come by, probably by 9 p.m. Gannon, like other cops before him, had some photos he wanted to show Stan and Julie, more "look-likes." Was it okay to get there so late? The Patzes were used to cops showing up at all hours. Sometimes they called first, as a courtesy, but not always.

When Bronx detective Don Gannon arrived at the Patz loft, Stan and Julie sat and looked through the pictures, but as expected, none were Etan. They had no reason to suspect this time was any different than all the others. There would probably be some press, they were warned, about an arrest that day in the Bronx. But since these were "look-likes," thought Stan, this would be yet another round of press to ignore.

———

John Miller waited out the police until they released the scene so he could get a closer look inside the length of the pipe. His flashlight danced around, to illuminate pockets of detritus the cops had left behind. Farther down the tunnel, the dank surfaces were completely blanketed with trash. Well into the second day of Ramos's arrest, police had barely touched the enormous volume of his belongings. Miller assumed there'd be more official digging the next day and he wanted to do some of his own before then. He considered hunkering down on his hands and knees to burrow in, then crouched low instead, balancing on the balls of his feet to spare his buff-colored pants. Moments into his inventory, his eye caught a stack of paperwork. It looked like old mail; a promising glimpse into the man's past. He picked up a wad of faded envelopes and examined them in the flashlight's glare. The most legible one was a letter from the Social Security Administration postmarked 1979. It was addressed to Jose Antonio Ramos at an apartment on the Lower East Side. The paper was torn, but the address was clear—234 East Fourth Street.

Miller flashed to a mental map of lower Manhattan. East Fourth Street was six blocks north of Prince, and that street address was just blocks east of the Patz apartment. Maybe a fifteen-minute walk, at a clip. If this guy was in fact Jose Ramos, and he was living in the neighborhood when Etan was snatched, Miller thought, the vagrant's interest in little blond boys just got much more damning.

The reporter's instincts were glowing bright red. Within an hour he'd extracted the "babysitter" angle from a source at the Bronx DA's Office, and landed an interview with the DA himself to ask him about it firsthand. Merola wouldn't go into further detail or give out Sandy Harmon's name, but he didn't deny the connection either.

That night, some twenty-four hours after Ramos had told the Bronx DA's Office of his connection to the Patz "babysitter," Channel 5 ran the story. Miller's report featured shots from inside the tunnel, as well as of the envelopes with the East Village address, and the other junk, now stacked outside. The camera lingered on the remnants of children's toys—a stuffed bear, a collection of blank-eyed, smiling baby dolls, missing their clothes and a limb or two. The report also broadcast pictures of Jose Ramos and all the boys whose photos were found in his wallet.

As it turned out, Sandy was the biggest real break the case would see for years. While she wasn't exactly Etan's babysitter, as his parents would be quick to point out, Sandy Harmon had been hired to walk Etan and his two friends Chelsea and Kyra home from school during that school bus strike in the spring of 1979. Sandy had been in the Patz home, she had spent time with Etan, was even at the Patzes' on May 25, picking up keys to the loft. She had intended to housesit over the long weekend while the Patzes went away. And then, of course, they never went away. Sandy was the one who'd been watching the news with her boyfriend in the first days after Etan disappeared, and then had seen him get up to leave, telling her he was going out to "help look for the boy." But she had never called him Jose; contrary to what Ramos had told Frank Carroll the day before, he did go by other names. He was known as Michael to most of his New York friends.

———

Stan Patz followed the explosion of coverage that started on Friday night. The story leapt at him from the TV screen and the tabloid headlines, assaulting his frayed nerves all weekend long. The pictures had not been Etan, but this was starting to sound like more than a simple "look-like." For the first time in quite a while, Stan and Julie were once again caught in that complex position, between two warring emotions. Almost three years into their ordeal, the half-formed scab covering their private life and private pain was being picked off yet again to ooze fresh blood. They greeted the news with the now familiar mix of trepidation tinged with the faint hope, one that could never be discounted, that new exposure could yield new information.

This time, though, was different. Unlike past headlines, now they ran next to pictures of the same tangible, sinister-looking face. The weekend that followed the drainpipe arrest marked the first time Stan's painstakingly constructed self-protective patina began to crumble.

For three years, since the day Etan disappeared, there had always been two basic scenarios Stan could choose to believe. In one, evil, unthinkable forces abducted and did his son harm. In the other, a deranged but well-intentioned motherly type, an infertile woman perhaps, was loving Etan somewhere in a parallel life. Stan had worked hard over time to ignore the first image and nurture the second. He did so with great skepticism, but it helped him get through each day. Now, as he stared at the disheveled, hollow-eyed man in Saturday's *New York Post*, Stan began to retrace his steps back to that carefully created mental fork in the road, to wander fearfully down the other path. A pedophile? In a filthy drainage tunnel? Stan longed for some facts, something real to bolster the media hype. But no one in a position to give him any called. All weekend long the press did, though, and he politely declined their interviews. He didn't want to add to the misinformation.

By this time, Stan Patz had reverted back to the days without sleep or food. On Monday afternoon when he finally worked up the nerve to call Missing Persons and put his fears into words, he had his first moment of relief in three days. "There's no possible way," he heard a detective say. "Just believe us." Stan wanted to believe, and so he did.

Ramos was held briefly for psychological observation, then released a few weeks later. The parents of the schoolkids weren't going to pursue charges, and the Bronx DA's Office turned their attention to the daily murders and rapes they needed to be chasing. Mario Merola's spokesman issued a statement concluding Ramos was not involved in the Patz case. The brief flare-up of interest died back down. But the jagged rent in Stan Patz's defenses could not be mended, and after that weekend, his darkest fears had a face. He and

Julie began to wonder about this abandoned lead. Talking to reporter Richard Rein a few weeks after the Bronx incident, they expressed their anger.

"We're very unhappy about the drainpipe case," Stan told Rein, who by now had interviewed the parents several times and written about them extensively for *People* magazine. "We haven't seen the toys they found, and we've argued that we'd recognize Etan's toys—the cops wouldn't. The woman who was the guy's girlfriend was, in fact, a woman who had cared for Etan." Why hadn't police contacted her? Stan and Julie wondered. And who's keeping track of this Ramos?

No one was, apparently, but authorities would later learn that over the next few months Ramos was living less than ten blocks away from the Patz apartment. Soon after his release, he went back to the Brooklyn room where he'd told Frank Carroll he kept the rest of his inventory and cleared it out. He set up a new headquarters back in the Patzes' Manhattan neighborhood, moving his junk to a vacant store in the West Village. There he slept on a mattress for a brief period, until the store's owner kicked him out. No one in law enforcement knew this at the time. And no one from the Manhattan DA's Office ever called Frank Carroll either. Ramos was another in a long string of briefly considered then disregarded leads.

Jose Ramos might never have been seen again, except for a New York vice cop who stumbled across him just a few months later. Officer Joseph Gelfand knew right away that he had caught the "drainpipe man." Ramos was carrying a newspaper clipping in his pocket that said so.

CHAPTER 7

Up on the Roof

[T]he defendant...directed informants to engage in an occupation involving a substantial risk of danger to their health, to wit:...Contact between defendant's mouth and informants penises with informants who are less than 14 years of age.
—*Felony Affidavit of P.O. Joseph Gelfand, Manhattan South Public Morals Division, August 24, 1982*

By the summer of 1982, police officer Joe Gelfand knew he was burned out, so he put in for a transfer from the New York Police Department's Narcotics Division to Vice. Working Narcotics was by turns hair-raising and mind-numbingly tedious, like a factory job bottling nuclear waste. Gelfand worked fourteen- to sixteen-hour shifts, each one the exact same. Every day a "buy and bust"; plus every day in court for the buy and bust the day before. He spent so much time at 100 Centre Street, he felt like he should just go to law school and be done with it. Plus the bad guys in Narcotics were more desperate than at Vice, since the hookers and numbers runners were back on the street in no time, but a drug bust could put you away for good. So the odds that some cornered dealer would pull a gun were that much greater. At thirty-two, Gelfand had been on the job over thirteen years, and although he was inured to the sense of danger, he knew it was there every single day.

Established in the early seventies, Vice's official name was the more genteel "Public Morals." In the Manhattan South Public Morals Division, or MSPMD, Gelfand could clock out after eight hours, and get his life back. Here they were a little more laid-back—on one of his first busts, a gambling racket, Gelfand cuffed his perp behind his back, the way he'd always done with the dealers. "Hey Sarge," the old-time racketeer said to Gelfand's boss, who was standing nearby. "What's with the cuffs?" "Oh," the sergeant replied, "he just came from Narco." In Public Morals, the cuffs went on in front; not quite by the book, more informal.

And there was more variety in the new job—there was prostitution, loan sharking, and illegal fireworks. MSPMD even had its own Pedophilia Squad, the only one in New York, created to meet the demand of the Times Square trade. Gelfand's first assignment was to the Pimp Squad, a name that made most people laugh when he mentioned it. Of course, there was nothing funny about the work. The victims were the hookers themselves, beaten, starved, or imprisoned by their pimps, and they weren't big on testifying against their "protectors." Gelfand would work on a long-range plan, visiting prostitutes in lockup for their own crimes. He would pass out his card and promise to do right by them in exchange for giving up their pimps. Sometimes they'd warm to him—he was unintimidating with his slight build, softly curling brown hair, and a pleasant, almost sweet voice that held traces of a faint stammer when he got worked up. Out on the street, Gelfand was known as a good detective with the ideal unassuming features for this kind of undercover work—one of his colleagues liked to joke that he looked like he'd be more at home playing the flute in the philharmonic. Plus, he was one of the fastest runners in the squad.

MSPMD covered nine precincts, from 59th Street east to west all the way downtown. It ran out of the makeshift fourth floor at Manhattan Traffic, a crumbling red-brick building in the heart of the fur district on West 30th Street. From the outside, the landmark building looked stately, a medieval castle right out of King Arthur's court. But inside, the officers sat in one sweltering room at worn desks shoved against each other, and got bragging rights for the biggest rat sighting. They carped constantly about what a dump it was, how nothing worked right, if at all. "Out of Order" signs usually hung on the bathroom doors.

Gelfand had barely been in Public Morals a week when Eddie Curry, a cop in the Pedophilia unit, took him on his first ride-along. "You don't know Public Morals if you don't know Pedophilia," was the gist of Curry's pitch. "Let's go see the sights in Times Square." On this unusually cool August night, wearing frayed cut-off shorts and T-shirts, Gelfand and his tour guide pulled up in an unmarked car across from the Playland Arcade at 47th Street and Broadway. In 1982, Times Square was still the dazzling,

Technicolor jumble of an earlier incarnation—of seedy strip joints, peep shows, and live! sex acts live! on stage live! parlors.

Amid this mecca of degeneracy, Playland stood out as a pedophile magnet. When cops from Curry's unit weren't actively investigating a complaint, they'd hang out across the street from the arcade, in the same building where the glittery ball dropped on New Year's. An empty office on the second floor provided a surveillance position for detectives peering through sooty blinds at the various games played below. If someone were lucky enough to witness a transaction, he'd pursue on foot. But catching a pedophile in the act was a rare occurrence, just by the crime's very nature and, in these cases, because of the ready compliance of its victims.

As Curry looked around for a place to park, he schooled Gelfand about the chickenhawks, older men who loitered casually behind the James Bond pinball game or the trendy new Asteroids machines at Playland, to offer kids quarters in hopes they'd see a return on their investment. Most of these young boys, some not yet in their teens, were actively soliciting; others just wouldn't turn it down if approached. These kids would hang out in Playland all night long, Curry told Gelfand, and their parents usually didn't care enough to miss them.

Before they even made it to a parking spot, Gelfand noticed a shaggy haired, Hispanic-looking male with a group of blond, preteen-looking boys. "Look over there," he told Curry. "It looks like the old guy is trying to pick up those kids."

It was 10:30, and the theater crowds jammed the streets. As the three boys and man began walking from Broadway toward Eighth Avenue, the unmarked car trailed them, but winding through the traffic slowed down the cops. "I'm going after them," Gelfand told Curry in a reflexive move, "and we'll meet up later." He grabbed his walkie-talkie and jumped out to follow on foot. He crossed west toward the bus terminal and checked in with his partner. "Curry, I'm heading into Port Authority." There was no answer. Public Morals, he thought with disgust; just like the toilets—nothing works. He lost sight of the car and, with it, his backup. But his targets were still visible, so he kept following. He was also losing his bearings, though, while trying to keep the man and boys in sight through the throngs of people streaming past him.

At Ninth Avenue, Gelfand turned south, and lost the four briefly, then saw them again crossing back and forth across the avenue. Are they trying to lose a tail? he wondered, pulling back a few steps. No, he realized and picked up the pace again; this guy's looking for a discreet spot to do his business. Finally, Gelfand followed as they turned east on 39th, where the foursome headed up a long garage ramp toward upper-level parking. Gelfand watched from fifty feet away as the group walked to the top of the ramp, then climbed over a low adjoining wall to the rooftop of a two-story building next to the garage. Gelfand started up the ramp too, treading gingerly as he approached the top. He could see the man talking to the boys, then unzipping his fly. The smallest boy was up close to the man. Almost to the end of the ramp, in the dark, Gelfand's foot went down hard on a loud piece of broken glass. Everyone turned. Gelfand pulled out his gun. "Police officer, freeze. Don't move," he yelled. "It's okay, just put your hands on the wall!" He wasn't sure it was okay. He was alone in the dark, on top of a building God knows where.

As Gelfand reached the rooftop, two of the boys took off, jumping over the wall back onto the ramp. They ran down to the bottom and out of sight. Waving his service revolver, Gelfand motioned the man up against the wall, while sizing up the remaining kid. He was clearly the youngest, and now he was crying. "Come here," Gelfand told the boy, then "Keep your fucking hands on the wall" to the man. The boy went toward Gelfand, who grabbed him. "How old are you?" Gelfand asked the quivering shape. "Nine," said the boy, who was really eleven. "Please, please don't shoot," said the man, who looked about to cry, too.

"Don't run away," Gelfand said to the boy. "I'm not going to arrest you. What did he say to you?" The boy looked terrified, but his words were clear. "He told me to suck his dick," he said. "First he asked us if we wanted to make some money. He said, 'I'll give you ten dollars to suck your dicks.'"

Gelfand looked around, trying to think straight. It was probably eleven o'clock by now. This was new territory for him, but he could tell they were in the Garment District. By day it was teeming with deliveries; double-parked trucks and clothing racks rolling through the streets. By night it was desolate. Gelfand realized he had jammed the boy up into his armpit, like a football. He knew that even if he could hold the perp, if he lost the kid he'd have no case. He looked at the man, the kid, and the wall, and thought, "What the hell do I do now?"

Suddenly a window opened in a building across from him, higher up, maybe the fourth or fifth floor, and he could barely make out the silhouette of a man's head poking into the night. Gelfand had a fleeting vision of an angel descending to rescue him. No one, he was sure, actually *lived* in the Garment District. "I'm a police officer," he yelled to his angel. "Listen—call 911. Tell them where I am, 'cause I have no idea. Tell them I need some help."

The head disappeared. Gelfand, still holding the boy tightly, moved backward and jumped over the wall again to the garage ramp. He kept his gun trained on the man, pinning him to the wall with the force of the unspent bullet. "Don't move," he repeated to his quarry. "Don't shoot," the man repeated back. "I got no gun on me, look, just a knife in my pocket."

How long, Gelfand wondered, do you wait for some stranger to maybe call for help, who will maybe come to the rescue? And just what do you do once you've decided you've waited long enough?

Gelfand turned slightly to the boy without taking his eyes off the man. "Who are those kids?" he asked of the other two, who he could now make out crouched at the bottom of the ramp. "One of them's my brother," the boy managed. The shadow down below was obviously the older sibling, maybe the reason he hadn't just taken off. He was probably breaking his little brother into the business, Gelfand thought, and might actually catch some hell if he went home without him. "Hey," Gelfand yelled down. "Get back up here. I've got your brother. I'm going to find out who you are anyways." The two older boys slowly moved back up the ramp.

"He told us to suck his dick," the youngest boy's voice repeated from the recesses of Gelfand's underarm. "First he was going to do it to us, but when we got up here, he changed it. He said if I didn't do it, something would happen. I thought he was going to kill us."

Now Gelfand could hear patrol cars arriving, sirens screaming. It sounded as though units were coming in from all over the city. A "1013" must have gone out, Gelfand realized, a call that brings everyone—"officer in need of assistance." He considered the logistics of reaching around his young hostage to take out his handcuffs, then remembered his handcuffs were back in the office. Boy, did he ever need assistance. But the man against the wall didn't look like a big threat, even without cuffs. He was crying audibly. Gelfand felt the cool air against his sweat-drenched face as he holstered his pistol. He never wore a uniform, and his streetwear could easily raise doubt in the minds of the approaching cops. Better not to be waving a gun.

Uniformed officers were now moving up the ramp. "This guy is under arrest," Gelfand called. "Attempted sodomy. He tried to have sex with the boy." One of the cops approached with his cuffs, and the suspect was led away down the ramp and into a radio car. Gelfand got in with them, and they headed to the closest precinct, as other officers followed, bringing the young victims.

At the station, Gelfand read the man his rights, and he immediately asked for a lawyer. So much for questioning him. He did give up his name—Jose Antonio Ramos. The name didn't mean anything to Gelfand, and he started going through Ramos's things. He found a wallet, and two knives; one the kind used for cutting carpet, the other a bone-handled hunting knife.

Gelfand pulled a Bible out of the suspect's worn brown leather backpack. "Please, give that back to me," the man pleaded, still crying. "I've been hearing things," Gelfand thought the man muttered, between sobs.

"I'm under a lot of pressure," Ramos continued. "I felt they were trying to lure me."

Gelfand mentally rolled his eyes. "Aren't you glad I showed up in time?" he asked.

"Oh, yes," said Ramos.

Gelfand looked at the Bible on the table. He couldn't resist playing with the guy's head a little. "Do you think God was watching you, and that's why I was there?" he asked.

Again, Ramos agreed. Well, what have we here—a *devout* child molester, thought Gelfand. Must pray a lot to be absolved from his sins. Gelfand went through the wallet and wasn't that surprised to find pictures of kids—six of them. These guys liked to remember their conquests. Some of the boys were blond and blue-eyed, most were smiling in what looked like separate photobooth snapshots. One was clearly taken in Washington Square Park—in the background Gelfand could see the identifiable arch at the entrance to the square.

The blond hair in some of the photos had immediately conjured up the name Etan Patz. Gelfand still passed the posters on the streets; one hung on the wall of his office at Public Morals. The Washington Square arch reminded Gelfand—that was just blocks from where the Patz boy had lived back in 1979. Not compelling evidence, he knew, but he felt a slight quiver, that proverbial gut feeling.

Then Gelfand unfolded a creased newspaper clipping and stood up straight. He stared at the picture alongside the written copy, of the man he'd just arrested, although the photo showed a bushy beard. "Tunnel Dweller Didn't Harm Kids," shouted a New York tabloid headline from late March, three months earlier. "Bellevue Examining Recluse." He's his own PR rep, marveled the cop as he read about the "eccentric recluse discovered living in a drainage tunnel." The article, unlike several that were written at the time, didn't mention a Patz connection. Even though this didn't confirm Gelfand's hunch, it pressed harder on his gut instinct.

Gelfand realized he knew very little about the Patz investigation, and he didn't want to blow it by grilling his suspect about someone else's case. He left Ramos to be booked, and called Missing Persons.

"P.O. Joseph Gelfand here from MSPMD," he started, giving his shield number. "I just picked up a pedophile in Times Square and he's being booked now. This guy had photographs of kids who looked like Etan Patz."

The voice at the other end could not possibly sound more condescending, thought Gelfand. "Oh, really?" said the detective, but what Gelfand heard was, "Who the hell do you think you are calling me with this bullshit? You locked up a guy with pictures of kids that *you* think look like Etan Patz, a kid who's been gone for three years? Are you kidding me?" Gelfand relayed the details to what sounded like dead air, then hung up the phone in disgust.

Typical, he thought. No wonder no one's found the kid yet.

Days later, Gelfand was out at a Queens precinct, working a gambling sting. The commanding officer of all of Public Morals happened to cross his path. Aaron Rosenthal was reputed to be tough on his cops, so when he stopped Gelfand in the hall, there was that momentary twinge of "oh-oh."

"Joseph," said Rosenthal, "that was a nice arrest you made last week." Gelfand was surprised the big boss even knew his first name, let alone his work. "I was only doing my job, Inspector," he said. "Well, you could have just looked the other way," said the man. "Good arrest."

Armed with the warm praise, Gelfand followed the progress of his first Vice case a little more zealously than an old hand might have. He waited for the DA's Office to call him to a grand jury. After the arrest that night, other cops in the squad had taken the three young victims home to Queens and reported back that they had no phone. Gelfand wondered how the witnesses would be contacted, but he figured he could always track them down just by going to the home. He looked forward to telling his story before a judge.

Once a suspect is arraigned, which usually happens within hours of his arrest, he must get a hearing within seventy-two hours, as his right to a speedy process. But if he makes bail, the hearing can happen on a more leisurely timetable. With the pace of the criminal courts, Gelfand knew how often "leisurely" slipped into "inert." After three days and no call, he assumed Ramos had made bail. But then months went by and there was still no call. Gelfand would periodically grouse about it. That night on the rooftop had taken a few weeks off of his life in adrenaline alone, and it involved kids, for Christ's sake. Maybe they weren't the best victims, but if nothing else, Gelfand could still remember the littlest one shivering under his arms. He wasn't going to let it go.

What he never knew was that Ramos had spent the entire fall in Rikers. The young ADA who took Gelfand's statement set bail at $15,000, BUT, she wrote, underlining the word twice in her initial report, she wanted him held anyway for a "730," or psych exam. She made note of Gelfand's account of the newspaper clipping and photos, but made no specific reference to Gelfand's instinct about the Patz case. "He seems like a real psycho," she finished the note.

The newspaper article Ramos kept in his pocket had traced his mental history, so in mid-September the DA's Office ordered psych records from several Bronx hospitals. North Central Bronx Hospital sent back an extensive report written in February 1982, the month before Ramos was arrested in the drainage tunnel, six months before Gelfand had him up against the rooftop wall. Ramos had come into the hospital requesting "individual psychotherapy, ... [and] secure living arrangements from welfare."

"Mr. Ramos stated that he struggles against voices telling him to harm others, that people upset him a lot, that he has trouble with his memory and needs a place to live," wrote the intake worker. Under *Current Life Situation and Brief Recent History*, she wrote, "Mr. Ramos has been unemployed since 1973. Prior to that, had worked in commercial arts. Presently he lives 'in the woods,' receives welfare, and eats at local diners. He has no friends and has not had a contact with family members for three years. . . . Last personal relationship was in 1968. He lived with a woman for 9 months. They had a daughter which he cared for. They had an argument over the child, he 'hit her hard,' and she left with daughter. No contact with them since. Hospitalized at Jacobi for 3 months (cannot recall when exactly). Reports that mother tricked him, and that he did not benefit from treatment there."

Describing his mental status, the intake worker wrote that "Mr.

Ramos...reports auditory hallucinations (male voice telling him to hit others when he is upset) and exhibits psychotic ideation (eg animal friends come to visit him in the woods)....Reports desire to jump in front of a bus (but suicidal intent questionable)."

She recorded a diagnosis of "chronic schizophrenia, undifferentiated," and suggested a "6 week evaluation to assess case further" as a course of treatment.

In mid-October Ramos took his "730" exam from behind bars and passed. He was found competent to appear at a grand jury. A date was set for early November. But Gelfand didn't know about any of this. He never got the call to come down.

Sometime before the end of the year, Gelfand called the DA's Office. "What happened to my case?" he asked. The young ADA he had spoken with before told him it had been dismissed. "We sent a letter to the victims and they never responded," she said. He was livid. "What do you mean, you sent them a letter? *I* wouldn't have shown up if you sent me a letter. If anyone had told me, I would have gone up there myself and just drove them down to court. We do that all the time." The ADA had nothing further to say. Ramos had been released. Nothing more to be done.

The other cops on the squad, with the patience of mother hens teaching a young chick, explained to the outraged newcomer that this was simply the way it worked. The Manhattan DA's Sex Crimes Unit, Gelfand was told, didn't like pedophilia cases. Especially when the victims were streetwise toughs, thirteen going on thirty. The kids don't show up, Gelfand heard. Hearings have to be rescheduled. And even if they do show up—only after the vice cops truck up to the broken homes where these lost boys live with their indifferent parents under heartbreaking conditions and drag them down to court—they do terribly with juries, who see them as hustlers asking for it, not as minors in the eyes of the law. Some cops who worked these cases felt that way too, but not all of them. Joe Gelfand didn't.

A month or so after he heard the case had been dismissed, Gelfand got a call from Missing Persons. "Do you know where Jose Ramos is?" asked the detective. "We want to talk to him."

"Well," replied Gelfand, unwilling to conceal his sarcasm, "I knew exactly where he was the night I called you guys back in August."

CHAPTER 8

New Life

WESTERN UNION TELEGRAM
...WHITE HOUSE DC OCT 8
MR. AND MRS. STAN PATZ
ON BEHALF OF THE PRESIDENT I AM INVITING YOU TO WITNESS THE SIGNING OF THE MISSING CHILDREN ACT...THE CEREMONY WILL BE HELD TUESDAY OCTOBER 12, AT 1:00 PM IN THE ROSE GARDEN...WE WILL NEED YOUR SOCIAL SECURITY NUMBER AND DATE OF BIRTH. GUESTS MAY BEGIN ARRIVING TO THE SOUTH-WEST GATE AT 12:30 PM
— *White House telegram for October 12, 1982, signing of National Missing Children's Act*

SEX CLUB CLUE IN HUNT FOR SOHO BOY?
Porn pix found—are they Etan Patz?
— New York Post, *front page, December 20, 1982*

Quiz ex-cabby in Etan Patz case: "Believe I picked up Etan & Man"
— New York Daily News, *front page, December 22, 1982*

Stan Patz was long overdue at the dentist, and he sat in the chair facing a new hygienist. She bent over him, made typical small talk while she cleaned his teeth. It was the kind of conversation two strangers usually started with, just not from this physical proximity.

"So, are you married?" she asked genially, scraping away.

"Uh-huh," Stan answered as best he could with the instruments in his mouth.

"Kids?"

Again, yes.

"Oh, how many?" And there it was—the question Stan didn't know how to answer, the one he'd been grappling with for some time now. One of the many unspoken topics in the Patz household was whether or not they should begin to acknowledge the possibility that Etan was no longer alive, and how. It had always seemed beside the point. They would continue to look for him, to return every phone call about sightings in New Mexico and Alberta and Spain. But after three years, it was during the small moments like this one that Stan could see the need for a position, one way or the other.

"Two, I guess," he answered the woman.

She laughed, assuming he was being playful. "You guess? What do you mean, you guess? Don't you know?"

"Well, no." Someone else might have artfully deflected, but Stan wasn't made that way, nor did he have the mental stamina to parse out an honest yet uncomplicated answer. "One of my children is missing, and we don't know if he is alive or not."

The woman stopped scraping. "That's terrible," she said. "Have you told the police about this?"

"Yes." Stan could speak clearly while the hygienist stood staring at him, her dental scaler unused in her hand. "We did, and they've been looking for him for several years now."

Sitting in the chair watching this woman stare at him, Stan decided in the future he would answer as Julie did:

"Yes, we've got two at home."

Three years into the case, that was still all that Stan and Julie knew for sure, but their feelings about what they knew were shifting. Interspersed with the stoic optimism Stan had always professed, he had begun to dwell on the harm that three years away would inflict on a small child. Even if Etan were to come home, his father sometimes thought, he would never really be theirs again. Under the best of circumstances, which after the drainpipe incident Stan was no longer able to blindly believe, he feared the damage would take a lifetime of love and healing to undo. As for Julie, she had often said that being in this endless limbo was the hardest part of their ordeal, but now she'd become more open about just how hard it was.

"I really believe that not knowing what has happened to Etan is far more difficult than even knowing the worst," she said in an interview marking the third anniversary.

"As horrible as that might sound," she continued, "I hope and I pray he's still alive, but even if I were to learn tomorrow that he has in fact been dead for three years . . . we could grieve fully and completely . . . we can be sad, we can cry, we can allow ourselves to feel the full pain of that death and be able to get it behind us."

Stan finished her thought. "Etan might have no more pain, but we do. We suffer on a daily basis."

This third year would be marked in a way designed to go beyond the plight of one New York boy, beyond even his home state. In the year since the gallery exhibit on missing and exploited children, Kitty Brown's advocacy group Child Find had come up with the idea of creating a special day, to focus annually on the problem. Let's not wait for the next horribly tragic announcement of a stolen child to grab people in a knee-jerk response, its advocates theorized, let's proactively mobilize public opinion. They picked a day to guarantee that anyone thinking about missing children would think about Etan Patz.

At Child Find's urging, governors from twenty-six states, including New York governor Hugh Carey, signed proclamations declaring May 25, 1982, National Missing Children's Day. Julie navigated a round of promotional appearances throughout the city, including a stop at City Hall to greet Mayor Ed Koch as he too marked the occasion. She made a carefully prepared plea for school programs to teach students how to avoid abduction, and a call to support the still pending legislation.

But while both Stan and Julie attempted public enthusiasm on that day, they were still reeling from the response that had bombarded them after the announcement of a reward for the first time the week before. Acting through an intermediary attorney, an anonymous donor had offered $25,000 for information leading to Etan's recovery, and the Patzes had finally taken this long-avoided step. The cops' earlier counsel that money would only bring the worst of humanity crawling out of the woodwork was immediately borne out. While the calls had always been heavier around the previous anniversaries, they now quadrupled in number, and many came collect. The Patzes felt compelled to accept the charges, fearing the even higher cost if they didn't. For every sympathetic soul and lunatic—literally—calling from a mental institution, the award also attracted the circling, flesh-eating vultures.

"I know where your fucking kid is," snarled a nameless male voice. "He's alive and I want $50,000 ransom.... I'm not bullshitting. King's Highway and Flatbush Avenue on Saturday morning at nine. Thank you."

When the hoopla of the anniversary day ended, the ugliness didn't. Perhaps the worst call came a week later. Julie scrambled to copy the message verbatim, in all its depravity:

"Male/female, trying to disguise voice," she wrote. "Has our f'ing son. Has fucked him up his ass. I'll cut his m'—f'—g neck off if you don't listen. I want $20,000.

"Listen bitch," the caller went on, "I'll send his severed head through the mail. Think about it and I'll call you back sometime. Next week. Or sometime." *Click.*

In the end, the reward offer brought fresh pain, but no leads. The case was in full stall. The task force was down to one detective, and the one development Stan and Julie felt merited further investigation—the drainpipe arrest two months earlier—hadn't seemed to register on the cops' radar as far as they could tell. The total dead calm was underscored a week after Julie was told to expect her son's head in the mail, when Stan called Bill Butler to report another semicoherent "tip" and learned the detective had been taken off the case. For all the "heads-up" calls the cops had made over the years, no one warned them about this development. Stan wondered if Butler had wanted to avoid a conversation acknowledging defeat.

When Ari Patz turned six a few weeks later, his mother took him to Coney Island for a full day of rides and arcade games. Ari had always been a very active "boy" boy, and Etan's disappearance added fuel to his fire. At three and four, he'd been surrounded by figures who were only fantasy heroes to other children, and he'd gotten caught up in the cops-and-robbers machismo of the detectives hanging around. At one point Ari talked about going off to find his brother himself, striking new fear in his parents' heart. When that proved impossible, he wanted to hang out with the older boys, and had even begged his parents to see if one or another of them could come live with him. Maybe, he'd ask, we could change his name to Etan?

He asked other questions, too, confronting as only a small child can the oppressive cloud his family lived under. One day, he solemnly crawled into his mother's lap.

"Are we ever going to smile again?" he asked her. Julie felt the gentle query like an open-palmed slap in the face, the proverbial wake-up call. She took it so much to heart that she found herself standing in front of the mirror, practicing. She found it very difficult and unnatural, and she was appreciative of her youngest son's candor and healing power.

But his sixth birthday saw a change. Ari grew fearful in a vague, unspoken way. After all, personal experience had taught him that six was a dangerous year for a young boy. His parents sent him to P.S. 3, rather than its offshoot Annex school farther downtown that Etan had attended; even though they thought the Annex school was a better fit, they too wanted to avoid all the associations there.

Every morning Julie either walked Ari to the bus stop, or all the way to his school in Greenwich Village. P.S. 3 was a cooperative program, nick-named the "Hippie School," with a progressive principal, known throughout the city for his creatively quirky methods. Parents were welcome in the spacious, shabby-chic classrooms, with their twelve-foot ceilings and separate play spaces for block building and dress-up. Julie took advantage of the liberal policy and often showed up several days a week. The teachers loved it—an extra hand who happened to be a professional. The kids loved Julie. She taught them new games, and held them when they cried. At Thanksgiving she organized a classroom feast, complete with turkey and all the trimmings, starting a tradition that later attracted other parents, grand-parents, and babysitters, who would all bow their heads in a nonecumenical thank-you for their blessings.

Ari was happy to have his mother around, too. He wouldn't run crying to her for special preference, but he sensed the grown-ups treated him a little differently. He was never sure if it was Julie's presence or because he was the boy with "that" brother. Maybe it was a little of both. Ari had never known life any other way, but how many kids' parents were constantly on television or were invited to the White House Rose Garden, to join the president as he signed a bill they'd helped pass? Ari liked it best, though, when his mother stayed nearby, where he didn't have to worry that she wasn't coming back.

On the last day of school before Christmas vacation of 1982, Julie did her usual stint at P.S. 3 in the morning, then hurried home to prepare for the holidays before picking up Ari at the bus stop after school. After a weekend of packing, gathering presents, and doling out plant-watering duties to the neighbors, the Patzes would make their annual holiday trek to Massachusetts, for a long-awaited week with grandparents, aunts, uncles, and cousins. Twice a year, as the New York City skyline receded and they were finally on their way home—which is what Julie still called it—she could always feel the tension leave her body. The house Julie had grown up in, then escaped from, was now a refuge; there the Patzes would be surrounded by family.

But by midafternoon Saturday, in a perverse twist of fate, news from Massachusetts would delay the family from traveling there. A Missing Persons detective was once again sitting in their front room with yet another photo to show them.

The cops typically didn't tell them where these photos came from. If Stan and Julie made a positive ID, there'd be plenty of time to fill in the details; if not, why bother? But the detectives had received a report that two weeks earlier Massachusetts police had raided a summer cottage in the beach town of Wareham. Three missing area teenagers, one from the Bronx and two from New Jersey, had been found there amid a cache of pornographic photographs, some depicting children in sex acts with adult men. Among the photos was a headshot of a handsome blond boy, his arm stretched to the side, elbow bent, his hand propping up his head. He was clothed and alone in the picture. He stared straight into the camera and wore a look that might be interpreted as sophisticated coy, with an ambiguous Mona Lisa curve to his lips. He had straight bangs that matched the ones in several pictures Stan had taken of Etan, and he bore a striking resemblance to the missing child.

Julie's first thought was, Oh, no, that's not him. It's just another picture. But as she and Stan shook their heads, they realized that if someone *were* to show them a current picture of their now nine-year-old son, after three and a half years he might not be familiar to them anymore. He had had baby teeth when last they saw him, and now those would be gone. He would have changed in other ways, and their shifting memories might have changed him, too.

Julie looked at the photo more closely, and thought how hard it would be to recognize their son from a two-dimensional piece of paper with no life and no animation; to make a judgment without all the things you use to really know people. Etan was full of life and animation. This couldn't be Etan, they said, this boy had a cleft chin and Etan didn't. Julie and Stan looked at each other. Or did he? Julie was suddenly panic-stricken. What if they said no to a picture of their own son?

Stan had suffered a similar attack of anxiety once, soon after Etan vanished, when a detective had brought him in to ID a boy. It was unusual to be looking at a real person—usually, like now, the cops showed the Patzes photographs. Stan had stepped up to the one-way glass and, right before the child had turned to face him, had felt that same desperate panicky sense—what if it's Etan and I don't know him? It had been completely illogical; his son had only been missing a month. But Stan was so lost himself at that point, in his self-doubt and confusion, he was terrified he'd get it wrong and reject his own child. The boy's face had come into view, and it wasn't Etan, and of course Stan had known it immediately. But now he comprehended Julie's current anxiety like no one else ever could.

As the detectives walked them through the boy's face, feature by feature, Stan and Julie became even more convinced this wasn't Etan. Yes, agreed the Patzes, some features were similar but some were not. Besides, Stan had his own extra assurances. The style of the photography dated it at least back to the 1970s. And then there was the paper. They were looking at an original eight-by-ten photo and the paper stock and borders just weren't contemporary. The detectives were less sure. The photo would be sent to an FBI lab in D.C. where analysts would compare it to Stan's pictures of Etan, examining facial shape and bone structure. Sorry to bother you, folks, the detectives said, as they always did. We'll let you know if anything further comes of it. The Patzes knew it wouldn't.

But the next day, a reporter from the *Boston Herald American* called to ask about the picture, which she explained had been found in the apparent hangout of a recently created organization advocating "consensual love" between adult males and boys. This group called itself the North American Man-Boy Love Association, or NAMBLA. The acronym would soon enter the lexicon, but this incident was the first most people—certainly Stan and Julie—had ever heard of it.

They were astounded an association existed that actually sought to legitimize child molestation. Stan considered himself as tolerant as the next New York liberal, but the idea made his skin crawl. Thank God the boy in the picture wasn't Etan, so the thought of their son being in NAMBLA's clutches wasn't something they dwelled on. The drainpipe incident of the previous March had sparked such damaging mental images that neither Stan nor Julie could afford more.

The phone started to ring sometime after dawn on Monday, just after the *Boston Herald American* ran the photo beside a headline nearly filling its front page: "Did Sex Club Trap This Boy?" At 6:45 a.m. *New York Post* reporters were ringing the Patzes' front buzzer, but the family had rules—no advance request, no interview. Ten pages of press calls were recorded in the Patz logbook that day, as the family pushed back their vacation plans, waiting to hear from the cops if anything had come of the photo. Camera crews and reporters milled around in the street below, in front of the door that still bore Etan's missing poster, one of the few left hanging in the neighborhood. It was a full-on siege, for a story that until the NAMBLA connection hadn't warranted more than a passing mention in months.

Late in the day, Stan finally ducked out the stairwell entrance to the building, eluding the crowd. As he reached the end of the block and slipped around the corner onto Greene Street, he heard the sound of high heels pounding the cement sidewalk behind him and realized he'd been spotted. He registered the strange sensation of being chased—by a woman, no less. He turned around finally and recognized her as an on-air personality at one of the local TV stations. As she drew nearer, he realized she was older than she looked on television, where the strong lights and heavy powder erased the fine lines he could see now starkly etched around her eyes and forehead. He was embarrassed—to be sneaking out of his own home, and to be evading her, someone he'd almost certainly invited into his living room on an earlier occasion, eager then to get exposure for Etan. He was embarrassed for her, too. She was the one driven to loitering on street corners in the winter chill, chasing people up the street. He dispatched her quickly with a few succinct quotes—no, there's really nothing new here today—and went on his way. The next day, having heard nothing further from the cops, he and Julie set their answering machine and fled for safe haven in Massachusetts.

As the Patz family were driving their rental car up the northern coastal route to the Boston area, a sixty-nine-year-old retired cabbie named Chester Jones walked into the newsroom of the *Daily News* and told a reporter that the old photo of Etan they'd run in their paper next to the NAMBLA story had prompted him to come forward. He may have been, he said, one of the last people to see Etan Patz.

"I believe that I'm the cab driver who picked up that boy in SoHo the morning he disappeared," said Jones, pulling on a cigarette. "I have very little doubt in my mind that he was the boy I picked up."

Daily News police reporter Jerry Schmetterer had covered the Patz case since the beginning, and he was skeptical to hear this lead coming in three years late, but he checked out the story through his sources. He was surprised to learn that there had been a very early report of a sighting that day, one of the hundreds that could never be substantiated, of a little boy and man getting into a cab. Jones explained that he hadn't reported the incident before because he'd doubted his own memory at first, and then later worried about getting involved. He had family problems, he said, and couldn't afford to make them worse. And he hadn't thought anyone would take him seriously anyway.

"Who's going to believe an old black man like me?" he asked Schmetterer.

The *Daily News* reported in the next day's front-page story that Jones described a man "in his 20s or 30s...not very tall....He had dark hair, with reddish or blondish tones. He was dressed well but casually. He had his arm around the shoulder of a small boy who was carrying a kind of knapsack schoolbag."

According to Jones, the two got into his cab and he overheard the man say something like, "I see you every morning from across the street. It's a shame your mother lets you stand here on the street corner all alone." The boy said, "My mother told me not to talk to strangers."

They rode a few blocks north on West Broadway, and at Houston Street, Jones said, the boy suddenly exclaimed, "This isn't the way to go to school." The man and the boy then got out of the car without paying and walked away.

Police questioned the cabbie for several hours. At the time they judged him a "credible witness," although the conversation Jones had related between the man and boy didn't match up with Etan's taking his first trip alone to the bus. This news, combined with the NAMBLA bombshell, brought Missing Person Case #8367 roaring back to life. The Missing Persons Unit recast the Patz task force, bringing in homicide detectives to start fresh, and adding back old hands. Bill Butler had returned to the First Precinct the previous June and was two days into a sixteen-day Christmas break when he got a call.

"Would you mind putting off your vacation to return to Missing Persons as part of the rejuvenated MPU task force?" the head of the force asked him.

"Of course not," he said. Suddenly the new group was eight strong, up from one detective just a month before.

The Patzes passed a relatively oblivious holiday week in Massachusetts, hanging close to the house and watching the two kids reconnect with their cousins. Uncle George, the former Marine and now a Sudbury fireman, took Shira and Ari for a tour of the station, and they were delighted to sit up in the open cab of the lemon yellow fire truck and ring the bell. They woke expectantly on Christmas morning to tear through stockings and gift-wrapped presents, welcoming the neighboring cousins throughout the day, as each arrived with a new round of presents.

The family saw the newspaper accounts of Chester Jones's story while still in Sudbury, and talked briefly to the police about it over the phone, but otherwise they worked hard to maintain a wait-and-see attitude so as not to spoil the holiday. But the Patzes arrived back in New York to a filled answering machine of media calls. Finally, an awkward press conference at One Police Plaza was convened, where Stan informed a roomful of reporters that there was nothing to report.

There really was nothing to report. Ultimately, police concluded that Chester Jones was one more dead end. After repeated sessions, they had begun to feel his story was changing—including his description of the man—enough to undermine his credibility. Jones couldn't even give enough details about the man's features to create a police sketch, and in one subsequent interview he told police the boy had actually given his name as Etan. Authorities considered hypnotizing Jones, but anything he said under hypnosis might jeopardize his testimony in court.

The NAMBLA picture was discounted by police as well, but not before two outraged NAMBLA representatives held a press conference at a midtown Holiday Inn to indignantly assert that the police were on a witch hunt. They held up a 1968 "Boyhood Calendar" issued four years before Etan's birth, with the same photo of the boy who looked like Etan, posing as January's model.

But both leads, fruitless as they were, served a critical purpose. As the new year began, two homicide detectives on loan to the newly energized task force to provide fresh eyes sat in the Patz apartment one afternoon for a whole new round of debriefs. At their behest, Julie had compiled a fresh list of friends or colleagues for them to reinterview, although she was surprised to learn later that some had never been questioned to begin with.

And she particularly stressed the connection between Sandy Harmon and Jose Ramos that had emerged the previous spring after the Bronx drainpipe episode. Yes, Julie said, this woman had cared for Etan briefly. She'd never been his babysitter, per se, but Julie explained the bus strike and Sandy's temporary part-time hours walking Etan and his two friends home from school. That was the time frame directly preceding Etan's disappearance, Julie pointed out, and if this woman was connected to Ramos as well as to Etan, then she was a direct link.

The cops were now eager to learn Ramos's whereabouts and question him again. They looked for him in Brooklyn, at the address he'd given authorities back in March. They talked to acquaintances of Ramos in lower Manhattan who reported last seeing him at a New Year's Eve party a few days earlier, looking fit, well dressed, and clean-shaven.

On January 12, 1983, Missing Persons detectives brought Sandy Harmon to police headquarters to ask about her relationship with both the Patzes and Jose Ramos. She later gave an angry account of this interrogation to authorities and described how police put her and her then eight-year-old son Bennett into separate rooms and grilled them both for hours. At one point, Sandy said, they led Bennett in and informed Sandy that her son had just revealed years of sodomy at the hands of Jose Ramos. Sandy told the cops she was shocked to hear this, but they didn't believe her. According to her later account they then threatened to have her son taken from her. Seven hours after they'd brought her in, they told her they needed her back the next day, and she and Bennett were driven home to her East Village apartment at 2:30 a.m.

After less than five hours of sleep, Sandy was back at One Police Plaza, where she was questioned again. Still dissatisfied with her answers, police polygraphed her. Although she'd agreed to the test, she showed "signs of deception" as she denied any knowledge of Etan's disappearance. Polygraphs are not lie detectors, and Stan Patz hadn't done so well on his either, but based on Sandy's results, police certainly wanted to pursue her role in the case, as well as that of her ex-boyfriend Jose Ramos. She claimed to no longer see or know where Ramos was, although she did disclose they'd been together for a last sexual encounter less than two months earlier, over Thanksgiving. Again, police ended this round of questions by telling Sandy they had more to ask, but by this point she'd had enough.

"I have a lawyer now," she said when they came to get her the following day. "Any more questions—you go through him."

Sandy Harmon had little more to say about the case after that, but investigators couldn't help seeing her as a nexus leading to tantalizing clues beyond their reach. At the very least, authorities thought, she knew more than she was saying.

———

BY THE PRESIDENT OF THE UNITED STATES OF AMERICA
A PROCLAMATION

...The date of May 25 has particular significance in the cause of missing children. On that day in 1979, six year old Etan Patz disappeared from his home in New York City. Unfortunately, Etan has never been found. His brave parents have fought to increase our awareness of this tragedy and to improve the agencies that work to solve this unique type of crime....

Now, Therefore, I, Ronald Reagan, President of the United States of America, do hereby proclaim May 25, 1983 as Missing Children Day....I urge all our law enforcement agencies to take particular notice of the danger that threatens any child who has lost his or her home. I urge every American family to take the proper precautions to protect their children.

—May 24, 1983

Stan Patz had always dreaded the days leading up to the May 25 anniversary, but by 1983 it wasn't just about the heartbreaking memories of the day itself. Inevitably, as Etan's disappearance was becoming increasingly synonymous with the missing children movement, May 25 meant requests for appearances, flashbulbs, and smooth soundbites to advance the cause. Stan especially hated hauling out his public face, preferring to mark the day quietly and to let Julie speak for them both. But when a national day had been named by the president after your family's personal tragedy, that felt inadequate, and he also felt he owed something to the others working so diligently to push for needed change.

In New York there were press conferences and a fund-raiser at a trendy midtown eatery. Actor Cliff Robertson chaired the event; John and Revé Walsh flew up with their new baby, Meghan.

"I believe my wife and I are symbols of the fact that this type of crime can happen to anybody," Stan told the press that day. But in the days and months that followed, the Patzes were beginning to consciously disengage from their role on the public stage. All along, Julie had been weighing the costs to her other children of the constant travel and media appearances, and at some point she'd decided that they were too high. Whether it was Ari's fears as he lived through the dangerous year of six, or Shira's persistent nightmares, Julie knew she needed to turn to her "two children at home."

She was grateful there were others, like John Walsh, or Jay Howell, a top Senate attorney who had led the fight to pass the National Missing Children's Act, who would continue to build on the momentum. From the sidelines she supported the push to move beyond the NCIC computer bank and finally create the national clearinghouse that she, Stan, and many others had been talking about for years. That dream was realized in the spring of 1984, when the National Center for Missing and Exploited Children was established. But when Howell called to invite the Patzes to appear with President Reagan in the White House East Wing for the center's unveiling, he got the same response he'd been hearing from them for the past months to these kinds of requests.

"I'm sorry," Stan or Julie would say, "we're just not able to do that now." The Patzes called it a "soft no," and if colleagues had pushed the need, they would make an effort to provide their services. But usually the "soft no" was answer enough.

Psychotherapist Gary Hewitt did attend the opening of the National Center, representing his own Center for Missing Children, a smaller entity established a year earlier in Rochester, New York. Hewitt's center focused on a narrow spectrum of the field that received little attention but demonstrated a huge need. He treated the families of the missing, as well as victims who returned, carrying the emotional baggage of their captivity. Hewitt had spent time with Steven Stayner, among others, who'd left home a freckle-faced seven-year-old and returned almost a full-grown man. Stayner was still struggling to adapt to a life that on the one hand was free of the abuse he'd suffered in his captor's clutches, but on the other was bound by the parental limits he'd shed during his time away. He chafed at his parents' authority, and cringed at the taunts from peers about his sexuality. Hewitt counseled Stayner's parents too, as well as many parents of children who had never returned.

Hewitt had also been in contact with Julie Patz over the past year, offering his services and seeking her advice. Now he called to invite her to an experimental retreat to take place over several days at the beginning of August. Hewitt would be bringing together several families of missing children, to talk, work, and play at a college campus in upstate New York. This was not an "appearance" in front of cameras, Hewitt assured her—no media allowed.

"I really hope you can bring the kids," Hewitt told Julie. "There's a pool and the lake, and we're planning lots of activities to keep them busy."

Shira was planning to be away with friends for part of the scheduled days, and Stan said he had too much work, when in reality he could have rearranged his schedule. He just found talk therapy and sharing feelings suspect. Hot-air balloons and speedboats were really, he thought, lures to get people like himself into a room and force them to talk about a painful subject. He'd prefer to get the post report. But Julie thought it could be helpful for Ari. He had come to her on his seventh birthday to express relief he'd made it through the scary age of six, but a year later he was still suffering the effects of his brother's loss. He'd recently spent hours up in the night weeping after a particularly bad nightmare. Now he would celebrate his eighth birthday in the company of trained therapists and the hopefully empathetic siblings of other missing children.

"HAPPY BIRTHDAY TO YOU! Happy Birthday, dear Ari, Happy Birthday to you."

On the first night, a group of some sixty strangers sang to Ari, then shared his birthday cake after a buffet dinner at Keuka College, 212 gloriously green lakefront acres in New York's Finger Lakes region. Gary Hewitt presented the boy with a newly minted coin set for his collection, and hoped the familiar birthday ritual would help to break the ice at this somber, awkward gathering of fourteen families. But it would take more than cake and party balloons to chip away their sorrow. These were mothers and fathers who had molded themselves rigidly into an unnatural public persona, or had kept an isolated vigil by the phone in hopes of a call. Many had completely lost sight of relating to other people. Looking around, Julie felt the oppressive weight of the collective tragedy in the room, and realized she was the veteran of the group. She doubted whether some of these people had smiled or laughed a single time since their child had disappeared. Over the past five years she had already learned some of the lessons this retreat hoped to impart, about the critical need to do just that; to talk to each other, and to listen. She didn't quite know what to expect, but she knew that nothing

like this had ever been done before, and that this group sorely needed it. She
needed it.

The next day, at the first working sessions, the adults were split off from
the children, as everyone divided their time between group therapy and
play. Parents talked to parents, kids to kids. Ari sat in a classroom with other
children ranging from seven to seventeen, who were encouraged to tell their
stories. Gradually, the youngsters opened up, but it wasn't until the evening
when the families came together again that the parents had their own shells
cracked, by their own children.

One after another, with safety in numbers, the youngest voices said what
they'd been holding inside. Our brother or sister may be gone, but we're still
here. We need to get out of the house, move forward, take a vacation, be
normal. Every aspect of life had been put on hold, and these children were
suffering for that too, not just for the loss of their loved one. As parents listened, and the tears flowed, they acknowledged the truth of what their children were saying. In the group therapy sessions that followed over the next
days, adults and children alike talked about their most private fears.

In the children's group around a campfire one night, Ari heard from the
others about how they grieved for siblings they barely knew or remembered.
Like everyone there, he'd never met anyone else in the same position. As one
of the youngest, the eight-year-old spoke up only occasionally, but when he
did, he felt a burgeoning sense of authority as a pro who'd essentially spent
his entire short lifetime dealing with Etan's absence. He warmed to the adult
therapists who praised his counsel.

In between the talking and listening was what Julie jokingly called the
"forced" recreation. These were people who had lost the ability to relax and
play, to feel unencumbered by their grief, or by the appearance they needed
to maintain, so that neighbors wouldn't find it unseemly, even suspicious, to
see them laughing. Here they were cajoled into waterskiing, swimming, and
canoeing. There was tai chi in the mornings for the most sedentary of the
adults, and counselors who doubled as clowns armed with balloon animals
for the youngest of the kids. And there were goofy parlor games, designed to
coax laughter from even the most grim.

Ari loved racing through the grassy fields outside the dorm rooms
where they slept at night. In an indelible moment, the boy and his mother
even peeked down from the basket of a striped hot-air balloon suspended

twenty-five feet in the air. They waved at the people in the truck that tethered them to safety, or gazed hypnotically upward to the roaring fire that kept them aloft but breathed dragon-fire heat on their heads. While Julie screamed in terror next to him, Ari was thrilled as for an instant the wind pulled the line taut and seemed to lift the back end of the truck clean off the ground.

It was a rare adventure for all the children, and an even rarer break for the parents. For Julie too, the entire Keuka retreat was a singular experience and one she would never forget. For the first time in five years she was spending time with other parents—besides Stan—who had shared the same horror she did, and they were free of media, law enforcement, or other "nonvictims." She didn't have to worry what anyone thought of her when she cried over an irrational fear, or, more importantly, laughed at a joke. The relief she felt at being able to express herself went far beyond anything she had ever expected. She was astounded at the commonality of their almost identical experiences. She took on a leadership position, as a role model for some of the other parents. And in the faces of mothers whose loss was more recent, she herself could recognize the Julie of several years ago, and realize how far she'd actually come in her "recovery." For the first time, she began to feel a grasp of her former self-esteem. And for the first time, she felt almost like the healthy, happy woman she barely remembered, the one who had disappeared on May 25 too.

Both she and Ari also spent time with eighteen-year-old Steven Stayner and his parents. She witnessed firsthand that the reunited family was functioning, and she knew then that it could be done. Ari thought Stayner was a cool guy, but for Julie their conversations were the antidote to a creeping paralysis that overcame her whenever she allowed herself to imagine Etan actually coming home. Speaking to Steven Stayner frankly about what he had gone through, she could envision her own son's ability to survive such horrors. And she began to believe in her own strength too. If she had to, maybe she could even learn to live with the unknown, of never finding out why Etan never returned.

"I at least carried home one clear message," Julie wrote years later in a testimonial letter to Gary Hewitt. "Reach out and grab at life again; take back your self-confidence and joy in what you do; stop hiding! I was not quite ready to do that then. But the seed of awareness had been planted, and I could not ignore it."

There was something else Julie Patz brought home from Keuka. She returned to face the rest of her family with a new understanding that each one was dealing with Etan's disappearance in his or her own way and time, and that was how it had to be. As she and Ari excitedly recounted their adventures to Stan and Shira, Stan saw how much they had benefited, and he too understood that he had missed out. But he was taking his own time, in his own way.

CHAPTER 9

∽

Reversing the Odds

To be an Assistant U.S. Attorney for the Southern District of New York requires commitment to absolute integrity and fair play; to candor and fairness in dealing with adversaries and the courts; to careful prepara- tion, not making any assumptions or leaving anything to chance; and never proceeding in any case unless convinced of the correctness of one's position or the guilt of the accused.

> —*certificate presented by U.S. Attorney Whitney North Seymour to his assistants, 1973; presented to all AUSAs for several years to follow, including AUSA Stuart GraBois*

Truth is on the march, and nothing will stop it. Today is only the begin- ning, for it is only today that the positions have become clear: on one side, those who are guilty, who do not want the light to shine forth, on the other, those who seek justice and who will give their lives to attain it.

> —*"J'Accuse," Emile Zola's open letter to the French president in the newspaper* L'Aurore, *regarding the Dreyfus Affair, January 13, 1898*

Assistant U.S. Attorney Stuart GraBois usually pulled into a park- ing space at One St. Andrew's Plaza and placed his government- issue permit onto the dashboard. He was at his desk by 7:30 in the morning, having retrieved his voicemail messages along with his second cup of coffee. He was an early riser anyway, and he liked to start the day before the halls were full. He got his best work done in the morning, although he rarely left the office for the commute home from lower Manhattan before 6:30 in the evening. AUSAs often juggled dozens of cases, and in GraBois's unit, Major Crimes, they might be interviewing witnesses for a fraud case in the morning and be in court for a bank robbery case in the afternoon, rarely seeing the same faces two days in a row. It was a full plate, but GraBois loved the variety, and he loved the work.

GraBois seemed taller than his six feet, and he cut an imposing figure. Everything about him bespoke a sense of strength. Steely hazel eyes with steel gray hair to match. A big man, not heavy, but solid; an immovable force. He dressed meticulously, in nicely turned-out conservative suits. The dark suits, the ever-ready dark shades, it all said: I am a Federal Prosecutor.

Stu GraBois had been in the U.S. Attorney's Office for three years, but today was his first full day on the Etan Patz case. The day before his immediate boss, chief of the Major Crimes Unit Barry Bohrer, had given him the assignment. It was late May 1985, the sixth anniversary of the boy's disappearance. Etan had now been missing almost as long as he'd been living safely at home, and the odds of his recovery were growing longer every day. The Patzes were still fielding requests from all over the country for his photo because of possible sightings, but his beautiful six-year-old portraits couldn't help much to identify him at age twelve and a half. Although New York artist Nancy Burson had created an experimental computerized age progression of the boy at the FBI's request, his parents were loath to distribute it. If it turned out not to look like him, searchers would be thrown off track.

Instead, it was the six-year-old image of Etan, measuring eight feet by nine feet, that looked down on Times Square. Chosen by the New York City Police Foundation, his was the first missing child's portrait to be displayed there on an electronic Diamond Vision billboard. His elfin visage—laughing broadly, head thrown back—blinked on the screen twice an hour that spring, to be replaced after a month by another missing child.

Indeed it seemed as though everywhere you looked there were now pictures of missing children. The previous year, a handful of midwestern dairies had begun featuring them on their waxy milk cartons and the idea had taken off. By the spring of 1985, more than seven hundred independent dairies—almost half the nation's eighteen hundred—were putting milk on the breakfast kitchen table along with small faces and toll-free hotline numbers. Missing children were showing up on every imaginable blank surface: pizza boxes, grocery bags, gas bills, highway toll tickets. And they yielded highly publicized results. A California runaway called home after her face stared back at her from a milk carton. An eleven-year-old whose mother had abducted her was returned home after an informant saw her picture and tipped off police. Two sisters whose parents were locked in a custody battle eventually turned up in Las Vegas with their father, who had kept them hidden inside his hotel room for fear that the advertising campaign would expose him.

Almost every one of these children, both the ones recovered and all those on the pizza boxes and milk cartons to begin with, were abducted by one parent from another in a vicious custody dispute. Or they were runaways. And while the parents of those recovered children were grateful for the massive public campaign, some were beginning to question the statistics that fueled such an onslaught of what critics called fearmongering hype. Contrary to public perception and these nebulous statistics, only a tiny percentage of missing children were snatched by unknown intruders, although actual studies didn't confirm that until some years later. Eventually, it would be determined that the figure for annual stranger abductions across the United States was not in the tens of thousands or even thousands, as some feared, but in the low hundreds. Child advocates were undaunted. Try telling a frantic mother whose abusive ex-husband has stolen her child that it's not kidnapping, they argued. And even if stranger abductions are a small fraction of the numbers, if just one child is returned to his parents unharmed, how can anyone be against taking action?

In fact, when Stuart GraBois took on the Patz investigation, it was the only open missing child case in the U.S. Attorney's Office of the Southern District of New York. Federal authorities had gotten involved back in late 1982, with the NAMBLA bust in Wareham, Massachusetts, which raised the specter of interstate activity. If someone had taken Etan across state lines, they could be charged with the federal crime of kidnapping. As a federal prosecutor GraBois would develop such a case for prosecution, aided by investigators who had already worked the case for some time. By this point his team comprised FBI agent Ken Ruffo, along with two NYPD Missing Persons detectives, Robert Shaw and Owen J. Byrne.

Ruffo came to see GraBois the Friday after Memorial Day. The agent handed the prosecutor a folder of background reports, to introduce GraBois to the major points of the case. "You'll get the rest of it next week, but this should start you off," the agent said.

"Okay, I'll read through it, get familiar with the other material when it comes and then I'll give you a call." GraBois took the papers home to read over the weekend. Typically, when he started a case, he'd read the briefing folder meticulously, making detailed notes, to be fully up to speed before adding his own paperwork to it.

The next week, a half-dozen brown cardboard storage cartons arrived in GraBois's office. Every one of them was full of folders thicker than the one he had already read. He stacked them up against a wall and pulled the first box over to his desk. He leafed through the chronological files to locate the first day, May 25, 1979.

On that day in 1979, Stuart GraBois was not yet an AUSA, but he was already with the Justice Department, as a senior trial attorney in the New York office of their Anti-Trust Division. May 25 happened to be his father's birthday, and the extended GraBois family would have gathered that weekend to mark it.

There had been another cause to celebrate: the recent birth of Stuart and Bonnie GraBois's son, Andrew. Arriving ten years after his sister, Melissa, he was a long-hoped-for baby. For the first time three generations of GraBois men would be at the birthday party, all three native New Yorkers.

Stuart GraBois grew up with his younger sister, Marsha, the children of first-generation Jewish-American parents, in the Bensonhurst section of Brooklyn. Theirs was an insular, close-knit neighborhood, where alliances formed not by religion or ethnicity but by block, even by building. The kids moved easily from apartment to apartment in a large complex that seemed more a small village, and they always felt protected. Everyone watched out for everyone else.

From an early age, GraBois internalized his family's deep reverence for those who upheld justice and contempt for those who did not, starting with the experience of his paternal grandparents, who had lived in France in the late nineteenth and early twentieth century. Before leaving Paris for New York in 1906, GraBois's grandfather had seen firsthand the damage of France's infamous "Affaire Dreyfus," and would often relate to his grandson with deep anger and sadness the decade-long travesty. The elder GraBois vividly recalled the injustice done to Jewish artillery captain Alfred Dreyfus, falsely convicted of treason and imprisoned for four years on the notorious Devil's Island off the coast of South America before his name was finally cleared. Dreyfus's superiors initially had believed he was guilty of passing state secrets to enemy Germany, but later lied and schemed when they discovered their error.

"That's why we came to America," Benjamin GraBois would tell his grandson. "Because justice is possible. Here you have a chance to go to school to make sure people get treated fairly."

The idea of justice by law captivated GraBois. In his middle and high school yearbooks he always wrote the same life goal: to be a lawyer. In his first month at American University's Washington College of Law he met his wife-to-be, Bonnie, an undergraduate studying political science, and by the time he got his law degree they'd already been married a year.

In 1967, fresh out of law school, GraBois worked as a Legal Aid investigator before taking the bar, using his new legal training to interview witnesses, gather evidence, and hone his persistent style. After admission to the bar, he stayed at Legal Aid and proved himself a feisty litigator with a bulldog reputation, no matter who his opponent might be.

Like most criminal defense attorneys, GraBois's cases usually ended in plea bargains, moving through the courts with conveyer-belt efficiency. Once, a client of GraBois's in a double narcotics charge bucked the system, refused the plea, and demanded a trial. The judge involved was renowned for his laziness. He had no interest in suffering through an actual trial, and became contentious when told the defendant wouldn't plead and planned instead to offer his mother as an alibi.

"That's ridiculous," the judge snapped in the court proceeding. "Mother, get up here."

GraBois watched the elderly black woman stand up and move timidly toward the front of the court.

"Her name is Mrs. Johnson, Your Honor," GraBois politely asserted.

"Don't tell me what to say." The air was getting charged. GraBois was already smarting at the idea that his client might be deprived of his right to trial. He thought the judge's words were demeaning to this woman, who clearly thought any authority figure was intimidating, let alone a black-robed white man on a raised bench who would probably send her son to prison.

"One more word out of you, Mr. GraBois, and I'll hold you in contempt of court."

"Come on, Your Honor, my client..."

"That's it!" The judge was livid. "Two hundred dollars or five days in jail."

"Judge, I work for Legal Aid." GraBois couldn't believe the man was serious, so he joked back. "I don't have two hundred dollars."

"Put him in!" roared the judge, who was nearly apoplectic. As the bailiff moved to lead GraBois away, the judge made him an offer. "If you apologize, I'll have you released."

"What am I supposed to apologize for?" GraBois asked.

After several hours behind bars, even the admiration of his fellow inmates wasn't making his stay any less miserable, but GraBois refused to accede to a man he himself held in contempt. GraBois's boss at Legal Aid, whom GraBois respected enormously, came to see him and made his own plea.

"Listen, don't apologize. The man is such an idiot; just say something that sounds good, and he'll buy it."

"Your Honor," GraBois announced in open court after being released from the cell, "I had no intent to be contemptuous of the court's robes." The judge seemed to chew on this, so GraBois repeated it.

"I'll take that as an apology," the judge finally said. GraBois's client went to trial and was found guilty, which he clearly was. "That's not the point," GraBois liked to say whenever he told that story. "He had a right to a fair trial, and if he wanted to exercise it, you shouldn't railroad him into a plea, just because you think it's a waste of time."

GraBois knew his days as a public defender were coming to an end when he found himself itching to prosecute some of his clients. The final straw came when he was interviewing a client in his cell and the man coldly detailed his physical and sexual abuse of a child. GraBois realized then that he still wanted to be a defender, it was just that he wanted to defend the victims.

When GraBois arrived at the U.S. Attorney's Office of the Southern District of New York in 1982, he knew it was where he'd always wanted to be. By this time, he was older than many of his fellow AUSAs, who often come to the U.S. Attorney's Office just a few years out of law school, and typically stay long enough to make their bones as litigators before moving on to high-billing private firms. GraBois came into the job not only having had several years' experience in the trenches as a Legal Aid investigator and defense attorney, but he was the kind of born and bred New Yorker who knew his way around town.

On the seventh floor of One St. Andrew's Plaza, GraBois's new office faced the church of the same name. Police bagpipers would practice in the church basement, sometimes preparing for the next funeral of a fallen officer, and the notes would waft up through the window. The poignant strains provided a fitting soundtrack as GraBois prepared cases against drug dealers, counterfeiters, and bank robbers.

But the prosecutor had a special affinity for pursuing criminals who took advantage of the most vulnerable victims—the elderly, women, and children. Maybe there was something of the white knight in his instincts, but all his life GraBois had believed in evening the odds, and, if he did his job right, even reversing them. A fraud scam that bilked senior citizens out of their Social Security checks was not a high crime, but he would picture someone his grandmother's age who couldn't buy groceries, and he would push hard for the toughest sentence. His unswerving, never-give-up, even-if-it-ends-in-a-head-on-collision mentality followed him from the Public Defender's Office, whether it meant facing down the criminals or a power-hungry judge.

At the U.S. Attorney's Office, Stuart GraBois felt that he was among his own. There was an ethos, a real spirit, that permeated the office. Many years before he'd arrived at the Southern District of New York, then U.S. attorney Whitney North Seymour had issued certificates—standards of performance—to each assistant, and the tradition continued beyond Seymour's tenure.

"To be an Assistant U.S. Attorney for the Southern District of New York is a badge of honor that must be earned," the dictum began, and then demanded a mix of virtues, both professional and personal: integrity, candor, and fairness; precision, thoughtfulness, decency; personal courage and conviction, among others. GraBois knew that some outside the office might think it corny, but he also believed every AUSA lived by those words.

He framed the certificate and hung it on his wall. The powerful words, especially the last sentence, served as a reminder of his grandfather's passionate defense of Alfred Dreyfus. Never proceed with a case, it cautioned, "unless convinced of the correctness of one's position, or the guilt of the accused."

In one of his early cases, agents working with him had wired an informant who then got his target on tape apparently making admissions to a series of armed robberies. The suspect had an extensive record and a history of pleading guilty. Despite the strong evidence, something bothered

GraBois—why this one time did the suspect not want to take the plea? Because I didn't do this one, the man was adamant.

Both the informant and the suspect were Hispanic and spoke Spanish on the tape, which made it harder to ID the voices. GraBois learned that with sophisticated technology, investigators in Washington were able to analyze Spanish-speaking voices, so he decided to go one step further and sent them the tape. The results revealed that the informant had deceived authorities—he'd been talking to someone else on the tape. The news came in late on a Friday night, as GraBois was headed out the door. He figured the judge was gone for the day, and by keeping the perp in for the weekend, he would probably prevent a few more crimes. But that would be wrong. He was surprised and relieved to reach the judge in his chambers, who immediately arranged for the man's release. It was the kind of thing GraBois knew anyone in his office would have done.

Before GraBois was assigned to the Patz case in 1985, it had been overseen by the AUSA in the next office over. GraBois would watch as agents and detectives filed in to see her from time to time, men he knew from some of his own cases, and he would chat with them after they left. Sometimes they'd stop by beforehand to run a line of investigation by him. "Do you think this has any legs?" they would ask, a dress rehearsal before they'd go onstage next door. When his neighbor left in 1985 for a judgeship, GraBois was eager for the challenge.

The Patz case had always been an enigma, with its crazy patchwork of leads and long list of amorphous suspects. Even with the unlikely prospect of a miraculous breakthrough, the issue of jurisdiction had always lurked beneath the surface. If after months, even years, of exhaustive labor, the investigation finally broke to reveal that Etan had never been taken out of New York, this wouldn't be the Feds' case to try. A subsequent prosecution would be turned over to the local district attorney. That would mean all of the work, and then a handoff.

But GraBois didn't care about any of that. He wanted the Patz case. Maybe it appealed to him as a father. How could a parent survive that? Or maybe there was something about the challenge of a case that had eluded so many before him, that had as much of an impact on him as it did on so many New Yorkers who'd felt violated themselves by this heinous crime. He'd followed the case in the press since he'd first scanned the chilling headlines over Sunday morning coffee in May 1979. He'd often thought of six-year-old Etan, walking alone on his own street for the first time, and how he'd seemingly vanished off the face of the Earth.

But before he could move forward on his new case, GraBois had to sort through its overwhelming history. It wasn't so much that there were no leads; there were too many leads and all of them frustratingly sketchy. They ran off in twenty different directions, dense paths he had to hack his way through, if only to post a "Dead End" sign. He got a morale boost in the first days when he ran into one of his bosses, the head of the Criminal Division, on the stairwell. The men stopped to chat, the usual talk about baseball and family, before turning to casual office talk.

"What are you working on these days?" Howard Wilson asked him.

"I'm taking over the Patz case," GraBois replied. "I'm really getting into it. There's so much there."

"You're kidding! C'mon, let's go upstairs," Wilson said, "and we'll tell Rudy."

U.S. Attorney Rudy Giuliani's office was one flight above GraBois's. His assistants numbered in the hundreds, so they were spread out all over the nine-story building. Giuliani's presence was keenly felt, though, from the early morning Pavarotti arias coming out of his large corner office with the expansive views of the Brooklyn Bridge, and his agile fielding on first base for the office softball team, to his hard-charging, high-profile attacks on the mob and Wall Street greed. Despite some criticism of his aggressive prosecutions, inside his office he was seen as a crusader with an intense loyalty for those who stood with him on his mission.

When GraBois and Howard Wilson stuck their heads into Giuliani's office to relay the news, the U.S. attorney brightened.

"That's terrific," Giuliani said. "You should know that this office is behind you 100 percent. Do whatever you have to do. I'll give you anything you need."

GraBois went back downstairs with the sense he'd just come away with a blessing from on high. He was passionate and eager to dig into this new case, but, looking at all the boxes spread out in front of him, it helped to know the big guns felt that way too.

CHAPTER 10

No Stone Unturned

Long-Lost Boy Hunted Anew;
New Yorker Gone 6 Years May Be Alive in Israel

..."There is no hard evidence, but there is a reasonable assumption that
Etan Patz might have been in Israel," said Giuliani, who reopened the
case six months ago....

...The Israeli investigation became public this week when a
Romanian-born woman in Queens noticed Patz's photograph in the current issue of a Romanian-language magazine from Israel....Federal officials said the photograph was published...at the request of Assistant
U.S. Attorney Stuart GraBois and FBI agent Kenneth Ruffo, who traveled
to Israel last month to follow up several leads.
    —Washington Post, *November 23, 1985*

Subject: interview of the mother Julia Patz....
...Mrs. Patz further stated that when the child did not return home on
schedule between 1530 hrs. and 1540 she called Karen Altman, a neighbor who usually walks the boy home from the returning bus which stops
on the northeast corner of West Bway and Prince St. When advised by
Mrs. Altman that she was informed by her daughter Chelsea that the
boy...
    —NYPD Police Report 5/26/79 (DD5) Bill Butler re: Lost Child #687

S he was informed by her daughter Chelsea that the boy..." Stuart
    GraBois was reading Bill Butler's first DD5, and when he got to
the end of page one, he flipped it over to continue reading. But the page
that followed...didn't. It was dated March 1983, four years later. "That the
boy...did what?" he thought with familiar frustration.

GraBois was trying vainly once again to read through Butler's earliest NYPD reports. In 1979, Butler could never have known when he wrote them that so many iterations of law enforcement, one after the other, would be piecing this case together with such fragmented artifacts, like archaeologists at an ancient dig moving around miniscule random remnants of pottery, hoping some of the jagged edges would click into place.

Ingesting all this material was making GraBois painfully aware how much this case differed from his others, and not just because it involved a young, vulnerable little boy and had attracted the nation's interest. Typically, by the time the federal prosecutor took on a new case, there was a clear-cut suspect, and whatever investigation had yet to be done related to building the prosecution. Although federal prosecutors were certainly part of that investigation, the FBI agents did the fieldwork. The Etan Patz mystery, GraBois had come to understand, was the sort of case that demanded more. It was a real whodunit. Not to mention where, how, why, and when.

Crouched in front of the open box of files, GraBois scanned the stacks of police reports, FBI summaries, and court documents, searching for the rest of that second DD5. Looking past the carton he was perusing, he eyed the five behind it. Sometimes it felt that no matter how much of the case he absorbed, no matter how many stacks of files he reviewed, more would take their place, as if from a magician's bottomless prop box. But he had given himself a mandate to tie up every loose thread, no matter how much of a stretch. If he didn't, he'd always be asking himself the worst of all the lingering questions: If I had only pulled at that one strand, would the whole case have unraveled?

Thank God for Ken Ruffo, GraBois often thought. FBI special agent Ken Ruffo was every neatly barbered, trim-mustachioed, deliberately nondescript Fed Hollywood has ever concocted. He had no hidden agendas, and on the job he rarely cracked a smile. But beneath his laconic manner lurked wry humor and genuine warmth.

GraBois welcomed Ruffo's impressive memory, which was like having access to a walking computer hard drive. To supplement his internal filing cabinet, Ruffo's secret weapon was an elaborate three-by-five index card system. Every fact in the case was logged and cross-cataloged. You could fire a name at Ken Ruffo, and he'd rummage around, then fire back with bullet points.

"Who was Monte Birnberg?" GraBois would call and ask. "And how does he relate to the case?"

"Just a minute." Ruffo would put down the phone, then read from the card he'd just pulled: "Monte Birnberg was one of the last people to see Etan on the morning of May 25. On May 26, 1979, Birnberg was interviewed and he told us the following…"

Like the rare beer can collection Ken Ruffo kept in alphabetical order in his Long Island home, the Patz files came in several neatly organized banker's boxes. But like GraBois, Ken Ruffo could only work with the material he'd been given, material that over the years and the changing guards had degenerated into the missing and misnumbered. The fragmentation seemed to be unintentional, with the sheer volume of interviews and separate investigations overwhelming an orderly system. GraBois was finding big gaps in the Patz paperwork, creeps who should have been checked out or may have in fact been checked out, although there was no record of it.

With the help of Ruffo and NYPD detectives Bob Shaw and O. J. Byrne, GraBois was beginning to learn the cast of characters and chart his own way. There were, of course, the Patzes themselves. Just like every investigator before him, Stuart GraBois needed to cross the Patz family off his own suspect list. But there were a lot of others.

Over the next weeks, he read through page after page of potential suspects, names culled from years of anonymous tips, interviews with friends, neighbors, and other law enforcement agencies, as well as known pedophiles and cons looking for a break in their own cases. In recent months, investigators had been following one informant's lead that had taken agents as far as Massachusetts, Florida, and even Amsterdam, but to GraBois it all seemed to go nowhere. He was, however, struck by an odd blip in Israel, where years earlier Etan's picture had mysteriously appeared in a magazine next to the name "Etan Ben-Haim." He also wanted to know more about the Patz "babysitter" and how she seemed connected to various shadowy figures he was also looking at.

GraBois was convinced Sandy Harmon could offer important clues, although he needed to hear them from her directly. Looking at a two-paragraph summary of a seven-hour police interrogation didn't tell him nearly enough. He was intrigued by her link to the man arrested in the Bronx drainpipe, especially when he learned that her son had been molested by Jose Ramos, and that no one knew where he was now. GraBois also noted that Sandy had been judged "deceptive" after she took a polygraph, and while he never counted on polygraphs, the evidence was mounting against her credibility.

Ken Ruffo had also told GraBois about the interviews he'd subsequently conducted with the two girls Sandy had walked home from school with Etan.

Both Chelsea Altman and Kyra Simmons had recalled that, contrary to Sandy's claims that she'd always walked alone, on several occasions the woman had met a man en route who would then accompany them partway home. The girls described him as tall, white, and in his mid- to late twenties, with light reddish brown hair and green eyes. He had severe acne and crooked teeth, talked slowly or with an unknown accent or speech defect, and walked with a limp. The girls used to quietly make fun of him, calling him Sandy's "boyfriend," after they saw the two adults holding hands.

GraBois also learned that after Sandy had lawyered up in 1983, detectives had tracked down Keith Browning, another man she'd been dating in the spring of 1979. Browning appeared to have nothing to do with the Patz case. But he corroborated that Sandy had indeed been involved with Jose Ramos, which Browning had discovered when he surprised Ramos and Sandy at her apartment one day in May 1979 and immediately broke up with her. Browning also told police Sandy had been afraid young Bennett's natural father might come to New York and try to hurt her or her son. Sandy's mother had once suggested that perhaps Bennett's father had taken Etan, mistaking him for the son he hadn't seen since infancy.

Ken Ruffo recounted to GraBois how in the summer of 1983, he and a Missing Persons detective had eventually found and interviewed Bennett's father in Arizona. A witness there had reported seeing him with a blond boy, which had immediately set off alarm bells. But after interviewing the man, they'd determined he was not involved in Etan's disappearance.

Just before the Arizona trip, Ruffo told GraBois, Missing Persons had also finally located Jose Ramos in New York City. Ramos had told the NYPD detectives he'd just returned from Coconut Grove, Florida, where his parents lived. But after extensive questioning and a polygraph, he'd been released.

Ruffo told GraBois he'd only learned all this after the fact. Ruffo wasn't happy about being left out of the loop, and had noted in his files that the police said they hadn't called the FBI agent earlier because they didn't think he'd be interested. When NYPD detective Bob Shaw was assigned to the case a year later, he reviewed the police files but never found a DD5 report for this session, if there was one. It seemed to have disappeared as mysteriously as Ramos then did.

There were a number of other neighborhood pedophiles on the list. GraBois studied hard and quickly learned them by heart: the "bubble man," who belonged to NAMBLA and attracted kids in Washington Square Park with his giant soap bubbles; the phony priest, who claimed to have supplied a false birth certificate for a child who might have been Etan Patz; and one man, who had joked about Etan being buried in a building around the corner from the Patz loft where he worked; and on and on.

A few months into the case, GraBois and Ruffo were standing outside Rudy Giuliani's office waiting to give him a status report. The biggest order of business that day was the Israel mystery. In 1981 a New Yorker visiting Jerusalem was taken aback to see a photo of Etan Patz in a Romanian-language magazine called *Revista Mea* that she happened to pick up while having her hair done at Dolly's Hair Salon in Jerusalem. Even more remarkable, the photo, found in a regular "family photo album" feature, bore the name "Etan Ben-Haim," which in Hebrew means "son of life." The picture purported to be from Kiryat Bialik, a small working-class city near Haifa. The tourist took the magazine to the American consulate, and when she got home from her trip she also sent the photo to the NYPD. The photo turned out to be one of Stan's, a series from which he'd distributed hundreds of copies, although this particular shot hadn't been circulated widely. How did it get into an Israeli magazine, and with that very significant name in the caption?

Questions had surfaced about Israel even before the magazine featured Etan's photo, when Stan Patz's brother, Rabbi Norman Patz, led a group of American children on a trip there just a few months after Etan's disappearance. There were those murky old rumors that religious differences among members of the Patz family might have led to Etan's being spirited away to the Holy Land.

Over the years, the NYPD had made attempts to follow the *Revista Mea* lead and had even solicited the help of the Israeli National Police. There's nothing there, the Israelis had said. When Ruffo got the case, he'd wanted to know more, and had gone after *Revista Mea* with his customary due diligence. But running leads in a foreign country without actually going there was a bureaucratic quagmire. Ruffo had to request—by telex—that an intermediary LEGAT, or FBI legal attaché, in Rome make inquiries to the Israelis, who in turn had to be relied on to investigate. The results—if any effort was actually made—also had to work their way back through the same channels to Ruffo. After two years of this complex game of "whisper down the lane," with much of the whispering in Hebrew, Ruffo had never felt satisfied enough to cross the *Revista Mea* angle off his list. Nor had GraBois.

That's the problem with a case like this one, GraBois thought as he summarized his progress to Giuliani. If this were your typical crime of tax fraud, or even a bank robbery, the investigative path would have been clearer, more obvious. But in this situation, getting one round of answers would invariably lead to follow-ups, so GraBois felt the need to ask all the questions himself.

"It bothers me," he said to his boss, his trademark phrase whenever something just didn't add up.

"So go," Giuliani said. "Why don't you two just go yourselves? Otherwise you'll never know for sure."

When GraBois came back to say the FBI wouldn't authorize Ruffo's trip to Israel, Giuliani wasn't fazed. "I'll take care of it," he said and dialed the phone.

"Hello, Judge Webster, how are you today?" Giuliani had a two-minute conversation with FBI director William Webster, and Ken Ruffo packed his bags.

"This is just stupid," Stan Patz said to Ruffo when the agent visited a few days before the trip. "You're wasting taxpayers' money to chase a copyright infringement case." Stan didn't hide his sarcasm. "*My* copyright of *my* photo, one I took when Etan was still safely at home in this very room. If the picture had been taken by somebody else, of an Etan lookalike, then I could understand it. But it clearly came from a series I took myself."

"This doesn't appear to be one of the shots you sent out, though," Ruffo countered, "and we need to understand this better than we do."

"Look at this proof sheet." Exasperated, Stan pointed to dozens of similar shots on one page. "Who really knows what I printed and didn't print? Anyone who got their hands on it could have sent it to the Romanian magazine as a joke." But as he had fumed, Stan realized that Ken Ruffo would only be incited by his protestations.

"Go ahead, go." Stan finally gave up trying to make his point. "Have a great time. Say hi to Ben-Gurion for me."

Ruffo dutifully reported Stan's protests to GraBois, and as predicted, told the prosecutor he didn't understand why Stan had his back up about Israel. GraBois didn't either, and Stan's attitude fueled them both further.

GraBois and Ruffo traveled to Tel Aviv in late October 1985, accompanied by General Joshua Caspi, the Israeli National Police liaison to the United States and Canada, who happened to speak not only English and Hebrew, but the Romanian of his native country. It was GraBois's first trip to Israel.

The three men left on a Saturday night, landed on Sunday morning, and went straight to the Israeli Police Headquarters, without a moment to catch their breath. In the Bible, God labored six days to create the Earth and rested only on the Sabbath, so Sunday in Israel was like any other day of the workweek. The ten days that followed were a nonstop blur of meetings, travel, and culture shock. GraBois and Ruffo were struck to see soldiers patrolling the streets with Uzis and the absence of public trash cans and mailboxes, any receptacle that could hold explosives. Every time the Americans returned to their parked car, their Israeli police chaperones ran a mirror attached to a stick the length of its underside, checking for bombs. And when Ken Ruffo saw an unusual beer can to add to his collection, the Israelis cautioned him to leave it alone. You never know, they said. How can people live this way? GraBois wondered.

The siege mentality occasionally made his job easier, though. Israelis didn't tend to question authorities knocking on their doors no matter the circumstances or time of day.

"But it's late," GraBois protested to one such intrusive visit, long after hours. Once they'd met with *Revista Mea* magazine staff, the team had pored through government census records to compile a list of Ben-Haims in Israel. Now they were crisscrossing the country to identify, firsthand, any matching Etans. They worked all hours of the day and night, and couldn't always time their visits conveniently.

"It's not a problem," their escorts assured GraBois, and sure enough, they were ushered into this Ben-Haim residence with no resistance. GraBois felt uncomfortable about their invasion, and not just because of the late hour. If strangers had showed up on his doorstep demanding documented proof that he was the parent of his own two children, he would tell them what to go do. But it didn't seem to bother the Ben-Haim families, who cheerfully produced their sons' birth certificates, and the sons themselves for inspection. The ultra-religious residents of Jerusalem's Old City were less receptive to GraBois and Ruffo when the two Americans visited as tourists during their one afternoon off. They threw stones at the two Americans for driving on the Sabbath.

Before GraBois and Ruffo left the country, they'd urged Israeli police to continue searching among other Ben-Haim families and asked *Revista Mea* to republish Etan's photo, in the hope that this would nudge loose its original source. In New York, an eagle-eyed reader spotted the familiar face and called the tabloids. When asked, the U.S. Attorney's Office confirmed a federal trip to Israel and then went one step further, asking major Israeli newspapers to publish an age-progressed photo of Etan.

The ensuing media blitz both in Israel and the United States launched a slew of New York reporters to Israel. John Miller, by now a crime reporter for Channel 4, NBC's New York station, followed in GraBois's footsteps and came back with an explosive interview. A woman in Kiryat Bialik, who had told investigators Etan's photo looked familiar, had given Miller a much stronger statement. Although her on-camera comments were later disavowed by Israeli authorities, they immediately made headlines.

MY SON PLAYED WITH ETAN, CLAIMS ISRAELI MOM. Stan Patz stared at the newspaper in his hand with disgust. He could not begin to fathom this trajectory of the case. Nothing will come of Israel, he assured Julie, and any minute we'll be under those swinging bare bulbs again.

GraBois had called Stan and Julie Patz into his office after the Israel trip, to give them a heads-up before the story broke in the American newspapers. This was their first meeting, and Stan had been in a combative mood, defending himself with that gruff, armored shield the early Missing Persons detectives had slowly seen through.

"Why the Hebrew names for all three children?" GraBois had asked him, making small talk, although he really was curious. "Etan is so unusual."

"My wife is part Native American," Stan had responded. "What should we have called him, Running Deer?" GraBois had laughed at that, but the glib response had left him unamused. He also had no interest in Stan's views on the Israel trip, which Stan was determined to share.

For Stuart GraBois this was a fresh start, and he was full of unbridled zeal. For Stan and Julie Patz this was the umpteenth fresh start, and their patience was wearing thin. They'd already had six and a half years contending with the homicide cops and the Missing Persons detectives and the FBI, not to mention hundreds of psychics and reporters. This time, the combination of what GraBois saw as the parents' insouciance and they saw as his overly aggressive demeanor didn't combine well at all, classic oil and water.

GraBois made no apologies for his aggression. He thought that after so many years it was exactly what this case needed. Ken Ruffo had spent his tenure reworking the case from the ground up, including new polygraphs of the Patzes in 1984—a year before GraBois got the case—and Stan's answers had once again raised suspicion. Two weeks later Stan had passed a second polygraph, after a crash course in calming meditation techniques. After that second round "on the box," being asked about his possible sexual perversions—"Have you ever masturbated in front of a minor?"—he told authorities he would no longer submit to these tests. I'm done with this, he thought.

But when GraBois got involved, he felt compelled to put Stan back in the spotlight. The many teams who'd preceded GraBois may have concluded that the Patzes weren't involved in Etan's disappearance, but those investigators also hadn't solved the case. It would be wildly irresponsible for GraBois to give the parents a free ride. By early 1986, he was dredging up all the old sore spots—rumors of marital strife, religious differences, financial burdens. He had to reassure himself that neither Stan nor Julie was a suspect. GraBois never came out and directly accused them, but the line of questioning was clear.

How did you get the money to buy your apartment in this up-and-coming neighborhood? Why were you taking photos of Etan nude from the waist up? "Because I'm a professional photographer," Stan had replied, bristling the most at that one. "Because my son was in his own home," was what he thought. "He wandered around in his own home in his shorts—my God, what a perverted thing to do."

But GraBois was not ready to dismiss those by now well-known photos. They had attracted everyone's attention and were beautifully shot, but he didn't care if Patz was an artiste. On the street, the shots of Etan posing shirtless would sell as "semi-nudes," and the sleazeballs who sold them got locked up if they were caught. GraBois had put some of those guys away himself.

"It bothers me," GraBois told the investigators, so he had them push hard on that angle, even though he knew how much it upset Etan's parents.

Imagine how ticked off Stan Patz would be, thought GraBois, if he knew the questions the Feds were asking *other* people about him and his possible predilections. The prosecutor had also contacted the manager of a number of bars, including one in Stan's neighborhood where all the older gay guys went to cruise really young flesh. GraBois wanted to know if anyone had ever brought Etan into one of them. "I got nothing to say to you," the manager told GraBois's investigators. Reportedly feared by his associates, this man was considered armed and dangerous, and protected by powerful mob interests. It was believed that the bar he managed was owned by an alleged gangster, who was himself a long-standing target of the U.S. Attorney's Office. GraBois had thought about it, then approached the alleged mobster's attorney. Would Matty "the Horse" Ianniello be willing to contribute his resources to finding this poor boy? Less than an hour later, the bar manager's attorney had called: He was now anxious to meet.

The prosecutor was slowly but surely working his way through every open-ended file, no matter how unlikely the prospect of a payoff. There was the Earth Room, an art installation around the corner from the Patz loft that consisted of a 3,600-square-foot second-floor room packed with two feet of dirt. The "sculpture" had been on exhibit since 1977, two years before Etan disappeared. GraBois's investigators learned that the building's custodian at the time of Etan's disappearance was a convicted pedophile, who'd allegedly made remarks suggesting that Etan was buried under the 280,000 pounds of dirt. GraBois wrote up a search warrant. Then he had to lobby, over the protests of his superiors, to bring FBI specialists and ground-search radar equipment from D.C. to sweep the room for any remains. Rudy Giuliani stepped in again and approved it. The men flew up, and after some selective digging, the Earth Room was eliminated as Etan's grave.

GraBois also returned to Etan's two afterschool playmates, this time hypnotizing Chelsea Altman and Kyra Simmons, whose memories of encountering different people on the way home from school with Sandy Harmon in 1979 again contradicted Sandy's version. There were certainly other reasons she could have lied to police, having nothing to do with Etan—fears about losing Bennett, mistrust of law enforcement, covering up some less egregious misconduct. But what if she'd inadvertently passed on information about Etan's wish to walk to school alone to the real suspect? She could have been directly involved, or the connection was much more innocuous but nonetheless could advance the investigation.

GraBois wanted to go at Sandy Harmon as hard as he had the Patzes, but she remained elusive. She was asked to take another polygraph, but she refused. Not even an offer of immunity changed her position. She had nothing further to add, she maintained. But GraBois was convinced she really did. It was a frustrating impasse, and it nagged at him.

He also didn't want to rule out any link to the extended Patz family members. While in Israel, Ruffo had obtained a list from the Israeli National Police of Rabbi Norman Patz's many visits. Throughout the next several months FBI agents pulled passport applications and overseas travel records for both Stan's and Julie's families. Stan and Julie weren't told about any of this, of course, but it was clear to them that everyone they knew and loved was under renewed suspicion, and the federal presence meant a more powerful microscope than ever before. Stan was especially sensitive about the shadow that continued to be cast on his brother Norman, who as a highly respected rabbi traveled widely, especially in Israel.

A rabbi's reputation is based on the strength of his character, Stan complained to an interviewing FBI agent. He was firm that under no circumstances would his brother have abducted Etan to be raised in a different environment. When GraBois told Stan agents were planning a trip to Massachusetts in the fall of 1986, he erupted.

"You're going to go harass my sick, elderly, grieving parents." Stan's normally calm voice was pitched higher as, a year after their first meeting, he sat in GraBois's office again. He was alone this time; Julie had begged off from the meeting.

"My mother is seventy. She has cancer. She has never gotten over losing Etan. If you grill her the way you grill us, it could kill her." Both Stan and Julie thought GraBois's efforts against the family were a huge waste of time, but Julie had given up trying to tell the prosecutor that.

"If we end up going, we're not going up there to harass anyone," GraBois countered. "Someone might be able to tell us something, some little throwaway piece of information that to them means nothing, but it could turn this case. It's not fun. I don't enjoy it. But we have to be thorough."

"You've gone after Julie and me for months; I know you think I'm turning out kiddie porn in my darkroom. Now you're telling us that you're spending more time and money, traveling hundreds of miles away, to go after the rest of our family? What am I supposed to think?"

There was a brief silence, as though both men were going to their mutual corners, to be toweled off and await the bell for the next round. Since Gra-Bois wasn't planning to divulge anything to the Patzes, he felt like a fighter with one hand tied behind his back. Still, he wasn't worried about the outcome of this match.

"My men are heading up to Massachusetts soon, that's all I can tell you." The irony was that Stan Patz's family was of little concern to GraBois. His men were primarily chasing another angle altogether, but he couldn't tell Stan and Julie about it. GraBois had strict rules about sharing information with the family, at least until he could cross them off his own personal suspect list. He knew it drove the Patzes crazy, but it couldn't be helped.

"You've spent more than a year looking at just me and Julie, and you're obviously not finished with the two of us," Stan Patz said before he got up and left the meeting. "When is this going to end?"

When he got home, he said to Julie, "This guy is the *worst*."

In recent years Julie had let her husband take over as point person to the investigation, around the time she'd begun to understand her further efforts wouldn't bring Etan home. Once she decided she couldn't be of any use to her eldest son, she'd retrenched, to tend to her remaining children, who needed her as badly as she needed them. Now Stan went to the meetings, talked to the cops, and reported back.

"You've got eight brothers and sisters," he said to Julie now, "and by the time he's figured out they're clean, Etan will be sixteen, and he'll just drive himself home."

In his moments of clarity, Stan understood he was directing his anger at the wrong person. There was a faceless demon somewhere out there who had stolen his son, but Stan had to settle for raging at Stuart GraBois.

United States Attorney's Office
Southern District of New York
Attention: Mr. Rudy Giuliani
re: Mr. Stuart GraBois
November 10, 1986

Dear Sir

My wife and I respectfully request that Mr. Stuart GraBois, of your office, be removed from active participation in our case.

In the time Mr. GraBois has been assigned to us, he has managed to antagonize all of my family, numerous law enforcement officials here and possibly some abroad. For the past seven and a half years, the time my son Etan has been gone, we have freely cooperated with almost anybody who could conceivably help us find our boy.... We are now openly hostile....

 ...Ostensibly, we all have the same goal: to find out what happened to Etan....We are anxious for an answer, yet we do not want to pursue that solution at any cost.

 If your office expects willing cooperation from us, relieve Mr. GraBois of his assignment.

Sincerely yours,
Stanley K. Patz and Julia B. Patz

cc: S. GraBois
cc: Howard Wilson
cc: K. Ruffo

GraBois took his copy of the letter and walked up to the eighth floor, to Giuliani's office. Rudy was finishing a conference call, his feet perched on the desk. Standing in the door, GraBois held up the letter. Rudy Giuliani looked at him, and as he hung up the phone, he nodded. "If you don't get complaints, you're not doing your job."

GraBois didn't need to hear any more. Giuliani's message was clear, and besides, GraBois already knew it: Stan Patz was looking for sensitivity and respect. Stuart GraBois was looking for a killer. As he headed back down the hall to the stairs, Giuliani's last words caught up to him: "Keep up the good work."

Back in his office, GraBois leafed through the documents spread out on his desk, detailing a cluster of Etan sightings in the Massachusetts area. He looked down at the handwritten list of possible suspects that he'd been compiling over the last year and a half. Stan Patz was on it but so were a dozen others. If and when Stan's name came off the list he'd be able to talk to him about the rest, and how he was working on them with the same force he had used on the Patz family. That's how GraBois could feel so confident that he was going to crack this case. He didn't care what they thought of him. He hoped someday the family would understand, but if they didn't, well, that was all right too.

CHAPTER 11

———

Welcome Home

We, Sisters and Brothers, Children of Light, friends of nature, united by
our love for each other and our yearning for peace, who call ourselves
the Rainbow Family Tribe, humbly invite everyone everywhere to join us
in expressing our sincere desire, through prayers, for peace on earth
and harmony among all.
> —*invitation to the Rainbow Gathering of the Tribes, Pennsylvania,
> July 1–7, 1986*

When the whole world is invited, anybody is likely to show up.
> —*"Quester," one of many Rainbow Gathering organizers*

Welcome home, brother!" "Welcome home, sister!"
Before Barry Adams had fully positioned his ten-year-old,
mud-splattered Chevy van into the Rainbow Gathering's designated
parking, off a soggy stretch of dead-end dirt road, he and his family were
besieged.

"We love you!"

This, from old friends and passersby alike, was the traditional opening line of a Rainbow conversation. Rainbow brothers and sisters of every
shade and hair length shouted greetings and extended their arms to the
Adams kids piling out of the van. The exuberant welcome party was a fraction of Barry Adams's "extended" family—the Rainbow Family of Living
Light—who would come together this year, as they did every July, for a
weeklong "spiritual event, an absolutely free, non-commercial celebration
held for the healing of all minds, hearts, bodies and souls." Thus proclaimed
the hand-lettered, hand-circulated brochure for the 1986 Fifteenth Annual

Rainbow Gathering of Tribes. "Come bring your light," it declared. "Let it SHINE!"

Like many veteran Rainbows, Adams, his wife, Sunny, and their two children were arriving ahead of time to Heart's Content, a remote outpost of northwestern Pennsylvania's Allegheny National Forest where white-tailed deer and black bear roamed freely under 400-year-old beech, hemlock, and sugar maples. Shielded by the protective embrace of these secluded old-growth forests and the anonymity of their Rainbow nicknames, some seven thousand pilgrims would soon be assembled, to let their freak flags fly. There'd be few outsiders on hand to be offended by the casual drug use, mostly pot and the psychotropics that Rainbows viewed as healing herbs or religious sacrament; few nonbelievers to gawk at the nudity that was neither de rigueur nor discouraged. Here, the Rainbows would say, they were in the sanctity of their own home.

Barry and Sunny unpacked the van between the breath-stealing, all-enveloping bear hugs from old friends they hadn't seen for a year, the "you've grown so tall" exclamations over their eleven-year-old son and six-year-old daughter, the gossip about goings-on that had preceded their arrival. Not all of it was lighthearted banter.

"There's some guy who's been giving off a negative vibe," someone told Adams. "He's handing out little toys and candy to the kids here. His energy is all wrong." A few other people had heard or seen this, and Sunny looked around to check that their own children were in sight.

They were still an hour away on foot from the Gathering's Main Meadow, deliberately chosen for its remote location, as far as possible from cars and highways, TV and money, and all the other strictures of mainstream society, or what Rainbows called Babylon. But after six long days on the road from Missoula, Montana, Adams knew the final destination was worth it.

He breathed deeply and soaked up the vibe. An infectious grin split his freckled, open face, recalling a hippie Howdy Doody. Clad in his signature outfit of handmade vest and buckskin chaps—with matching breechclout modestly covering the crotch—Barry Adams was a landmark at these Gatherings. He wore his long brown hair in twin plaits, clamped tightly to his head by a multihued bandana and his tortoiseshell Buddy Holly glasses.

In Babylon, Barry Adams's look stood out; here alongside brothers like Buffalo and Quester and Peace Ray, Barry "Plunker" did not. His Rainbow nickname derived from the single-stringed instrument that doubled as a walking staff he strapped across his back. The four-foot, feather-trimmed wooden "plunker" was the musical accompaniment to his Rainbow "hip-story" lessons, rambling discourses to extol "the largest non-organization of non-members in the world." Adams would never call himself a Rain-bow leader—he'd be the first to say the Rainbows *had* no leaders—but he was an elder, a passionate devotee who'd helped organize the very first Gathering in 1972. Inspired by Native American prophecies, some two thousand hippies had climbed high into the Colorado Rockies to sacred Arapaho ground. Since then, the Rainbows had journeyed annually to far-flung sites—the Burnt Coral Canyon of New Mexico; the Virgin River of Utah; the Antelope Hills of Wyoming; a different National Forest wilder-ness every year.

Today, Adams looked up and down the line of vehicles with a mixture of pride and wonder, and thought of how the Gathering had evolved since that first Rocky Mountain high. Now the Day-Glo VW buses held together by strapping tape and karmic energy were just as likely to be parked head to toe with a late-model four-by-four, a suburban family wagon, or a Harley hog. Adams watched approvingly as the all-volunteer parking crew motioned vehicles into neat slots and delivered their orientation, "Rap 107," which laid out Rainbow doctrine to each newcomer.

"Keep the balance," the crew recited earnestly. "Earth, Sky, Trees, Water, and People!" Old-timers who arrived mid-rap joined in. "Alcohol is discour-aged, guns are inappropriate, violence is contrary to the Spirit."

Adams soon added his distinctively hearty western twang to the chorus. "Freedom with responsibility," he'd preach to the uninitiated, strumming the plunker for emphasis. "Common sense, faith, and elbow grease."

Indeed, everything at these Gatherings was free or bartered, a "Magic Hat" routinely passed through the crowds to subsidize food, entertainment, childcare, security, sanitation, and medical attention. It often did seem like magic, but peel back the anarchy and the Rainbows hid a surprisingly com-plex infrastructure. Every year a shining new, fully functional paradise rose from the dust, complete with consensus government, nursing stations, slit-trench latrines, and dozens of individual camps centered around communal kitchens, with names like Moondancer's Enchanted Forest or Earth Moth-ers' Kitchen.

Adams finally hoisted a spartan mess kit onto his back and disengaged from the group around him. Trained nurse and midwife Sunny gathered her homemade liniments, antibiotic tinctures, and bottled oxygen for the Rainbow version of a M.A.S.H. unit called the Center of Alternative Living Medicine, or C.A.L.M. Then she rounded up the kids and they all headed down the trail.

The path that led to Main Meadow was deliberately long and meandering. Folks needed the time and distance every year to shake off societal layers, to make the transition into a holy place. Rainbows saw the Gathering as a sanctuary. "How would you feel if we brought a rifle into *your* church?" they would say to the uniformed officers who inevitably hovered near the scene. With thousands of transients massing in their backyard, authorities saw it differently, and as at past Gatherings, state troopers in Pennsylvania had established a mobile outpost some three miles away, ready to move in if necessary.

Rainbows had little use for the law enforcement officers, or "LEOs," who flashed their guns, took pictures, and otherwise killed the buzz; although to be fair, the troopers largely ignored the illegal herbs. The Rainbow Family looked to their own internal security force, Shanti Sena—Sanskrit for "peacekeepers"—armed with little more than goodwill and, occasionally, walkie-talkies. In theory everyone at the Gathering was a Shanti Sena peacekeeper, but a small band of stalwarts, like Barry Adams and his compadres, held a certain status born of experience and commitment.

Over the next few hours, Adams and his family made slow progress toward the Gathering's center. At every turn of the path there were more old friends and new strangers to embrace, including the roving Hug Patrol. As the group drew nearer, they breathed the pungent smoke from the kitchens and campfires mingling with the aroma of damp earth and incense. The muffled patter of drums and the occasional strum of a solo guitar broke the silence from time to time, but otherwise the forest's natural tranquillity prevailed. Finally, the four skirted an industrial-looking gate that had been transplanted mid-forest to straddle the dirt path, marking the official entrance. A street sign fluttering above, with an arrow pointing forward, proclaimed FREEDOM.

They were home.

Main Meadow—already dotted with tents, teepees, even a wood-framed, open-roofed yurt or two set into the spongy field—stretched ahead. The surrounding trees were draped with tarps for simpler cover.

A scraggly-bearded young man passed by, blowing footlong soap bubbles;

a bare-breasted woman suckled her child nearby. Days of rain had created natural mud baths, and one group now lay in the hot sun clad only in dried clay, ferns tied to their hair.

Adams split off from his family as they headed to C.A.L.M. and he to Shanti Sena camp. He stopped to check the Welcome Center, a battered surplus NASA trailer once used to store missile launch tracking equipment. Flower garlands and an ancient Sanskrit banner now replaced the hardware. A rainbow of colored posters announced the week's offerings: ayurvedic yoga classes, tantric meditation workshops, herb walks and woodcarving, acupuncture, massage, and more—all free.

Adams planted stakes at the Shanti Sena camp, and ran into his old friend John Buffalo, who'd driven in from San Diego a few days earlier. With a solid two hundred pounds on his nearly six-foot frame, fiery red hair, and full beard, Buffalo was a security force unto himself. While the two men caught up, Adams related the unsettling report he'd heard in the parking lot, about the mysterious man handing out toys and candy to the Rainbow kids. He and Buffalo talked about the best way to check out the rumor, and in the meantime they'd be on the lookout.

But there were other duties and distractions, and this summer the Shanti Sena was operating short-staffed. Although veterans Garrick Beck and Joanee Freedom had arrived from New York, she was hobbled by crutches after a near-fatal car accident, and he was busy looking after her. It wasn't until a few days later that Barry Adams found himself in Kid Village, looking at a pile of toys on the ground.

Kid Village was the center of the world for the youngest members of the tribe, a fairytale night-and-day care center. The Rainbows, who prized the qualities of childhood—innocence and unbridled emotion, not to mention an underdeveloped superego—fiercely protected their children. At Kid Village, junior hippies romped in open spaces, fed by their own kitchen, shielded from all-night bacchanalia by the stream that separated them from the main meeting area, by a screen of Christmas-tree-sized evergreens, and by their families' tents ringing the Kid Village perimeter.

This year, youngsters played hide-and-seek among the trees and tangled themselves in a homemade spiderweb jungle gym. But now, the Shanti Sena were learning, the web might have sinister overtones. A man, perhaps the one Adams had heard about earlier, was spotted hanging around nearby with these action figures, talking to the kids. "It just feels funny." Adams heard the same kind of talk as up in the parking lot. "This dude has no kids of his own, but he's hanging around here a lot."

Barry Adams picked up a four-inch, hard plastic Obi-Wan Kenobi figure still in its sealed plastic wrap and turned it over and over in his hands. These weren't scuffed-up castoffs; each one looked to be worth a few bucks. He asked parents at Kid Village to alert him if the man was seen again. Anyone might be welcome at the Gathering, but not to harm children. The question had suddenly become pressing: Who was handing out these mysterious gifts, and at what price?

Adams and Buffalo were finishing breakfast around a Sunday morning campfire when another Rainbow man approached. "I hear you've been looking for the fellow passing out stuff to the kids," he said.

"We're interested in talking to him, yeah. What do you know?"

"He's up in Bus Village. I saw him with the Taylor boys on his bus, and I told him he had to leave. But he's still there."

This was serious news, not only because it pinpointed the mystery man's location, but because one person unilaterally forcing another from the Gathering breaks one of the few rules of the rule-resistant Rainbow Family. Adams at first condemned the informant's actions, but then realized he couldn't ignore his information.

"We better go up to Bus Village and see what's going on," he told John Buffalo.

Folks who drove to the Gathering in mobile homes of any kind could choose to stay in them through the week, only semi-roughing it in Bus Village, which this year was nearly an hour's trek uphill to a ridge overlooking Main Meadow.

"I can't stop thinking about the dude John Wayne Gacy," Adams said to Buffalo as they walked, referring to the infamous Chicago serial killer who dressed like a clown to entertain the neighborhood children.

En route, the two men met another friend, who was carrying her camera. In the absence of weapons, the Shanti Sena had learned that photos proved useful, so they asked her to join them. The three had reached the top of the path when they heard the sound of an engine. Coming into view of the parking lot, they saw a blue converted school bus revving its motor. The trio drew nearer and spotted a vaguely familiar figure at the wheel, so they ducked around to the front, cutting off the bus's escape route. From this closer vantage, Adams and Buffalo looked at each other in dismay.

"Oh, man," said Barry Adams. "That's Jose Antonio Ramos."

"I know this dude from Michigan," John Buffalo said. "And he's up to no goddamn good."

———

John Buffalo was one of a handful of Rainbow Shanti Sena who had a history with Jose Ramos, starting three years earlier at the 1983 Michigan Rainbow Gathering. On one of the last nights of those festivities, Buffalo found himself in the main supply area closest to the road out of camp, standing guard over a dark-haired, disheveled Ramos as the rest of the Shanti Sena Council assembled.

Shunning a central authority, Rainbows only took action by consensus, so at Gatherings every decision—no matter how small—required a council. Bigger councils often numbered in the hundreds and they took hours, sometimes days, before agreement was reached. Moving around the circle, one speaker at a time held a feather or shell—a rock off the ground would do—and no one could interrupt until the sacred object was finally passed on. But on this starless, overcast northern Michigan night, a core circle of Shanti Sena members crouched on logs around the fire pit, and there was no need for a feather to keep order. This group had known each other for years. Well-spoken, urbane Garrick Beck, one of the first organizers, was a renowned Rainbow figure with deep roots in New York's counterculture movement. Calm, measured earth mother Joanee Freedom, another New Yorker, recognized the man being watched by John Buffalo from the streets near her home in the East Village. Dave Massey, a relative newcomer to the Shanti Sena, just sat quietly and listened.

Carla Breen had summoned the group together, despite the late hour. Days earlier a distraught mother had left the Gathering abruptly, claiming this man had "messed with her kid." But that wasn't enough to go on, until a twelve-year-old boy had come to Carla to report another incident. The boy was in a sleeping bag in Kid Village, when Ramos lay down next to him, reached into the child's bag, and touched him. It was unclear from the boy's account whether the advance had been sexual.

"I pretended to be asleep," the boy went on, "and he finally took his hand away."

"Could you have been mistaken?" Carla had asked him gently. The boy looked her straight in the eye, and she believed him. He wasn't hysterical and he wasn't terrorized. He just didn't like what had happened.

"What he did was wrong," he said.

Carla agreed, and she grabbed Ramos the next time she saw him coming back into the Rainbow camp late at night from a trip to town with Saxophone Sonny, a New York street musician who was Ramos's traveling companion. She had both men sit with John Buffalo to wait while runners went out through the various camps to gather the Shanti Sena. As the group straggled in and learned why they were meeting, reactions were wildly mixed, from "String him up!" to "Healing crystals!" In 1983, the Rainbow Family, as much as the outside world, was just learning about the prevalence, indeed the very existence, of child molesters. Around the fire pit, the vibe of tolerance and acceptance that characterized the Family now clashed with moral outrage and disgust. Finally John Buffalo brought the man over for the council to begin.

"What were you doing with this boy?"

"Why would you put your hand on a child?"

"What were you thinking?"

"How do we know you're telling the truth?"

Ramos seemed surprisingly unfazed as he faced more than a dozen accusers, like it was almost a big joke to him.

"Oh, c'mon, I didn't do nothin' wrong," he said. The collection of amulets and colored pins that hung from his worn black vest jangled as he raised his hands in a what's-the-big-deal gesture.

"It was all a misunderstanding, just a mistake." He'd found this tent, he was cold, he stumbled in and fell asleep next to this kid. "It was no big deal. I was just trying to keep warm."

"This kid said you put your hand in his sleeping bag. That you touched him."

"Naw, I didn't mean nothin' by it. What's the big deal?"

"It is a big deal," Carla said. "This is really serious. You might not have hurt him, but you can't even play around about this kind of thing." Even for a Rainbow Gathering, this man's affect was odd, out of place, like he was detached from the scene and any sense of personal responsibility.

"People are always mistaking my sense of humor, and it gets me in trouble. I wish they would just understand me. Remember, Sonny"—he turned to his friend sitting nearby—"it was like that in Palm Beach? And the same with that Etan Patz thing, remember?"

There was an audible gasp from Joanee Freedom. Later she took Carla aside and explained. "That's that famous missing kid from New York. If he's mixed up in that, it's serious shit."

Still in the circle, Ramos tried a different tack. "You're going to make me a victim, too," he said, and finally one woman took his hand as if to soothe him. This was the Rainbow way, to heal instead of judge. The people around this campfire had all been victims of bigotry and preconceived notions for the way they lived their lives. And if others at the circle weren't in a healing mood, there was still no evidence of a crime.

"We'll give you a choice," Carla told Ramos. "We want your word you will not go near a child here again. By rights we can't force you to leave, but if you stay, you must agree to be walked." It was glorified babysitting, an oft-used technique, especially effective in domestic disputes. If he chose to remain, Shanti Sena would stick by Ramos's side around the clock through the rest of the event. Ramos looked contrite and said he wanted to stay.

"You're my family now," he said. "You're the only family I have. I'll do whatever you say."

John Buffalo started the first shift, watching over Ramos until morning, to keep him from disappearing back into the crowd. In the morning, when Ramos announced he'd changed his mind and was leaving, Buffalo walked the man out of the Gathering, gave him some loose bills and a look of disgust, and left him on the side of the highway.

Back in New York later that summer, both Garrick Beck and Joanee Freedom would run into Ramos in the East Village. He peddled his salvaged wares on Second Avenue, one of the area's many makeshift street vendors who laid their goods out on blankets off St. Mark's Place. Ramos's large white Akita, Jesse, attracted passersby, especially the children.

Beck would pass him on the street on his way home from work, and they'd nod companionably or say hello. Beck didn't make the connection to the fireside council in Michigan. One day, Ramos pulled him aside.

"You're a spiritual guy, I know." Ramos leaned toward Beck. "Do you ever hear voices?"

"No," Beck replied, going for the joke. "Maybe you've heard me described as visionary or something, but not visions. Not like that. Why?"

"Because I hear voices sometimes." Ramos had a confiding tone. "I try to resist them, but they tell me to do bad things."

Beck was stumped. He didn't know whether to laugh it off or try to say something visionary. He said the first thing that came to mind.

"Well, you appear to be a strong person, who can speak well for himself. Talk back to those voices, and tell them to leave you alone." Ramos seemed to accept this counsel and went back to leaning against the parking meter next to the ragged cardboard sales counter. Beck didn't think much about the incident as he walked home. New York was filled with characters. He prided himself on being one too.

———

Two years after their first encounter in Michigan, Ramos found his way to the 1985 Missouri Gathering, but his presence wasn't immediately apparent. Instead, the Rainbow Family confronted a different threat to their children when a teenage girl was sexually assaulted by someone else in the early days of the celebration. This time they convinced the girl's parents to bring charges. Ever since the Ramos incident in Michigan two years earlier, Shanti Sena like Joanee Freedom, Garrick Beck, John Buffalo, and now Barry Adams had become informally pegged as the de facto vice squad. The Missouri incident was resolved in a delicate series of maneuvers, as Shanti Sena corralled Rainbow Billy, a.k.a. William Bonine, led him to the edge of the Gathering, and turned him in to the Missouri State Police, who charged him with rape and sodomy.

Maybe the security force's resources were diverted by all this, or maybe ten thousand revelers proved effective cover, but no one spotted Jose Ramos in Missouri until the week was well under way. As dawn broke on July Fourth, adults began to assemble in the Main Meadow, hands joined in silent meditation for the Gathering's capstone Prayer Circle. At high noon, the stillness was broken by thousands chanting "Om" in one voice.

Then, as every year, worshipers heard high-pitched laughter and childish singing punctuated by horns and drums. The Kid's Parade swarmed onto the meadow, where children with elaborately painted faces, draped in flags and feathers, giddily signaled the meditation's end.

Amid the noise and spectacle, Joanee Freedom spotted someone whose large aviator shades and rainbow-bedecked, wide-brimmed hat enveloped most of his face, but what was visible looked suspiciously familiar. This time Joanee had a camera. She tried to maneuver around, to see him clearly and take his picture, but he kept turning away. Joanee's friend Stephen Principle watched her moving erratically.

"What are you doing?" Stephen asked her. Joanee explained, and Principle walked over and put his arm around the man, turning his body toward Joanee for a clearer look.

His hair was longer and his beard was thicker. He'd been calling himself Michael Rainbow. But it was Jose Ramos, his face covered by the hat and the oversized shades. Joanee raised the camera as he moved his head away again.

"Stand still and look at me," she told him, pointing and clicking.

"I don't like my picture taken." That was a common refrain among the Rainbows and it was usually respected. But there were times the Shanti Sena reserved the right.

Ramos turned his head. Stephen Principle tightened his grip on the man's shoulder and turned his head back to face the camera.

"I don't like my picture taken either," Principle said. "It's a special day, though, so smile. The two of us are taking our picture together." For the rest of the Gathering, Ramos was walked. Joanee passed the picture around as a warning, then filed it away with her other Gathering memorabilia, a matter of Rainbow record.

A year later, in 1986, two months before Barry Adams and John Buffalo would come upon Ramos at the Pennsylvania Gathering, he showed up at an annual New York Central Park Picnic. Joanee Freedom wasn't there—she was recuperating from her car accident. But there were other folks who knew to watch out for Ramos, including Dave Massey, one of the group at the Michigan council back in '83. Instead of demanding that Ramos be walked, Massey, a slight man with a quiet intensity, sat back and observed him, unnoticed, until the crowd of children surrounding Ramos seemed to swell in numbers, growing louder and more boisterous. Massey suddenly had the uncomfortable sensation he was watching the Pied Piper. Hoping to avoid confrontation when the kids were nearby, he began talking softly to individual parents, and little by little they removed their children from the mix. Finally Massey moved closer, with a mental image of herding his prey. Now he wanted the man to notice him, and Ramos did. As Massey came within arm's length, Ramos picked up a weighty oak table leg from a nearby pile of garbage and made a threatening gesture. Massey stopped, but didn't retreat.

"It's important that you come sit and do some business," Massey said quietly. "There've been some things said, some accusations leveled. Why don't we straighten these things out?"

They stared at each other for a long minute. Massey calculated Ramos had the reach to move forward and swing at him. For his part, the smaller man didn't step in to risk getting his head cracked open. Finally, Ramos backed away and left the area.

Later that day, Massey sat up on a hill with a friend and watched the hundreds of people blissfully dancing to an impromptu band in the late afternoon sunshine. "The problem is," Massey said, after he'd told his friend what happened, "this brother sure seems like bad news, but who really knows if he's done anything wrong? We just don't have the evidence."

———

Dave Massey hadn't yet arrived at the Pennsylvania Gathering, but in the parking lot, both John Buffalo and Barry Adams had no trouble IDing Jose Ramos, both from Buffalo's personal encounters with him and from the old photos the Shanti Sena had passed among themselves, their version of a mug shot. Now the engine of Ramos's converted school bus was idling, ready to take off, but Adams and Buffalo stood in front of it.

"Open up, Jose," Barry Adams said as he banged on the door. "We'd like to talk with you."

The door folded in slowly to reveal Jose Ramos, his hands clenched on the wheel, looking ready to bolt. *Click.* Once again, a camera caught his defiant expression, as the woman who'd accompanied Adams and Buffalo moved in for a close-up. In the three years since Michigan, Ramos had transformed his look into the full-blown hippie prophet, with flowing, matted beard and hair that blended together in the dim light, obscuring most of his face. A red beret hung over sullen eyes.

Adams's words were friendly enough, but the acid tone made his displeasure clear. "Brother, are you the one with these Star Wars figures we been seeing all around? You been giving them out to our kids?"

Ramos mumbled inaudibly.

Adams tried again. "Hey, I heard tell that you've been with our kids, which is against our agreement. You remember that agreement you made not to be with our kids?"

"Oh, no, no." The denials were clearer. "No, I haven't been with any kids. Everything's cool."

There was a scuffling noise from the back of the bus.

"What's that?" Adams stiffened. "Who's back there? Come on out."

Adams and Buffalo craned their heads around to look inside the dark recesses of the bus. A small shape emerged and took focus, seven-year-old Billy Taylor.

Out of the thousands of Rainbows gathered here, Adams just happened to know this boy well. The curly head moved forward into the brighter front space, squinted his blue eyes against the light, and acknowledged his parents' longtime friend.

"Hey, Plunker," he said.

"Are you okay?" Adams asked.

The boy nodded.

"Get off the bus, son. Go find your folks."

"We're just riding around," Billy said. "We're going to get some gas." The boy seemed a little defensive, a little defiant. Adams knew Billy wasn't old enough to understand the danger he could have been in if the Shanti Sena hadn't arrived when they did.

"Your folks'll be looking for you." Adams's words brooked no argument. "You need to go to them. I'll come around in a little while."

Reading the expression in Adams's face, Billy scrambled down the bus steps and ran off, but by this time another boy, this one much older, had also come forward from the back of the bus and now moved to stand in the door. He looked to be a teenager, but one of an unreadable age—he could have been anything from a tough-countenanced thirteen to a baby-faced twenty. Adams didn't recognize him, but later others would realize they'd spotted him with Ramos at past Gatherings. For a moment the only sound was the click of the camera, as it freeze-framed his dirty-blond mullet, his shopworn, dissolute mien and indifferent pout. He wore his jeans slung low with a hunting knife strapped on the belt loops; a wide expanse of skin showed below his gray short-sleeved T-shirt. His expression was vacant, his pose slightly provocative, like Ramos's. He remained silent.

"I'm leaving," the older man said in an injured tone. "I don't want to stay where I'm not wanted."

"Just hold on a minute, brother." Barry Adams stifled the instinct to happily accede to his wishes. "Folks here need to counsel some and come to an agreement."

The council of three considered their options. They wanted Ramos gone as much as he wanted to leave, but should they try to make him stay long enough to call in authorities? The benefit of the doubt was wearing thin.

Adams turned back to the bus. "We might have us an attempted kidnapping. You were leaving with one of our young'uns."

"That's just crazy." Ramos turned and gestured to the empty interior. "That kid and his brother been practically living on this bus. I fixed their meals and watched over 'em like they were my own. His folks are my friends. You heard him, we were just going to get gas. I promised him I'd take him into town." Ramos looked restless. "I'm leaving, and you can't stop me."

They couldn't and they knew it. Ramos was free to go. If not, the Shanti Sena were well aware they themselves could face kidnapping charges.

"You're no longer welcome in our home," Adams finally told the man. "Even if you didn't hurt anyone, you made an agreement and you broke it, so we can't trust you. You better go on down the road and don't come back."

"I'm telling you, nothing happened," Ramos reiterated one last time. "I didn't hurt nobody." The older teen glared at the Rainbows and moved farther back inside. As Ramos closed the door, Adams's friend with the camera circled around. From behind the bus just before it pulled away, she snapped the curlicued letters advertising TAROT CARD READINGS, and the numbers off the license plate.

The Rainbows walked down the road to follow until the bus turned out of the encampment. Then they went off to "A Camp" to talk to Billy's parents.

Joe and Cherie Taylor were mainstays at the rough-and-ready "A Camp," which usually set up at the edge of the Gathering, to enjoy a beer or two . . . or twenty, away from the disapproving eyes of most Rainbows, who frowned on alcohol as a Babylon drug. Joe Taylor ran the "A Camp" kitchen by day, a well-maintained, crowd-pleasing mess, and drank lustily by night. Well respected by many, he was more likely to break up a fight than start one; a man who knew the difference, as he liked to say, between peeing on someone's tires and peeing on someone's car.

Cherie Taylor was his wan shadow, whose cornflower blue eyes could occasionally still brighten a once luminous face. But at thirty-one, she looked a decade older, and the ravages of her family's marginal existence, coupled with years of ill health, showed in the deep lines etched into her pale complexion.

During the rest of the year, the Taylors were inveterate road dogs, living off day jobs, the state, and the kindness of strangers, but the Gathering was an annual refuge that briefly anchored them in community. Cherie told folks there that she came every year to regain her strength. It's what keeps me going, she'd say. Her family had been on-site as far back as mid-May, living out of and serving meals from a broken-down mobile kitchen, a gift from sympathetic locals. By all accounts, they were loving parents who, even if caught up in their excessive lifestyle, tried to do right by their children, seven-year-old Billy and eight-year-old Joe Jr.

When Barry Adams and John Buffalo came to see Joe and Cherie Taylor after the run-in with Ramos, the parents listened with alarm.

"We've been watching this brother on account of trouble with him in the past," Adams said. "He might be a child molester, he might not. We've never been able to prove anything. We'd talked to him, though, and he wasn't supposed to be alone with our kids. But Billy was on his bus."

"We met him in Missouri last year," Cherie said, "and he hung out with us a lot. We knew him as Michael, and he seemed like a nice guy. I think he brought that older kid with him, but I don't know much else about him." And yes, she said, Ramos had been minding her two boys, especially after hours, when their kitchen turned into a bar scene. Cherie had been relieved when they'd slept over on his bus two days earlier, safely at a distance from the late-night carousing. But just the day before, she recounted, she'd told the boys to stay away from Ramos. Another friend, the man who'd warned Barry Adams earlier that day, had seen the boys on the bus, and had dragged them kicking and screaming back to their mom. There, the friend had warned Cherie too that Ramos wasn't to be trusted.

"Stay off of his bus, and go down to Kid Village," she'd told her sons. When Joey had come to ask her if he could go with Ramos to get some gas in town, she'd said no. But his younger brother didn't bother asking permission. Even if he had, everyone knew that if you wanted Billy to do something, you only had to tell him it wasn't allowed.

"Why don't you talk to your youngsters and let us know if they report anything bad happened. They may be just fine," Adams said now. "We're going to track this dude down the road a stretch, while we put out the word to see who else might have information. I'd hate to think he messed with some other kids, but if so, we should know about 'em."

It was several miles from Bus Village to the first paved road, and as Adams and Buffalo covered the terrain, stopping to spread the word, they were relieved to see no sign of their quarry. It looked as though Ramos was gone for good.

CHAPTER 12

⌇⌇

Hard Evidence

The VICTIM'S mother and father appeared on station with the VIC-TIM, and advised this officer that their 8 yr. old son had been sexually assaulted by the above mentioned SUSPECT. SUSPECT apparently made friends with the child by giving him toys and candy and letting him stay in his bus, which is apparently set up for living....

...VICTIMS parents then discovered from other members of the Rainbow Family that the SUSPECT was alleged to have a past history of attempted child molesting. VICTIMS parents at this point questioned the VICTIM about any touching with the SUSPECT and the VICTIM at this time related to the parents what had happened. SUSPECT departed the Rainbow Family Encampment on the 22nd of Jun 86 at approx. 1500 hrs.

    —Initial Incident Report, PA state trooper Blaine Kuhn, June 23, 1986

Pt is an 8 yr old male who alleges five incidents of sexual abuse on June 20th and 21st, 1986....Verbalizes well about the incidents and his history is lucid and consistent....I would recommend an evaluation of the alleged perpetrator for venereal disease, including determination of the HTLV III status.

    —physical evaluation of Joey Taylor by Barbara E. Barnes, MD;
      Forest Area Family Health Center; June 23, 1986

I t's 2:22 p.m. on June 23, 1986, and we're here at the Pennsylvania State Police Barracks in Tionesta."

Trooper Blaine Kuhn sat in the small room off the front entrance and started the interview tape. Facing him across the desk was a little boy in a raglan-sleeved baseball shirt, sweet-faced, eight-year-old Joey Taylor, Billy Taylor's older brother.

"Joey," Kuhn began gently but without any coddling, "do you know the difference between right and wrong?"

"Yes." Joey nodded, speaking so quietly Kuhn strained to hear.

"Don't add anything to it, just say exactly what happened. Do you understand?"

The boy nodded again.

"Tell me what happened," Kuhn went on. "You're going to have to speak up now."

While Billy Taylor had continued to tell his parents that Ramos had left him alone, that morning Joey had finally retracted his own denials.

"He touched my pee-pee." Joey's soft chirpy voice cut through any preliminaries. "And he stuck his pee-pee in my butt."

"And where were you?" asked the trooper.

"At the Rainbow Gathering."

Kuhn had been down to the Rainbow encampment in Heart's Content. Relatively speaking, the boy and his parents, who sat in chairs flanking their son, looked pretty ordinary—no Middle Earth costumes or multiple piercings in sight. Joe Sr. had a full beard and shoulder-length hair beneath his knit cap, but he wore a white golf-collared shirt and seemed respectfully subdued. His wife was in jeans and a neat floral top, her straight brown hair pulled back to the nape of her neck.

She turned slightly toward her son, arms crossed, listening intently to his account, nodding encouragement as Joey answered the trooper's questions.

"What did he say to you?"

"He said, 'Will you tell?' and I said 'No.' But then I did." The boy looked chagrined, as if he was well aware he'd broken his word.

He certainly was composed, though, Kuhn thought, not like some kids who get hysterical. No sign of coaching—fearful looks to his mother or father to check if he'd said it right. They weren't riling him up either, the way parents can do in these sensitive interviews. The trooper knew how these Rainbows felt about involving the law in Family business. He was surprised but grateful that they had brought in their son.

Young Joey went on to describe the candy and toys, the mini Donkey Kong computer games, the Obi-Wan figures that Michael—as he called himself—handed out to the kids. The man had long curly hair and a beard and sometimes he wore glasses. The eight-year-old put his own fingers into a "junior birdman" pose around his eyes to illustrate. When asked about hair color, Joey was stuck, until he pointed to the salt and pepper at Kuhn's temple. Kuhn thought he showed no signs of dissembling and was clear about his story, even when Kuhn himself had trouble keeping it straight.

"Did he have his clothes on or off?"

Joey considered this. "On Saturday he had his clothes off."

"What about Sunday?"

"It wasn't Sunday," Joey unself-consciously reminded the man. "It was Friday and Saturday."

On both days, Joey recounted, Michael had invited him and Billy onto the bus to play with his big dog. On the bus, Michael told them stories and let them listen to music. Eventually the man suggested they lie down and rest, Billy on the floor and Joey on the daybed.

"Michael told me that he got the boys to take a nap," interjected Cherie Taylor, "and I said to him, 'How did you get them to do that?'"

It was during the naps, said Joey Taylor, while lying on the daybed as his brother slept on the floor, that Michael did these things to him.

"That would have been Friday, the nineteenth?" the trooper asked.

"Then again, Saturday," added Joey, "on the first day of summer."

That stopped Kuhn short for a minute. "It *was* the first day of summer on Saturday, wasn't it?" he mused out loud. "The longest day of the year." The things kids remember, he thought.

On Friday night, Joey went on, he and his brother Billy had slept over on Ramos's bus.

"When he put his pee-pee up your butt, this was Friday night?" Kuhn was trying to cement the order of things in his head.

"Yes," replied David.

"And then on Saturday?"

"Yes."

"How many times did this happen in all?" asked the trooper, and Joey spent a moment doing the math, an addition problem in his head.

"Five," he finally said.

"Five times?"

"Okay." Joey scrunched up his face and splayed out his hands as if he were trying to break it down for this man who wasn't understanding. "Two times-es on Friday and three times-es on Saturday."

Three times on Saturday, thought Kuhn, the longest day of the year. Five times in two days.

"Who else was there on the bus, besides you, your brother, and this man Michael?" the trooper asked.

"Oh, Jesse James was there too," said Joey. "The dog."

Through the session, Joey's parents sat immobile, arms crossed, looking tautly controlled, almost blank, as though they were either dazed, wildly defending against any feeling, or trying to contain their rage. Joey himself appeared remarkably straightforward and unself-conscious. The only signs he might be ruffled were the occasional swing of his arms to grip the chair behind him. The boy really only hesitated once during the entire line of questioning.

"Did you do anything to Michael?" Trooper Kuhn asked Joey.

"He turned around," answered Joey, "and he said, stick your pee-pee up my butt."

"And did you?"

It was just a brief pause, but then Joey nodded, answering in what was almost a question.

"Um...yes?"

"Just tell the truth," Kuhn prompted gently.

Joey's mother added, "Don't be afraid." She patted him awkwardly on the shoulder.

"Don't be afraid," Kuhn repeated, relieved to hear the mother respond so calmly. "It's not your fault."

Kuhn had worked dozens of these cases, and parents sometimes reacted badly when they heard this part of the story. Co-opting the victim into his own seduction was the favorite tactic of a clever pedophile. Complicity begets self-recrimination begets silence. There was no way to know for sure whether the Taylors would take this boy home and beat the crap out of him outside the presence of the law, but Kuhn doubted it. These two seemed typical of the Rainbows he'd come across—earnest folk, rough around the edges, but with their heart in the right place. They'd clearly been easy prey. The Taylors told Kuhn how Ramos had come to their bus the night before he was chased out. He was already talking of leaving, but he was stuck.

"He had no gas," Cherie explained, "so my kids went out and got him some, and they gave him some money that they had."

"Your kids gave him money?" Kuhn was amazed at the man's audacity.

"Yeah," said Joe. "He asked them to go out and hustle him money and he sent 'em out to get gas."

When Kuhn explained to the parents that Joey would have to testify if the case moved forward, Joe Taylor looked determined. He didn't know where they were going after the Gathering, maybe to Maine—they'd heard the coast was beautiful; or up to Woodstock, to help friends build a house. They were going to look for someplace nice to put the kids in school come fall. But wherever they were, he said, they would bring the boy back when he was needed, no matter what.

Cherie Taylor provided the numbers of two relatives who could keep them in touch and assured Kuhn they'd check in with him before they left the area when the Gathering ended. Then he ran the license plate numbers the Shanti Sena had given him, and came up with a Florida address, date of birth, and Social Security number for Jose Antonio Ramos. With all this information, a vivid description of their suspect and his bus, Kuhn told the Rainbows he was optimistic.

"We're going to send this all out," he said to Joe and Cherie Taylor. "He's got a twenty-four-hour head start, so he could be back in New York or halfway to Florida by now. But if he hasn't left his bus, we'll get him. The way you describe that thing, it's like he's driving a blimp down the road. He's going to be noticed wherever he goes."

———

Jose Ramos hadn't gone far. When he and his teenage passenger had left the Gathering a day earlier, he'd cut south on country roads heading for I-80, the east-west interstate that divides Pennsylvania. East would be a straight shot to New York, west led across the border first to Ohio, where his young companion lived, and then I-80 could take him all the way to San Francisco, if he wanted to get that far away. But maybe his bad karma was finally catching up to him, because Jose Ramos made it no farther than the entrance ramp to I-80 at Shippenville, Pennsylvania, when his engine sputtered, then died, and he was forced to veer off into an adjacent parking area. The teen hitchhiked away, leaving Ramos behind, stuck in his bus through the night and the next day. He hadn't made it twenty miles from the Gathering.

Carl Reese owned the Exxon station that looked out onto the I-80 entrance ramp. From his front window he could see the blue school bus sitting idle most of the day, and watched with distaste as the ragged man picked his way across the road to Reese's cramped gas station office. Reese liked to say to anyone who'd listen that he'd served four years in the Navy defending this country in 'Nam, and then returned home to find it overrun by lowlifes, like the one now walking into his garage. Greasy hair pulled back into a ponytail, pockmarked face covered in a full beard. Even if Reese had known that Jose Ramos was a Navy man too, it wouldn't have made any difference to him. People who went around looking—and smelling—like that showed no respect, and didn't deserve any in return. Creeps, is what Reese always called them.

"Hey man," the creep said. "Can I get the key to your bathroom? I'll be quick."

"Sorry. Out of order." Reese would have lied about it, but he didn't have to. The electricity was cut so the pump wasn't working. But the man didn't want to take no for an answer.

"C'mon," he kept saying. "I've got my own toilet paper. I really need to get in there."

Like a little kid who thinks he's right and won't listen to logic, Reese thought, the man kept pushing the same line, until he finally gave up and went back across to his bus, where he sat for the next several hours.

———

Later that afternoon, Joey Taylor's parents took him to be examined at the local clinic, after Trooper Blaine Kuhn explained to them that he was turning the case over to the state police in the next county, who technically had jurisdiction of Heart's Content.

The Warren State Police responded to Kuhn's call by dispatching a regional "Uniscope" with a physical description of Jose Antonio Ramos, his distinctive bus, and the numbers of its Florida license plate. The computerized message went out at 5:06 p.m.

Patrol cars in twenty-six counties heard "Be on the lookout..." and Blaine Kuhn was right about the blimp effect. When the BOLO came over his radio, State Trooper Franklin Wills was less than a quarter of a mile from where he'd seen a bus matching that exact description earlier in the day. The trooper simply swung his patrol car around the highway and pulled into the parking area. The bus was still sitting there. At 5:09 p.m. word came back from the Shippenville barracks that the suspect had been spotted and police were in pursuit. Wills pulled up perpendicular to the bus's front windshield and nudged the patrol car's front door open, drawing his service revolver to point through the small space created by the doorjamb.

The driver of the bus appeared at the top of the stairs, but Wills didn't register a physical description, his attention drawn instead to the full-size Akita the man held on a short leash. The dog was harder to target than the man and could do more damage.

"You let go of that leash," Wills warned the man and waved his gun to show his intent, "and I'll kill the dog first. Then I'll kill you."

Jose Ramos didn't say a word, just lay down on the ground, clutching the leash tightly. Both man and dog were taken into custody in the Shippenville barracks. The bus was towed to the impound lot there, and the dog, Jesse James, was sent to Orphans of the Storm, a local animal shelter. Jose Ramos sat in the local jail until he was transported up to Warren County later that night. There he was charged with involuntary deviate sexual intercourse, statutory rape, and indecent assault, and held on $50,000 bail.

It was after midnight when Ramos was shown to his eight-by-ten single-bunk cell in the Warren County jail. With the same disconnected affect he'd shown in the Shanti Sena Council in Michigan, he didn't seem to understand his predicament. All he could talk about was how the dog was worth thousands of dollars and they'd better be taking good care of it; how miserable the day had been, first stuck for hours in a broken-down bus and now this; and how he needed his bus back, because it was the only home he had. Ramos had no way of knowing that he'd never see his dog again, that the day spent sitting by the highway with no place to defecate would be his last day of freedom in a long time. He wouldn't need his bus anymore. He'd found a new home.

> Mr. Ramos noted that Joey pulled his penis out of his pants first, and then pulled his pants down....Mr. Ramos also fondled Joey throughout, and at one point during this contact, told Joey he wanted to stop but could not. Mr. Ramos reports that Joey stated to him that it was okay and that he did not mind this contact....Mr. Ramos claims that at no time the child seemed hurt or upset by this action, and in fact appeared to enjoy this.
> —Interview with Perpetrator by John Bowler, Associate Director, Forest/Warren County Children and Youth Services, June 26, 1986

Three days into Jose Ramos's jail stay, John Bowler came to see him about Joey Taylor. Bowler was a supervisor at the county's child protective services, and this interview was not part of the criminal investigation, but for a parallel, civil complaint of child abuse automatically triggered because the alleged crime involved a minor. As a social worker, Bowler's job was not to determine guilt, but to safeguard the child. He was simply there to investigate whether abuse had occurred and whether Ramos could be defined as a caretaker, someone whom the parents had entrusted with their child. Because he wasn't a law enforcement officer, Bowler wasn't required to read Ramos his Miranda rights and he didn't. In fact, he reassured his subject at the outset that he couldn't incriminate himself. Bowler just wanted to understand what had happened, he explained, in order to seek help and treatment for the victim—maybe even for the alleged perpetrator himself.

After a first few defensive moments, Ramos relaxed and startled the counselor by making a rambling, full confession, clearly stating that he had sexually molested Joey Taylor. But, he maintained, Joey had initiated all sexual contact, had been unharmed, and had even enjoyed it. Joey's parents, Ramos explained, were either alcoholics or drug addicts, and left their children unattended and vulnerable, so they were clearly responsible for their son's misfortune. It was at the Rainbow Gatherings, Ramos said, that he was first made aware of his "problem with sexual addiction," when he'd watched young boys "exposing themselves." He made this claim despite a handful of prior arrests for child abuse crimes. It was a textbook case of "blame the victim."

As Bowler listened and took notes, he considered which of the two standard categories Ramos fit into as a child molester. "Situational," or "regressed" molesters can successfully carry on adult sexual relationships, but simply put, they will take whatever they can get. Often emotionally immature themselves and with low self-esteem, they turn to children sexually as relief from stress in other parts of their lives. Their victims often appear post-pubescent; a childlike countenance is less of the appeal to this type, like the adult who hits on his fifteen-year-old stepdaughter because his wife doesn't understand him, and the teen is around and willing, especially after he plies her with drugs or alcohol. Some of these characteristics fit Ramos's emerging profile, but Bowler knew that the two types overlapped, and he saw Ramos more as a fixated molester, the second of the two categories.

"Fixated" or "preference" child molesters are sexually attracted exclusively to prepubescent children. Often they're drawn to a particular type—nothing will do for them but a narrow age range, a certain look. Fixated molesters are much more likely to see themselves as unfairly misjudged

victims themselves; victims of their own troubled childhood, the bad hand
fate has drawn them, their own uncontrollable urges. The fixated molester
identifies himself with his child victim, sees himself on equal footing, no
different, for example, than the five-year-old "lover" who "wanted it as much
as me." A fixated molester typically sets out to woo his victim, seducing him
into behavior that doesn't necessarily feel bad, at least not at first, and that
might even feel very good. Often such young victims don't have feelings
of guilt and trauma until they grow older and come to realize what they'd
been led to do. The very fact that it feels good can cause damage in itself,
and leads to self-condemnation and self-loathing. It didn't surprise Bowler
to hear Ramos describe his MO of first performing the sexual acts on his
victim before asking for the return favor. Bowler didn't necessarily believe
Ramos's version of the order of things, but if it were true, pleasuring Joey
had almost certainly been a deliberate ploy.

> The perpetrator admits to sexually assaulting the child in several fash-
> ions, including fondling, oral sex, anal sex.
> —*Interview by John Bowler, June 26, 1986*

John Bowler took his notes in the most clinical fashion possible as he
listened to Ramos talk about raping Joey Taylor. Bowler often heard this
kind of frank talk in his work. There was nothing extraordinary about the
graphic language, the laundry list of perverse acts. But the counselor was
struck by Ramos's relish. Bowler left the jail with one clear thought that
stayed with him for over twenty years: that Jose Ramos was a very dangerous man. He knew from both his training and experience that there were
really only two ways a pedophile would stop targeting children: if he felt true
remorse or if he thought the consequences of getting caught were not worth
the risk of repeating the act. Bowler didn't think Ramos had ever considered
either thought. The counselor was convinced Ramos would hunt down and
molest kids for the rest of his life.

Later, Bowler checked in with his friend State Trooper Dan Portzer.
Their paths regularly intersected on cases, and when Bowler told Portzer
about the interview, the trooper immediately obtained a copy of the report.
The confession would be a mainstay of the case against Ramos. Portzer was
a twenty-four-year veteran of the Pennsylvania State Police, a quiet, even shy,
but diligent investigator. Cases involving kids were often directed his way,

because of his gentle manner with the young victims. He was the officer who'd gone down to Shippenville and brought Ramos up to be charged in Warren, and was now assigned to follow up.

In the days immediately following Ramos's arrest, Trooper Portzer went to great lengths to track any leads. He pulled Ramos's rap sheet and sent word to police in Miami, New Orleans, and New York, where the man had priors—both to alert them and to help build his case. New York advised that they had no outstanding warrants on Jose Antonio Ramos, although a man with the same birthday but no other relationship to Ramos *was* wanted. Portzer wouldn't learn for years that New York City detectives and FBI agents had been interested in Ramos since at least the year before, when AUSA Stuart GraBois had taken on the Patz case.

Trooper Portzer got little else back on his inquiries, although he did hear an account of a Florida woman whom Ramos had conned into buying the bus, putting it in his name. Ramos, his friend, and her two children had then driven to Washington, D.C., where he'd dropped her and the kids off, told her he was going to park the bus, and was never seen again.

Portzer also interviewed Cherie and Joe Taylor and asked the Rainbows to search out any other families at the encampment whose children might have come in contact with Ramos. When Portzer met with the Taylors the following Saturday at the temporary command post the state police had set up at the Gathering itself, he was introduced to Serena Landry and her live-in boyfriend, Brian. The couple had driven several hours to the Gathering from Erie, hard in the northwest corner of Pennsylvania. They'd come without Serena's five- and nine-year-old sons, who'd flatly refused to attend any more Gatherings. "No more crazy Rainbows," the two boys had said, and when pressed, they'd finally revealed why.

The man they knew as Michael might be there, the boys told their mother, and they didn't want to see him. Michael had come to stay with them after the previous one in Missouri, the Landrys' very first Gathering. He was welcomed by the whole family, who'd all enjoyed hanging out with him in Missouri, and he was given a place to stay in the basement bedroom for a few weeks. He'd cooked and run errands, taken the boys fishing, and then he'd touched them in ways they didn't like. It didn't hurt, and he didn't force them when they wouldn't do it back. But when he rubbed them through their clothing, it felt bad, even though Michael said it wasn't. He must have known what he was doing was wrong, though, because he'd told both five-year-old Jake and nine-year-old Jason he'd kill them if anyone found out.

Both boys took the threat seriously and kept the secret for months, although in retrospect their distraught mother realized they'd shown typical signs. One had become less outgoing, while the other grew more hostile to authority figures. When it was time for another Rainbow event, they finally spoke up, but Ramos was long gone from their home, with no way to track him. Serena and Brian dropped the boys off with their grandparents and went alone to the Pennsylvania Gathering, planning to look for Ramos and to spread the word, but when they learned about the Taylor incident, they offered to do more.

"We'll press charges, too," they told Trooper Portzer, "anything to help." When they returned home to Erie three weeks later, they did as Portzer had instructed and contacted state police there, who charged Jose Ramos with corruption of a minor and indecent assault.

The Erie County charges—which were both misdemeanors and, therefore, lesser counts than the two felony charges for the rape of Joey Taylor in Warren County—would nonetheless turn out to be critical. Both cases were moving forward toward trial in the fall of 1986. But while the Erie case proceeded in a straightforward manner, Ramos's surefire confession to John Bowler in Warren ran off the rails. The judge had ruled in favor of Ramos's public defender's motion to suppress the confession on the grounds that as a social worker John Bowler had acted as an arm of the state and state policy should have dictated that he read Ramos his Miranda rights.

Unfortunately, the Warren County prosecutor had built his case around that confession, believing that although Joey Taylor's parents had left contact numbers and assurances they'd return as needed, an eight-year-old's testimony was not the slam dunk a confession would be. As the Warren County district attorney filed an appeal against the suppression of his key evidence with the Superior Court in Harrisburg, it looked like the case would drag on well into 1987.

In January 1987, the Landry trial against Jose Ramos began in Erie, Pennsylvania. The older of the two victims was now living out west with his father, but the Erie district attorney had no problems relying on his younger brother as his star witness. Then-six-year-old Jake Landry took the stand in a one-day trial and testified about Ramos fondling him the previous summer. Ramos's lawyer tried to discredit his testimony, saying a child that young couldn't possibly be reliable. Jake Landry didn't waver, and told the jury how Ramos threatened his life. Ramos himself testified, denying everything, so that in the end it became nothing more than a "he said/he said" between a six-year-old and an alleged pedophile.

After less than an hour of deliberation, the jury concluded that Jose Ramos had perjured himself and found him guilty on both counts, corruption of a minor and indecent assault. He was sentenced to a total of three and a half to seven years, his first real prison time ever. It was a victory for the Rainbows. But as Jose Ramos was processed into the Pennsylvania State Correctional Institute at Rockview in May 1987, they were still waiting for final resolution in the Warren County case against Ramos for the rape of Joey Taylor.

———

Ramos had been arguing all along that the Commonwealth of Pennsylvania had no right to commandeer his bus and personal belongings, but once he started serving time on the Erie sentence, the bus became abandoned property. In early June 1987, state police made plans to dispose of the vehicle, and inventoried its contents. There were sixty-six items on the list, including one pair of Pony gym shoes, one pair of jeans, one T-shirt, and underwear (listed as dirty). It was all considered junk, and the troopers called Himes Sales and Auto Wrecking to take everything away for disposal.

Himes Sales had a new owner, Carl Reese, who remembered Jose Ramos well from their meeting off the interstate exactly one year earlier, when Ramos had come into his Exxon station asking to use the men's room. I knew he was a creep, Reese thought, when he learned what had happened to the man since then.

Reese and one of his workers, Tim Reitz, towed the bus to the salvage yard and cleaned it out, sweeping the refuse into a burn pile in one corner of the lot. Reese had Reitz crawl around inside, dumping things out of the back of the bus, which was overrun with vermin and filth. Reitz gathered together a pile of small plastic toys, still pristine in their cellophane wrappings, and he and his boss speculated about Ramos's devious intentions. Reitz pocketed a handful to give to his mother, who collected such trinkets for her annual Easter egg hunt. Better to do some good with them, he thought. This guy sure has no use for Darth Vader action figures anytime soon.

But just a few months later the Rainbows were angered to learn their children wouldn't be safe from Ramos for as long as they'd hoped. In October, nearly a year after the Warren judge had ruled to suppress Ramos's confession, the Superior Court of Pennsylvania upheld the judge's decision. Ramos's admission to John Bowler that he'd had sex with Joey Taylor could not be used as evidence. Trooper Dan Portzer and the other state police who'd worked on the case saw the ruling as a travesty of justice. After months of hard work they watched a known predator, who in no uncertain terms had confessed to his crime, beat the system on a technicality.

Two weeks after the Pennsylvania Superior Court's decision, Warren County district attorney Rick Hernan moved to drop the prosecution altogether. He didn't feel confident he could rely solely on victim testimony, and bringing the Rainbows back to Warren from across the country would tax his limited budget. Besides, Ramos was already locked up on the Erie case. Trooper Dan Portzer chafed at the decision, but his own hands were tied.

When Jose Ramos got the news, however, he was ecstatic. He was now free and clear of the outstanding felony charges, and his earliest release date was less than two years away.

"This is God's way of showing me that prayer works," he wrote that night.

———

Over the months, the Taylors had moved around, staying with different friends and relatives. Everyone could see the difference in both Taylor boys. Joey had always been the slower, softer, sweeter of the two, but now he was shutting down, becoming withdrawn and defensive. In their naturally affectionate family, Joey stopped giving and receiving hugs. His younger brother Billy, who'd been the more outgoing and exuberant of the two, had become angry and hostile toward Joey. You're a fag, Billy would say derisively, in the cruel way of children who want to distance themselves from possible contamination. The other kids soon echoed Billy's taunts, and Joey suffered in silence. He went from A's and B's in school to D's and F's, and he woke up sweating from nightmares that Ramos was coming to hurt him.

The children weren't the only ones affected. Cherie and Joe Sr. fought over his increased drinking, and Cherie's health suffered too. Bouts of depression exacerbated her physical problems, and the family sunk further into the debt brought on by her growing medical bills. They called the DA's Office periodically about the status of the case, but at first were put off, and then one day they were told it had been dropped. Angry and demoralized, they felt betrayed. This is a hard lesson, the parents told each other, about what happens when you try to play by the rules.

CHAPTER 13

Help from All Over

NOTES—Etan Patz

1. License plate 36806—AEL or ABI belongs to a Yonkers man. . . .
3. Doesn't think Etan is living—sees skeletal remains in shallow water. . . .
7. Sees a buoy or navigational aid—#19—red with white flag or light—body or remains is near area.
   —*Bill Sillery's notes on Denise Cealie's visions*

Bill Sillery was just finishing up with the commanding officer at NYPD's Missing Persons. He'd been in meetings all day, as he usually was on these frequent road trips, and he wanted nothing better than to start back to Albany. If he left right now and caught the 4:30 train he'd make it home by seven. He wasn't sure if he should even bring this last bit of business up. What the hell, he thought, I'll probably regret it later if I don't.

In late 1987, William J. Sillery had been working for the state government more than fifteen years, and was head of both the New York State Missing and Exploited Children Clearinghouse as well as Criminal History Operations and Special Operations. He looked the part—conservative dresser, short, neatly groomed graying hair, the appearance of a responsible professional administrator, who after a long career now oversaw three programs and a staff of more than a hundred. Just now, though, he found himself shifting uneasily in his seat. He knew what he was about to say would undoubtedly raise eyebrows.

"I've got this bizarre thing that happened a while back, some information that came to me from a rather unorthodox source, and quite frankly, I don't know what to do with it, but I don't feel right just sitting on it. It's about the Etan Patz case."

Detective Al Doyle perked up. Everyone in Missing Persons knew all too well about the Patz case. Sillery told his story, about hearing from a cop he respected and dealt with regularly at one of the police departments upstate. This cop had passed on a letter from a woman who said she was a medium. A good friend of hers had done some valuable work for the department and sent her to them.

"Hundreds of psychics have taken a crack at the Patz case," the detective said, laughing. "Every one of them has a different story and they all contradict each other."

Sillery repeated what the woman had told him when they'd first spoken a few months earlier. "She's not just any kind of psychic. She's a medium. It's different. I'm not saying I believe in all this, but mediums supposedly communicate with people on the other side. It's a different skill set." He knew that would get a look, but he forged ahead.

"I know, I know, it sounds crazy; that's what I thought too, but just listen."

Sillery told Doyle of the mysterious clues the letter contained—about Etan being taken somewhere in a cab, about skeletal remains buried in shallow water near where two bridges could be clearly seen. The writer saw a license plate with very distinct numbers, the name "East Park," and a navigation buoy in some kind of water marked by the number 19 and a red-and-white flag. The letter said a body or its remains would be found there.

The letter had also listed this medium's phone contact, so he'd called her, a young woman named Denise Cealie. Sillery introduced himself and told her he wanted to know more. He didn't know what to believe, but he was willing to listen with an open mind. If nothing else, he found the whole topic fascinating, and of course he'd followed the Patz case over the last eight years.

Cealie explained that she both saw things and sometimes heard voices. They came to her mostly at night, she said, not full conversations, just cryptic phrases that weren't spoken so much as they appeared, kind of like jigsaw puzzle pieces, leaving her to fit them together on her own. Her information had come solely from the voices at first, until one day she'd actually heard from Etan himself, introduced to her by a boy she'd known growing up, who'd died as a child.

She knew how it sounded, and she'd heard horror stories of people like her who approached the cops with this kind of information. She didn't want to cold-call the NYPD. She wasn't even sure she wanted to tell anyone. But she also felt like a witness, and if she'd seen a person murdered in her backyard, she'd have certainly felt obliged to report it.

"If someone can take this further," she'd told Sillery matter-of-factly, "great. If not, then at least I've passed it on."

Other than the topic of conversation, Sillery thought she'd come across like a perfectly straightforward, sane person. He was curious about the clues she'd provided. He wondered if the number 19 referred to some kind of marker. Sillery took notes, and then, with a great deal of skepticism, he did some follow-up research on his own. He called around looking for navigational maps and finally spoke with the Coast Guard's Office of Navigation. Was there a buoy or navigational aid in the water with such a flag or number? Yes, the woman said after checking, we have one aid numbered 19, a light structure in the East River off Astoria, Queens, not far from Hallett's Point. Intrigued to learn he'd found his buoy in New York City waters, he spoke to someone at the city's Parks and Recreation Department and asked about "East Park." There was an East River Park several miles farther down, on the Lower East Side of Manhattan, running along the FDR Drive and under the Williamsburg Bridge.

Sillery looked at the two detectives. "And here's the wildest part. Hallett's Point, where the number 19 light structure is? It overlooks a particular area in the water that's got a hell of a lot of history. Literally. It's a narrow channel where hundreds of ships have sunk over the centuries. You've got tides hitting each other from at least three different directions, and together they can wreak havoc. It's called Hell Gate."

"Hold on," Doyle said, and he picked up the phone. He talked to someone for a few minutes, then hung up.

"Stu GraBois's sending his people over to get you," he said. "He'd like to meet you." Two men appeared soon afterwards and Sillery was escorted to One St. Andrew's Plaza.

By late 1987, along with a full, unrelated caseload, Stuart GraBois had been working the Patz case for over two years, and within New York law enforcement circles the two names were usually mentioned in the same sentence. He cast the net as wide as he could for new leads, and lobbied aggressively for support. At cocktail parties, he was wont to corner anyone with the resources to help his cause. He would stop at nothing. No matter whom Bill Sillery might have approached with Denise Cealie's information, they probably would have picked up the phone to call Stu GraBois.

And it wasn't just the Patz case that made people turn to GraBois. Over the last several years, federal interest in sex crimes in general, and child exploitation cases in particular, had grown. Interstate travel of abused children, the possibility of linked networks; child porn mailed cross-country through the U.S. postal system; these cases were all getting more scrutiny. Within the Southern District of New York, the uptick of new cases was being funneled to GraBois, because of his experience in the Patz case. Eventually, he was asked to oversee all the cases generated by the Sexual Exploitation of Children Task Force, a joint venture between New York police and the FBI that also called on the U.S. Marshals, the Customs Service, and the Postal Inspection Service.

Now GraBois was learning about heinous crimes he'd never before even conceived of. Earlier that year, he'd prosecuted a New Jersey man whose victims were infants as young as *four months*. The crimes against such small victims so appalled him that GraBois had gone at his defendant particularly hard, asking for the absolute max after the man had pled out. And in one sense the defendant got the max. He shot himself the week before sentencing, and left a lengthy note blaming GraBois's tough stance.

"I'm assuming prosecution will not be proceeding with this case," said the judge at the subsequent court hearing where the defense moved to dismiss.

"That depends, Your Honor," GraBois answered coolly. "I need to see proof first. Does defense have a coroner's report?" He had no sympathy for the defendant—and he wanted to be sure the man wasn't pulling a scam.

GraBois had also heard plenty of far-fetched stories like Bill Sillery's. Soon after he'd finished with the baby molester, the prosecutor and one of his investigators had even flown to Chicago to hear from an institutionalized woman with multiple personality disorder who claimed she'd witnessed her father sacrificing Etan in a ritualistic cult murder. Although none of her personalities would speak to him when he got there, GraBois comforted himself with the knowledge that at this point, anyone with information on the case knew he was the one to call—even someone who was hearing it from the great beyond.

"What do you mean, she has information?" GraBois asked Sillery now.

The man didn't seem like a wacko, but he'd have him checked out before going much further, just on the basis of how seriously he was taking this woman's claims. "She *thinks* she has information, or she has firsthand information?"

"She's got this vision in her head of a place somewhere on the water, and you can see two bridges from this location. Somewhere, on a pier or breakwall, she sees the number 7 or 8. She thinks Etan is buried right under there." Sillery talked about Hell Gate and described other tidbits Cealie had offered up: the mental pictures that Etan's killer was a cab driver who drove him from the point of pickup to an unknown location. That he'd already been interviewed by the police, and that she thought the letter M—a name sounding like Michelob—connected the man significantly. The remains, either a body or bones, would be found in a location strewn with garbage, including some kind of shirt, all of which was near shallow water. She saw a wooden post or stick in the ground, too, and some kind of hook. Sillery read off a long list of observations. It sounded like the typical "one from column a, one from column b" psychic list where odds were good that something amid all the details would pay off.

GraBois listened to the account and immediately presumed either Denise Cealie was a quack or she must somehow be involved in the kidnapping, either explicitly or indirectly. Maybe she wanted to get it off her chest, and had come up with this tactic. If, on the other hand, she really thought she was getting her information from across the great divide, well, GraBois had been approached by psychics in the past, and he usually dismissed them out of hand. He'd found they often had their own agendas and were searching less for lost children and more for legitimacy by affiliating themselves with reputable law enforcement. But he wanted to know more, especially since Sillery had bothered to do such intriguing follow-up.

Over the next week, GraBois did his own research, using contacts in Albany to check out Bill Sillery. The man was in good standing, a career government man with no crackpot history. Now GraBois wanted to learn about the area Denise Cealie was describing. Could such a location exist? He had to narrow it down from the entire length of the Hell Gate channel and a vague mental image of two bridges. He talked it over with a fellow prosecutor down the hall one day, his friend Louis Freeh.

Freeh put on his coat. "Let's go across the street and talk to Jim. He'll have some ideas."

James Kallstrom ran the FBI's Special Operations Division. He was renowned as the guy who once put a bug the size of a quarter under a sofa cushion at mobster John Gotti's favorite hangout, the Ravenite Social Club. Special Ops could not only find the needle in a haystack, but they could then get close enough to hear it confess to a gangland slaying. In Kallstrom's office, Freeh introduced GraBois, who wondered if he'd see some eye-rolling from the small group in the room when the problem was explained, but Kallstrom quickly agreed to send up a plane to take surveillance pictures. Days later, the photos came back with views of the two bridges spanning Hell Gate channel that directly corresponded to Denise Cealie's vision. Spray-painted on one of the bridges was the number 1978. Weird, thought GraBois, shaking his head as he looked at the pictures.

In mid-December, GraBois called up Sillery and asked if he could get Denise Cealie to meet with him in New York. He also arranged to have NYPD detective Al Sheppard there, who was assigned to what had become known as the Devil's Squad. Originally tasked to investigate child porn cases, the squad had morphed into the realm of the occult, which overlapped when pedophilia cases were tied to cults and ritualistic crimes. Sheppard and GraBois had worked together on other child exploitation cases, and the prosecutor asked him to weigh in on Denise Cealie and her special gifts.

A few days before the Christmas break, both Sillery and Cealie took a day off from work and trained down to the U.S. Attorney's Office, where GraBois was able to form his own impressions.

On the short side and a little stocky, Denise Cealie looked to be in her late twenties, with shoulder-length wavy dark brown hair, large, expressive eyes, and a pleasant smile. Neatly attired in dress pants and blouse, she was perfectly "normal"-looking; no tarot cards, incense, or zodiac references. She had no criminal history and was gainfully employed as a special ed schoolteacher. She presented herself well and spoke as an articulate schoolteacher would.

"Start from the beginning," GraBois said simply, "and tell me your story."

Cealie talked of becoming aware of her "gift" as a teenager, that her mother accepted it, her father not at all. For a year or two now, she said, she'd been hearing about Etan, from the voices, then from the boy himself. Sometimes she heard the voices in her head, sometimes out loud. There were also "pictures" that presented themselves, so that she knew what things looked like. And no, she'd known almost nothing about the Patz case when this started, and still didn't. She'd brought notes with her and referred to them as she began to repeat the details she'd already given to Sillery.

GraBois was gracious and took pains to minimize any outward sign of his doubt in her tales from the supernatural, but he peppered her with questions. Who did she know in New York? How often did she come there? Did she have a boyfriend there? How could they verify her statements? He was looking to uncover any tie she might have to the case, but it wasn't immediately apparent.

"Can we get a car?" Cealie finally got the chance to ask her own question. It was getting late and she was itching to move out, to look for the site. And off they went, GraBois and Sillery, Al Sheppard and the medium, in the direction of Hell Gate. GraBois knew where it was in the water, but not how to get there, and they drove across to Brooklyn, then uptown through Queens, until they reached a point in Astoria that looked out over the East River. At Cealie's request, they piled out of the car and regarded a scene that included two bridges spanning the water. One was the Triborough Bridge, connecting the Bronx, Manhattan, and Queens via Ward's Island. The other was a picturesque steel arch railroad bridge named after the Hell Gate channel it rose 135 feet above. At low tide, the channel descended six feet farther and looked more like a glassy lake sheltered from the wind, but when the tides clashed, sparring from the Hudson and East rivers, the Long Island Sound, and the Atlantic Ocean via the Hudson estuary, its name was appropriate. Cealie searched the skyline with a puzzled look.

"Something's not right," she said. "This doesn't look like the picture." Then her face cleared. "We have to cross over," she said.

GraBois was too annoyed to make "crossing over" jokes. He squinted at the sun, estimating no more than a few hours of daylight left, and he wasn't sure where this wild ghost chase was going to end. Cealie was pointing to the other side of the steel span bridge. Ward's Island was a sparsely populated speck on the map, once a pauper burial ground, and still home to a psychiatric institution for the criminally insane. That was where Cealie wanted to take them now.

"In the picture that I see, that bridge is on the left, not the right. We're on the wrong side." The scenery all looked the same to everyone else, snow covering the most distinguishable characteristics, and it was miserably cold. Cealie shrugged her shoulders, they got back in the car, and since they couldn't actually cross the railroad bridge, they had to laboriously work their way around, then across the Triborough Bridge. Once on the other side, Cealie assuredly started to direct them, convincing GraBois she'd been there before, despite her protests to the contrary. She's playing us, he thought, but he let himself be guided to see where they'd end up. They finally approached the southern tip of the island.

"Stop the car!" Cealie screamed suddenly. She was pointing at a chain-link fence that surrounded the outer edges of the land.

"Bill, you need to go over to that fence," she commanded Sillery. He did as she asked, aware that he had no boots, just the dress shoes he'd worn down from Albany. When he got to the fence he could see an embankment to the water's edge, a rocky, muddy scramble from where he stood. He looked back at Cealie and followed her hand as she motioned him down the fenceline to a short section he hadn't noticed where the fence had pulled away to allow access to a narrow path that led precipitously down to the rocks below. Cealie waved him toward the water.

"Go down, go," she yelled, and he carefully picked his way on the almost vertical trail, sliding partway until he reached the bottom, rough stones and gravel that led to the shoreline. He took just a few steps forward before he stopped short, flabbergasted.

He stumbled frantically back up, motioning the others out of the car. GraBois told Cealie to stay back and he and Al Sheppard joined Sillery.

"You've got to see this." He wouldn't say anything more.

Sheppard went down first, as GraBois and Sillery watched him struggle to keep his balance before disappearing down the trail.

"Holy shit, holy shit." GraBois and Sillery heard his epithets and GraBois quickly followed. At the bottom, all three finally stood stock still, taking in the sight. In the background lay a clear view of the two bridges, and closer, the water lapped at the rocky shoreline. But only a few feet directly in front of them stood a makeshift wooden cross. Draped over it, the worn pattern of teddy bears running in a wide strip across its middle, was the tattered remnants of a child's sweater.

"How could she have known this?" Sheppard marveled. "You can't even get to here without risking your neck." The men looked back up the steeply graded hill toward the car now out of sight.

"She's got to know something," GraBois asserted, circling around the cross for a closer look. "Where is she getting her information? It's just too much of a coincidence, and there's no way she could have gotten down this steep of an incline on her own to know about it otherwise."

"Come look at this," Sillery called. He was standing in front of a flat-topped rock covered in graffiti. GraBois peered at it. His mind was racing. He was at a loss for words.

"Does that say 'Prince St. Kid'?" someone asked.

When Cealie was brought down to join them, the others were busy looking around for any more traces that people had been there before them. Sheppard found a plastic bag filled with old clothes. But GraBois was staring at the rock. He just didn't know what to think. There were some battered abandoned cars lying farther down the rocky shore. Was this a dumping ground, and if so, was it a convenient location for the dumping of human remains? Was this a makeshift headstone? And how could Denise Cealie have predicted this?

"Did you know that Etan disappeared from Prince Street?" he asked Cealie.

"No, I didn't."

It was getting dark, and they were all frozen and splattered with mud. GraBois could see through the dim light that the woman was shivering. They still needed to sidestep their way back up the narrow incline and drive all the way down the length of Manhattan to GraBois's office. He would have to arrange for photographs.

"We're going to need you back here in New York again." He had a lot more questions for her now.

"It'll have to be after Christmas," she replied, and he nodded.

"This time we'll fly you down," he added.

———

There was no way around it. They would need a polygraph, for many reasons, not the least of which was that GraBois wasn't going to get anyone to authorize a dime spent on Denise Cealie's information first. But they couldn't let her know in advance. GraBois gave Bill Sillery a heads-up, so he wouldn't be taken by surprise, but made him promise not to say anything. Sillery and Cealie arrived in New York the first week of January, and Cealie showed no qualms about going off with the FBI agent as soon as she walked in the door. I expected as much, she told everyone. She was gone for what seemed like hours, while the others speculated endlessly about what was really going on. When the agent returned without her, he looked a little taken aback.

"She passed," he said. "She appears to be telling the truth."

"Can she have figured out a way to fool the polygraph?" GraBois wondered.

"These are highly sensitive systems," the man said, "but they're designed to pick up deception. If the subject truly believes he or she is telling the truth, they can pass, even if they're spinning out-and-out lies. So this woman believes she's a medium and has this gift. Whether she does…" He shrugged.

GraBois didn't have the answer to that, but at this point he couldn't afford not to believe that Denise Cealie might somehow know there were remains buried where she said. That's how he found himself on the next day, on a below-zero morning, stamping his feet and wincing as he sucked the icy air into his lungs. With the Hell Gate Bridge as dramatic backdrop, Gra-Bois, Cealie, and Sillery watched as the NYPD divers adjusted masks and submerged themselves in the frigid waters off the Ward's Island shoreline. Because of the temperature, the men could only stay down for a few minutes at a stretch before they were forced to surface and warm up at a nearby dive truck. Bundled into his heavy jeans and blue down parka, the hood pulled snugly around his ears, GraBois was still freezing and couldn't imagine how the divers could force themselves into the water. But he heard no grumbling as the officers prepared to go back under. Denise Cealie feared they couldn't help but miss the right spot, because they needed to wait until later in the year, when the shoreline receded in the spring. After repeated dives and what seemed like an eternity in the deep winter weather, a sampling of bones was recovered, but when later tested, they proved to be animal remains. Searchers returned days later to dig up long trenches in a wide swath around the cross site. Again, nothing. It all proved a futile exercise, just one more chapter in the long and storied case. But ultimately, as these things often happen, the voices from beyond inadvertently set off a chain of events and led to the most fruitful development in the case to date.

Joe Veltre, a supervisor in the Federal Probation Office, was an old friend of Stuart GraBois's. He and GraBois had known each other for years, and he was one of the legion who would stop by from time to time to fan the prosecutor's heated interest in the Patz case. What's new, he'd ask, and then sit back while GraBois thought out loud, hashing through the latest piece of the puzzle together. Veltre was a good listener and made helpful suggestions whenever he could. When he could lend a hand with a little extra fact-finding, GraBois was always happy to let him. He would take all the help he could get.

The license plate number Denise Cealie had envisioned did in fact turn out to be a registered plate, but it had been reissued more than once. By this point, GraBois had stopped caring about where the medium got her information, he just knew it needed to be checked out. Maybe Cealie *was* trying to signal she really knew someone with a car who'd been involved in the kidnapping. Or maybe bigger forces were trying to tell him something. Cealie had also envisioned an Hispanic man and Veltre was on the trail, looking for the particular Hispanic man to whom the plate number had been registered. Veltre had invested considerable time in the project, his own time, just like all the other cops and government officials who volunteered their experience and insights gratis.

Veltre was in GraBois's office one day with the latest results of his search, and he picked up some of GraBois's case material lists, leafing casually through them.

"Who's this Jose Ramos character? What's his story?" Veltre asked the prosecutor.

"Yeah, he's always been interesting to me. He dated the babysitter, but it looks like it was so he could get to her four-year-old son," GraBois replied, looking over Veltre's shoulder.

"Have you ever talked to him?"

"Don't know where he is. He's a transient; went to ground before I got the case, and no one's seen him for years."

Veltre wrote down Jose Ramos's name and date of birth. "I'll nose around a little and see if I can find anything." He knew a lot of people, who in turn knew a lot of people. "Have your guys run a rap sheet on him? I'll take a look."

"Let me check the files, and I'll get it to you." GraBois started toward one of the cabinets where he stored his paperwork.

Veltre waved him off. "Don't bother. I'll just run it again."

He called GraBois a few days later. The excitement in his voice was palpable.

Etan with Julie Patz in their home, at his sixth birthday party, October 29, 1978. (©Patz Imaging)

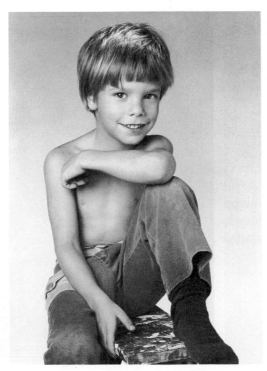

Etan perches on a ladder to approximate the proper height as he sits in for a professional model yet to arrive at his father's photography studio. Stan Patz is later horrified to learn some found the photo salacious and suspicious.

(©Patz Imaging)

In March 1982 New York City police arrest drifter Jose Antonio Ramos, after a young boy accuses him of trying to lure the boy into the Bronx drainpipe where Ramos had been living. Charges are later dropped, but this is the first time a public connection is made between Ramos and the Patz case. (ABC NEWS/PRIMETIME)

When Jose Ramos is questioned by the Bronx DA's office after his 1982 drainpipe arrest, he tells Asssistant DA Frank Carroll that at the time of Etan's disappearance, he'd been dating a woman who looked after the boy.

Assistant U.S. Attorney Stuart GraBois and FBI Special Agent Ken Ruffo travel to Israel in October 1985 to investigate the appearance there of a mysterious photo of Etan. (STUART GRABOIS)

The converted school bus where Jose Ramos lured at least one young victim in 1986 sits abandoned today in a western Pennsylvania salvage yard. (LISA R. COHEN)

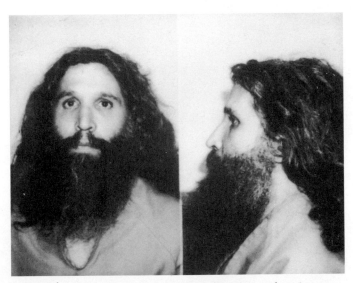

Jose Ramos mug shot following his Pennsylvania arrest and rape charge involving eight-year-old Joey Taylor, June 24, 1986.

Based on a medium's vision, in January 1988 NYPD divers search the frigid water of New York's East River for Etan Patz's remains. (WILLIAM J. SILLERY)

Bill Sillery, Denise Cealie, and Stuart GraBois huddle in the cold as the NYPD searches the Ward's Island shoreline, January 1988. (WILLIAM J. SILLERY)

PA Special Prosecutor/AUSA Stuart GraBois and PA Chief Deputy Attorney General Marylou Barton walk to court for Jose Ramos's sentencing in Warren, PA, November 29, 1990. (ABC NEWS/PRIMETIME)

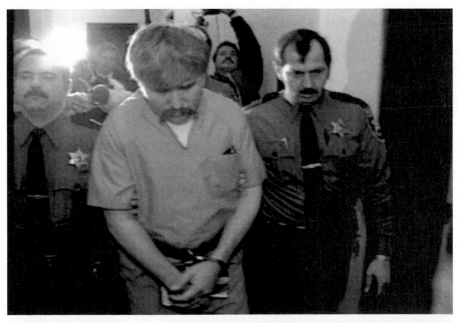

A furious Jose Ramos is trailed by the press as he is led from the Pennsylvania courtroom after being sentenced on November 29, 1990. (ABC NEWS/PRIMETIME)

Assistant U.S. Attorney Stuart GraBois works the Patz case from his New York office in May 1991, while from the Otisville federal prison, his planted inmate informants report to him on their progress. (ABC NEWS/PRIMETIME)

Julie Patz poses proudly with Lev Sviridov at his middle school graduation, June 1993. (FROM L. SVIRIDOVA FAMILY ARCHIVE)

Stan Patz is interviewed on *60 Minutes II*, May 2000. "He's a predator," he says, describing Jose Ramos. "And he should never be allowed to be near children again." (CBS NEWS ARCHIVES)

"I found him," he told GraBois. "Jose Ramos is in." It was much easier to track someone down who had a prison address.

Between the time investigators had last come up blank on Ramos's whereabouts and the moment in 1988 when Joe Veltre ran his rap sheet, Jose Ramos had preyed on the Rainbow Family of Living Light, and they had put him somewhere Stuart GraBois could easily get his hands on him. With one look at his rap sheet GraBois could now pinpoint Ramos's exact whereabouts—the State Correctional Institute at Rockview, Pennsylvania.

Veltre brought the sheet over. GraBois saw the Erie misdemeanor sentence, which would hold Ramos in place for at least one more year. But when he turned to the sheet's last page, he saw an entry that interested him just as much. There was another charge, a felony rape, which had been dropped the previous year. The sheet didn't reveal the whole story of Joey Taylor and the suppressed confession, but it raised some interesting questions that bore further research. While the prosecutor immediately began to make plans to writ Ramos into federal custody so the two could meet, he also wanted to know more about the charge that had gotten away.

The next week was exhausting. Knowing that a potentially promising suspect was so close, GraBois began the necessary paperwork to have him brought closer. But that was just part of his workload. In just that week, he appeared in court against a defendant so unruly he had to be carted to his hearing in a wheelbarrow, and questioned a suspect in a grisly sadomasochistic murder involving bondage masks and violent sex games. By Friday, GraBois was grateful for the weekend break, as he left his office early to pick up his family and get back into Manhattan in time for a Passover seder there. He'd been feeling under the weather for a few days, which he credited to his hectic schedule. But by the time he arrived home, he was having searing chest pains and trouble breathing. A trip to the local ER was reassuring—it looked like nothing more than a pulled muscle, and he went on to his holiday meal.

GraBois took it easy that weekend, and would have stayed home Monday morning, but members of his task force were bringing him a suspect to interview. By the time he drove home afterwards, the pain had returned, now so severe he was forced to pull off the road and wait until the worst of it subsided. He made it inside his apartment before collapsing on the living room floor. This time the hospital stay was weeks, not hours, as doctors shook their heads, fed him more antibiotics, and ordered more tests. IVs

laced around his supine body, and an oxygen tube was his lifeline, as his
lungs grew weaker, ravaged by the worst case of double pleurisy his physi-
cian had ever seen. GraBois spent the days in a fog, although he remembered the hospital clergyman leaning over him at one point.

"Get your affairs in order," the man counseled.

Two weeks after he was stricken, doctors tried one last test and discovered the reason he wasn't responding to treatment. It was a rare case of
Legionnaires' disease, contracted either on the icy Ward's Island shoreline,
or from a germ-filled air conditioner in the Syracuse hotel room where he'd
gone the previous month to question a small group of Denise Cealie's fellow mediums. GraBois made steady if slow progress after that, but it would
be two months of bed rest and working from home before he was back in
the office and operating at full capacity. During those months, Jose Ramos
had gotten a brief reprieve. As GraBois was heading to the emergency room,
Ramos was being upgraded to a coveted new status that allowed him to
work outside the prison fence.

"It means that I now have a little more freedom," Ramos wrote to a pen
pal. "Thank God for this."

CHAPTER 14

90 Proof

SUBJECT: MISSING PERSON ETAN PATZ M/W/6
CONTENTS: INTERVIEW OF JOSE ANTONIO RAMOS

1. On this date the undersigned and Detective Cavallo interviewed Jose
    Ramos. Also present at the U.S. Attorney's office where this interview
    was conducted was US Attorney Stuart GraBois....
3. Ramos at the end of the interview slouched down in his chair and
    said he was glad to get this off his chest. He then said that he never
    told this to anyone else.
    —DD5 Report of NYPD Missing Persons detective Robert Shaw,
    June 28, 1990

Stuart GraBois walked into the U.S. Marshals' holding area on the
third floor, four flights down from his office, accompanied by two
NYPD detectives. Three months had passed since GraBois had first looked
at Jose Ramos's rap sheet and learned Ramos was just a writ of habeas corpus away. Now, in late June, GraBois was returned to his full strength; he
was back pitching for the office softball team, and the only remnants of his
near-death encounter with Legionnaires' disease were a lingering shortness
of breath and scar tissue in the lower left quadrant of his lung. As he had
reviewed Ramos's background in the weeks since he'd come back from sick
leave, he'd become increasingly convinced that the pedophile was the biggest potential lead in the Patz case thus far. The previous week, Ramos had
finally entered federal custody, arriving at the Metropolitan Correctional
Center, adjacent to the U.S. Attorney's Office, from Pennsylvania's Rockview state prison.

Normally, the detectives would bring a subject upstairs to a prosecutor waiting in his office, but this time GraBois had come along for the pickup. He was sure he would recognize Ramos immediately, even though the video-tapes he'd been studying all weekend were six-year-old grainy black-and-white VHS, at least a few generations degraded from the originals. He'd pulled the two nondescript tapes, marked simply "Ramos Q&A," out of a file the previous Friday before leaving the office. On the tapes were Bronx ADA Frank Carroll's March 1982 session with Ramos—the one and only time he'd been questioned by a prosecutor about the Patz case—after two boys said he'd tried to entice them inside his drainpipe home. Over and over that weekend, Gra-Bois had hit rewind, scribbled notes, and mulled them over with his social worker wife, Bonnie. Two things in particular had struck him. The first was that on the tape Ramos claimed to have heard voices back in 1979, inner voices that goaded him to violence. "I had to hold it back," Ramos had told Carroll, "'cause I was ready to explode." To GraBois, this predilection to violence was key—Ramos was someone capable of harming a child.

The second revelation on the tape was Ramos's direct connection to the Patz family. Listening to him volunteer that he'd dated a woman who had cared for Etan, GraBois was amazed. Ramos had even claimed on tape that Etan Patz had played with Sandy Harmon's son Bennett, and that Ramos himself babysat for Bennett on numerous occasions. To GraBois, when Ramos said "babysat," it was easily broken code for "molested."

Preparing for today's interview, GraBois had reread the files with new purpose. He'd always known the cops had questioned Ramos back in 1982; that they'd felt they didn't have enough evidence to hold him. He also knew that when they'd talked to Sandy Harmon ten months later, not only had she failed a lie detector test, but her son had revealed to police that Ramos had abused him. At that point, GraBois thought, Jose Ramos should have been the number one suspect. But he also recognized that he was looking at the situation in hindsight, with nine years of fragmented information gathered neatly together for him and fresh in his mind. What was so clear now would have been less obvious at the time. He didn't even know if anyone else had ever seen this tape. But now that he had, he was looking forward to his meeting with Ramos.

Charles Manson. That was GraBois's first reaction as the detectives cuffed Jose Ramos to take him upstairs. In person, Ramos's resemblance to the serial murderer was uncanny. The same narrow, dark face, the same beard and hair, the same disturbing look in his eyes, like he was inwardly laughing at a cruel joke no one else would ever find funny. Eyes that darted from side to side, evasive and restless. Standing in front of him, GraBois once again had the thought he'd been harboring all weekend—how could a man who looked like this win the trust of children? Of their parents?

"Mr. Ramos, my name is Stuart GraBois." GraBois always started politely. "I'm an assistant U.S. attorney in the Southern District of New York. Do you mind if I call you Jose?"

"No, go right ahead," the man replied, with a cavalier smile, "and I guess I'll call you Stuart."

Ramos's menacing appearance was tempered by a softly melodic voice, warm and soothing; a kid-show host's dream. That's how he does it, Gra-Bois thought as the men ushered Ramos upstairs. Charles Manson meets Mr. Rogers.

In GraBois's office, Ramos sat with one hand cuffed to a heavy metal chair, directly in front of the prosecutor's desk. NYPD detectives Bob Shaw and Dan Cavallo sat in chairs flanking their subject. As they all made pre-liminary small talk about his background and his family, GraBois again was struck by what he was hearing, and not just the soft-spoken voice. Ramos was also much more articulate than he'd expected. He was in visibly high spirits—like a schoolboy on a field trip. He seemed happy to be back in his hometown of New York City, no matter the circumstances. At certain points he even affected a Jackie Masonesque New York Jewish accent.

"So what's new?" he asked in broad tones. GraBois just sat there and looked at him, not sure how to answer. He was saving that for later.

At first, GraBios had the odd sensation he was convening a collegial business meeting. There was the chitchat about the weather, about Ramos's trip up to New York, how things were for him in prison, his entrepreneurial previous life. He boasted of his past success: how he'd once found $4,000 in a trash can, which funded a lengthy European vacation. Then Ramos got a knowing expression on his face, a preemptive "I know you're going to get me so I'm going to beat you to it" look.

"I betcha I can tell you why you guys brought me here," he said.

"Oh, why's that?" GraBois asked. This might be even easier than he'd anticipated.

"Okay...I guess I forgot to pay my taxes on that stuff I sold on the street." He had the mischievous, confessional look of someone who'd been caught with his hand in a very small, inconsequential cookie jar.

No need to disabuse him of his theory, GraBois thought, and he used it as an opening into his interrogation.

"Well, we would like to ask you a few questions, if that's okay with you," he began.

"Sure, fire away," Ramos answered.

GraBois waited as Shaw read Ramos his rights and then asked if he wanted a lawyer. The prosecutor was praying the interview wouldn't end with Ramos's next word.

"Nah, nah," Ramos said. "That's not necessary." GraBois inwardly exhaled.

"So, Jose," GraBois said, starting with a blunt warning. He picked up the dense, softcover U.S. Code book lying open on his desk at the relevant page. "If you're willing to talk to us, you need to understand one thing. If I catch you in a lie, I will prosecute you to the full extent of the law under Section 1001, Title 18 of the United States Code." The "thousand and one," as it was known in shorthand, worked like the threat of a perjury charge in court. GraBois read aloud about the five-year sentence for lying in a federal inquiry. He placed the open book back on his desk, and paused to check his subject's reaction. Ramos looked surprised that the mood was suddenly so serious, and GraBois backtracked, to cushion his threat with a string of softball questions.

Tell me about yourself: your background, your family, your work history. In smooth succession the prosecutor eased Ramos into familiar territory, into the same spiel Ramos had recited at any number of precincts and prisons. As he began to relax, Ramos grew expansive, like a patient reveling in his life story during a free, unlimited therapy session. He ran through the intricacies of the "salvage" business; GraBois and the detectives nodded sympathetically as he vented about his family—how he hadn't seen them in years. He boasted of his legal prowess from behind bars, and his audience acted suitably impressed as he misused terms and talked about the legal filings he wrote for other inmates.

"You seem to really know your law," GraBois told him, at the end of one convoluted story. He looked at Shaw and suppressed a wink. "You ought to be a lawyer." Ramos responded with a big grin. After nearly ninety patient minutes, they were nearing the point in the interview GraBois had been watching for.

He picked up a piece of paper and pretended to be looking at a particularly incriminating spot on the page. It was a trick he'd used in the past.

"How many times did you try to have sex with Etan Patz?" GraBois's tone had abruptly shifted, and now a different person was asking the questions, not the friend offering career advice.

There was an electric pause. Ramos went white, and his smile was gone.

"Don't lie to me, Jose." GraBois picked up the U.S. Code book threateningly. "And before you answer me, I'm going to read the thousand and one again." When GraBois finished the part about the five-year jail term, he looked up at Ramos.

GraBois could see him weighing those extra years behind bars. "I guess you have a witness," the inmate finally managed.

GraBois didn't say a word, just examined the blank page in his hand.

"I guess you know everything," Ramos said, his voice cracking.

Suddenly Ramos slouched back in the chair. He took a deep breath and began to cry, loud sobs that made his body heave.

"I'll tell you everything," Jose Ramos wailed. "I never told anyone this before."

It was GraBois's turn to be stunned. He and Shaw looked at each other from across the room. This was how you dreamed it would go, though it rarely did. Every once in a while you push the right button and your man falls apart, like a cornered animal. He thinks we have a witness, and now he can't afford to lie his way out of it, GraBois thought, elated. He'd been doing this job for a long time and had seen his share of con artists. This was either the real deal or an Academy Award–winning performance. GraBois felt pretty sure it was the real deal.

"Start by telling us what happened the day Etan Patz disappeared," GraBois said. "And Jose, you better not be lying to us." He looked pointedly at the U.S. Code book again. Ramos followed his gaze and nodded.

"I remember that morning, I made my rounds, looking for garbage to sell." Ramos's sobs had subsided but his voice was still shaky. "Then I went over to Washington Square Park, and I saw a little boy bouncing an old tennis ball. And now I think it was the kid who went missing that day."

"What did he look like?"

"Blond and blue-eyed, and he was around six years old."

"Do you remember how he was dressed?"

"He was wearing a dark jacket, I remember, and he had on a belt with a western buckle. And those sneakers, the kind with bright stripes on them."

Etan had been wearing blue sneakers with fluorescent stripes when he'd disappeared. But Ramos could have known that from the missing posters. GraBois reserved judgment on the significance of that detail.

"Did you know this boy?"

"No, no, never seen him before," Ramos answered. "But I'm telling you it was the kid."

"How do you know?"

"Because I was over at Sandy Harmon's apartment…"

"Who's Sandy Harmon?"

"She was my friend, her and her son Bennett. We hung out a lot together back then." Just like he'd told Frank Carroll back in 1982, Ramos explained how he'd met Sandy on the welfare line, that she was his lady friend, and that he was a "close" friend of her son Bennett as well. Ramos would visit them both two or three times a week back then, and on the night of May 25, 1979, or maybe it was the next night, he'd dropped by as usual. Sandy was watching the news, he said; about how authorities were scouring the city for Etan.

"She told me that she knew him; that she used to take care of him. They showed his picture on the TV, and I'm 90 percent sure that kid was the kid I talked to in Washington Square."

"You talked to him?"

"We talked a little, and then I asked him if he wanted to go back to my apartment."

"Um-hmm." GraBois looked down at the fake notes he held, and made a check next to an imaginary witness statement. If Ramos could keep thinking someone had seen him that day, all the better. GraBois worked to keep a matter-of-fact tone in his voice.

"Why would you take him back to your apartment?"

Ramos hesitated, perhaps in recognition that he was about to step over a line. "For sex," he said.

No one spoke for a brief moment. With no expectations or fanfare, the case looked to be breaking wide open right here in GraBois's office. My God, he thought. He's just admitted to soliciting a minor for sex. But the statute of limitations on a nine-year-old molestation crime had run out. GraBois needed to keep the momentum going and to ignore the goosebumps running up and down his flesh. We can't give Ramos the breathing room to consider a lawyer, he thought.

"What happened in your apartment, Jose?"

"I gave him some apple juice, I remember that. Then I picked him up and started to feel around his legs."

GraBois steeled himself against that mental image. "How high off the ground did you pick him up?" he asked. What if he'd picked him up above his head, then thrown him down hard enough to kill him?

"This high." Ramos gestured indiscriminately in the air.

Bob Shaw moved to a filing cabinet along one wall of the office. He drew a line on it some three feet off the ground.

"That high?" GraBois asked.

"No, higher," Ramos said. "His belt buckle was about here," and he gestured at eye level, then nodded when Shaw moved the pencil farther up.

This meant something to GraBois. Ramos wasn't just saying the first thing that came into his head. The prosecutor held up the thousand and one statute again.

"Then what happened, Jose? Remember, you don't want to lie to me."

"I'm not lying, I swear it. I tried to have sex with the boy. I admit it, I did some things back in '79 that I'm ashamed of. There were kids I took to the movies in Times Square because I wanted to have sex with them, and I messed around with a boy once in the tunnel. But I never hurt nobody, and I never forced any of those kids. This boy said no. He wasn't interested. So I put him down. And then he said he wanted to go to school."

The tone in Ramos's voice had suddenly changed. GraBois could sense he was getting his control back, could almost feel the instant that his panic-driven candor shut down, replaced by agenda-driven dissembling.

"So we left," Ramos went on, "and we got in a taxi that took us back down to SoHo. But he changed his mind before we got there, and said now he wanted to go see his aunt in Washington Heights. I walked him to Sixth Avenue and put him on the uptown subway. I remember I waved goodbye to him from the other side of the turnstile as he got on the train. And that's all I know."

"That's bullshit, Jose!" GraBois's outrage burst from him. He couldn't contain it as Ramos's tale spun into absurdity. The idea that Ramos would politely acquiesce to a six-year-old's resistance, let him go unharmed, and then cheerfully wave goodbye as Etan jumped on a city subway to visit an aunt GraBois knew didn't exist was ludicrous. Ramos must believe we could prove he was seen taking the boy into his apartment, he thought, but it's a lot harder to prove Ramos never took him out.

"No, it's true. Look, I want to tell you everything," Ramos said and started to cry again, "I want to get it off my chest. But I guess I need a lawyer for this. I'll answer all your questions then, even if he tells me not to."

What GraBois wanted to do at that moment was to lock the door and go at Ramos even harder. This was not the time to stop, when his subject was still vulnerable, and the seasoned prosecutor knew he could squeeze out of him what really happened. He knew guys like this, and he could bet that by their next encounter, Ramos would have recovered, and he would shut down tighter than a cell door. Countless times, in the months and years to follow, GraBois would second-guess his next words, but really, there was no other option. He just didn't do things that way.

"We'll get you a lawyer, and we'll take this up again tomorrow."

The session was over. Shaw unlocked Ramos from the chair and the four men walked down the hall to return Ramos to the U.S. marshals. Only two elevators were working that day, so they stood in the hallway longer than usual. As they waited, Ramos turned to Bob Shaw and said with a baleful stare, "By the time I tell you everything, you're going to be the police commissioner."

He looked at Detective Cavallo and promised him a promotion. Then to GraBois he said, "And you, you'll be famous. You'll have Giuliani's job." Less than a minute later the elevator doors opened to find the U.S. attorney himself standing inside. The four men crowded on and rode next to Rudy Giuliani, who must have been on his way out to lunch.

GraBois was astounded to hear his prisoner pipe up.

"Mr. Giuliani," Jose Ramos said. "I seen you on TV. The camera makes you look heavier." GraBois's boss cast him a glance as if to say, Who's this bozo? GraBois was dying to tell him, but knew he'd have to wait. This news was bigger than a four-floor elevator ride.

———

What do you think?" GraBois asked Shaw, sitting with him and Cavallo back in his office.

"What do *you* think?" All three men were thunderstruck, trying to make sense out of what had just happened.

"He's our guy," GraBois said. "There's really no doubt in my mind. Did you see his body language? The look on his face when he said he let him go. That was such bullshit."

Shaw was still shaking his head. He and GraBois didn't always agree on everything. The veteran detective had been on the case well before GraBois, and sometimes they butted heads on tactics and theories, but on this one there was no dissent.

"I think he's our guy," he agreed.

The men speculated about what Ramos had really done with the boy he'd taken to his apartment, the boy he'd all but admitted was Etan Patz. There was little doubt they were now looking at a homicide case. Yes, there was always the chance he'd sold him to some pedophile ring, but to Gra-Bois's mind it was unlikely. Ramos came off as a lone operator. The men kicked around the more feasible scenarios. Maybe Ramos had killed his victim because he'd put up a fight, or maybe he'd panicked when he saw the extent of the search. He'd told Sandy Harmon he was running out to look for Etan after seeing the TV news. Maybe that's when he'd gone back to dispose of the body, or that's when he'd realized he couldn't afford to keep the boy alive.

GraBois called a defense attorney he knew and arranged for him to come in the next day. Despite Ramos's promise to tell him everything, GraBois knew the man's moment of vulnerability had passed. A door had opened, but had it now closed?

CHAPTER 15

⌒

"Just Watch Me"

Dear Rainbow Family Members:

It has come to our attention that an individual known as "Michael" whose true name is Jose Antonio Ramos has preyed upon the young sons of Rainbow Family Members. We ask your help in identifying incidents where your children have been sexually abused.
—*November 6, 1988, letter from Stuart GraBois requesting a notice be placed in the Rainbow Newspaper* Always Free

Jose Ramos arrived at the U.S. Attorney's Office the next day sporting a Jewish yarmulke and a serious attitude. As predicted, gone was the acquiescent demeanor. In its place was an invocation of his right to remain silent. Twenty-four hours across the street in the MCC had given Ramos time to regroup. At Giuliani's suggestion, GraBois had set up a camera to record the next session, but Ramos refused to be taped.

He was still performing, though; his fake New York Yiddish accent grew more pronounced from that day forward. Leonard Joy, then a public defender with the Legal Aid Society, was assigned to represent Ramos, who was brought back to GraBois's office several times over the next months with Joy present. GraBois and his team played the requisite good cop/bad cop; tough-guy talk mixed with trips to the street vendor to bring Ramos back New York's signature Sabrett's. Ramos ate the hot dogs with gusto, then continued to play coy.

"Listen, Jose," GraBois would say, "you own up to everything, let the Patz family finally get some peace, and I'll work with you. I understand you haven't seen *your* family in a long time. I'll try to locate them and arrange for you to see them. You'll do federal time for everything, always a nicer way to go. And that outstanding felony case in Pennsylvania won't be prosecuted again, I'll speak to the authorities there. But if you won't give me what I want, I'll push them hard to bring the case back."

Ramos didn't seem to think much of those terms. He showed no signs of concern whenever GraBois mentioned the felony charges against him in Pennsylvania. As far as he was concerned, the Taylor case could not be resurrected. Although Ramos never recanted his "90 percent confession," as GraBois and his team took to calling it, he would never again let down his guard.

Frustrated by Ramos's stonewalling, GraBois was nonetheless reenergized by the near confession. All that summer and into the fall the prosecutor conducted a systematic review of the case, plugging in Ramos as the prime suspect. Letters went overseas to Interpol, trying to track Ramos's travel in Europe. GraBois talked to the Pennsylvania prison authorities and had them comb through Ramos's personal property and his visitation lists for clues.

GraBois brought in Sandy Harmon. Sandy was stick thin and sallow-faced. To GraBois, who'd spent years either defending or prosecuting narcotics cases, she wore the familiar look of a junkie losing her health. She was lucid but tight-lipped, bitterly condemning her past treatment at the hands of authorities. Sandy did cooperate by confirming one part of Ramos's story. He *had* been in her apartment one of those first days after Etan disappeared, and he'd left once she'd told him the boy was missing, saying he was going out to help look for him. But as far as she knew, she said, Ramos had never actually met Etan, although he'd seen Etan in Washington Square Park.

Yes, she admitted, her son Bennett had slept at Ramos's apartment several times, and Ramos had stayed at her place sometimes too, but she again claimed no knowledge that her then boyfriend was molesting her young son. She did recall one occasion when she was walking with Bennett and realized Ramos was following them, hiding behind parked cars and in phone booths to avoid detection. She was afraid, she said, and had ducked into a store with Bennett.

Bennett came in the following week. He was a pleasant-looking young teen, clean-cut and well behaved. At thirteen, his small talk was peppered with references to the many girls he dated. GraBois couldn't help but think that was a response to the fear of Ramos's taint, and he felt badly for the boy.

Bennett claimed little knowledge of events from 1979. He acknowledged spending time with Ramos; they'd watched a Muppets TV show together once, but he couldn't say if he'd ever been in the man's apartment. GraBois knew that the boy wouldn't be expected to remember much from the age of four, and even if he did, if there were any sordid revelations, it would take time and considerable patience on the prosecutor's part for them to surface.

By the summer of 1988, GraBois had kept his interactions with Stan and Julie Patz to a minimum. The tension of previous encounters notwithstanding, the detectives and FBI agents were the Patzes' usual point of contact anyway. But now GraBois felt that he himself should let them know of this new development. Ramos's partial confession was not only the first real break in the case, but it also presented a highly disturbing scenario to any parent. GraBois waited out the summer while he pushed Ramos for more information, but finally he called Stan Patz one day in September and asked him to come in.

"I wanted to tell you in person that there's been a significant development." Stan took a seat and sat quietly as GraBois recounted his meeting with Jose Ramos, how Ramos had walked into the U.S. Attorney's Office prepared to confess to tax fraud, and had walked out leaving the investigators speechless. For GraBois, Ramos's admissions had erased any lingering doubts about Stan's culpability, so the prosecutor didn't hold anything back. When Stan asked him for the worst of it, GraBois told him Ramos had admitted taking the boy he thought was Etan to his apartment for the purpose of molesting him.

"I really think we got the guy who did this," GraBois finished.

Stan Patz felt more than heard the weight of this news, a heavy, sickening thud. His vigil in 1982, while the press had trumpeted the "drainpipe man," had been the second worst weekend in his life. He'd never quite been able to banish the tabloid sketch of Jose Ramos, and what that represented, from the dark pit of uncertainty in which he'd blindly groped for almost ten years. Now he struggled to digest the idea that what he'd most feared was proving most likely. It just made sense.

If the 90 percent confession had erased GraBois's doubts about Stan Patz, it had done the same for Patz's animosity toward the prosecutor. As much as Stan had felt bulldozed by GraBois in the past, now he saw real results. This wasn't an investigator heading off to Europe with a nebulous "Well, we're looking…" This was a suspect with a name, whom Stan could actually picture in his head. A man with a real connection to the family.

Most importantly he was a man in custody, GraBois laser-focused on building a case against him.

The prosecutor had Stan bring Julie back the following week and asked both of them a series of questions—about their recollections of Ramos, his girlfriend Sandy Harmon, and her son Bennett. Had Bennett played with Etan? Had he been up in the loft? Did Etan tell either Bennett or his mother about his plans to walk to school alone? Did Etan ever meet Ramos before? But Stan and Julie had been asked these questions before, and could offer little about the woman Stan didn't think he'd even met and Julie knew only to feel sorry for. Sandy was a quiet woman; she was neat and unobtrusive. She didn't really register in a downtown artists' colony filled with flamboyant characters who deliberately dressed and acted to be noticed. Her son was a sweet kid, a few years younger than Etan, and the two boys had had little to do with each other.

GraBois had more luck with Bennett Harmon himself the second time they met in November. This time GraBois was able to coax out buried memories of those sleepovers at Ramos's apartment, a sixth-floor walk-up dump in the East Village section nicknamed Alphabet City, so called because the avenues there were lettered, not numbered. At that time Alphabet City was known as a top New York drug supermarket, and Ramos's building was a haven for junkies and hoodlums, who hung out in the cramped hallways, terrorizing the tenants. Ramos would bring Bennett there after a movie in Times Square or a trip to the Empire State Building. Before bed, Bennett revealed, on many nights the older man would tell him it was time for a bath in the ancient claw-footed tub that took up half the kitchen. Then they would play an "adult" game Ramos had agreed to teach Bennett once the boy promised not to tell his mother. A mortified Bennett told GraBois how Ramos would undress too, and join him. The man would sit Bennett on top of him, fondle him, and then fellate the boy on the studio couch afterwards.

Bennett said he couldn't recall Ramos penetrating him, but the investigators weren't so sure. A four-year-old might not even understand that it was happening, let alone be able to talk about it nine years later. GraBois was a grown man, a hardened prosecutor, and it made *him* sick to his stomach just to ask the questions. "It's not your fault," he said over and over to reassure Bennett. "You were a little boy, and he took advantage of you. What he did was wrong, and you are the victim."

By this time, after four months in federal custody, Ramos had already returned to his Pennsylvania cell, taking his yarmulke and his newfound Jewish religion with him. GraBois knew he could bring the inmate back to New York at any time, and while at SCI Rockview, Ramos's movements were being closely monitored. But GraBois was well aware of his deadline: Ramos's first possible release date was less than a year off, and once his suspect was freed from the system, he could easily slip away.

So GraBois was working on a parallel track from the Patz investigation. Since his first look at Ramos's rap sheet, he'd been intrigued by that entry on the last page—the Warren County case that had been "nolle prossed" by the local district attorney the year before. *Nolle prosequi*, Latin for "we shall no longer prosecute," meant not that the case was irrevocably dismissed by the judge, only that it would no longer be pursued by the prosecutor. This left a door open. A "nolle prossed" case was rarely resurrected, but GraBois just needed to get his proverbial foot in. In October 1988, GraBois called the Warren County DA.

Warren County's district attorney, Rick Hernan, seemed surprised to get a call from a New York federal prosecutor about a case he'd given little thought to in over a year. He explained the facts of the case to GraBois and the circumstances surrounding the suppressed confession. He'd gone as far as an appeal to the State Superior Court. Child molestations were tough, he said, and even if the victim was prepared to testify, without the confession they just didn't have enough.

GraBois disagreed, and Hernan's attitude rankled.

"I don't think you need a confession," GraBois said. "You've got this kid's testimony. Maybe you can't use Ramos's confession in court, but one thing it does is tell you for sure that he's guilty as hell. So you know for a fact the kid's telling the truth."

"I'm not saying I won't do it," Hernan countered. "I'm just telling you what we're up against. If you want to go find the kid, go right ahead. We haven't been able to in a long time."

GraBois hung up the phone in disgust. This DA did not appear at all interested in prosecuting the case. He found a more kindred spirit when he called Dan Portzer. The Pennsylvania state trooper had never been satisfied with how the Warren case had ended. As far as Portzer was concerned, Ramos should have sat in the electric chair for what he'd done to young Joey Taylor. Instead he'd gotten clean away with it.

GraBois told Portzer he needed his help. "I want to keep this piece of garbage off the street as long as I can. My interest is the possible murder of a six-year-old in New York," and then he filled Portzer in.

"I'm with you," Portzer assured GraBois. "Whatever you need, just ask." Portzer sent GraBois copies of his files and gave him a brief primer on the Rainbow Family of the Living Light. Sounds interesting, GraBois thought, maybe even entertaining. He saw lots of con artists and pedophiles in his typical cases—a bunch of flower children might be a refreshing change. He turned to Jim Nauwens, an investigator in the U.S. Attorney's Office.

"Can you find me some Rainbows?" he asked.

On the day that GraBois sat with Bennett Harmon and heard what Jose Ramos had done to him, Jim Nauwens drove up the New York State Thruway to Woodstock, New York, looking for Rainbows. Had he been aware of them, Nauwens could have taken the subway twenty blocks north to the East Village, where the Rainbow Family flourished, and even had their own P.O. box at the local post office, but up to this point, Rainbows were an unknown entity to the U.S. Attorney's Office of New York's Southern District. All Nauwens had to work with was the name "Barry Adams" and a hefty briefing book the U.S. Forest Service had put together on how to prepare for a Rainbow Gathering. Nauwens thought the extensive backgrounder resembled no less than a defense for the invasion of Normandy, but it offered few clues to help find Rainbows in their off time. If Nauwens was hunting hippies, Woodstock was as good a place as any to start.

"I'm looking for some help," he'd say, working his way from head shop to hair salon. Everyone listened politely, if blankly, to the straitlaced blond Fed. "Could you get me to Barry Adams? We're on the same side with this one, and I think he would want to help." After a few days of spreading his card and affable demeanor around town, he came back to New York City feeling defeated. Two days later the phone rang.

"I hear you want to talk to me," said Barry Adams, calling from his home in Montana. "When the Feds come looking for me, I don't usually want to be found," he told Nauwens. But he listened as the investigator detailed his interest in Jose Ramos and what the Rainbows could say about him. Adams agreed to talk to GraBois, and told Nauwens that the Taylor family was pretty disenchanted with the whole judicial process.

"These folks have been waiting more than two years," Adams said when he had the prosecutor on the line. "They feel like justice is for other people, not poor folk who don't have a nice home with a white picket fence, near Main Street in Warren, Pennsylvania. That DA threw the case away."

"I'm not the DA," GraBois countered. "Let's meet and talk, and you can make your own judgment. If you don't want to cooperate with me, then you leave." Adams agreed to meet with the prosecutor. He'd fly into New York for a parley, he said, a feeling-out process.

"But I'm not coming alone." He was adamant. So GraBois arranged to bring in John Buffalo from San Diego, and added in a New York contingent as well.

The Rainbows met an hour early in front of One St. Andrew's Plaza: Joanee Freedom and Garrick Beck, the New Yorkers; Barry Adams and John Buffalo; Dave Massey, up from D.C.; and another Rainbow who called himself "Peace Ray," a graduate student at Drexel University.

By far, Adams was the standout, in his cowboy hat, leather chaps, and plunker, but as a group they drew stares from the stream of uniforms and pinstriped suits that usually crossed the square. The Rainbows held an abbreviated council, and agreed to listen without judgment, say little, and come to consensus later. They were walking into a possible ambush on the basis of little more than a phone conversation between Barry Adams and GraBois.

The group filed into the modern U.S. Attorney's Office building, feeling as far away as possible from the familiarity of a smoky drumming circle.

"Welcome to the 'House that Giuliani Built,'" joked Joanee, to break the tension.

The security guard picked up the phone and dialed Jim Nauwens's extension. He'd been around a long time, had seen some real fringe types come through over the years. But he'd never seen anything like this.

"Jim," the guard said, a note of incredulity in his voice. "There are a bunch of people down here to see you. Are you sure you want to see *them*?" Nauwens went down to collect the new arrivals. He waited while they checked a few knives, vouched for the ones who didn't possess ID, and ignored the "Who the fuck is that?" from agents walking by.

Up in his office, Nauwens stashed the group in his office until he could move them into a vacant conference room. They wandered around the investigator's cramped quarters, filled with boxes of paperwork; cases in progress. Joanee peered at the crime scene photos and diagrams from different cases, blown up and taped to the walls or mounted on easels. She wondered how the investigators looked at this all day and then went home to their families at night. She spied one posterboard mounted with photos of the small blond boy she immediately recognized as Etan Patz. It featured two duplicate photos side by side, one untouched, the other computer-enhanced to show age progression. "That face looks familiar," she thought, and called over the others to look, before they all adjourned to wait in a bigger room nearby.

When GraBois walked through the door, he introduced himself with a welcoming smile. He was careful to work the crowd, passing out his business card, with a handshake and direct look for each one. Now he understood why for the last twenty minutes staffers had been sticking their heads in his office to playfully inquire about the motley crew gathered in their conference room. GraBois took the ribbing good-naturedly. He knew that those passing the open door saw little more than a group of aging hippies and hoodlum bikers, but he saw them as potential colleagues.

"I asked you to come because I need your help," GraBois started. "I'm trying to stop the worst kind of scum. He's hurt a lot of kids, and I believe he molested and murdered a six-year-old in New York. I've now come to learn he molested at least two boys among your people. Who knows how many others he's hurt?"

"Well, we're glad you brought us in," drawled Adams. He leaned back, took off his hat, and looked to be settling in. "A free trip to New York City is always a treat. But at the same time, you got to understand it's a rare occasion when we visit the Feds on a voluntary basis. Usually when a federal officer goes to shake my hand, he's putting the cuffs on." Barry Adams loved a good audience, and he had a lot to say.

"Our people are considered outlaws by law enforcement in general, and the Feds in particular," he continued, then spoke at length about the Rainbows' history with federal authorities, their legal battles around Gatherings on federal land, and their hassles with the Forest Service. When he was finished, he pulled out a sheaf of paperwork and handed it to GraBois.

"We've been taking advantage of our freedoms in this great country of ours," he said. "Especially the Freedom of Information Act. And we come to find out the government keeps files on us. I expect—no, I'm sure—they've got way more than this, but this is what we've gotten our hands on so far."

GraBois took a quick look. It was a heavily redacted file that spanned several years. It seemed largely unremarkable, but he saw the word "drugs" on one page, "runaways" on another. He put it down without reading further. "I want to be very clear about this," he said, addressing the whole crowd. "I don't give a damn about anything you have in your past, including what might be in this." He swept his hand toward the report.

"When I asked you to come in, I told Barry that I wouldn't pull your records or look into your backgrounds. I think you'll find out I'm a man of my word.

"I don't have to look into your background to know who the Rainbows are," he went on. "I know there are people who look askance at the way you choose to live your lives, or the baggage that you come with. I couldn't care less."

The Rainbows listened without interruption as GraBois ran down his agenda—he needed them to find the Taylor family and convince them to come to New York, too. GraBois would hear their story and evaluate the case. If he felt it could go forward, he would take the Taylors to Warren, and ultimately expect them to testify against Ramos in court.

"How can you do that?" they wanted to know. "You're a Fed and this is a state case."

GraBois explained the concept of "cross-designation," whereby in special circumstances, state and federal prosecutors swapped jurisdiction back and forth. What he didn't say was that he'd seen state prosecutors come to the federal level, but he wasn't sure he'd ever heard of an assistant United States attorney going out of state, especially a state outside of his purview. The Southern District of New York was more than 350 miles from Warren, Pennsylvania, and if GraBois were to get directly involved, it would take some serious finessing.

"Why are you doing this?" Adams was blunt. "We know why *we've* pursued this case for more than two years. This family wants justice, and we're not going to stop 'til they get it. But what's in it for you?"

"I have my reasons. Many of them coincide with yours. This guy is a menace, and what he did to Joey Taylor is unconscionable. As a father myself, I can't imagine what this does to a family."

GraBois saved his own stake in this for last. "I'll be honest, though. I'm trying to put so much pressure on Ramos that it'll get him to open up on the Patz case." GraBois gave them the bare bones of his investigation, and the name Etan Patz brought a flash of recognition to the New Yorkers' faces.

"But even if he doesn't say another word, if I can do anything to keep Ramos behind bars, it's worth it."

The meeting ended on a hopeful note.

"We're in town for a few days," Adams said. "We've got some things to do. In the meantime we'll counsel amongst ourselves. But we should definitely talk about this some more." They arranged to meet again the next day, and after another round of handshakes, the crew left to do some sightseeing. Barry Adams had never seen the World Trade Center.

———

Here's a present for you." Adams had barely gotten through the door of GraBois's office the following day before handing GraBois a picture. It was the photograph of the older boy who'd been on the bus the day Ramos had been discovered with the younger Taylor brother.

Joanee Freedom had seen that photo sometime after the '86 Pennsylvania Gathering where Ramos was thrown out, and she'd realized right away Ramos had a long history with this boy. She knew him as P.J. and had first seen him at the Michigan Gathering with Ramos in 1983. When Ramos had left the Gathering so precipitously, P.J. hadn't gone with him, and as the Gathering had wound down, Ramos's friend Saxophone Sonny had come to Joanee with P.J. in tow to ask her for a ride back to New York.

"I need to take this kid home to Ohio on the way," Sonny had told her. "Ramos and I brought him, but since he's gone, I've got to get P.J. back myself." So Joanee and Garrick Beck had dropped Sonny and P.J. at an exit on the Ohio Turnpike. Riding six hundred miles together between Michigan and Ohio had given Joanee enough time to remember a face, and when she'd seen the age-enhanced composite of Etan Patz in the investigators' office the day before, she'd been struck by the resemblance to P.J., the teenager on Ramos's bus. Now GraBois was, too.

"You just never know," said Adams. "See what comes of this."

He also told GraBois they had all conferred.

"You looked us in the eye when you talked to us," Adams said. "I appreciate that. We feel a good vibration here, and think we can work together. But we've gotten screwed before, and if at any point we think that's what you're doing, we will walk."

"That sounds fair," GraBois said. "I really don't foresee any problem. I'm going to pursue this case as far as it goes." He had no intention of backing out, especially since he'd already given his word to someone else.

———

One week earlier, Jose Ramos had arrived back in New York to meet with GraBois again. This time, the prosecutor had a surprise for him.

"Jose," GraBois said. "You remember Pennsylvania state trooper Dan Portzer?" GraBois had arranged for Portzer to fly up, to show Ramos he meant business. The trooper was in plainclothes, but Ramos clearly recognized him. His attorney hadn't yet arrived, but GraBois wasn't looking to engage Ramos in a dialogue.

"I don't want you to say a word, Jose. Just listen carefully to me. Trooper Portzer is eager to help me reopen the case against you in Pennsylvania. I want you to understand just how serious I am. If you won't tell me what I need to know, make no mistake, this will happen. I will do whatever it takes. Even if I have to go down to Pennsylvania and try the case myself."

At first, Ramos had looked shell-shocked. But his characteristically cagey expression quickly returned. He laughed derisively. "Do you know where that place is?" He leaned forward and lowered his voice, as if to confide in GraBois out of Portzer's earshot. "It's some backwoods little hole out in the middle of nowhere. You're never going to go all the way down there."

GraBois leaned forward too, but his reply wasn't hushed.

"Just watch me," he said.

CHAPTER 16

More Lost Boys

CASE REOPENED:
On date of 01-03-89, this officer was contacted via telephone by U.S. Asst. Attorney, STUART R. GRABOIS...New York, NY and he advised that he had information to lead him to believe that the Accused RAMOS in this case was involved in a kidnapping and possible homicide in that city....He was having a Subpoena issued for this officer and the subpoena would include a photo album and papers that were located in the bus of RAMOS by the members of the Shippenville PSP Station at the time of RAMOS's arrest in 1986 in this State and all records pertaining to this case....

Asst. U.S. ATTORNEY GRABOIS advised that he was going to contact Warren Co. Dist Attorney, Richard A. HERNAN in regards to this case as he felt that it should not have been Nolle Prossed and after doing so would be in touch with this officer.
—Trooper Dan Portzer, DD5, January 22, 1989

T wo months after Barry Adams told Stuart GraBois he could track down the Taylor family, they were sitting in the prosecutor's lower Manhattan office. Adams had found them a few days after putting the word out on the Rainbow drumline, and now he and John Buffalo had accompanied the family to New York. Adams wasn't yet completely sold on GraBois, but he encouraged his friends to at least listen.

"He says the right things, and then he seems to back them up."

GraBois would have the chance to give the Taylors a similar pitch to the one he'd given the original Rainbow scouting party. He also needed to decide for himself whether Joey Taylor, now ten years old, and two years away from the crime, would make a good witness.

His immediate first impressions of Joey himself: pleasant kid, quiet; GraBois imagined someone had told the boy and his younger brother Billy to behave themselves in this forbidding office. The parents were as he'd expected—frayed around the edges, with the world-weary look and demeanor of the well-trodden-upon underclass. Joe Taylor was a big man, with a sure grip when the two men shook hands. But he sat far back in his seat, wary and stony-faced through much of the conversation. His wife Cherie moved around more, like a fluttery hummingbird; her nerves were more apparent. The passage of time since Ramos's attack on her son hadn't dulled her raw response, and she cried as she talked about how Joey had changed since then, how withdrawn and mistrustful he'd become.

GraBois asked the parents if they minded giving him some time alone with their son. As he gently talked Joey through what he needed him to do, the boy hesitated at first, and GraBois sensed that Joey felt some responsibility for what had happened to him. He'd gone on the bus without being forced, he told GraBois.

"You had no control over this," GraBois said, working hard to dissuade him. "He was an adult and he was bigger and older than you. He knew better. He's the bad guy here."

Joey seemed to hear him, and within a few minutes the story was out. With little prompting he was able to give a lucid account of his rape. In a heartbreakingly clear, childish voice he explained the sequence of events in much the same way he had with the state trooper two and a half years earlier. He'd knock it out of the park on the stand, GraBois thought to himself.

GraBois told the boy much the same thing. "You did exactly what I needed you to do, Joey. If you can tell your story, we'll make sure Ramos stays in jail. Together we can get this guy. But remember, I can't do it without you." It was true. GraBois hated to put that kind of pressure on a ten-year-old, but he couldn't sugarcoat this.

The prosecutor stood up, and asked Joey to stand too. "Raise your right hand," GraBois said, "and I'll swear you in as my deputy."

The boy looked at him solemnly, held up his hand, and repeated GraBois's improvised pledge.

"Welcome to law enforcement, Joey." GraBois shook the boy's hand. "Now you're my partner.

"Okay," Joey said, and his face was brighter, like a light had turned on inside, illuminating a dark place. The prosecutor was pleased to see that Joey was taking the conversation very seriously. So was GraBois.

GraBois brought Joe and Cherie Taylor back in, and told Joey he could go out to the conference room to play with his brother.

"He should do fine," GraBois said. "Here's the bottom line. You speak to Joey, and if he doesn't want to go forward, I won't do anything to force the issue. But if you agree, then I'll arrange to have the DA in Warren meet with you while you're out here, and we'll take it from there."

"We already know that Joey will do this," Joe Sr. said. "We've talked about this more times than you can imagine. Our family has been torn apart by Ramos. We all want him to pay for what he did."

As the Taylors were leaving, Joe Sr. took GraBois aside.

"I appreciate everything you're doing for us on this." The father paused. He was uncomfortable, but he wasn't going to leave before he finished his thought. "I want to ask you... Is there any way you can arrange to get me and Ramos in a room together, alone, just for a few minutes?"

GraBois laughed. He couldn't help himself. "To be honest, Joe, I think that's a great idea. But I can't let you do that."

Afterwards, GraBois had called Rick Hernan, the DA, who suggested setting up a meeting in the future.

"No," GraBois insisted. "They're here now. Let's just do this. I'm sending them down, and I expect you to let me know what the next step is after you meet with them."

There was just one problem. Warren was a seven-hour drive from New York, and between them, neither the Taylors nor their Shanti Sena escorts had a credit card or any other means to rent a car. GraBois looked to his team of investigators, who in turn all but pushed Jim Nauwens forward into the line of fire. "You're going to have to give them your car."

Letting a government car out of your hands was serious business. Allowing virtual strangers with little to recommend them drive it out of state was right up there with handing over your gun. Nauwens drove a white sedan that, at least to him, screamed "unmarked car." He sat down and composed the Rainbows a "To Whom It May Concern":

"The bearers of this letter are NOT law enforcement agents. However, they have been authorized to be in possession of this vehicle, for the express and only purpose of traveling from New York City to Warren Pa and back, solely to perform business in the interest of the U.S. Attorney's Office." Then he and his fellow investigators laid odds on getting the car back.

With that the Taylor family, Barry Adams, and John Buffalo were en route to Warren. When they called GraBois several hours after they'd left for Pennsylvania, he assumed they were reporting in on how the meeting went.

"We're here," Joe Taylor said, "but we're still waiting to see him. We've been waiting a few hours."

GraBois was outraged. He hung up the phone, called the DA's Office directly, and tried to contain his anger. The Taylors were ushered in to see the DA soon afterwards, but the episode left a bad taste in GraBois's mouth. I got him everything he asked for, GraBois thought, and he couldn't care less.

The Rainbows were due back on Monday. GraBois had put on a good front to his men, but he couldn't contain a sigh of relief when Barry Adams called to say they were downstairs parking the car. In a way, the Rainbows had just passed a test. If there were going to be any more anxious moments, GraBois would remember this one, and know that despite their outward appearance the Rainbows could be counted on. When he followed up with the Warren DA later that day to get Hernan's impressions, it was clear he felt differently.

"Have you actually seen these people?" Hernan said. That was all GraBois needed to hear. He didn't care whether the DA was making a personal statement or whether in practical terms he was concerned about their ability to make good witnesses. With that one sentence, taken in any context, GraBois knew this was not the man to win against Jose Ramos. Hernan went on to say that he had no objection to recharging Ramos in the Taylor case—as long as GraBois and the Feds were prepared to assume all costs.

This is all about money, GraBois thought disgustedly. Once again, he was profoundly grateful to know the expense was not an issue in his office, and he assured the DA the Feds would handle the witness costs and any other expenses. But maybe not right now, not while this man was running the office.

"If you're not chafing at the bit to prosecute a bum who sodomized and raped a little kid, what kind of prosecutor are you?" GraBois had worked himself up into a state by the time he told Nauwens about it later. "Who cares what they look like? Okay, maybe if you're going to trial and they have to testify, you dress them up a little for the jury; get Barry Adams to trade in his chaps for a suit." GraBois had heard with his own ears that Joey told his story clearly and credibly, so he knew the family's appearance was irrelevant. He couldn't help but take it personally, not only for the Taylors, but because it reflected badly on his profession.

GraBois explained his reluctance to involve the local DA to the Taylors, who'd returned from Warren freshly reinfused with the zeal of the righteously wronged. "I'm completely on board," he told them, "but I know from experience that everyone involved has to be as well. We're better off waiting for a new DA."

GraBois was well aware that the Taylors might see those words as yet another stalling tactic and he worked hard to convince them that, on the contrary, it was a tactic designed to ensure the best chance to win. He'd already heard that the DA's Office was likely changing hands at the next election, slated for the end of the year.

"Don't give up hope," he urged the Taylors before they left to go back west. Unlike the Warren DA, meeting Joey Taylor had strengthened GraBois's resolve, and seeing how Joey and his family had been treated had moved the federal prosecutor one step closer to traveling outside his turf.

———

GraBois picked up the picture that had been sitting on his desk since Barry Adams had brought it to him, the photo of the teenage boy who'd traveled with Ramos at the Rainbow Gathering, and who'd reminded the Rainbows so much of the computer-aged photo of Etan. P.J. Fox, the Rainbows had called him.

GraBois was skeptical about the P.J. connection. The prosecutor had no doubt that Etan Patz was dead, and this boy was probably another in the long list of a certain type Jose Ramos was drawn to. Besides, Etan would have been thirteen in the summer of 1986 when P.J. stood at the door of Ramos's bus and had his picture taken. The teenager glaring at the camera looked considerably older and more mature. But even if P.J. Fox *weren't* Etan Patz, GraBois had now met Joey and heard what Ramos had done to him. If nothing else, P.J. might know something—about Ramos, about what happened at the Rainbow camp—and GraBois wanted to find him. He might even be an eyewitness to Joey Taylor's rape.

As tidbits of information began to stream in, P.J. Fox became more inter-

esting. There was a report that the teen had been involved in male prostitution in the Columbus, Ohio, area, and he also had a healthy rap sheet,
complete with an outstanding warrant. When GraBois learned that P.J.'s
mother had worked at a foster care home, it raised the obvious question:
Was P.J. adopted? If so, it lent more credence to that next-to-impossible
thought: Could P.J. actually be Etan? GraBois was taking it seriously
enough to want to know what Etan would look like now, in 1989. The 1984
computer-enhanced portrait that the Rainbows had seen in GraBois's office
depicted a prepubescent boy. This year was the tenth anniversary of Etan's
disappearance. He would be sixteen years old now, fully adolescent. At that
age, youngsters physically transformed.

GraBois called Stan Patz, and while assuring him this request was just
in the service of eliminating yet one more "look-like," he asked Stan to dig
up teenage photos of himself and Julie. Together with a current picture of
Shira, these were sent to the FBI Special Projects Unit in Quantico. There
the graphics whizzes who prepared exhibits for trial and worked techno-
magic, re-created a computer-enhanced estimate of a sixteen- or seventeen-
year-old Etan.

They gave the teen an unkempt mullet haircut, to match P.J.'s, but otherwise worked entirely off of the Patz family's facial features. Only after they
were finished did they set eyes on P.J.'s actual photo. Even to the naked eye,
the resemblance was astonishing. Next, Special Projects overlaid a grid on
each face, dividing them into several distinct areas. Then each individual
square of the grid was compared side by side, one square at a time. Every
separate grid section matched.

"Oh my God." GraBois held the two photos next to each other and listened to FBI special agent Lisa Smith describe the grid process. The two
faces staring back were twins. For the first time in the four long years of his
investigation, he allowed himself the unthinkable thought: "What if the
kid's alive?" He'd been so sure it wasn't possible, knowing Ramos, knowing the odds. Then the moment passed, and the logical, methodical side of
GraBois's brain reasserted itself. It just didn't add up. Still, he needed to see
that for himself.

In late October 1989, GraBois and Bob Shaw, along with Agent Smith,
headed to Ohio. They flew to Columbus with a collective air of contained
excitement. P.J.'s mother had an apartment in nearby Portsmouth, and the
team drove to her trim, well-groomed garden complex to interview her,

hoping she'd lead them to her son. At one point, GraBois and Lisa Smith were standing outside the apartment house while Shaw and a local FBI agent were inside talking to P.J.'s sister. Suddenly, the two spotted a young man walking toward the building, and they realized he matched P.J.'s description. But in the next moment he saw them, glanced around wildly, and turned as if to run.

"FBI, P.J. Don't run, we just want to talk to you." Smith, a tiny but toned long-distance runner who habitually ran six miles, took off after him, quickly reaching P.J.'s side before he could get away. But everything after that dramatic moment was anticlimactic. Inside his mother's apartment, it quickly became apparent that P.J. was not Etan Patz. A copy of his birth certificate was produced. Even if it were forged, the age difference, as GraBois had suspected, was obviously too great. Later there would be confirming fingerprints, even DNA, and the Patzes themselves, when eventually shown P.J.'s photo, would shake their heads right away. But the follow-up was all just a formality—the evidence was clear that day. P.J. was not Etan Patz. Worse, in GraBois's mind—since he'd been skeptical all along—P.J. professed to know nothing further to help them in their case against Ramos.

Afterwards, the three investigators—GraBois, Smith, and Shaw—went to dinner and spent most of it staring at each other in disbelief. How many more highs and lows could there be in this case? Later, after he talked to Bonnie on the phone back at the hotel, GraBois found it easier to put things in perspective. His own frustration was nothing compared to what the Patz family had gone through every day of their lives for years. Then GraBois thought back to his encouraging words to the Taylor family not to give up, and he turned them inward.

CHAPTER 17

⌒

"I Told You So"

Dear Mr. Ramos,
  I have reviewed your letter of October 16, 1989 wherein you ask whether the District Attorney will refile charges. This is to advise that once charges are nolle prossed they cannot be refiled.
  —*letter from Thomas Bonavita, assistant public defender,*
  Warren County, to Jose Ramos, October 23, 1989

On a miserably wet November morning a week after the Ohio trip, Stuart GraBois was back in his office. Jose Ramos was back there too, for one final visit before the end of his latest stint in federal custody at GraBois's behest. This was the third time the prosecutor had writted Ramos from Pennsylvania's Rockview prison, each time for several months at a stretch, each time in the futile hope the inmate's resolve would crack. As the two men waited for Ramos's attorney Leonard Joy to arrive, GraBois as usual cautioned Ramos not to speak without his lawyer present.

"You just need to listen," GraBois said, "and understand that your situation is about to change. The decision you make today in my office will affect you for the rest of your life, because by tomorrow, word will be out all over this city—and then beyond—that you are the guy we're looking at in the Patz case."

GraBois knew that Channel 4 reporter John Miller planned to break a big story on the case that night, a story that for the first time in ten years would put a name and a face on its prime suspect. Never mind that Jose Ramos's near confession was over a year old by November 1989; to a still fascinated public, it was the first news in years. From his reporting in the days following Etan's disappearance, then slogging through the drainpipe in

206

1982 and trekking to Israel three years later, Miller had been a presence at several pivotal moments. He liked to refer to himself as the Patz case's Zelig, recalling the Woody Allen character who'd been cleverly edited into newsreel footage of real-life historical events.

In Ohio, GraBois had pointedly ignored the large white satellite uplink truck with the "WNBC—New York" logo emblazoned on its side that was parked outside his hotel every day. Tipped off to the Ohio trip, Miller had hauled a producer, camera crew, and the company truck across state lines to Columbus, where they'd all cooled their heels for several days, staking out the Feds.

By this time, Miller had become a high-profile reporter at Channel 4, the NBC network's flagship affiliate, where he'd made a name for himself with his irreverent, ballsy coverage of New York mobsters. He was often seen on camera in his signature trench coat, trailing after feared crime boss John Gotti and lobbing pointed questions. But now the reporter had taken a long-shot bet, hoping to roll the camera, knock on a door, and record history when it was opened by a seventeen-year-old Etan Patz. It didn't happen. After delicate negotiations back in New York both the disappointed GraBois and the persistent Miller agreed that it was finally time for the Ramos angle to surface. Miller would get a big scoop to help mitigate his wild goose chase out of state. For his part, GraBois hoped a new lead would result from getting the word out. Press was always a tricky proposition, but as the Patzes had found out in those first few days, it was often the best way to mobilize resources. Plus, GraBois hoped the publicity would have the extra benefit of putting added pressure on Ramos.

"You and I both know you could have a real hard time after the evening news tonight," GraBois said to Ramos. "I can make it *easier* time by putting you in a federal institution, but you have to give me something in return. Think about it, and remember, we're not talking about just the next few years. If I get the Taylor case reopened, you'll be looking at a lot more time than that."

When Leonard Joy arrived to join his client at the U.S. Attorney's Office a few minutes later, he confirmed that the press had been calling his office for comment. Ramos knew then that GraBois wasn't just playing with him, and that his life would be in danger once the story aired. But the warning only seemed to make him more defiant. He'd been hearing GraBois talk tough since the two had first met, and so far that was all it had been—just talk.

For months the prosecutor had been waving the dismissed 1986 Pennsyl-vania charges under Ramos's nose, but the inmate had done some research. He'd written to his former attorneys at the Warren County Public Defender's Office to ask if there were any teeth to the threat. An assistant public defender had written back just the previous week to say those charges couldn't be refiled and the Joey Taylor case was over and done with.

Ramos kept his mouth shut in his characteristic, stony glare and left GraBois's office for the last time before being returned to Pennsylvania's Rockview prison a few weeks later. If you think this is over, GraBois thought as he watched the marshals lead Ramos out of the room, you are so wrong, pal.

John Miller's story was heavily promoted all day and led both the five and six o'clock broadcasts. It was more than ten minutes long, a standout for the local nightly news, and it recapped ten years of the case, prominently featuring its prime suspect. The story was picked up in the next days by the New York print press, and by the time Ramos left for Pennsylvania his name and face were out there.

GraBois called Rockview to fill them in and learned that was unnecessary—some of the inmates had seen the news coverage. Just to be sure that the authorities knew who they were dealing with, GraBois sent the warden a letter in anticipation of Ramos's coming bid for parole, detailing his full record with children and advocating against parole.

On his return to Rockview, Ramos was placed in segregation as a safety precaution, banished from other human contact. The solitary cell was pro-tection, but it was also a punishment.

———

Soon after that, GraBois cold-called the Pennsylvania attorney general in Harrisburg. He didn't know anyone in that office, but he introduced himself to the person at the other end of the line and made his request. They must think I'm crazy, he recognized with some humor, as he waited for the return call. But he needed the attorney general's help with his plan. The Novem-ber elections had put a new Warren County district attorney in office, and GraBois had once again put out feelers to resurrect the Rainbow case. DA Joseph Massa was a well-known, well-respected attorney who'd practiced in Warren for twenty-one years, but he could not prosecute the Joey Taylor rape case. Massa had revolved straight through the courthouse door from the Warren County Public Defender's Office one floor below. While there, he had ably defended Jose Ramos, arguing successfully for the suppression of his confession. With such a clear conflict of interest, there was no point in GraBois even approaching him. When he called Massa to introduce himself, it was only to ask if the new DA would make a formal request, as protocol dictated, to the Pennsylvania attorney general asking him to take over the case. Massa agreed immediately, and he told GraBois that conflict notwithstanding, he'd be more than willing to help in any way he legally could. But this was now a case under the jurisdiction of the attorney general of Pennsylvania, Ernest Preate—if he chose to take it on.

GraBois planned to make it easy for the Pennsylvania AG, because the New York prosecutor would offer to do all the work. He would come down there and try the case himself, if the attorney general would swear him in as a temporary deputy.

"What do you make of this?" Preate had summoned Marylou Barton to his office to discuss the request he'd just been told about from this unknown federal prosecutor.

Barton looked incredulous. "It's absolutely bizarre."

Chief Deputy Barton ran the attorney general's new Child Abuse Unit, the logical place to place this request, but she had to feel it was merited. "Bizarre," she went on, "but exactly the kind of case I created the unit for. If this man is so serious about it, we should by all means pursue it."

The diminutive Barton was outwardly no-nonsense and reserved, until she climbed onto her very tall soapbox, the one that had brought her to this office. Crimes against children were as old as bound feet and slavery, but talking about them—let alone prosecuting them—was a relatively new phenomenon, unfamiliar and uncomfortable legal territory. Barton was battling judges who didn't know how to rule on these cases, lawyers who didn't know how to present their evidence, and untrained testifying physicians who showed their gross ignorance on the stand. Once, at an autopsy, Barton had watched a forensic pathologist examine a young victim with forty-four broken bones, then announce that the baby had died of SIDS—the mysterious catchall of sudden infant death syndrome.

Barton was on a crusade to recruit and educate medical specialists, police, and attorneys to recognize abuse, then use special interview techniques for children, and move aggressively on these crimes. She held workshops and training sessions, and watched the new methods begin to take hold across the state. But along the way, even though the AG's Office didn't officially have jurisdiction over actual cases, actual cases started finding them. Cops who weren't satisfied with a coroner's rulings, grandparents who balked at cursory findings, would come to plead for a champion and a second hearing. In its first few years, Barton's unit had revived and resolved ten unsolved cases.

Sexual abuse presented a particular challenge. There was often little evidence, sometimes no more than the word of a child, who might have waited weeks or months to come forward. Beyond any other barrier, Barton was up against the "ick" factor—no one wanted to enter into the nightmare world of pedophiles, to hear the acts described, or to meet the human beings who perpetrated them.

The Joey Taylor rape case presented all these problems, and more. Barton walked back to her office shaking her head in doubt. Not because the case was being shifted to their office—in small towns, conflicts of interest were fairly common. But this was a nearly four-year-old crime, with a transient young victim, and lots of moving parts. And then there was the wild card of Assistant U.S. Attorney Stuart GraBois, coming in from another jurisdiction in an altogether different state and asking to take the case himself. Barton had practiced law for seventeen years. She'd argued—and won—in front of the U.S. Supreme Court. But she had never in her life heard of anything like this. That a New York federal prosecutor cared enough to pursue a small-town crime all the way to Pennsylvania was unheard-of to start. But that he wanted to prosecute it personally? Barton suspected she'd either be dealing with a wacko or some Kojak type from the big city, thinking he was coming down to rescue the small-town folk from their own ineptitude.

Then she met Stuart GraBois. The actual meeting place was a halfway point, at a conference room in a Philadelphia federal courthouse. Barton brought her chief investigator, Larry Gerrard, a crusty former Philly homicide detective. Gerrard had already started his own investigation—calling old friends on the force in New York—to check out GraBois. Although the federal prosecutor got high marks all around, neither Barton nor Gerrard knew what to expect before the meeting. And they didn't want to take this case any further if it was going to turn into a turf war.

"If he walks in and pulls the pushy Fed routine, I'm going to tell him he can kiss my ass as I walk out the door," Gerrard vowed to Barton on the drive to Philadelphia.

But their concerns were unfounded. The stakes were high for Gra-Bois, and he was charming and solicitous. He'd brought his half of the team—Barry Adams and the Taylor family, whom he'd flown in again, this time from Texas. GraBois didn't feel quite like he was walking into an audition, but he badly wanted the face-to-face to convey personally what a bad guy Ramos was, and how crucial it was to keep him from getting released. If this didn't pan out, he'd played his last card and Ramos could be gone in a matter of months.

GraBois had one more goal. Underneath the surface of the easygoing team player he presented, GraBois believed the prosecution was only going to work if he could run it his way. After all his effort, he wasn't prepared to take a backseat to anyone else's direction. He just had to convey all that…in a nice way.

Luckily, Barton cared about winning, not who took the lead. She was immediately struck by GraBois's knowledge of the case, the absolute certainty with which he was pursuing it, and his utter lack of hesitation amid the unknown legal territory of a state prosecution. He never once seemed to question himself or the cause, and she couldn't help but be swept up in the force with which he commanded the room. She was also moved by his willingness to pour his heart out to a total stranger about the years of work he'd put into the Patz case and the passion he felt for its resolution.

Joey Taylor was twelve now, a chunky, slow-talking boy with a sweetly sad demeanor who seemed younger than his years. When Barton herself questioned him, it was clear he'd make a good witness. She also saw how despite their obvious differences, GraBois had already built a rapport with the Taylor family. And she walked out of the meeting all but certain a jury would too. Before she left the room, she told GraBois that she was going back to Harrisburg to recommend to the attorney general that the case go forward, with GraBois as her partner.

COUNT 1: Involuntary Deviate Sexual Intercourse 18 Pa. C.S. 3123 (5) (F-1)

Defendant Jose Ramos did engage in deviate sexual intercourse with Joseph Benjamin Taylor, age 8, on more than one occasion, June 20–21, 1986, in that he did have anal sex with the victim, said victim being under the age of 16 years and not the spouse of the defendant….

COUNT 2: Involuntary Deviate Sexual Intercourse 18 Pa. C.S. 3123 (5) (F-1)

Defendant Jose Ramos did engage in deviate sexual intercourse with
Joseph Benjamin Taylor, age 8, on more than one occasion, June 20–21,
1986, in that he did have oral sex with the victim, said victim being under
the age of 16 years and not the spouse of the defendant.
   —*Criminal Complaint*: Commonwealth v. Jose A. Ramos, *July 9, 1990*

On a hot, sticky July morning two months later, Stuart GraBois left his
office to catch a flight to central Pennsylvania. He could have gone directly
to the airport from home that day, but knowing he could finish a good two
hours' worth of work in the morning, he drove into lower Manhattan first.
Then at 10 a.m., he sorted, shredded, and otherwise cleared his desk as
he did every day before leaving, and headed to LaGuardia. He had a one
o'clock flight to Harrisburg, and calculating the drive time to the airport,
he was allotting himself the usual two hours to check in. His wife and kids
loved to joke about all the extra time he spent hanging out at the gate, but it
was a good place to catch up on his reading, and with thunderstorms in the
forecast, he was leaving nothing to chance. Ninety percent of operational
success was contingency planning. If this trip went the way he had meticulously planned it, he thought, as he bought a paper and sorted through his
sheaf of legal documents, tomorrow would be the best day in his long and
successful career.

GraBois was going down to Rockview prison, to be there to look Jose
Ramos in the eye when they finally arrested him. It was the week after
July Fourth, and GraBois loved the irony of Independence Day. He almost
wished he could have done it on the Fourth, but it wouldn't have been worth
giving up the long weekend with his family. And of course the folks in the
Pennsylvania Attorney General's Office wouldn't have tailored the dates just
for the sake of a little poetic justice. Justice all by itself was good enough.

GraBois scanned through the headlines and tried to focus on the news
of the day. It looked as though New York would be home to the next Democratic convention. The Marion Barry trial was in full swing in D.C., as witnesses testified they'd delivered cocaine to his mayoral office and watched
him snort up at least thirty times. And the jury was going into deliberations
on the second trial of Raymond Buckey, one of the accused child molesters
of the infamous McMartin preschool case in California. Along with the
first trial, which had ended in acquittal, the case had cost the state more

than $13.5 million. GraBois smiled as he read this, thinking of the $42 hotel room he'd reserved in State College, Pennsylvania, for the night.

Off the plane in Harrisburg, GraBois headed to the Pennsylvania Attorney General's Office and temporarily traded his federal prosecutor's hat to be officially sworn in as special deputy attorney general. It sounded much more dramatic than it was—there was no "Raise your right hand and repeat after me," just a stack of paperwork to sign. But each piece of paper gave him the authority to pursue his goal over the last two years: to keep a promise he'd made to his prime suspect.

When GraBois had told Ramos he was going to have him rearrested and prosecuted for Joey Taylor's rape, he had meant it. Over and over, Ramos had laughed at him. But GraBois never bluffed. He firmly believed that bluffing was the worst thing a prosecutor could do. It made you lose credibility, a precious commodity.

The paperwork signed, newly appointed Pennsylvania special prosecutor GraBois got into a car with Marylou Barton and Larry Gerrard, his brand-new colleagues, and headed deeper into the Pennsylvania countryside. "Keep your eye out for bears," Gerrard said to GraBois, who thought he was having some fun with the city kid until he saw a black, clawed figure, looming taller than the car and not ten feet from the side of the road.

Two hours later, they stopped for the night at the nondescript motel in State College and had dinner across the street on the Penn State main campus, home to more than forty thousand students. Dead center in the state, the university was some ten miles south of SCI Rockview, the medium-security state prison where GraBois intended to keep his appointment the next day. He slept fitfully, with the alien thrum of crickets threatening his sleep, and awoke to a gray, muggy morning. GraBois, Barton, and Gerrard drove to the prison's gates, to be met by troopers Dan Portzer and Gene Casasanta, who had driven in from Warren, two hours in the opposite direction.

Stepping out of the car, GraBois craned his neck and looked up. As a veteran prosecutor, he'd been in a lot of prisons. This one was right out of a Lon Chaney movie. Rockview was built in the early 1900s and boasted a seven-story rotunda building at its entrance, flanked by five-story cellblocks on either side. From the outside, the rotunda's front façade gave the appearance of one giant, seven-story-high room, entered through a small mousehole of a door, like the front gate of a Gothic castle or a Victorian workhouse. So this was where Jose Ramos had been hiding from New York authorities, thought GraBois.

Ramos had already served three of his three-and-a-half-to-seven-year sentence, and he was doing everything he could to shorten his stay. He was hoping to move into a job that gave him more freedom, and he had even been talking about weekend furloughs and work release. GraBois's sense of urgency had been growing.

This was the prosecutor's first visit to Rockview prison. After all of Ramos's trips to the U.S. Attorney's Office in New York, it seemed only right that GraBois would reciprocate for this event. He had choreographed it so carefully.

The folks at Rockview had never seen a prosecutor come to witness an arrest. Usually he charges the crime from back in his office, then a sheriff or state trooper shows up to take the prisoner quietly out the back in handcuffs for arraignment before the judge. But GraBois had deliberately staged the scene differently. He wanted Ramos to remember this day, to have the image of Stuart GraBois breathing down his neck ingrained in his mind. A power trip? GraBois thought it was an effective way to keep the pressure on him. His own experience from the day Ramos came close to confessing in his office told him to do anything he could to throw Ramos off kilter.

The guards in the room watched the prosecutor with curiosity. The Rockview staff wasn't aware of the Patz case, but Ramos himself was a familiar character. Most inmates there were processed in and out without much notice. Even the child molesters, who were notoriously singled out, could go low-key if they chose to. Ramos, however, made an issue of anything and everything. He was very much in the public eye—as a weirdo to the other inmates, as a nuisance to the staff. He claimed now to be an Orthodox Jew, one of the lost tribes that had ended up in Spain. This meant special privileges; he balked at haircuts and filed grievances claiming religious persecution. SCI Rockview was happy to see him go.

The cell door opened.

"C'mon, you've got visitors."

"Who?" No one came to see Ramos. He hadn't had a visitor since he'd been there.

"You'll see." Ramos was told nothing of what lay ahead, just brought down a flight of stairs leading off his tier. The stairs led to a holding area separated by steel doors from a control center where GraBois had positioned himself—the man in control. As Ramos reached the stairwell landing, a gray-haired figure appeared through the glass window cut out of the doors ahead. Coming down the last steps, the face came into clear focus; the hard stance, the familiar features... still closer, until only the two locked doors kept both men apart.

When Ramos first saw GraBois, his mouth automatically curled into that familiar half smirk he seemed to save just for the prosecutor. Jose Ramos liked to tell people GraBois was obsessed. GraBois himself bristled whenever the term was used. He himself thought obsession was pursuing little boys to violate their bodies; it was following them home from school, dating mothers to get to their kids. GraBois had no doubts about who was obsessed.

For a brief moment, the two men stood regarding each other through the glass windows separating them. Then Trooper Portzer stepped forward and snapped on his handcuffs. "Jose Antonio Ramos," said Portzer, "you're under arrest for involuntary deviate sexual intercourse in Warren County, Pennsylvania. You have the right to remain silent," he continued. As Ramos was read his rights, he turned white, the smug look replaced by one of total shock.

Then, when he was finally brought through that last door and within earshot, GraBois couldn't help himself. As Ramos was led past to the waiting patrol car outside, the prosecutor leaned in to whisper, "I told you so."

CHAPTER 18

On the Record

Ramos was arrested at Rockview State Correctional Institution at approx
0945 hours and then returned to Warren Co by these two officers and
Agent Larry GERRARD of State Attorney Gen'ls Office. Upon return to
Warren Co ACCUSED RAMOS was arraigned before Dist. MAG. Dalton E. HUNTER...and committed to Warren Co Jail in lieu of $1 million
bail....PRELIMINARY HEARING was set for 07/17/90 at 1330 hours.
[postponed to 8/15/90]
　　—*July 13, 1990, Supplementary Report of Pennsylvania state trooper*
　　Daniel L. Portzer on Jose Ramos, July 10, 1990, re arrest

A month after that first trip to Warren, Stuart GraBois was at the
airport again, early as usual. He was flying to Pennsylvania a
second time, for Jose Ramos's preliminary hearing, but this time he wasn't
alone. He was watching his traveling companions from across the waiting
area in front of the gate and trying to control his temper. He could understand the stares—he was getting used to them by now. If Barry Adams didn't
stand out enough with his braids and leather ensemble, or his propensity for
exhorting total strangers to love each other, when he whipped out that flute
to play Native American songs of healing, he got everyone's attention. No, it
wasn't the raised eyebrows that upset him. It was the attitude.

Up until this point, GraBois realized, it had been clear to everyone else
that he—the man in the well-tailored suit—was part of this group, but now
he suddenly got a sense of what the others faced when he wasn't around.
Adams and Joe Taylor Sr. were trying patiently to get the gate attendant's
attention, and from what GraBois could see, neither one of them looked
"normal" enough to rate it. He noted the woman's apparent disdain as she

216

ignored the two men, one shabby, one cosmic, asking their polite questions. It was as if they didn't exist.

GraBois approached the counter in time to hear the attendant tell his party the flight was overbooked. They were being forced to bump passengers and the Taylors et al. would have to take a later plane. Sorry, nothing we can do. It was her snotty delivery as much as the message that put GraBois over the edge.

He yanked his federal ID out and angrily thrust it in the woman's face.

"Who the hell are you to talk to them this way?" GraBois used his hardass voice. "I am a U.S. federal prosecutor from the Southern District of New York and these individuals are my witnesses in an important case." Other passengers were looking at GraBois now, who until this moment had been the unremarkable one.

"It is imperative these people be at their destination on time in order to testify. They are holding prepaid full-fare tickets, and I don't care who you have to bump to get them on. Get me your manager."

Joey Taylor watched as the woman's superior, who had been summoned, and now fluttered around GraBois, gushed apologies. He felt like a big deal when they were ushered onto the plane, and he saw the AUSA in a new light. Joe Sr. was impressed too.

"Nobody ever treated us that way before," he said to GraBois. "No one ever showed us that kind of respect. If you weren't here we would never have gotten on this plane."

"I wouldn't care if you were wearing monkey costumes," GraBois replied. "No one deserves to be talked to that way."

As the group drove through Warren later that day to get to their hotel, GraBois got his first real sense of the town—he'd been too focused on Ramos the last time to pay much attention. He remembered—as if he'd ever forget—the words Ramos had said to him in New York.

"You know where that place is? It's some backwoods little hole out in the middle of nowhere." It had been muggy and miserable back in New York, but here in Warren, the air was fresh and cool on this mid-August day, and it carried the fragrant scent of late summer roses, yarrow and daylilies from flowerbeds laid out neatly on manicured lawns. Nestled into a bend in the Allegheny River, Warren was picture-postcard small-town USA, with its two-hundred-year-old faded brick buildings, a centerpiece clock tower, and a founder who'd died defending Bunker Hill. This placid town, with an average annual murder rate of zero, was overwhelmingly white, middle-class, and churchgoing. Even though everyone GraBois had met so far was unfailingly polite and friendly, they must have wondered how their home had been chosen to play out a scene whose cast of characters defined the word "stranger." There was the New York City Fed, the Puerto Rican child molester, and the Wild West hippies. It could get stranger, but not much.

Before dinner, GraBois took the Rainbows over to the courthouse. He always liked his witnesses to get the lay of the land in advance. He was glad the hearing tomorrow would not be in the elegant but highly formal main courtroom of the Warren courthouse, with its walls all dark inlaid wood paneling, its story-high glass windows draped in somber dark red velvet, and its imposing judicial bench towering over spectators and litigants alike. Gra-Bois walked the Taylors through the more intimate, third-floor multipurpose space across from the District Attorney's Office, which looked more like the small conference room it often functioned as when not in use for hearings.

The whole group ate dinner together at the hotel, and afterwards Gra-Bois planned to spend the evening preparing his witnesses for the preliminary hearing. The next day's court appearance would be Ramos's first since his July 10 arrest, and GraBois went over again how the judge would listen to the prosecution's case, then decide if it merited proceeding to trial or dismissal. The evidence itself was pretty straightforward. GraBois might introduce the photos of Ramos from June 22, 1986, which Barry Adams had supplied, and Adams himself would testify about finding Ramos on the bus, heading out of camp with Joey's brother Billy.

But the most important voice would be Joey's. It would also be the biggest wild card. Four years had passed since his assault, a long time to retain an accurate memory of events. Yet even if it had happened yesterday, a child's testimony was never a sure thing. Sitting on the stand, facing their attacker, victims had to relive the intimate details of the attack out loud in a courtroom full of strangers. Although uniformed men might be standing by to protect a boy like Joey, their guns sometimes had exactly the opposite effect of making him feel safe. There was always a risk the testimony would fall apart.

GraBois and Marylou Barton sat with Joey in GraBois's room conducting one more in a string of mock interrogations, stopping as they went along to reassure the boy.

"Will he be there tomorrow? Will he talk to me? Will I have to look at him?" Joey had a string of questions that betrayed his nerves.

"Yes, he'll be there; no, you absolutely don't have to say a word to him. I'll probably ask you to identify him, but just briefly, so you'll point to him, and then you can look away. Just look at me the whole time, or at the judge. But if you're feeling funny, look at me. I'll be there to protect you."

Joey nodded and seemed more comfortable. In court the next day he would wear a suit his parents had bought him specially—a present for his thirteenth birthday one week earlier—but right now he was a boy in shorts and sneakers, looking like he just wanted to sit in his room with his little brother Billy and fight over the hotel TV remote.

"The other attorney is going to ask what I told you to say," GraBois went on. "This is very important, because I'm not telling you what happened, *you're* telling *me* what happened."

They went through all the questions that would be asked, one more time. The hardest part was always the moment Joey had to go over the actual rape. GraBois hated making his witness dredge it all up, and Joey was clearly embarrassed.

"Do I actually have to say it in front of the whole room? Like, use the words and everything?" He was fidgeting again, and his soft features were shuttered.

"You really have to," GraBois said gently, "but don't worry about it, no one's going to say anything, you're a kid, everyone knows it's not your fault."

"I'm not a homo," Joey said. He was suddenly close to tears. "The other kids call me that, and they won't hang out with me. I've gotten used to it from Billy, but I just wish the others would stop. Could you make them stop? Could you make it better, like it was before all this?" He looked hopefully at the man who had stood up for his family at the airport earlier in the day. GraBois thought his heart was going to break. He didn't know what to answer, but he tried.

"I can't tell the other kids what to think," he said gently. "But I'd tell them what *I* think; that you're a hero, Joey. You are doing one of the bravest and strongest things anyone could ever do. *You* are the reason we're going to lock this man up so he can't hurt any other kids for a long time. I would be proud if you were my son. And I'll always be proud to hang out with you."

His words didn't get much of a reaction from Joey, but GraBois thought he detected a fleeting smile at the corners of the boy's mouth. Or maybe it was just wishful thinking. Joey finished his practice testimony with no further hesitation, and GraBois knew he'd do well the next day. By now the boy had told it so many times in the practice runs, it would help him to feel like it had happened to someone else.

GraBois had deliberately booked connecting rooms, and before Joey left, the prosecutor told him if he needed anything, if he got nervous, or if he just wanted to talk, he should knock on the door. A few minutes later, GraBois heard soft tapping, and when he opened the connecting door, Joey stood there.

"Everything okay?" GraBois asked.

"Oh yeah," said Joey, looking a little sheepish. "Um...I just wanted to say hi."

———

Every Wednesday was preliminary hearing day at the Warren County Courthouse. On Wednesdays District Judge Dalton E. Hunter traveled from his storefront office in the neighboring town of Tidioute to Warren's 150-year-old, historic landmark building. Hunter was a stocky, beer-bellied ex–police chief. Like the six other district judges in this judicial district, Hunter had no law degree; in fact, he'd never gone to college. But he took the responsibility of meting out justice seriously. It was Judge Hunter who'd arraigned Ramos one month earlier, who'd been astonished to see the determined New York Fed present himself with his prisoner, and who'd promptly set the astronomical million-dollar bail. Now Judge Hunter would listen to the prosecution's argument that this case had enough evidence to be bound over for trial.

Until today the only press coverage had consisted of a short paragraph in the *Warren Times Observer*, but word had spread about the big-city prosecutor who'd come to town, and a handful of area reporters were wedging in to sit facing the judge behind the two simple counsel tables. Jose Ramos himself would just be traveling around the corner, from the cell where he'd spent the last month in the modern, low, brick county jail adjacent to the courthouse.

That morning Joe Sr. had given his son a pep talk while they'd gotten dressed. Joey donned the new blue suit his mother had hung carefully overnight to smooth out the suitcase wrinkles. His father didn't own one, but he spent some time looping a tie around the collar of his dress shirt. They'd discussed all of this so many times before, and Joey seemed calm, but he'd clearly been thinking about what lay ahead.

"I know this guy shouldn't be out wrecking lives," he told his father, "so I feel like I can do it. But I don't know how I'm going to do it. That's the hard part."

"It *is* hard to tell the truth sometimes," Dave Sr. said. "All I can say is that in my experience, telling the truth is always better than lying."

But a few hours later, when the boy and his parents arrived, Joey Taylor wasn't sure. His first moment in the courthouse was a scene straight out of four years of recurring nightmares. As he and his parents reached the top of the stairs to enter the hearing room, they nearly bumped into Ramos, who was being led off the elevator and down the hall into a waiting area. Clad in an orange prison jumpsuit, his hair was shorter and grayer than the last time the boy had seen him. Unruly waves framed his face and his beard was longer and wilder, a massive clump of frizzy gray brush. Unseen, Joey fled into the hearing room, following his parents. Jose Ramos had been in leg irons and flanked by deputy sheriffs; still, his proximity gave the boy a shock.

When Ramos finally entered the room, he was himself confronted by the Rainbow contingent waiting there. Normally, witnesses were secluded across the hall in the DA's Office until they were called to testify, but GraBois had planned it differently. He wanted Ramos to see his accusers right from the start, to hammer home his message. This is not a game, the message read; I'm here—and I'm not alone. The boy you raped is here too and he's not afraid. He's going to tell the judge under oath, right now, exactly what happened to him on that bus when he was only eight years old. You are dead in the water.

As a tactic, this psychological warfare seemed to have hit its mark. While Ramos had known the witnesses were scheduled to be there, he appeared transfixed by Joey, his parents, and Barry Adams, who now all sat quietly at the prosecution table. GraBois hoped actually seeing the Rainbows would provoke Ramos into a panicked, confessional state, like the one that had netted the 90 percent confession on the Patz case two years earlier. The room was so small that Ramos stood not six feet from Joey, who interpreted his look as a menacing glare and shrank back in his chair. GraBois asked the judge to order Ramos not to look at the boy. Judge Hunter in turn instructed deputies to stand between the two, screening Joey from his assailant.

As often as not, defendants waived their right to a preliminary hearing, even though that guaranteed the case would proceed to trial. But because it was the only chance to see how the witnesses might fare on the stand at trial, a defense attorney might also use the hearing to reconnoiter the prosecution's case. If Tom Bonavita, Ramos's public defender, got under Joey's skin, intimidated him a little, and made him slip up, every word today would go on the record. It would create a huge problem for the prosecution if later at trial the boy flat-out contradicted his first testimony. And in the defense's best-case scenario, if Joey crumbled on the stand today, so would the case. Besides the obvious benefits to the defense, GraBois half expected Ramos just wouldn't be able to resist going up against him. But it didn't happen.

"At this point," Bonavita said to the judge when the hearing got under way, "Mr. Ramos has indicated he wishes to waive his preliminary hearing."

"You wish to waive it?" The judge asked Ramos for confirmation, and he nodded.

"Mr. Ramos, you have to answer yes or no. Is your answer yes?"

Ramos nodded again.

This wasn't good enough for GraBois. Exasperated, he went into what he called "busting chops" mode.

"Your Honor," he said, "I do not believe a response other than a mumble was made on the record. I ask it be stated clearly by Mr. Ramos, not counsel, that he wished to waive."

At that, Ramos's attorney bristled.

"May it please the court," Bonavita said, "this individual has not entered his appearance; he is not the attorney of record. I don't even know who he is, and I respectfully request any request for procedural points be made by the deputy attorney general, not by this individual who has not entered any kind of appearance whatsoever." This was partly a nod to the record, to lay the groundwork for a future appeal, but the defense attorney was also annoyed enough by GraBois's condescending tone to challenge it.

"What a wiseass," GraBois muttered to Joey. He rose from his seat and addressed the judge.

"Your Honor, *this* individual is a special deputy attorney general from the Commonwealth of Pennsylvania. That individual has not told me who *he* is. I assume he is counsel for Mr. Ramos. I will state my name for the record, and that individual can then understand who this individual is."

Next to him, Joey seemed to perk up at the prospect that his team was taking on the "other" side.

"My name is Stuart R. GraBois." He spelled it, articulating each letter, taking care, as he always did, to capitalize the B. "I am a special deputy attorney general for the Commonwealth of Pennsylvania in charge of the prosecution of Jose Antonio Ramos. Thank you." He wants to play games, I can play games too, GraBois thought, and persisted until Ramos confirmed his decision out loud. But the prosecutor wasn't finished.

"Before we recess, may we have a minute to consult in the hallway?" he hastily asked the judge. "We'll be right back."

GraBois wasn't blindsided by Ramos's move, but he had gone to enormous trouble and some expense to bring his witnesses to Warren. Joey had been through those grueling rehearsals, and if they ended things now, it would all be for nothing. GraBois wasn't going to lose the Taylors' testimony just because Ramos was a coward. While the family had kept up their end of the bargain thus far, he was well aware a Rainbow in the hand...was an ephemeral thing. GraBois and Marylou Barton huddled in the corridor.

"I was afraid he might pull something like this," GraBois fumed. When he got worked up, he would put one hand on his hip and run the other one through the hair at his temples. "What a punk. Here he is with this opportunity, and now this little kid's scared him out of his wits. But I have a backup plan." He quickly explained.

"Will that work?" Barton had never heard of this before.

"We do it in the federal system. So I don't know why we shouldn't be able to here."

They walked back into the hearing room.

"Your Honor," GraBois addressed Judge Hunter. "The Commonwealth would request that we be allowed to take depositions from the witnesses who are present here."

Judge Hunter looked perplexed. He had never heard of this either. Depositions were for civil cases.

"You want them to testify, or what?"

"Yes, sir, under oath, be allowed to depose them at this time on the record for the purposes of preserving the testimony."

"I think," Bonavita piped up, "that is out of the realm of your jurisdiction."

"It sure is," the judge agreed, looking relieved someone else had said it first.

———

Marylou Barton felt like she'd had the air knocked out of her. This was all quite extraordinary. Depositions were never taken before trial in a criminal case in Pennsylvania, unless a witness was dying. But GraBois had been undeterred and he'd approached the judge once the hearing was adjourned. He was going to act on the presumption that he had a right to stay and depose the Rainbows. These folks move around, he'd argued. They don't have phones; they're hard to reach. We may never get them back here, and the prosecution can't afford to lose their testimony. Ramos had been taken back to his cell, the room had been cleared of spectators and press, and the judge wasn't needed. Only the defense attorney stayed in the room, although as far as GraBois was concerned, if Bonavita had protested, he was welcome to leave and forfeit his opportunity to cross-examine on the record. But he could never claim he hadn't been given that chance.

Barton had no idea if any of this was even legal, but GraBois seemed to know what he was talking about. I guess we'll just do it and ask forgiveness later, she thought, retaking her seat.

"You okay, champ?" GraBois looked down at Joey. He explained the change in plans to the Taylors and Barry Adams.

"I'm going to ask you all the same questions, but it's actually going to be easier, because the judge won't be there, and more importantly Jose isn't going to be there, so you can take it easy."

Joey already looked more relaxed than when he'd first walked into the courtroom. Whether it was Ramos's absence or the shot in the arm of watching GraBois cop an attitude with the defense, he had assumed a cool, composed game face.

GraBois squeezed the boy's shoulder. "Let's go get 'em," he said.

"We call Joseph Benjamin Taylor Jr."

Joey stood up and moved just a few feet away to a witness chair near the now empty judge's bench. He raised his hand and was sworn in.

"Do you know what that means, swearing to tell the truth?" GraBois began the well-rehearsed set of questions.

"It means tell the truth, not tell a lie."

"Do you know what a lie is?"

"It's not to tell the truth."

"If you told a lie in this courtroom today, would something happen to you?"

"Yes," Joey said. "I would probably be punished."

"Do you remember my asking you questions or asking you anything?"

"To tell you what Jose did."

"Did I tell you what happened, or did you tell me what happened?"

"I told you what happened."

"Did I tell you anything at all?"

"To tell the truth."

It took only a few minutes to get to the hard part.

"Joey, did anything bad happen to you on that bus with the man you then knew as Michael and you later learned was Jose, the man you saw today in this court?"

"Yes."

"Can you tell us in your own words what happened to you?"

Joey didn't hesitate, he didn't look down, and he used all the words. "He stuck his penis in my butt, and he stuck his mouth on my penis, and he stuck my mouth on his penis."

"Now, you mentioned butt. What do you mean by butt?"

"My behind."

"I have no further questions." GraBois gave Joey a look of encouragement and ceded the witness to Tom Bonavita.

His cross-examination was even shorter, for the most part a series of questions about whether Joey had been coached, and who might have coached him. Joey himself was firm and consistent. He fidgeted a little, and shuffled his feet, but otherwise looked at ease throughout, answering questions about his attacker.

"Can you describe him for me? What did he look like?"

"He had a little bit longer hair than he did now. It was still black, and he had brown eyes. I can't describe any clothes, because I don't remember what kind of clothes he wore."

GraBois was impressed. Joey wasn't going to say anything he didn't know for sure. All this preparation had paid off.

"Do you remember if he had a beard?"

"Yes."

"You are definitely sure about that?"

"Yes."

"You are absolutely certain that the person that you saw today was the person four or five years ago?"

"Yes."

When the cross ended, GraBois rose again for another short round of redirect. He wanted to establish that each separate "bad" act, as he called them, had happened multiple times. He wanted Bonavita to go back and tell his client that the prosecution had hinted at additional charges.

"So for the purposes of the record, what you described about the penis and the behind, that happened more than once?"

"Yes."

"The fact that he put his penis into your mouth, and you put your penis into his mouth, happened more than one time?"

"Yes."

"Are you certain how many times?"

"No, I am not."

"But are you certain it was more than once?"

"Yes."

"No further questions."

"Is it over?" Joey asked. Barry Adams had also been deposed and now they were all packing up to leave the courthouse.

"For now," GraBois said. "There's still the trial, if it comes to that. But I wouldn't worry too much. You all did just great."

It could not have gone better if Jose Ramos *hadn't* waived the hearing. Now, if the Taylors dropped out of sight tomorrow, Joey's testimony was forever preserved, and could be used in trial. Even without the suppressed confession that had torpedoed this case the first time around, GraBois had no doubt they were in good shape. But exactly one hour after the hearing ended, the evidence suddenly got even stronger, when a handwritten letter arrived in the office of Judge Robert L. Wolfe, who was slated to preside over the trial. The letter was from Jose Ramos, begging the judge to stop GraBois, in consideration of Joey and the suffering a trial would cause him. Ramos had written the letter two days earlier, with no way to know he'd soon be facing Joey Taylor himself, and that Joey would breeze through his testimony.

"I am asking your Honor that you not make the child who had sex with me go through the experience all over again in your Court Room. I didn't force this child to commit these acts with me, and I didn't force myself on this child."

In his convoluted ten-page plea to dismiss the case, Jose Ramos had just made a full confession, this time directly to the judge.

CHAPTER 19

Done Deal

Howdy,

Along about a year ago, I was preparing to travel to New York to answer witness concerning evidence on Jose Antonio Ramos. I was spending some time with my children explaining to them the reasons I was going. My son, 14 years old, listened for awhile, went into his room and returned with a small Star Wars figurine. He said, "Dad, I got this from that guy, at the Gathering." (Meaning Ramos, in 1986, in Pennsylvania.) Looking at the Star Wars Figure, a chill ran up and down my spine. I realized how close it could have been to Ramos pursuing his aims with my son. It scared me then, and it scares me now.

—*November 19, 1990, victim impact statement from Rainbow Barry "Plunker" Adams*

Two months later GraBois was en route to Warren yet again. It was his third trip there in as many months, flying west to connect through Buffalo before a shorter flight south to Jamestown, New York. From there it was a forty-five-minute drive across the Pennsylvania border to the Warren Holiday Inn where he was now greeted by name.

The interim weeks had seen an arraignment hearing on August 31, where Ramos had—predictably—pled not guilty. GraBois had used the opportunity to reveal in court that the prosecution was considering filing a third felony count, arguing that since two different kinds of *oral* rape had occurred, both giving and receiving, they could be charged separately. A conviction on all three counts could bring a maximum sentence of sixty years. Afterwards, defense attorney Tom Bonavita told the press he saw this as a clear ploy to pressure Ramos on the Patz case.

GraBois wouldn't deny the New York case was never far from his mind, and he kept the Patzes updated on his comings and goings to Warren. Stan always had a noncommittal "wait and see" reaction to the idea that Pennsylvania would crack his son's case, but GraBois remained optimistic. If his prime suspect were to buckle under such pressure and cough up more on the Patz case, well, that would be ideal. If the prospect of sixty years convinced Ramos to plead guilty on the Joey Taylor case, that was good too. GraBois hoped on this trip the Warren public defender would be willing to talk plea. Both he and Marylou Barton were open to that, but so far the defense didn't seem ready—during the hearing that had brought the prosecutors to Warren, Judge Wolfe would rule on a long list of motions Tom Bonavita had filed to derail the prosecution's case altogether.

GraBois's flight out of LaGuardia landed in Buffalo, where he'd change planes for the twenty-minute hop to Jamestown, and he walked over to the gate. He was the only passenger there. He assumed the flight had been canceled because of the nasty fog cover that had made landing in Buffalo difficult enough. He walked to the counter to reschedule, but was told the thirty-seater was due out on time. "Then where are the other passengers?" he asked the attendant. "Oh, *they've* canceled," was her reply. "What about the fog?" asked GraBois. "Not a problem," she assured him. "The pilot flies strictly by electronic navigation."

GraBois was scheduled to interview eight potential witnesses as soon as he arrived at the Warren Holiday Inn, mostly state troopers who would have taken time off from work. Barton was driving from Harrisburg, and GraBois couldn't afford to get behind schedule. He was also looking forward to his regular confrontation with Ramos the next day. Every time GraBois saw the man, it fueled the fire in his belly. So they boarded the plane, just he and the pilot, who had to rearrange GraBois's seat assignment to distribute the weight properly.

Airborne, the prosecutor mapped out his next few days, going through notes to prep for his witnesses. He liked to make efficient use of travel time; he'd been on the road constantly in the past months. The previous week he'd flown to San Diego to question one of Ramos's constant companions during the seventies, a man who called himself "Cochise" and favored swathing himself in pink fabric. Cochise claimed to have found religon and given up his unsavory past associations; he'd married and settled down with his wife out west, where GraBois's investigators had finally tracked him down. The interview had netted little new information. Cochise denied any knowledge of Ramos as a pedophile. Toward the end of the disappointing session, however, Cochise's wife had made an offhand reference to the journals Ramos often kept close at hand. She remembered him holding the books up to his face as he wrote, and how he would fill each page with cramped spidery handwriting,

Diaries were a trademark pedophile accessory. Child molesters were known to keep detailed accounts of their victims, compulsively cataloging descriptions and ages, dates of the abuse, even the sexual acts in great detail, to pore over afterwards. Could Ramos have recorded his crimes too? GraBois immediately worked his way through the chain of custody in Pennsylvania looking for Ramos's belongings, which led him to Himes Sales and Auto Wrecking. Tim Reitz had worked in the shop for years, and he'd be happy to come meet with the prosecutor when he got to Warren.

Yes, Reitz confirmed on the phone, they'd cleaned out the bus and disposed of Ramos's property, nothing but a bunch of old garbage. And yes, come to think of it, there had been a book. He thought some more and recalled a hard-covered eleven-by-fourteen notebook with the word "Journal" stamped on it. Reitz had found it in a pile on the floor of the bus, and had shown it to his boss, Carl Reese. They'd flipped through, scanning the indecipherable notes. On one page, Reitz distinctly remembered, the writer talked of sitting by a fire with a group of other people, but then the handwriting abruptly changed. Guy must have taken drugs, the two men surmised, and this is where they kicked in. They couldn't make any sense of the chaotic, childish block letters after that. They talked about what to do with the journal, and briefly considered calling the state police barracks before deciding that since the authorities had already combed the bus, they must have kept what they'd wanted. So they threw the book on the fire with the rest of the junk.

GraBois looked out the airplane window and saw nothing but dense white fog. It was exactly how he'd felt when he'd heard the journal was gone. It had taken a long, painful moment before his mind had cleared. Now he realized they were an hour into what was supposed to be a twenty-minute flight. Something was wrong. Almost at the same moment, the pilot spoke to him through the doorless opening separating the cockpit from the cabin.

"Sir, I believe we have a problem." GraBois waited. "I can't find the airport."

"Well, that is a problem." Apparently, it was one thing to fly by electronics, but to land you had to actually see the airport. GraBois asked about returning to Buffalo and learned there wasn't enough fuel to make it back. The pilot's best plan was to fly around a little while longer, hoping the fog would lift enough to afford a glimpse of the runway below. Knowing the limited prospects of that scenario, GraBois gripped his armrests and willed his life not to flash before his eyes.

"That son of a bitch," GraBois found himself thinking. "What if he gets away with it now?" That one outrage, along with thoughts of his wife and children, distracted him for the long tense moments before the circling plane took a swift, almost vertical drop, to land with a thud that left him hobbled by back pain for days.

After the hearing the next day, GraBois and Barton stood in the hallway comparing notes. The defense had filed several motions, and only won one: Ramos's million-dollar bail was cut in half—a hollow victory, since five hundred thousand dollars was still wildly prohibitive. Plus, in opposing Bonavita's request for bail reduction, GraBois had seized the opportunity to paint Ramos as a serial pedophile, listing offenses dating back to 1971. This included, for the first time ever, an official confirmation of both Bennett Harmon's molestation and the 90 percent confession linking Ramos to the abduction of Etan Patz.

"Ramos has also sodomized a five-year-old" GraBois had written in his response to Bonavita's motion, "and has admitted to taking a 6-½ year old boy to his apartment on May 25th, 1979 for sexual purposes."

Now Bonavita approached the two prosecutors and signaled he was ready to raise the prospect of a plea.

"What do you have in mind?" Bonavita asked them. The three went over the terms. While the prosecutors were adamant about not bargaining the charges down from Felony 1, they would be willing to drop the count of anal sex and agree not to file the additional count of oral sex. That left the single oral sex charge, which carried a minimum mandatory five years, and a maximum of twenty.

Even though they were confident in their case, both prosecutors were also realists. While Stuart GraBois would have been happy to see Jose Ramos in jail on two counts for forty years—essentially a life sentence—he knew a trial was always a gamble. On the other hand, this plea agreement carried a stiff sentence, and it was a sure thing. Besides, by refusing to reduce the remaining charge, they might not have given up anything in the deal. Even if Ramos had been convicted on the two charges in the original indictment, there was a good chance the judge would have sentenced Ramos to concurrent prison terms—a two-for-one deal. In the meantime, a trial would force Joey Taylor back to Warren, and this time he'd have to tell his story in an open court full of press and spectators. The choice was clear.

GraBois and Barton wasted no time. They went immediately upstairs to the District Attorney's Office and wrote up a letter outlining the plea. Putting the screws to Ramos, they gave him less than a week to make up his mind. If he met the deadline, they would be back in Warren ten days later to watch Ramos plead guilty. Otherwise, the trial would move forward, starting with jury selection on Monday, October 22.

GraBois arrived back in Warren the following week. This time, when he landed at the Buffalo airport, he rented a car and drove to Warren—no more puddle-jumper connections into Jamestown.

At the eleventh hour, Ramos had agreed to the prosecutor's terms, and the next day he was scheduled to plead guilty to the Felony 1 oral sodomy of Joey Taylor. His change of plea hearing was set for 3:30, and some twenty minutes ahead of time, Jose Ramos was brought over to the courthouse from his cell next door. He'd cleaned up considerably from his first appearance, smooth-faced now except for a thick Pancho Villa mustache, his hair shorter and neatly groomed. A few minutes after he was locked into a grate-covered prisoner holding area off the courtroom, Tom Bonavita walked up to Gra-Bois, looking chagrined.

"There's a problem," Bonavita said uncomfortably. "He's changed his mind, and he doesn't want to plead."

"Let's have a brief discussion," GraBois said to Bonavita, trying to contain his fury, "just the two of us...and your client." When the three men walked into the courthouse law library, GraBois startled Bonavita by moving immediately toward Ramos, who in turn edged backward, until he was literally up against the wall. GraBois was careful not to touch him physically, but he leaned in, prompting Ramos into a defensive posture.

"Well, wait a minute here..." Bonavita started. Even if both attorneys wanted to resolve this quickly, he thought, it was highly improper for the prosecutor to be talking to his client directly like this.

"Why don't you just listen." GraBois motioned to the public defender dismissively, not taking his eyes off of Ramos. GraBois was fifteen years senior and a head taller than Bonavita, who stopped talking.

Turning to Ramos, he continued. "You too, Jose, don't talk, just listen. The time for waffling and bullshit is over. I'm sick of this crap. You either plead today, right now, or we go to trial on Monday. It's that simple. Your choice."

"I need more time to think about it," Ramos said.

"You've had enough time, and you won't get a better offer. Or we will pick our jury on Monday, and I promise you it won't take long."

The two men stared at each other—a battle of wills. As always, GraBois wasn't bluffing. If he closed his eyes, he could almost see the incriminating words of Ramos's tidily written confession to the judge: "I was in a terrible state of mind with my addiction. I couldn't control myself."

"Well?" GraBois prompted him. "Are you ready to plead?" Ramos just nodded reluctantly. He looked like he was about to cry.

But just a few minutes later when he walked into the courtroom, Ramos seemed to have recovered, or at least assumed a mantle of false bravado. Spotting some now familiar reporters, Ramos reveled in their attention.

"No comment," he announced, without ever being asked for one, then tried to identify individual reporters. *New York Daily News* reporter Joanne Wasserman, newly pregnant and already fighting to keep her lunch, felt a fresh wave of bile rise up the back of her throat when Ramos greeted her by name before moving on.

"Associated Press? *Warren Times News*? *Daily Bugle*? No comment," he said. "Size 38 uniform, shoes 10½, brown socks, trifocal glasses. I'd invite you all to shrimp dinner. That's what we're having tonight—shrimp.

"They want to know everything," he said offhandedly to no one in particular. A few minutes later, when District Attorney Joe Massa entered and took a seat in the gallery, Ramos singled him out.

"Ah, Joe Massa," Ramos proclaimed when he saw his former public defender. "Enter the dragon."

But when the judge himself entered, Ramos and the whole room fell silent. Judge Robert Lea Wolfe, president judge of both Warren and Forrest counties, brooked no nonsense in the courtroom he had called his for the last twenty-one years. He was known for holding defendants in contempt for wearing inappropriate clothing, and attorneys in contempt for daring to perch comfortably on the edge of a defense table during closing arguments. Things were done by the book in Judge Wolfe's courtroom.

A handsome man with dark wavy hair and mustache, he was stern, fiercely independent, and known for his prodigious work habits. When Wolfe walked out his back door in the morning he was standing in front of the courthouse parking lot. He took the last two weeks of July off every year for summer vacation, but otherwise he was in his court, and in his court, he was God.

Judge Wolfe began by reading Jose Ramos the charges against him and then discussed the plea agreement. The judge was a stickler at pleas, and he led Ramos through a lengthy recitation of his rights, before hearing his guilty plea.

"And can you tell the Court briefly, Mr. Ramos, what you did that brought this charge upon you? What did you do?"

"Well, Your Honor, I conducted myself in a very heinous manner, and it was because at the time I was really under a lot of mental strain."

"All right, but what did you do?"

"Well, I conducted myself in a sexual manner with a child."

So far the judge had yet to hear Ramos confess to anything specific, and in order to accept the plea, he needed to hear him admit to the exact elements of this particular crime. He tried again.

"...What does it mean to you to have oral sex? What's that mean to you?"

"Well, I put my mouth on the child's penis."

This admission threatened to derail the hearing yet again, because Ramos had just pled guilty to the wrong crime, to the third charge that had never actually been filed. He corrected himself, and the hearing continued. Ramos had now admitted to giving oral sex as well as receiving it, an additional felony crime that carried another five to twenty years in prison. At that point, though, any thoughts of further prosecution were overcome by the relief of hearing him actually make his plea in court.

"It's done." GraBois's voice held a note of triumph as he spoke on the phone afterwards to Cherie Taylor. "He stood up and admitted his guilt in court. All that's left is the sentencing. But this is a felony crime he pled to, and he will serve serious time, no matter what."

"Bless you," Cherie said. "God sent you to protect our children." She was overcome then, and she put Joe Sr. on.

"How long can we keep him in?" Joe asked, and GraBois went over the window of jail time. It was complicated, because it depended on the actual

time Ramos would serve on both the Erie sentence he was currently in for
and the new Warren conviction.

The minimum mandatory sentence for one count of involuntary deviate
sexual intercourse was five to ten years. If the judge ruled the Warren sentence to run concurrent to the time Ramos was already serving for the Erie
charges, five to ten could see his release anywhere from 1995 to 2000. But if
the sentence was consecutive, and he had to serve first one then the other, he
faced a possible fourteen years. It could go even higher if the judge slammed
Ramos with the max—ten to twenty years—but GraBois cautioned the
Taylors against that hope. He never allowed himself to think beyond the
minimum mandatory.

"It's not quite putting you in a room alone with the guy," GraBois said to
Joey's father, "but it's a real victory." Then he asked to speak to Joey.

"We got him, kiddo," GraBois said. "You should know what a great job
you did. *You* got him. You put him away."

"Wow," Joey said. GraBois wished he could see Joey's face, but the tone
in that one word felt very rewarding.

"There will be one more hearing where the judge will sentence him, but
you don't have to be here. You don't ever have to see him again. He'll be in
jail for many years, and if he ever gets out, they have to let me know first.
You're safe now."

"Thank you, Stu, thank you," Joey said.

———

Glimmer of Hope in Patz Case Dimmed by Child Molester's Plea Bargain,"
read the caption under a photo of Ramos in the brief *New York Times* mention of the guilty plea the next day. GraBois put the newspaper down with
disgust. His moment of triumph had been reduced to this? A little boy and
his family were vindicated. Jose Ramos was going to serve hard time for his
crimes now, and the press painted this as failure. Of course he was disappointed Ramos hadn't crumbled and fully confessed to the kidnapping of
Etan Patz. But short of that, GraBois thought, he'd achieved an important
objective—he'd locked this bum away behind bars for a long time.

Not only that, but his hopes for solving the Patz case were far from
dimmed. GraBois knew this wasn't his last shot at Ramos; to the contrary,
the Warren case had already led to two new leads GraBois had barely begun
to pursue, but both held promise. Ironically, even though he couldn't share

this new development with the press, he had the press to thank. Because of the coverage on the Pennsylvania case, two different men who knew Ramos had learned of GraBois's investigation into the Patz case, and both had now come forward separately to offer potentially valuable information. The Warren case also guaranteed the Patz case prime suspect a known address for at least five years, and hopefully more. Now that the hurdle of the guilty plea was past, GraBois focused his efforts on the sentencing.

The judge would consider both the defense and the prosecution's recommendations. He would also review a pre-sentence investigation report, which included the defendant's history and impact statements from the victims. GraBois put the Taylors in touch with the victim advocate in Warren, and he asked Barry Adams, as a longtime friend of the family who'd observed them over the years, to provide additional written testimony. GraBois himself had already started drafting the prosecution's sentencing memorandum on the flight back from Warren to New York.

Ramos was busy with pen and paper too. The day after he pled guilty, he wrote another long letter to the judge—ten pages on a standard yellow legal pad—asking him to revoke the plea. "'We should judge by the standard of truth, never on any account, by any other,'" he wrote, quoting Plato.

Here was the real truth, he said: Joey's father knew "fully well that I told him...that I did not want him to let his children come near my Mobil [sic] Home, because I was mentally unstable...and I was afraid something might happen." Ramos believed he himself should be absolved of any guilt: "The father is the real criminal," he wrote. "I am now made to pay for a crime that he knew could have been avoided. What kind of Justice is that."

In the six weeks leading up to sentencing he wrote a good half dozen of these letters, each more frantic than the last, and started filing his own motions to revoke the plea, refusing to deal further with his defense attorney. He requested a psychiatric evaluation to pursue a mental illness defense, and he was penning notes to the press, negotiating for big money to tell his exclusive story, trying to play different reporters off against each other in a bidding war. He responded to a request from the *Daily News*'s Wasserman by flaunting other offers from *Inside Edition*, *Current Affair*, and WCBS-TV in New York. "As I have stated [to them], unless your Editor is willing to give me $40,000 for an exclusive interview with a possible book option, that I will not conduct any interview with members of the Media, both Print and Visual."

Ramos, who evidently figured the tony magazine *Vanity Fair* could afford a higher price, demanded $50,000 from Ed Klein, who was writing a long feature piece on the Patz case. "Then I would maybe consider doing an exclusive interview," Ramos wrote Klein, "that would go down in History as the greatest work of journalism that anyone has ever written to date." In Klein's letter back he asked if the price included Ramos's connection to the Patz case.

"Personally," Ramos responded, with the same "blame the victim" mentality he evinced in Joey Taylor's case, "I think the Parents should have been charge[d] with Criminal negligence, for allowing that child to be by himself on the streets."

———

On November 29, 1990, Stuart GraBois and Marylou Barton parked their rental car on the street outside the Warren County Courthouse. The first time they'd been in this courthouse for the preliminary hearing, the tree-lined streets of downtown Warren had been shaded from the summer sun by a leafy green canopy. Now it was cold enough to see your breath, the otherwise bare trees and the small shops were dressed in Christmas lights, and huge red-and-green wreaths hung from the fourteen-foot carved courthouse doors. Yellow ribbons tied in giant bows festooned the two-story lampposts that flanked the courthouse entrance, in support of Warren County reservists who'd been called up to sit at the Kuwait border, awaiting President George H. W. Bush's order to invade Iraq.

GraBois and Barton had arrived for the 9:30 a.m. sentencing forty-five minutes early, with enough time to sit in District Attorney Massa's office—the staging area on their periodic visits—drink a cup of coffee, and go over last-minute details of the case. GraBois had been up late the night before in his Holiday Inn room, putting finishing touches on his remarks before the judge, and now he added a few more lines, changed a few words.

GraBois wasn't nervous—he hadn't felt nervous in a courtroom for over twenty years, not since his very first appearance three hours after being sworn in as a Legal Aid defense attorney, when his hands had shaken and his voice had cracked. But he had been reading drafts of his speech out loud for the past two weeks, to himself, then to his wife, incorporating her advice on editing and delivery. He was not expecting to get his wish of the maximum ten- to twenty-year sentence, but he was going to make his very best argument for it.

Outside, a cadre of Rainbows who had traveled to Warren to represent the Taylor family stood on the sidewalk, dressed in their establishment best. New Yorker Garrick Beck wore the classic version of a business suit, accessorized with a ponytail; and the other three men were in corduroy and leather. But under the cowboy hat, Barry Adams had brushed out his braids. Walking toward the courthouse, past the Civil War cannon guarding justice on the stately lawn, Adams surveyed the gray day and caught a glimmer of sun hiding behind the cloud covering.

"We're going to see a rainbow today if we're lucky," he said to his friends. But first, as they lingered outside a side entrance, they saw Jose Ramos. He was being walked from his jailhouse cell to the courtroom with the press following along. It wasn't hordes of paparazzi chasing after a celebrity scandal, but even the jostling of a handful of news crews combined with the tension of Ramos's ankle chains to throw him off guard, and he stumbled once, trying to shield his face from the cameras.

Inside, the courtroom wasn't packed, but it wasn't empty. Besides the press and the Rainbows, a sizable group of curious townspeople had gathered. The mood, as always in Judge Wolfe's chambers, was muted and respectful, but there was a curiosity to see how this would finally resolve. Even without the novelty of the Rainbows, the outside attorneys and the sensitive child molestation charges, sentencing day in Judge Wolfe's court was often newsworthy. The stories were legion. Once, Judge Wolfe had sentenced a man who'd represented himself and brought his entire church congregation to fill the spectator benches in his support. When the man had pointed that out in a show of his good faith and respectability, the judge remained unmoved.

"Eleven and a half to twenty months," he'd declared, giving him a harsher sentence than expected. To the deputies leading the defendant away, he'd added, "And make sure there's a Bible in his cell."

Today the judge quickly dispensed with Ramos's most recent round of motions to dismiss. Defense attorney Tom Bonavita began by making his recommendation of the minimum mandatory sentence—five to ten—and he asked for it to run concurrent to Ramos's Erie County term. He argued that more than a lengthy sentence, what would be most appropriate was the psychological treatment Ramos had never received. Then it was GraBois's turn.

"Your Honor, may it please the Court?" GraBois began, stepping forward. It felt strange to him, standing shoulder to shoulder with Ramos at the front of the courtroom. In federal court, these remarks were made from the counsel table, with the defendant seated several feet away. GraBois spoke directly to the judge.

"Jose Antonio Ramos appears before you today for sentencing for having committed one of the most horrible acts known to our criminal law, the sexual violation of a young child. Instead of using weapons or fear, Ramos used kindness, friendship, and gift giving to lull his young victims into a false sense of security, and then he struck."

These courtroom speeches were always a performance, the prosecutor's big moment to impact the judge with his spoken words. But today, for Stuart GraBois, this was more than just a show. For a man who shunned the press, whose public comments were of necessity terse and perfunctory, it was the first time he'd ever been able to speak publicly about everything he'd learned and felt about Jose Ramos. There would never be a trial, and in his capacity as prosecutor he certainly would never have testified even if there had been, but now he was getting his chance to bear witness to the misery caused by the man beside him.

"Your Honor, Joey Taylor is a victim for life, he will never be the same. He is treated as an outcast, he is the brunt of other childrens' jokes, he no longer has any friends. His own brother, William, Your Honor, won't be seen with him in public for fear he, too, will somehow be ridiculed"—GraBois gestured to the man by his side—"as a result of what this person did to him."

There was something so powerful about putting voice to his feelings with Ramos standing at his right shoulder, so close he could hear the man breathing. GraBois reminded the court that even as Ramos had pled guilty to his crime and claimed he didn't want to put the child through more pain and suffering, his actions spoke the real truth.

"What truly amazes me, and I've been prosecuting for a number of years, is on the day that he entered his guilty plea, he was sitting over there; he was bantering with the reporters and he still is corresponding with news people, negotiating fees to tell his story, and it's all a big joke to him, Your Honor."

Everyone in the courtroom could hear the genuine outrage in GraBois's voice.

"There is no conscience in this man, there is no remorse. Joey is still suffering, Your Honor, and this man shows no remorse..."

GraBois paused to let his last words sink in, and to give his next words their due.

"Your Honor, the Commonwealth respectfully requests that this monster standing here, who stands here so smugly, be put away in prison where he can never again harm a child, and therefore most respectfully recommends to Your Honor that he be sentenced to the maximum allowed by law of twenty years' imprisonment consecutive to the sentence he is now serving."

To GraBois's right, Ramos then made his own case, speaking so softly at first, spectators strained to hear his voice. "I am very remorseful...I understand that this is a very, very traumatic situation for a child to go through. I myself have been abused all my life, too. Nobody helped me out, now you want to put me away for twenty years, well..." His voice broke, then rose sharply. "It ain't right."

For his part, GraBois looked straight ahead, but he was acutely aware of the white-hot rage spilling off of the man next to him. Ramos was now swaying slightly from side to side. Growing up in his Bensonhurst neighborhood, GraBois had learned from experience that such body language sometimes signaled an impending attack, and he moved into a defensive stance, raising his arms slightly and leaning back. One of the sheriff's deputies stood up and walked purposefully toward Ramos, as his voice rose and took on a keening quality. Ramos motioned him back.

"You don't have to stand here like he's going to hit me or something, I'm not going to do nothing," Ramos said to the deputy.

Marylou Barton also stood up to her full five-foot-three height and walked to stand between the two men. She would tell GraBois later she'd expected at any moment both of them to be rolling on the courtroom's thinly carpeted floor.

"I'm just upset because nobody helped me when I asked for help," Ramos said. "Mr. GraBois accused me of molesting everybody in the United States, well, if that's the case, you know, well, charge me with that, too."

Ramos was defiant but he was now also weeping openly. "Where's the justice at? I'm asking for justice, I've been asking it for three years now," he wailed. His eyes raked the front of the courtroom, moving from the judge to the other officers of the court.

The deputy had moved up to Ramos's other side, and he reached out to put his hand in restraint on the prisoner's shoulder.

"No." Ramos pulled away. "I want to say what I have to say, I have a right to say what I have to say."

"I'm not stopping you," said the deputy. "Just settle down." Ramos seemed to compose himself, but another officer standing outside in the gallery area quietly undid the latch and cracked open the gate in readiness. Everyone who worked here knew the last time things had turned violent in this courtroom. Forty years earlier a divorce hearing had ended badly when the plaintiff, Norman Moon, shot and killed Judge Allison Wade as he dived under his bench, then later turned the gun on himself. Bullet holes in the desk and wall were a prominent reminder of the first and only assassination in Pennsylvania of a sitting judge.

But Ramos had lost his fire, and he slumped into himself, his voice dropping back down. "I don't know how to express my hurt inside me, I don't know how, I'm trying to ask the Court for help. I'm trying."

"All right," Judge Wolfe responded, his voice devoid of all sentiment. "Is that all?"

"Yes sir." Ramos sounded defeated, as though he could tell the judge was unmoved by his emotional outburst. It *had* been emotional, gut-wrenching to listen to, even coming from the mouth of a serial child molester. Some in the court simply thought it was manufactured, a calculated ploy to sway the judge or bolster Ramos's claims of mental illness. GraBois himself thought it was real. He'd seen Jose Ramos emotionally implode in similar situations—when he first admitted he was 90 percent sure that the child he took back to his apartment for sex was Etan Patz, and again just one month earlier when he'd finally agreed to the plea. But his breakdowns evoked no sympathy from GraBois. He reserved his sympathy for Ramos's victims.

Before pronouncing his sentence, Judge Wolfe took some pains to explain his decision. He had read all the paperwork, the pre-sentence investigation, the half-dozen multipage letters Ramos had sent directly to the judge, and now he cited specifically the clear admissions Ramos had made in those letters of his sexual abuse against children.

"You have indeed told the Court," began Judge Wolfe, "in your own writing, of your sexual activity prior to this charge with male juveniles."

The judge had also read in great detail the examining psychiatrist's report, and referred to the doctor's conclusion that Ramos could not rest on a mental illness diagnosis to mitigate his criminal history.

Citing directly from the psychiatric evaluation, the judge acknowledged Ramos's reports of childhood abuse, then read aloud the doctor's assessment that nevertheless, "there is no evidence that he was psychologically impaired at the time of the assault in any way that would make him any less responsible for his actions.

"In the Court's opinion," the judge now told Ramos, "you're a predator upon young males, and your writings have acknowledged that."

Predator. As soon as GraBois heard that word, he knew the judge was going to come down hard.

Turning to Ramos's tearful assertions of remorse for what he had done to young Joey Taylor and his family, Judge Wolfe said, "The Court does accept the Commonwealth's position that you have shown no remorse whatsoever. You haven't denied your acts; you haven't justified your acts except by attempting to shift the responsibility to your victim and his parents. This Court concludes from all of the evidence: Yes, you do know right from wrong; you know these acts are wrong and you continue to do them."

The judge pointed out that this was not Ramos's first offense, and he signaled the need to protect society against such repeat offenders.

"For these reasons, Mr. Ramos, you are sentenced to pay the cost of prosecution; you will stand committed to the Western Diagnostic and Classification Center at Pittsburgh for a minimum period of ten years to the maximum period of twenty, that sentence to run consecutive and not concurrent to all of the sentence that you are now undergoing."

Ten to twenty, consecutive. GraBois was exhilarated. The judge had ruled in favor of every one of the prosecution's wishes. Standing there, he told himself it had all been worth it.

He thought about Joey and Etan and Bennett, and all those boys in the little photo-booth pictures from the drainpipe. Ramos would serve the full twenty, GraBois promised himself. He'd do whatever he could to make that happen. And because the sentence was consecutive, it meant, at the very least and barring parole, that Jose Ramos would sit behind bars well into the next century, possibly until 2014. He'd be at least seventy years old then, if he lived that long. Joey Taylor would be thirty-six, and hopefully he'd spend the interim growing up and out of his trauma.

GraBois glanced toward the gallery. Barry Adams had that face-splitting grin, and he flashed a thumbs-up. GraBois felt himself grinning back. He exchanged congratulations with Marylou Barton, and they gathered up their papers to leave.

As he was leaving the courtroom, GraBois asked Tom Bonavita whether he and his client would meet with him again in the law library, just to listen to a final offer. All along, GraBois's bargaining chip on the Patz case wasn't how much time Ramos would do, but how he'd do that time—hard or easier. There was no easy. But the federal prosecutor could arrange for Ramos to serve his sentence in a federal rather than state facility where there was less overcrowding, healthier food, and a better all-around class of criminal. Most murders, rapes—all the worst violent crimes—came through state court, so those murderers, rapists, and an entrenched gang network were for the most part in state prisons. For a child molester vulnerable to attack, a forty-seven-year-old thinking about how he'd be spending his next twenty-four years, this was far more than a simple quality-of-life issue.

"Jose, you're going away for a long time," GraBois said. "I'm willing to try to see that you do federal time. I can also reach out to your family and put you together with your parents. I know you haven't seen them in a long time. But you have to do the right thing and help the Patz family."

He half expected to hear Ramos tell him to fuck off, but the man said nothing, simply stood there, glowering. He had clearly heard the offer, but he was either not going to give GraBois the satisfaction of acknowledgment, or he was in understandable shock. When all of this had started in GraBois's office back in June 1988, Jose Ramos had been looking forward to the possibility of parole in November 1990. Instead, with one day left in that month, twenty-plus more years now stretched bleakly ahead of him.

"I don't want an answer now. Just think about it," GraBois said as he ended the brief meeting. Ramos was then led out of the courtroom, and the press crowded around, eager to get his reaction. John Miller's question followed Ramos down the hall.

"Do you think this ten to twenty might give you an incentive to consider a deal on the Etan Patz case?" That was exactly what Miller thought the prosecutor was going for in the Pennsylvania courtroom.

"I got no comment on that."

"Do you think you got that stiff sentence because of the Patz case?"

Ramos had nowhere to go with the cameras trained on him as he waited for the elevator. "Yeah," he said. "But I have no comment whatsoever on the Patz case." At the shouted follow-ups, he stepped into the elevator. "Why don't you ask GraBois about that? Why don't you ask GraBois why he had me arrested..." The door closed on his words.

When GraBois spoke to the reporters some twenty minutes later, the question was asked again about the Patz case and its connection here, but he echoed Ramos.

"I cannot comment on that" was all he'd say. Instead he talked about his satisfaction at the sentence, and what it would mean to the victim.

"A little boy was injured," he said. "Psychologically, emotionally, physically, and this was judgment day. For a man that thought he could get away with it, he was now humbled by the judge."

In his last comment to one local Erie reporter, who persisted in asking about the Patz case, he finally gave her what she needed, the soundbite guaranteed to make it on the air.

"The U.S. Attorney's Office is not finished with Jose Ramos."

CHAPTER 20

Another Door Opens

Dear Stuart,

Hi, hope that this letter fines [*sic*] you and your family well and a merry Christmas, this coming new 1991 New Year. My family and I wants to thank you very much for all your help.

—*Cherie Taylor's Christmas card, December 20, 1990*

To Mr. Stuart R. GraBois and Family

"Especially for You:

May Hanukkah be a season of beauty, shining with warmth, joy and love."

[handwritten:] "Thou shall take no Vengeance (Leviticus 19:18)"

—*Jose Antonio Ramos's Hanukkah card, December 28, 1990*

T he year wound down slowly, compared to the pace of the fall. Little could compete with November's crescendo in the courtroom. Jose Ramos remained safely locked away at Rockview state prison, serving out the last four years on his Erie conviction. Any chance for early parole on that charge was blown to pieces by this new conviction. Ramos was working himself into a state, trying to find a loophole in the sentence he'd just been handed. Within days he'd filed an appeal, then furiously filled even more long yellow sheets with invective and pleadings to the judge, citing mind-numbing precedent, the Greek goddess Themis, and Plato. Jose Ramos held one person responsible for his personal nightmare, and boxed up in a fifteen-by-ten-foot world at SCI Rockview, his enmity was festering.

Stuart GraBois stayed in touch with the Rockview administrators. Once again, GraBois's ability to see setbacks as opportunities kept him moving forward. The fact that Ramos hadn't broken down further and coughed up the missing pieces to the Patz case was a bitter disappointment. But it was mitigated by the prospect that far into the foreseeable future, GraBois could count on dealing with a stationary target. GraBois hoped it wouldn't take twenty-five years, but he wouldn't think that far ahead, just to the next step in his work-in-progress.

There were other payoffs, smaller perhaps but powerful in their own right. GraBois opened a stack of Christmas mail in late December 1990 to find a card addressed from a rural route postbox in a small midwestern town. "May the faith and hope of Christmas light your way the whole year through" was the inscribed message. The Jewish prosecutor was touched by the sentiment beyond the words. A long, heartfelt note was folded into the card.

Cherie Taylor thanked him not just for taking on the court case, but because "it was also a part of our life that made my family stronger and closer together in love and in heart.

"Thank you very much once again," she wrote in a large, loopy scrawl. "I am sending a school picture of Joey and William for you." Thirteen-year-old Joey was still a round-faced, cherubic-looking seventh grader; at twelve, Billy's eyes were warier. The typical overlit, stilted studio photos portrayed two scrubbed innocent faces. GraBois had spent the previous months with these boys, and knew it wasn't like that; you can't go back and change things. But, he now thought, their expressions hinted at a life retrieved.

"When you look at them," Cherie wrote, "remember that the hope and faith we put in man's law is really the love God has for his children."

It was a slightly garbled but lovely thought. Cherie had talked before about how this prosecution had given the Taylor family a new, if guarded, belief in the law, and that's how GraBois interpreted this sentiment. Prosecutors aren't often afforded such appreciation, he thought, and he tucked the note away in his files.

It helped rinse away the bitter taste of GraBois's most recent exchange with Jose Ramos. The week before Cherie Taylor's letter arrived, GraBois had taken his last shot of 1990, launching the next phase of his campaign. In search of a bargaining chip, GraBois's investigators had tracked down Jose Ramos Sr. at his Florida home. He was deeply ashamed of his son, Ramos Sr. told GraBois over the phone. In fact, the family had had nothing to do with him since the early seventies. He often wondered if his son's problems stemmed from an accident during his Navy stint, some kind of explosion on board ship that might have damaged him this way. "He was regular before that," said Ramos Sr. As GraBois filled him in on recent events, he sensed a dignified elderly man whose family had thrown up their hands. Ramos Sr. told GraBois that his wife was very ill in Florida, but if the prosecutor thought he could help, he would make arrangements to travel to New York.

GraBois thanked him, and the next day he called Jose Ramos Jr. It was a terse, awkward exchange.

"I had a long talk with your father," GraBois started. "Your parents are willing to come up to see you. I would bring them up." But the Patz family need something as well, he went on. They need to hear about *their* son.

"I am no longer interested in prosecuting you in New York," GraBois continued, which was not the truth. He simply wanted to know if Ramos would take any kind of bait, whether there was even any point to keep on fishing. Given the decades facing Ramos, "to try to prosecute you here on something else makes little sense now. And we think you can help us out on this end." The prosecutor offered to get Ramos a lawyer to work out a deal.

"So I throw that out to you, for what it's worth. If you want to tell me to go to hell, go ahead."

Ramos listened in silence, but he wasn't buying it. "You have a Happy Hanukkah, yourself and your family," he replied. "I have nothing else to say to you. I don't know what you want and I've told you I don't have anything more to offer you."

"You certainly do." GraBois wasn't going to just let that go. "Look, I'm talking about the Etan Patz case, you know that and I know that. You told us what you told us . . . and I have other facts too, now. You could help to put this case to rest once and for all for that family, and I could help put you together with your family. That's your call. I'm not dealing with you here, I'm just asking you to listen." GraBois gave him new contact numbers and could hear the sound of Ramos writing them down. "You can call collect anytime."

GraBois hung up in frustration. The phone rang a few minutes later. "I don't know what you said to him," Jack Allar, the Rockview superintendent's right-hand man, reported, "but he was crying when he got off the call." Some small satisfaction, thought GraBois. This is working on him. I just need to find more of the same.

When the card arrived from Ramos just days later, wishing him and his family a Happy Hanukkah, GraBois felt sure that the inmate wasn't ready to walk away from their game just yet, which was good because GraBois wasn't either. He left for the holidays, after making an appointment for January with the FBI agent currently assigned to the case.

"Does this mean you're going to have to get him a gift?" Special Agent Mary Galligan had just read Ramos's greeting card and it made her laugh out loud. She was twenty-seven years old, and just two years out of the training academy. She was now juggling the Patz case with several others, but it was particularly close to her heart. Galligan had only assisted on other investigations before this one, her first solo flight.

Galligan's parents had worked hard to send her to the Sacred Heart Academy, an all-girls Long Island college prep school where the sisters didn't use rulers, just plenty of rules. No clogs, no dark nail polish, no listening to Billy Joel's "Only the Good Die Young." There was no rule, however, that a girl couldn't do a boy's job, because there were no boys to cede to. Tall, strong, and athletic, with wavy brown hair and a scathingly sarcastic wit, Galligan had been the editor of her school newspaper and a standout on the swim team. At Sacred Heart she'd developed the inner confidence that would allow her to handle a position with the prestigious FBI Bank Robbery Squad only a year after she joined the Bureau. Timing played a major part too—the only woman on the squad, Lisa Smith, was leaving, so there was room for her replacement. That's how things worked back then in the most sought-after ranks of the Bureau. Named when stickups—white-collar and otherwise—were the most serious crimes in the FBI's purview, Bank Robbery would later be rechristened Violent Crimes, and include interstate kidnappings, extortions, and product tamperings.

As a rookie agent, Galligan had inherited the Patz case sometime around its ten-year anniversary from Smith, the departing agent. Growing up on Long Island, she was only vaguely familiar with the name Etan Patz. But her mother, who'd raised four kids, knew it by heart. Read up on the files, Galligan's boss told her, and sent her to the twenty-seventh floor where the research was kept in floor-to-ceiling rotor cabinets.

"Can you direct me to the Patz files?" she asked.

"Over there," the clerk said. Galligan looked at an entire tower labeled "ETAN PATZ 7-NY-186181."

"And over there, and there and there," the woman pointed.

Galligan tackled all of it, but it wasn't until she was sent to meet with

Stuart GraBois that it began to fit together. As Ken Ruffo had once done for him, GraBois now walked Galligan through the case, and he did so with such a passion and fervor that it proved infectious. In the early part of her involvement on the case, Mary Galligan dealt with P.J. Fox, who was brought to New York for follow-up; interviewed Sandy Harmon to hear her story and her denials; and chased a number of other leads while GraBois's attention was on the Pennsylvania chapter. Every part of her first case had proved challenging, but the day she met Stan and Julie Patz in the summer of 1990 affected her most deeply.

It had become clear by then that P.J. was not Etan. The birthdates weren't right, and other details didn't fit, but in order to rule him out definitively and move on, the FBI wanted to compare his DNA to the Patzes'. Galligan was charged with ensuring the integrity of the blood samples, which would be taken and tested at a Madison Avenue lab the Bureau contracted to conduct the then-cutting-edge procedure.

By this point, she'd spoken with the Patzes over the phone several times. But while she was perfectly pleasant whenever she answered, Julie always handed the phone to Stan, and Galligan didn't know what to expect the day she met them at the lab. She wasn't prepared for how unsettling the surprisingly private moment soon became.

The agent watched as Julie Patz rolled up her sleeve. The nurse swabbing Julie's arm doesn't know, Galligan thought. She's the only one in this room for whom this could be a simple blood test to check for drugs, or a parasite. But the rest of them were all too aware they were here to rule out the rough petty criminal P.J. Fox as Stan and Julie's son. Stan said next to nothing, and Julie made little reference to what was really going on.

"People don't understand," she said sadly at one point, "what it's like to have one day change your life so much."

Galligan felt the discomfort hanging in the air. She didn't want to make small talk; it felt so oppressively banal. She thought of making some effort to break the tension, but was at a loss.

"How long have you been an agent?" Julie Patz's voice interrupted Galligan's thoughts.

"Two years," she answered, as the nurse labeled and packaged the vials. Julie continued to chat quietly, asking more questions as she and Stan waited patiently to be told they were through. She's trying to put *me* at ease, realized Mary Galligan incredulously. She attempted to follow the other woman's lead and respond politely, but all she could think about was the one thing she wanted to ask, but knew she couldn't. Would Julie Patz want this boy to be her son, or hope to God that he wasn't?

When GraBois came back from Pennsylvania with the triumphant news of Ramos's lengthy sentence, Galligan was pleased, but she couldn't help but be a little disappointed. The investigation seemed to be over without having been able to unravel the mystery of what had happened to Etan, at the very least for his parents' sake. Until GraBois set her straight.

As the new year began, he laid out another avenue that had been slowly developing all through the previous fall. As it had in the past, whenever the Patz story surfaced in the public eye, it held out the promise of a ripple effect that could push the case along. The Pennsylvania case had gotten people talking. Certainly there'd been a buzz in the prison, as inmates realized they had a notable in their midst. GraBois appreciated that, not only because it meant tougher time for Ramos—even cold-blooded ax murderers treat child molesters like scum of the earth—but because his notoriety might also engender new information.

The prosecutor had been intrigued when, back in July 1990 in the midst of Ramos's rearrest, a federal inmate serving time in upstate New York by the name of Jon Morgan had written to GraBois out of the blue, to hint at a connection to the Patz case. Or at least to Jose Ramos.

"He was my roommate in Otisville," Morgan had written. He and Ramos had spoken often there, and although he didn't want to "get involved," he might be willing to talk to GraBois about those conversations.

GraBois had read the letter with interest. The Federal Correctional Institution at Otisville was an hour and a half outside of New York City; Ramos had in fact been there several times, whenever GraBois would bring him up from Pennsylvania for questioning. And GraBois had met Jon Morgan before when another AUSA had brought him into the office. Morgan had stuck in GraBois's mind because when he wasn't in prison, he lived in the same nearby New York suburb. He was also, GraBois recalled, a real piece of work.

Jon Morgan had a sordid, if not violent, white-collar history. He and his partner were an audacious pair of "entrepreneurs" who had skated the boundary between life in the fast lane and life behind bars, until they careened wildly over the line and went away for thirteen years each. The two men had made a fortune buying up chemicals for cheap that didn't pass muster in the United States, then reselling them at a huge profit in the Third World where standards were much lower and oversight virtually nonexistent. They saw it as a win-win-win. Chemical companies got rid of expired product without expensive, annoyingly safety-conscious disposal costs. Businesses in developing countries got material that their governments sanctioned, or at least looked the other way from. And the partners pocketed more than a million dollars a year, for over fifteen years. Until they got caught. It turned out oversight served a purpose; in at least one case the two were selling pure poison in the guise of legitimate chemicals—unknowingly, they claimed. There was at least one toxic spill, and large oozing canisters were dumped in suburban East Coast warehouses. Jon Morgan was being tracked by at least eight government agencies when the Feds finally caught up with him.

Back in the mid-eighties, before he started on the Patz case, GraBois had met the "Biohazard Boys," as they were known around the office, when the AUSA prosecuting their case had them in for questioning. From those previous dealings, GraBois knew Jon Morgan as smart, coherent, and open to working with the Feds. He was not someone you'd want your daughter to bring home, but informants never are. GraBois didn't care. As long as his info was sound and verifiable, GraBois would welcome it. He was never going to torpedo a case with information he couldn't corroborate. Trust but verify, as the last president liked to say. GraBois knew all too well that informants could be more trouble than they were worth, because you had to carefully vet what they were offering. But he also knew you didn't look a gift horse in the mouth. Or at least you didn't turn the horse away without a careful examination of his teeth.

If Ramos had indeed been in Otisville at the same time as Morgan, the two might very well have come in contact, and GraBois had wanted to follow out the lead. So, at the end of the busy summer, once Ramos had been arraigned, charged, and was awaiting trial, GraBois had talked to Morgan on the phone and learned a bit more.

Morgan and Ramos had become acquainted while hanging out in the Otisville law library, where they both spent time working on their cases. At one point, Morgan told GraBois, the two had even briefly been cellmates.

When they'd first met back in 1989, Morgan said, Ramos had spoken good-naturedly about GraBois, almost bragging that he knew him. He made it sound as though he was the model cooperating witness. "The reason I'm here at Otisville is because an AUSA brought me in from state custody to help on this Patz case," Ramos had told Morgan. He'd talked about sitting in GraBois's office for hours, even getting the red-carpet treatment of Sabrett's hot dogs from a nearby vendor. "The agent went down and brought them back up to me," Ramos had said, "and they were the best hot dogs I ever ate." That was significant to GraBois, because the hot dog story had actually happened during the summer of 1988, in one of the meetings that followed Ramos's "90 percent confession." It was a small detail, but it added some credibility to Jon Morgan's account.

Ramos had also spoken openly to Morgan about his link to the Patz case, explaining that he knew all about it because his "wife," as he called her, had been the Patzes' babysitter.

As Morgan relayed Ramos's claims, GraBois scrawled, "Had info— eventually make deal" on his ever-present notepad. Ramos had led Morgan to believe he was just waiting for the right time to reveal all and solve the case. "Kid might be alive," GraBois had noted. Indeed, Ramos had stressed this, Morgan had said. He'd also asked Morgan a lot of questions about federal law, about a statute of limitations for murder. "I don't know how it is now," Morgan had told GraBois, "because I hear from other inmates up here that you're going after him on some Pennsylvania thing, but back when we met he was acting like your pal."

Besides conversations in the law library, Morgan had said, he also knew Ramos from Jewish services. Ramos, Morgan had scoffed, was a self-styled Jew, who'd told Morgan he'd uncovered his roots during a trip to Spain. Ramos had taken to growing out his bangs, his version of the long curly locks—*payes*—that religious Jews dangled over their ears. GraBois also knew that to be true; Jack Allar at Rockview had regaled him with tales about Ramos's nascent faith. But, Morgan said, Ramos was the most ignorant Jew he'd ever met, and the other Jewish inmates resented his "playing Jewish." Ramos seemed harmless enough at first, Morgan had believed, but he'd later learned the man had two sides.

"He's a lunatic," Morgan had told GraBois in that first phone call, "and he's got a hair-trigger temper." Morgan had witnessed that temper once when several other inmates had to restrain Ramos in the law library from smashing in an elderly inmate's skull with a typewriter. GraBois took notes on a yellow legal pad. "Absolute lunatic," he wrote, "mentally deranged."

In the summer of 1990, when Morgan had first sent his note to Stuart GraBois, he hadn't seen Ramos in months, but he'd been hearing about him. Arriving up at his current home in FCI Ray Brook, a medium-security prison tucked in the Adirondacks, Morgan had met up with some old friends from Otisville. "How did it feel to be roommates with a cannibal?" one of them had asked Morgan. The other inmate had seen a news story about Ramos that made the Patz connection. "He killed a bunch of kids and ate them," the man had misinformed Morgan, who then went on to learn about the Pennsylvania charges. Suddenly what had seemed like boastful jailhouse bullshit seemed worthy of passing along to authorities. Of course, it went without saying that for any inmate, it never hurt to be on the good side of a federal prosecutor.

At the end of that September conversation GraBois had told Morgan he'd be in touch, and he turned once again back to the outstanding Pennsylvania case. Then, mid-October, GraBois had gotten a nibble from another source.

An old friend, an investigator in the New York County District Attorney's Office called one day. "We got a guy over here in on a local charge. I think you should come and hear what he has to say." By that time, Ramos had finally taken his plea, and GraBois was preparing for November's critical sentencing hearing. Still, he went down the street to meet a check-kiting career confidence man named Jeremy Fischer.

Fischer, trying to get some leverage on his state case, had a strange story to tell. At first, GraBois couldn't believe his ears—and not just because, with his slicked-back hair and ponytail, cool delivery, and ready banter, Fischer immediately radiated con artist. GraBois's incredulity stemmed just as much from the bizarre coincidence that Fischer, too, knew Ramos from Otisville, from the same Jewish prayer group as Jon Morgan. In fact, Fischer even mentioned Morgan's name offhandedly when he was listing other inmates he knew in the group. What are the odds, GraBois had wondered.

Unlike Morgan, GraBois had no prior knowledge of Fischer beyond what was on paper, and he had no particular reason to trust him. In fact, it was quite the opposite. But he listened to Fischer's story.

Fischer said he and Ramos had spent a lot of time together in private conversation at Otisville in the yard, the cafeteria, at services. It was a weird friendship, said Fischer, filled with fantasy- and mysticism-laced talks. Ramos would give him books to read, with sections on pederasty underlined. But the talk wasn't pornographic, Fischer was quick to clarify, more intellectual, philosophical—long discussions about life in ancient Greece, for example.

Again, GraBois was completely unconvinced, but one word he heard gave credence to Fischer's story.

Fischer recounted how the previous year, he'd seen Ramos after a Jewish holiday service. He was coming out of an area of the chapel behind Ramos, who didn't see him. They were the only two in the room, Fischer said, when suddenly Ramos began to cry, then got down on his knees to pray. "I did terrible things," Fischer heard; then something about how everyone was after him, that someday he'd be famous. At some point later Ramos began crying again, and wailed, "It's gonna happen," then, "Oh, Etan, Etan, I never meant to hurt you, Etan. I loved you." Fischer said that at the time he didn't understand what Ramos was saying, because of his pronunciation. "He said, 'Eat-en,' 'Eat-en,' and I thought he was talking about food or something. It wasn't until I was down at MCC on this new charge that I saw a story John Miller did on the news about this case in Pennsylvania, and I finally made the connection."

GraBois perked up at the boy's name. Now he took Jeremy Fischer more seriously. Very few people could know that Jose Ramos pronounced Etan's name exactly that way. GraBois had learned about it only from talking to Ramos himself the day he all but confessed in the prosecutor's office.

Fischer had incriminating things to offer up about other inmates, too. GraBois learned later that this was Fischer's MO—picked up for his latest scheme, he would immediately roll over if it meant working a deal. He was always looking to make his information work for him, greasing whatever tight spot he was in. GraBois left thinking the Ramos information wasn't going to help in and of itself, but maybe there was a way to put it to good use.

A jailhouse informant posed even more challenges than a snitch on the outside, although one advantage was he couldn't drop out of sight; until he's released, you always know where to find him. The downsides were numerous: An inmate was invariably attached to his lawyer, adding—really, multiplying—to the complexity of the negotiation. Communication was a bigger problem, and the loop of people who'd have to know about such an arrangement was wider. Most critically, you couldn't easily *solicit* an inside informant; it wasn't like you could make an announcement over some prison loudspeaker. So the fact that two separate sources in different locations had reached out was not just a gift horse, it was a surefire tip in the Belmont Stakes.

In the first weeks of the new year Stuart GraBois and Mary Galligan were on the phone nearly every day, strategizing. Could they get either one of the informants inside to get next to Ramos? How, without making him suspicious? This all had to be orchestrated very delicately, since Ramos was both paranoid and clever, and would be automatically on his guard. Was Jon Morgan a good candidate? Jeremy Fischer? Galligan needed to meet and assess both, but it was good to have options, and either way it certainly kept the door open.

CHAPTER 21

Confidential Witness

COMMONWEALTH OF PENNSYLVANIA
VS.
JOSE RAMOS

ORDER

AND NOW, to-wit, this 17th day of January, 1991, the defendant's motion for reconsideration of sentence is denied.

BY THE COURT

Robert L. Wolfe, P.J.

J on Morgan was talking to his mother from a pay phone, in one of his carefully apportioned personal calls at FCI Ray Brook. It was the start of the new year, but it felt like the same-old same-old. His mother was fretting about some problems around the house, and Morgan was only half listening, until she remembered the letter he'd received that morning from his old cellmate, Jose Ramos. Morgan figured it might be another tidbit to pass along to GraBois, so he had his mother read it to him. For two pages, it went on about the injustices Ramos had suffered recently in Pennsylvania. "I was forceably coerced into pleading guilty," Morgan's mother read. "I got ten to twenty years to run consecutive to the sentence that I was serving." That's a bad deal, thought Morgan. "So anyway, how are you?" the letter continued. Morgan was starting to tune out again, but then he heard his mother read a familiar name, and in a split second he was ramped up to a near panic. "Remember you told me you knew where Stuart GraBois lived? Could you send me his address and any other information you might have on him?"

"Stop, Ma," Morgan broke in, his voice drowning out the last part of the

255

sentence. "Don't read another word." Those words should never be heard over a Bureau of Prisons phone line. He knew they recorded this shit. They might even be listening in right now. He was sweating. "Put the letter down, Ma. Don't even touch it. It could get me in a lot of trouble. I'm going to call GraBois right now, and I'll let you know what he wants me to do."

When GraBois took the collect call from Morgan he was surprised to hear him so agitated. In his few dealings with the man, he'd perceived Morgan as fairly measured. True, he normally talked in a nonlinear fashion, but now he was approaching a rant.

"This guy Ramos, I don't even know him that well," Morgan said. "I just hung out with him for a few days at Otisville. I thought he was harmless, but I was wrong. Now he is trying to get me involved in his craziness and I want nothing to do with it."

"Okay, calm down," GraBois said, "and tell me what happened."

"This guy doesn't like you," Morgan said.

"The feeling is mutual," GraBois replied. Then Morgan told him about the letter.

"He wrote this whole thing about what a bad deal he was forced to take, how he got fucked, and now he's trying to get an appeal."

"Yup. He did. And I await his appeal with pleasure. He's got nothing," GraBois told Morgan. "He even wrote to the judge to complain and ended up confessing in the letter."

"There's a problem, and I wanted you to know about it right away," Morgan said. "Ramos wants to know where you live. He's asking me to find out."

"Why would he be asking *you* that?" GraBois was surprised, although he enjoyed the notion that Ramos was thinking about him.

"Well, I might have told him we lived near each other," Morgan said uneasily.

"Why the hell would you do something like that?" GraBois was remembering back to the one time he'd met Morgan, when they had, indeed, talked about being neighbors.

"Look, when I first met the guy, he was fine with you." Morgan said. "He was all about helping you out." So Morgan had thought little of his casual mention to Ramos that he and the prosecutor came from the same part of town. It was a status symbol of sorts to have connections with a federal prosecutor. Morgan was just making conversation. Now Ramos seemed to have seized on that connection.

"He sent this letter to my house. To my home. To my mother, for God's sake." Morgan was working himself up. "So my mother is pulled into this too, now. He's heading for criminal conspiracy, and he's put me smack in the middle of it. Who the hell does he think he is? I want nothing to do with this, and I want you to know about it, from me, up front."

"Okay, Jon," GraBois said, "I appreciate your bringing it to me, and it may be useful. I think you should come down and talk to me some more about this."

"I don't need this—I've got my own problems," Morgan continued. "This guy is seriously mentally ill, and I think he could be really dangerous. I told my mother not to even open any more of his letters."

"That's exactly what you should have told her," GraBois assured Morgan. "I'll go get the letters from your mother. Tell her just to call me when she gets one, and I'll come pick it up. She shouldn't even touch it. Have her put it in a plastic bag and set it aside." If Ramos had anyone on the outside helping him who might have handled the letter, GraBois wanted a shot at getting prints.

This might just do it, thought GraBois as he hung up. Now that Ramos was looking at his twenty-year stretch, he was reaching out in desperation. Desperation was good. GraBois called Jack Allar at Rockview and told him what was going on. They agreed the prison would put a mail cover on all of Ramos's correspondence, screening everything going in and coming out of the prison. GraBois also wanted to be alerted to any visitors going down there, and especially if anything was being said about him.

GraBois went to Jon Morgan's house a few days later on his way home from work and picked up the letter. Jon's mom invited the prosecutor in and he took an immediate shine to her, a mother in distress. Mrs. Morgan was a birdlike, fretful little woman, in a panic about one of the problems Jon had mentioned to GraBois—a deadbeat, erratic boarder, who was now threatening her. GraBois felt sorry for the elderly woman, and a bit protective. Her middle-aged boys had taken the hit for their crimes, been shipped off to prison, and they'd left their mother living alone and vulnerable. The prosecutor listened sympathetically, told her he'd have an agent make some calls, even gave her his home number, something he almost never did. She was grateful and promised to call him about any other letters from Ramos. "Don't even open them," GraBois cautioned her. "If you see that return address, put it away and call me. And don't worry about your son either. I'm looking out for him."

It was Morgan who called him the next day. He had heard from his mother, and she'd been impressed. "Thanks for treating her so well," he told GraBois. He agreed to come down to New York for a meeting.

GraBois didn't wait. Just five days later, the prosecutor sent up the order to move Ramos from state custody in Pennsylvania to the federal prison in Otisville. Now, at least, Ramos would be in position for whatever came next.

————

As best he could with his hands cuffed in front of him, Jon Morgan pulled at the coat some pitying soul had thrown loosely over his head and shoulders to shield him, ineffectually, from the biting February chill. Once the cuffs go on, the coatsleeves can't get past them, but at least he had an extra layer over his thin prison jumpsuit. In the early morning hours, Morgan had arrived from Ray Brook, caught a few hours' sleep, then been roused for more paperwork and waiting. He felt seriously sleep-deprived, miserably cold, and pissed off. He blamed Ramos for all of this.

Now he followed the U.S. marshals as they walked him across the street from the Manhattan Correctional Center into 26 Federal Plaza, where GraBois had been temporarily moved while his offices were under renovation. For the next months, the U.S. Attorney's Major Crimes Unit would be housed in the same building as the New York FBI. It was there that Morgan was to meet today with AUSA GraBois and agent Mary Galligan. He wasn't sure exactly what the Feds wanted from him, or whether he was going to be willing to do it, but he was angry enough with Jose Ramos to at least listen. He had little more than a year left on his sentence and had fully expected to serve it quietly, except for the mountain of legal filings he was preparing. When Morgan took on the system, he did it legitimately, not violently. He just wanted to do his time peacefully and go home. He could easily work himself up into a lather every time he thought about Ramos and his bullshit.

Stuart GraBois ushered Morgan in, and told the marshals it was all right for them to step outside. GraBois felt it was important to act respectful to Morgan, without piling it on. He had looked through Morgan's files. In person, he wasn't at all the dramatic character that his international criminal past conjured up. GraBois had always suspected that Morgan's partner, the law school graduate, was the dynamic half of the duo. With his lank, unkempt hair, doughy frame, and prison pallor, Morgan looked anything but the dangerous criminal. The two men waited for Mary Galligan to arrive and made ineffectual small talk. When Morgan started to talk about the case, GraBois quickly stopped him.

"Let's wait for the agent," he said, and they talked about the neighborhood some more. Nothing of any substance was to be said without a corroborating presence. That was the golden rule in federal law enforcement.

Galligan arrived soon afterwards. Unlike GraBois, she had never met Morgan and knew virtually nothing about him, other than his white-collar criminal status. That was how she and GraBois always played it. "Don't tell me anything—I'll start from scratch," she would tell the prosecutor. Gra-Bois knew a fair amount about Morgan; he'd checked into his background thoroughly. So Galligan was the one without preconceptions, and GraBois would very consciously let her ask most of the questions today, to let her form her views independently. It would be her show. Plus, it would provide a chance for Morgan to trip himself up if his story today was in any way inconsistent with what he'd told GraBois earlier. If they were going to pull Morgan into this operation, both of them needed to be convinced he was the right guy.

Galligan hadn't been impressed with Jeremy Fischer when GraBois had taken her down to meet him at the DA's Office a few weeks earlier. Fischer had gotten his story straight with her, nothing changed or scrambled from the time he'd met with GraBois. But Galligan had simply pegged Fischer for what he was—a con born and bred, and it remained to convince her he was a reliable source. That made Jon Morgan's part in this even more critical.

"Date of birth?" Galligan asked, starting as always at the beginning. GraBois and Galligan had different interviewing styles; their separate lines of questioning drew out added bits and pieces. GraBois's style was more staccato, and he often liked to cut right to the chase. "What did Ramos tell you?" might be his first question. It was the prosecutorial pounce, and he could throw a subject off guard to effective use right off the bat. Galligan might start slower and work up to things. One wasn't better, they were just different.

Morgan was thirty-nine years old and he looked older. As the man continued to answer her standard questions, Galligan took stock. Working violent crimes, most of her interviews were worst-case scenarios, real bad guys who robbed banks at gunpoint and kidnapped helpless victims. People could fool you, she knew, but this one didn't have a threatening vibe. Nor did he look desperate. He sat calmly and still, not like the cons she often dealt with, whose knees shook as Galligan nailed them dead to rights on a bank robbery—caught on camera with their hands covered in red dye. The ones who knew if they couldn't make a deal, they were going away for the rest of their life. This guy looked like he didn't need to be there.

Morgan told Galligan the same story he'd related to GraBois over the phone, and more:

At the law library in Otisville, both men had worked on their cases. Ramos, Morgan explained, had spent all his free time there, because he also helped out a clientele of other inmates, writing briefs and "advising" them.

Breaking an unwritten law this time—that inmates didn't discuss their crimes (especially pedophiles)—Ramos had told Morgan how a woman he'd stayed with in Pennsylvania had unjustly accused him of messing with her kids. "Don't tell the others," Ramos had said to Morgan. "Even though I didn't do it, it sounds bad."

Morgan learned more from Ramos, in the course of hours spent either over law journals or at Jewish services. "He told me he was from a lost tribe or something," said Morgan, "that he had discovered a Jewish grandfather when he was in Spain." They saw each other at services and in a study group, but again, Morgan reiterated how the small cadre of Jewish inmates were suspicious of Ramos's true roots.

Then Morgan talked about Ramos's broad knowledge of the Patz case. He knew, for example, that GraBois was looking for a boy in Ohio, because of some picture the prosecutor had found. Although this boy looked a lot like Etan, Ramos enjoyed watching GraBois on a wild goose chase, because he knew for a fact the kid was not Etan.

This is important, Galligan thought, making a note. She knew what was in the newspapers and what wasn't. There was no way Morgan could know about P.J. Fox unless Ramos had really told him. She also noted that Morgan didn't know the Ohio boy's name, and didn't act like he thought he should. When the answers weren't pat and complete, it was often a sign of the truth.

"Tell me again about this boy and his picture," she prodded Morgan, watching to see whether he would embellish. Would he tie together the picture of P.J. Fox taken on Ramos's bus and the composite "aged" photo of

Etan? But Morgan stuck with what he knew. "Just that there was this picture somewhere of a kid in Ohio who GraBois thinks is Etan Patz. That's all."

"How is this conversation going?" Galligan asked Morgan. "Is he just rambling all this at you?"

"No," Morgan replied. "Mostly he was answering questions; he would give me info if I would ask him a question. Like I would ask him, 'Why are you in Otisville?' And he would answer. It was a conversation."

Yes, thought Galligan, a conversation two people had, freely. No government coercion. No possibility of entrapment. This is better than if we had put the two together.

Ramos, Morgan went on, asked a lot of questions about the statute of limitations. He wanted to know especially about murder, and about kidnapping. "So I looked up that statute for him, and whatever it said, that's what I showed him," Morgan said. Galligan also thought this spoke to Morgan's credibility. It was a particular incident—a story—that would account for why Morgan remembered it specifically. Another good sign—if Morgan were spinning a tale, he would have thought it important to account for the exact law, not say "whatever it said."

GraBois sat on the sidelines and listened for inconsistencies. He heard none. It was a welcome break to have Mary in the lead, he thought; Morgan was clearly knowledgeable and seemed to have a savant-like facility to recall obscure details. But following his train of thought could be exhausting.

"Tell me your impressions of Ramos," Galligan asked Morgan. "What's he like?"

"He's got a temper, I'll tell you that," Morgan replied.

"Why do you say that?"

"I try to stay out of his way when he's mad." Morgan described once again watching Ramos going after an older inmate in the law library, how his hands shook as he grabbed the typewriter and brought it up over his head, how at least three inmates had to restrain him.

GraBois and Galligan looked at each other, poker-faced. "And how do you feel about Ramos, Jon?" Galligan continued.

"He's a real creep. I'm pretty mad at him myself these days, getting me mixed up with all of this. I've got next to no time left. It could get me in serious trouble if someone thought I was involved in a plan to take out a federal prosecutor. Plus, if he had something to do with this Patz case, that's horrendous. When Ramos first told me about his charges, I was willing to give him the benefit of the doubt. He's pretty convincing. But then I hear he catches this other Pennsylvania case, and I start to think maybe he did molest all these kids. And maybe he did molest Etan Patz too. Makes my stomach turn."

GraBois leaned in closer to the man. It was time for him to talk. "He's a bad guy, Jon. He's in for a long time because he has hurt a lot of little children."

This was the cut-to-the-chase moment. "Let me ask you straight," the prosecutor said. "Would you be willing to help us with this? You know I can't promise you anything, but if it comes up, I'd be in a good position to vouch for you. I know you've got this other New Jersey case. I'd try to help you with that. And it would get us closer to giving this guy what he deserves. It wouldn't be fun, I'll be honest, but he clearly feels like he can tell you things he isn't telling others. I would put you back in Otisville and you'd see what you could get."

"Yeah, I could probably do that," Morgan responded without waiting more than a beat. "He's been dancing to the music with those kids—I think he should pay the piper."

"He's in seg right now," GraBois pushed. He had to know how serious Morgan was. "He may not get into general pop. What if you had to go into seg to get near him?" Seg was administrative segregation. Lockdown twenty-three out of twenty-four hours, very few privileges. You landed there if you acted out, or if you feared for your life and had to be kept away from the others. For some inmates it was hell.

Now Morgan was silent for a moment. He was either thinking, or gearing up for a speech.

"Listen, you didn't put me into this," the inmate finally answered. "I didn't ask to be put into this. Ramos put me into this. He made it so that I had to report the letter or I could have gotten stuck with a conspiracy charge. I might be a pain in the ass, suing everyone, but I'm sure as hell not interested in a conspiracy to injure a U.S. attorney. Or attempted murder, or however this could have gone. Once Ramos sent me that letter, and my mother read it, I knew I was stuck. And once Ramos decides to stick me in the middle, if I'm *in* the middle, I want to be on the good side."

Somewhere in there was a yes, thought GraBois. "We'll have to figure this all out carefully," he said. "If you can get close enough to him, you would have to maneuver it so that he asked you to be his roommate. If *you* ask *him*, he'll be suspicious. This is tricky."

"He asked me before, the last time," Morgan said. "He's got no reason to think we're not still okay. I think it's doable. He wants me to help him with his legal papers."

"You'd have to take a polygraph." GraBois didn't ask, he stated.

"No problem."

"The next thing to do is to answer his letter. Mary would work with you to make something that matches your style, written on paper like the kind you would send yourself."

"Knock yourselves out," Morgan said. Another yes.

"We'll be in touch. You'll be around for a few days, at least. I can arrange for you to come back up here to visit with your mother if you want, that'll be more pleasant than her seeing you at MCC." MCC was a godawful place for a mother to see her son. "Thank you for coming down." The two men shook hands, Morgan's clanking as the cuffs knocked against each other. Galligan stood up and walked Morgan down to hand him off to the U.S. marshals. Then she came straight back up to GraBois's office to compare notes.

"Well?" she said. "Did you hear anything that didn't match?"

"He gave the same thing to you as he did to me." GraBois was convinced, and waited to hear if Galligan would concur. She did. Their guts were in sync about Morgan. If he passed a polygraph, he'd head up to Otisville within the week. And if they tried Morgan out with Ramos and he got nothing, they would still have Jeremy Fischer waiting in the wings. They would both feel more comfortable with Fischer if Morgan could corroborate. As long as one didn't know a thing about the other. The best part—Fischer and Morgan could provide a sort of checks and balances. If Fischer reported he was in the library with Ramos at the same time Morgan said he saw Ramos at the gym, someone was lying.

"Let's see what Jon's letter back to Ramos gives us." GraBois got up to walk Galligan to the elevator. "And Mary, can you do me a favor? Can you put something in the letter that says I've moved out of the neighborhood?"

CHAPTER 22

Into the Hole

Jon Morgan: Ramos must have said it ten times—the kid will turn up one of these days.... He will take out a whole building.... He will get plastic explosives.... If he goes down to your office and you uncuff him he'll try to choke you.
—*phone conversation between Stuart GraBois and Jon Morgan in Otisville segregation, March 20, 1991, 1:50 p.m.*

D id Jon Morgan call you yet today?" Special Agent Mary Galligan knocked at Stuart GraBois's office and stuck in her head.

"I can't help it if he keeps calling me." GraBois put his hands up. "I tell him to talk to *you*. But I'm not going to hang up on him."

Ever since Morgan had gone up to Otisville a few weeks earlier, Galligan kept reminding GraBois that the case could be jeopardized if the two men were in direct contact without her. "Stu, you know I love you," she would say, "but if he tells you something and I don't hear it, and it comes to a trial, you know damn well you'd have to testify, not me. And if you're a witness, you can't be the prosecutor. It would kill you if someone else took this case after everything you've gone through."

Now Galligan glanced out the window ten flights down to the line of people waiting to get through the metal detector at the building's entrance, then turned to face GraBois. She shook her head. "No, no, that's not what I meant this time," she said. "I meant, has he told you what he got from Ramos? I just got off the phone with him, and I figured he'd have called you in the time it took me to take two elevators and cross a lobby."

"He called me for a minute earlier this morning, but he couldn't really talk. What's going on?"

"Ramos told Jon that he plans to blow you up."

"Right." GraBois liked to hear Ramos's ravings.

"I know, I know, but this sounds like a legitimate threat." She recounted Morgan's story.

Within a few days of arriving at Otisville, it had become clear to Jon Morgan that Ramos was in protective segregation, and he wasn't getting out. Too many people knew who Ramos was and what he was in for. Prison management didn't want to risk any violence if another inmate went after him. Morgan could understand that. Technically Ramos was "on loan," and if the state facility in Pennsylvania sent over a live inmate and got back a pine box, someone at Otisville would have to answer some awkward questions. If Ramos wasn't coming out of seg, Morgan would have to go in after him.

I've gone this far, he told himself, I may as well finish it up. Besides, he'd already been warned by Galligan and GraBois what it might take. To avoid any suspicion that could arise if GraBois arranged it from the outside, Morgan simply wrote an anonymous letter to the warden saying another inmate in general population was after him. Guards picked him up coming out of breakfast the next day, and he was off to protective custody—the hole.

Morgan knew that most inmates hated the hole, but he personally didn't mind it. It was quiet, and you were left alone. The word conjured up the dark, waterlogged hold of a galley ship filled with slaves, but the reality was starker and more sterile. You landed in segregation for two main reasons—in *disciplinary* seg as punishment, or in *administrative* seg to protect at-risk inmates by separating them from the rest of the population. Either way, you were moved out of the general "Compound" to the SHU, or Special Housing Unit. Physically, the SHU wasn't that much different from the rest of the prison. It featured the same cinderblock cells, linked by antiseptic corridors where the sound seemed to carry for miles, so a whisper at one end of the tier mingled with every other noise to reach your ears at the other end in a cacophonous riot. There were small distinctions—the sink and toilet in the SHU were stainless steel, not ceramic, which made for a colder seat but one that couldn't be broken into weapon-sized pieces. The bed and chair were bolted down. The biggest difference between seg and general population, though, was the amount of time you spent in your cell and the privileges you enjoyed when out of it.

In general population at Otisville, they cracked the cell doors first thing in the morning, and until the four o'clock count you were free to move around—to the library, to the track out in the yard, maybe to the gym. There you could lift weights, ride the stationary bikes, play some hoops or even tennis once your "workday" was over. After the count you were on your own again until an hour before lights-out at ten o'clock; then you were shut back in your cell for the night.

By contrast, seg meant total lockdown, trapped with one roommate in an eight-by-fifteen-foot space for basically twenty-four hours a day. You got tougher time in disciplinary seg, where you couldn't open the windows, smoke, or turn on the lights at will, but even if, like Morgan, you were placed in the hole purely for your own protection, you ceded your movements to the guards. Cuffs were de rigueur outside the cell. Showers were rationed to three a week—if you were on the guards' good side—and exercise to one hour daily—again, if you weren't on anyone's shit list. You could breathe fresh air during an outside workout, but you were still caged, in something like a giant dog run. But since Morgan passed most of his days prepping for his labyrinthine lawsuits, and couldn't remember the last time he'd worked out, it was all truly academic to him. Besides, he thought, this was a short-term gig, just a week or so, no sweat. He counted on GraBois to spring him upon request. Ultimately, he didn't really feel like he had a choice, so he'd just make the best of it. And buried down deep, so deep perhaps he didn't even recognize it himself, Jon Morgan relished the idea he'd been singled out as the linchpin of a special team. Who wouldn't enjoy being on a secret mission, even if it turned out to be impossible?

The hardest part of the assignment for Morgan was finding Ramos in seg. Trapped in your cell, you could go your whole stint without catching sight of a particular inmate if he wasn't on your tier. Even if he were, he could be four cells away and you would never know it. Morgan's task was complicated by the fact that only the warden and a couple of his key staff were in on the operation. In general you could never know if the guards would keep their mouths shut. There were just too many side deals in prison. Besides, guards were known to do things like grab your letters and read them out loud to the rest of the inmates, just for entertainment. A slip of their tongue could get you killed.

The problem was solved a few days after Morgan arrived. In a rare moment, he was out of his cell, sitting in the legal phone booth that fronted the law library. Even in seg, inmates could not be denied access to either

legal calls or legal resources. Inmates were eligible for one legal call a day
as needed, and up to one hour a day in the library. Of course, "law library"
was a misnomer—no hushed stacks filled with tomes of jurisprudence, just
a converted cell furnished with one regulation prison desk and chair, one
typewriter, and the basics: *Black's Law Dictionary*, a *Corpus Juris Secundum*
law encyclopedia, and a set of the federal regulations.

As Morgan was finishing up his call, he nearly missed guards leading
his quarry into the library a few yards away. But Ramos himself banged
on the window to get his attention. Morgan's escort wasn't back yet, so the
two could reunite through the glass. Morgan showed surprise that was only
partly feigned, since he'd never dreamed it would be this easy. "I'm down
in Otisville from upstate to be closer for one of my cases," he explained to
Ramos, who was just happy to see his old friend.

Ramos looked about the same as he had when Jon Morgan last saw him,
a little better groomed, perhaps. His wiry gray hair hadn't grown back completely to its straggly mane in the three months since he'd cleaned up to prepare for sentencing in Warren. As usual he carried a thick pile of paperwork:
court transcripts, subpoenas, and his ubiquitous press clippings. There
were more of these to come, Ramos said, showing Morgan his collection of
media pitch letters. *Vanity Fair* wanted to talk to him about his link to the
Patz case, as did *Inside Edition* and the local New York CBS News channel.
The inmates at Otisville might hate him, but outside the prison he was in
demand.

"What's happening with that address you were going to get me?" Ramos
asked Morgan. "I'm still interested."

Morgan looked around; they were alone, but at first he wished Ramos
wouldn't speak so recklessly. Then he remembered—he was allowed, even
supposed to be talking this way.

"Listen, if you get it, be careful; I know they're watching my mail,"
Ramos instructed Morgan, despite the irony of saying this loudly enough
to penetrate a solid wall. Ramos appeared not to notice, nor to care. "Here's
what you need to do. First send me a letter with the stamp upside down, so
I know that you got the address, and then send me another letter and write
the address under the stamp."

"Got it." Morgan only half listened to this Rube Goldberg–esque plan,
thankful he had no intention of complying. One thing is sure, Morgan realized: Ramos had really thought this through.

"Why do you want GraBois's address?" he asked.

"You don't want to know." Then Ramos told him anyway.

"I know a guy on the outside. He's a demolitions expert, and he owes me a big favor," Ramos said. "I did a writ for the guy in here." He went on to describe a suitcase of explosives and his plan "to blow up GraBois's building, when the time is right."

"I think it might be an apartment building," said Morgan.

"Doesn't matter," Ramos told him. "I'll take out the whole place."

Of course, Morgan could never tell what was real and what were the ravings of a pathological liar. Ramos had spun a lot of tales in the past, each one more grandiose than the last. The bus he sorrowfully spoke of losing in Pennsylvania, the one Morgan later found out was a junk heap filled with garbage, had been described by Ramos as a moving Four Seasons. Still, explosives and an outside contact who knew how to use them? That was a viable threat. The fact that Ramos would talk about it openly out of the cell meant he'd lost all reason.

Mary Galligan had listened to Morgan tell her all this in his furtive call, then got off the phone and headed to the U.S. Attorney's Office. Whether Ramos *or* Morgan was full of crap, she thought, GraBois needed to be protected.

"He's asking Morgan whether you have any kids." She had finished recounting the conversation, and now watched for GraBois's reaction. She knew if anything was going to get to GraBois, it was this last bit.

"That son of a bitch." GraBois felt the outrage any mention of his family in the same conversation with a perp could elicit. This was a hot-button topic for any prosecutor, and GraBois was no exception. Like most of his colleagues, he had a strong stomach for taking on the vilest of the human species. He'd met all kinds in charge of the prosecutions of the NYPD–FBI Joint Task Force for the Sexual Exploitation of Children. He'd screened the child porn; he'd heard the victim statements. Those were the days when GraBois didn't flinch. But bring his *own* family into it? That just made him crazy.

"Look, Stu, this is not the kind of guy who can pull off killing an assistant U.S. attorney. He's not connected; he's one guy. I mean, he's begging someone just to come up with your address." For the most part, Galligan believed the soothing sounds she was making to calm him down. But she had also just been assigned the Cathy Palmer attempted assassination case.

Palmer, an assistant U.S. attorney in the Eastern District of New York, had narrowly escaped a .22 caliber rifle with a sawed-off barrel that was spring-loaded in an attaché case and then sent to Palmer's office, so Galligan knew these weren't always idle threats. At this point, though, Ramos's seemed rather vague and ill-conceived. "Look how many steps he'd have to take to pull this off. It's all puffing, I'm sure of it."

There was, of course, the small part of her that said: A guy can get lucky. That's why she'd put the phone down from Morgan and raced over to see GraBois. The U.S. Marshal Service needed to be flagged along with the Bureau, and an order placed in the prison files that GraBois be notified upon Ramos's release. Shortly after that, GraBois began to drive his car with a remote-control key chain that started the engine from yards away.

In the meantime, that day in GraBois's office, he and Mary Galligan briefly imagined pursuing Ramos on charges of threatening a federal prosecutor, but in the end rejected the notion; they didn't want to jeopardize Morgan's tenuous position. So when Jon Morgan called GraBois the next day and repeated the same information he'd given Mary Galligan, the prosecutor listened, calmly making notes. GraBois kept his cool even as Morgan warned him that if Ramos were brought down to Manhattan for questioning, he planned to attack GraBois and choke him. Let him try, thought GraBois, it'll give us grounds to bring new charges. It wasn't personal risk that lit GraBois's fuse, but the prospect of inadvertently bringing the danger of his work home. He told Morgan to keep going.

The plan progressed just days later, when Ramos's cellmate was moved out and Ramos requested Jon Morgan replace him, although Morgan couldn't figure out why. Maybe, he reasoned, Ramos considered him a known quantity since he'd already confided that his conviction was for sexual deviance. Or maybe Ramos figures that if Morgan knew GraBois, he was only one degree of separation from something he badly wanted. Over the next few weeks, Morgan got to hear just how badly, as he listened to Jose Ramos's endless tirades against his "oppressor." The prosecutor, Ramos would say, was clearly just using the Patz case as a career stepping-stone—how else to explain his perseverance?

Morgan had to admit this spying game was entertaining at first. "You know," he'd say to Ramos, at GraBois's instruction, "you were arrested in a National Forest. That's federal land. The Feds can come after you now on separate charges, and they probably will."

Ramos looked shocked. "They can't do that. That's double jeopardy."

What a moron, thought Morgan. "No it's not. Double jeopardy is when you beat a charge and the same people try to go at you again. This is different—there's no double jeopardy between the state and the Feds."

"He was so upset, he almost died," Morgan told GraBois later, during a call from the legal phone.

During such calls GraBois and Galligan would play at being Morgan's attorneys, even acting the part on their end of the phone. These conversations were all recorded, monitored intermittently, and there was always the risk that someone listening in would inadvertently—or deliberately—pass on the juicy tidbit that Jon Morgan was on the job. Morgan tried to call GraBois and Galligan regularly, reporting the latest details first to whomever he could get on the phone, often to both. The parallel calls were consistent with each other, and little by little, comparing notes, GraBois and Galligan were able to fit more pieces of information into the puzzle.

Despite the risk, Morgan occasionally called GraBois right from the cell, to speak cryptically as Jose Ramos sat on the bunk below him. A guard would dial the number—to what Morgan claimed was his lawyer's office—and then pass the phone through the meal slot. Inmates in seg got a certain allotment of calls weekly. Morgan was working the phones prodigiously, so when he used up his time, Ramos would sometimes offer Morgan his own personal minutes for Morgan's nightly call to his mother. Ramos himself had no one to call. He just had Jon Morgan.

When Ramos's nonstop, mostly useless prattle did merit a trip to the legal phone, Morgan passed on whatever information he had deciphered. GraBois and Galligan found some of it useful for building the case against Ramos. Almost as important, these bits and pieces solidified Morgan's own credibility. When Ramos talked about his days in the Navy, on board an aircraft carrier, GraBois subpoenaed his military records, and it all checked out. When Morgan reported that Ramos bought his bus in Florida for $2,500, that also checked out. Morgan heard stories of Bennett, Sandy Harmon's son, and how much the boy loved his friend "Michael." He also heard about the drainpipe where Ramos was hunted down and persecuted. Still, GraBois and Galligan needed to hear him talk about their case. For whatever inexplicable reasons, Ramos had felt comfortable discussing the Patz case with Morgan in the past, and now the Feds were counting on a reprise. There were random fragments, but they were elusive, almost lost among disjointed, irrelevant mutterings, like Ramos's elaborate, fanciful plans to stage a prison break.

"He knows Etan's school bus route," Morgan finally called one day to tell GraBois. It was April 1, more than two weeks since he'd arrived in the hole. Morgan and Ramos had been talking about landmarks around New York, with Ramos boasting he knew the Village like he owned it. He'd started drawing maps of some of his favorite hangouts, which grew more and more detailed, including one of the Patz neighborhood. Somewhere in the midst of this, Morgan told GraBois, the school bus route came up. "He knows all the stops the bus made back in 1979," Morgan told GraBois, "and he says Etan's was the third stop in SoHo." Ramos knew the name of Etan's school and told Morgan he was surprised they didn't alert the parents when a child didn't show up. As with all their communications, GraBois listened impassively to this first taste of progress and said little—he couldn't afford to give his informant a reason to embellish. "See if you can get more details on how real this planned prison break is," he told Morgan, "and get us the map Ramos drew."

But Ramos was starting to wear Morgan out, jumping from one subject to the next, the traces of worthwhile information like slivers of gold embedded in a slag pile of useless stone and rubble. While it was true Morgan himself meandered in conversation, Ramos was just plain incoherent, and he would contradict himself from one moment to the next. The first time he told Morgan that they'd never be able to charge him for Etan Patz's murder because there was no body, Morgan was both repulsed and elated at the revelation, until a minute later when Ramos then announced, "The kid will turn up alive." It's like a television with a remote gone haywire, Morgan reported back in exasperation.

He'd been warned it was dangerous to take notes, but at a certain point, Morgan felt he had no choice. It was getting tougher every day to make the calls, and he couldn't keep the disparate fragments in his head. Yes, it was a risk—he'd seen the razor blades Ramos secreted in the binding of a book. But he was bigger than Ramos, Morgan reasoned, and a blade might cut, but chances were it wouldn't kill. Perched on his top bunk while Ramos read a Stephen King novel below, Morgan began to keep written accounts on the sly. Some pages he stashed in the two worn paper bags that comprised his personal property. Some he'd smuggle out in letters to his mother, folded into an envelope thin enough to avoid suspicion. Mrs. Morgan in turn would forward them on to the Feds.

Morgan made reference to Ramos's dramatic "90 percent confession" in GraBois's office, which Morgan could not have known about except from his cellmate. "He claimed he gave a statement because he was pressured," Morgan later passed on, "by three grown-ups who extorted him for more than eight hours and then let him go." At another point, Morgan referred to a woman he could only know about from Ramos.

"He doesn't know for sure where Harmon is, she's probably in the same dump on 13th Street." Morgan was struck by Ramos's ill will toward his former girlfriend. "She is a bitch cunt. Every woman Ramos talks about is a bitch, a cunt, or some other derogatory name. He apparently does not like women."

But Morgan told GraBois on several occasions that Ramos reserved his real venom for the prosecutor himself.

"He would blow up the whole U.S. Attorney's Office with a suitcase of plastic explosives if he could," Morgan once stated. Ramos's escape plans grew more detailed. "Ramos thinks he'll get out one way or another," Morgan reported. "He knows he can escape from Rockview eventually. They'll give him outside custody and then he could get to Ohio and then Texas and off to Mexico." According to Morgan, Ramos had clearly thought his route through, concocting a whole scheme to live in the jungle near the Colombian-Brazilian border, traveling through Mexico with some Rainbow friends to get there.

One week sequestered in the close, confining cell turned into two, and Morgan's amusement was dissolving with his frayed nerves. With no clocks, no calendars, and no control over his sleep schedule—Ramos often insisted on keeping the lights on all night to read, then sleeping in a darkened cell all day—Morgan began to feel that insanity was infectious. When he found out he would miss a court date for one of his many lawsuits because of the undercover operation, he took out his frustrations on GraBois himself.

"I'm livid," he told the prosecutor halfway through his stint. "Without my knowledge you put off my depositions in Danbury." Morgan wanted out. "I agreed to stay in seg one week, I have now been here more than that. Passover is coming next week and I do not intend to spend it in the hole."

GraBois calmed him down while spurring him on. "You're doing such good work, we need you," he exhorted the inmate. There were no Passover seders for Jon Morgan in seg that year, just a box of matzoh and Morgan's fervent, unspoken plea for "next year in Jerusalem," the traditional Passover prayer.

The holiday fell toward the end of Morgan's stint, fortunately, because what really crystallized Morgan's rage was watching Ramos play the Jewish card at Passover. As a boy in the North Bronx, Morgan had often used his fists to defend his faith, so it was increasingly difficult to go along while Jose Ramos masqueraded his devotion. When the rabbi came to the SHU for a special pastoral visit, Ramos picked a fight with him about the matzoh he'd brought to pass out. Morgan couldn't hear the details—maybe it wasn't the right kind of matzoh, or the finest quality. Standing in the back of the cell where he'd retreated out of earshot to give them some privacy, he silently seethed as he watched Ramos berate the elderly rabbi. For all the talk of Ramos-the-child-molester—and possibly worse—on some level, to Morgan it was just that: talk. It had happened elsewhere, out of sight, out of his experience. He was a direct witness to this scene, however. In a strange yet explicable way, it hit him the hardest.

Morgan had spent time with this rabbi, and knew the man was traveling the thirty miles each way between his home and the prison from a genuine concern for his inmate congregation, not for some paltry stipend. How dare Ramos—who pretended at his convenient faith—lecture this Orthodox rabbi? How dare he make a mockery of Morgan's religion? Worst of all, how dare Ramos affiliate his sleazy, depraved soul with Morgan's people? Jose Antonio Ramos was, as they said, "not good for the Jews." He was ready to get out of there. He was done.

"I don't think I'm going to get any more out of him," Morgan told Gra-Bois in a brief phone conversation a few days later. "He won't talk about Etan Patz, he won't talk about anything."

"It's okay," GraBois replied. "I'm really happy with everything you got. We'll talk more when we bring you down to New York next week."

GraBois *was* grateful for Morgan's efforts, but he was ready to see him go. GraBois was already working the bullpen. Unbeknownst to Jon Morgan, his relief was warming up in a nearby cell. Sometime in the previous days, Jeremy Fischer had arrived in the SHU at Otisville. Fischer was the next phase of the plan.

~

CHAPTER 23

Take Two

Many sexual offenders lie about their crimes....Hopefully as you read this workbook you will understand that you must accept responsibility for your crime, recognize that you have a problem and want help in order to change.

—*section underlined in pencil in* Who Am I and Why Am I in Treatment? *sex offender workbook Fischer "helped" Jose Ramos complete while in his cell, April 1991*

Y ou have to get over here," the disembodied voice echoed into Jeremy Fischer's cell. "C'mon, we can live together. I need to be near another Jew."

For what felt like the twentieth time that week, Fischer found himself crouched in front of the toilet, as though he were paying the consequences for an overindulgent night out. But here in segregation at Otisville, drunken binges that ended by praying to the porcelain god weren't even an option. Instead, prison toilets were useful for other things. You could wash clothes, tie dental floss to a makeshift weapon and temporarily flush it for later retrieval, even drink from it in a desperate moment. And sometimes, as in this case, if the acoustics were right your voice would carry the length of the sewage pipes and end up in the cell of the inmate downstairs.

Like a ventriloquist with his grotesque dummy, Jose Ramos had been speaking to Fischer through the commode for the last several days, and now he was urging Fischer to move in with him. Jon Morgan had just been sprung from segregation, leaving Ramos alone and unwanted by any other inmate. A pedophile is never "A list," and Ramos was especially unpopular.

Just as it had in Morgan's case, Ramos's request neatly sidestepped the challenge of inserting Fischer into the cell without arousing suspicion.

Jeremy Fischer and Jon Morgan were two very different animals. Both were educated, white-collar criminals, both were Jewish; but while Morgan was brusquely artless, Fischer was a slick talker, a real craftsman. As an informant, this had both its advantages and its drawbacks. On the one hand, it made Fischer inherently less believable to authorities, so both GraBois and Galligan had set the bar higher for him to prove his worth, carefully looking for corroboration of anything he said. On the other hand, he more naturally suited the task. Like the best three-card monte dealers, Fischer possessed an agile mind, a golden tongue, and a performer's instincts, all of which served him well at Otisville in April 1991.

After he accepted Ramos's invitation, the cell they shared was Fischer's stage. Like Jon Morgan, Fischer kept copious notes while Ramos slept, grateful for the loud snores drifting up from the bottom bunk. What he found irritating in other cellmates worked here as an alarm system. After he finished each page, he would tuck it into the waistband of his pants. It grew increasingly uncomfortable to move around with as many as ten or fifteen pages pressed against his stomach, but the thought of Ramos discovering his true intent was infinitely more painful.

Unlike Morgan, Jeremy Fischer was not inured to the general discomfort of segregation. The cell was dank and dark, and he shrank at the sound of rats and bugs scurrying in the night. In such close quarters, the rank odor of two bodies, each limited to three showers a week, was not quite overpowering, but it was certainly unpleasant. Mondays were the worst, especially if either of them exercised in the yard; there were no shower privileges on the weekend. Fischer tried to keep sight of his goal, and the prize it would earn him—a federal prosecutor in his corner and the chance to beat a parole violation. GraBois had made no promises, but Fischer was optimistic.

From the beginning he approached the mission differently, more strategically than Jon Morgan. He went about his task systematically, following a predetermined plan. Part of the time he was Jeremy Fischer, Esquire, coaching Ramos on legal strategy. When they'd first met, Fischer had told Ramos that he was in fact a lawyer, thinking that Ramos would be more open if he viewed their conversations as free counsel.

"I'll get my own lawyer involved too, and I have contacts with Kunstler and Kuby," Fischer told him, invoking the name of famed New York radical and underdog defender William Kunstler and his partner Ron Kuby. "This is a case they'd definitely want. It's a high-profile, overzealous prosecution. It reeks of misuse of power.

"We'll start a defense fund for you. I'll contribute, and I know others who would too. Don't worry, I'm going to help you. We just have to figure it all out."

This seemed to strike the right note with Ramos. He was eager both to appeal his Pennsylvania sentence and to elude the Feds on the Patz case. He'd already filed the next round of appeal papers himself for the Warren case, and as for the Patz case, Fischer listened to him muse aloud endlessly about how to recant his near confession to GraBois without incurring perjury charges. The thousand and one statute GraBois had read to Ramos repeatedly that day in his office must have made a lasting impression. Sometimes it seemed to Fischer that Ramos hadn't forgotten *anything* GraBois had said or done to him. Clearly, the point of intersection between both of Ramos's legal cases was the all-consuming animus he felt for his tormentor, Assistant U.S. Attorney Stuart GraBois.

Fischer later told GraBois that Ramos's desire to recant the 90 percent confession was as much about derailing GraBois's case as it was for the inmate's obvious legal benefit. "His obsession for you is total," Fischer marveled.

Fischer's legal conversations with Ramos would invariably disintegrate into revenge fantasies. "The next time GraBois hauls me down to his office, I'm gonna be ready for him," Ramos would tell Fischer. Now he was actively looking forward to seeing the prosecutor. He would talk relentlessly, gruesomely—of hitting GraBois over the head with a hammer; of biting off his face; of ripping out his liver. Ramos would lie in the dark after lights-out, filling the space between his bottom bunk and Fischer's mattress with invective. His favorite image was delivering the "Ramos Award," conferred with a hard-driving baseball bat.

"Let's give him the 'Ramos Award,'" he'd say of GraBois, and anyone else on his lengthy shit list. With no actual bat in sight, his ravings would have been comical, except Fischer had good reason to think he was locked in with a serial child molester who had raped and murdered a helpless boy. He had no choice but to take Ramos's threats seriously...and then had no choice but to ignore them.

When he wasn't playing jailhouse lawyer, Fischer's parallel role was

as therapist/confessor. Back at the state facility in Rockview, Ramos had
repeatedly failed his applications for parole. The commonwealth of Pennsylvania was not going to approve a known sex offender who refused treatment.
Now facing a twenty-year maximum sentence, Ramos had finally relented,
so when he'd arrived at Otisville he'd brought with him course material for
the treatment program. *Who Am I and Why Am I in Treatment?* asked the
title of his workbook. Fischer was hoping that by helping Ramos answer
that question, he would ultimately answer another one: "Did you molest
and kill Etan Patz?"

With each passing day, as Ramos gradually relaxed his guard, Fischer
offered a sympathetic ear. He cajoled and flattered, he soothed and empa-
thized. If it helped Ramos to think that Fischer too felt these same shameful
feelings, then the good doctor obliged.

"You know, in ancient Greece," Fischer counseled, "it was the most normal thing in the world. Socrates, Plato, Aristophanes—they all had boy lovers." Ramos liked to hear that he was in good company. Fischer also offered
to put him in touch with a NAMBLA chapter he pretended to know about.
Anything to help lower Ramos's guard.

During these informal counseling sessions, the two pored over the workbook. Disclosure, the book emphasized, was a critical first step.

"In your notebook," read chapter 6's assignment, "make a list of all
of the different sexual offenses you have committed.... Write down how
many times you did each type of offense and how old you were at that
time.... Share this assignment with your friend, group, or therapist."

"Okay, Jose, tell me what happened," Fischer would say. "Tell me why
you did this. Tell me what you were feeling when you were with this child."
The two inmates set aside a prescribed time period each day—a mock
therapy session—to work on the notebook. Ramos didn't speak about Etan
Patz, but he quickly began to reveal other incidents, other horrors. Fischer
tried to ferret out names, identifying details, but Ramos didn't always know
himself.

"Where did this happen? What did he look like?" Fischer would pump
Ramos for whatever he could get, then scribble it down afterwards, until the
pencil stub would lose its point and he'd have to petition a guard to sharpen
it. He'd relay all this information to GraBois and Galligan later. There was
Joey Taylor, whom Fischer knew as the "boy on the bus." There were boys
with Down syndrome Ramos had met while living two blocks from a New

Orleans children's hospital. And there was the camp for retarded children in Ohio. On the third day in, Fischer was able to steal away to the phone to call Stuart GraBois.

"I think I'm on first base." Fischer had been given a code to use. For every hit he was getting closer to a full admission of guilt—the home run.

"He's got plans to escape. He's even drawn me a map and it leads straight to New York—and you." Fischer didn't know that the prosecutor had already heard this from Morgan, so he hastened to tell GraBois the details of Ramos's plan.

"He knows where you used to live," Fischer continued, naming the town. Fischer couldn't himself know where the prosecutor lived—score one credibility point, thought GraBois. "All he talks about," Fischer cautioned, "is that once he escapes, he's coming to your office to get you, now that you've moved out of your neighborhood. And he takes no small pleasure out of knowing you moved because you were afraid he was coming after you." That, in turn, pleased GraBois. It sounded as though Ramos had believed Jon Morgan's story that GraBois was no longer his neighbor.

"I'm getting some results from the workbook," Fischer went on. "It's not what you're looking for, I know, but it's progress." He reported the atrocities he'd heard, including a few names. GraBois recognized one, someone Fischer couldn't have made up. Hearing Fischer pass on the name Bennett Harmon was significant. Fischer had to work hard to earn his trust, and Sandy's son was authentic coin.

"He's got a serious plan for blowing you up," Fischer warned again. "It's all he talks about. I'll try to get more details. Just be careful."

"*You* be careful. Let's stay in touch."

That wasn't going to be easy. Soon after their call, the segregation phone broke, and Fischer could only track his progress in sporadic notes. His sense of isolation almost complete, the days took on a tense routine. Daily "therapy" sessions with Ramos became increasingly frenzied; Fischer suspected his "patient" was using their sessions partly to exorcise demons, and partly to reexperience the sex. He even wondered sometimes if Ramos did feel a spark of actual remorse, and every once in a while he would catch a glimpse of another lost child. After their first few sessions Ramos started lobbying Fischer first thing in the morning.

"When can we get to the book?" he'd say.

"Wait awhile," Fischer would stall. "I've got my own things to do. We have to conduct our work on a schedule, just like the professionals." Instinctively, he sensed that putting off Ramos would bring him to a faster boiling point, so when they did sit down, Ramos's tightly held secrets would spill out uncontrollably. It was strangely satisfying for Fischer to use his con artist talents to good purpose. He was all too aware that they usually landed him in trouble.

During the sessions themselves, Fischer sought to tread a fine line between amateur shrink and amateur detective, knowing if he pushed too hard he would tip off Ramos. Mostly he just listened, sympathized, and tried to keep the conversation going. He'd come to realize that Ramos had no friends; that the only people his cellmate talked to regularly were in law enforcement, and Ramos knew they were only listening to build a case against him.

"This is good," Fischer would prompt when Ramos slipped into confessional mode. "Tell me more. What about Ohio? What about Florida? Were there young girls involved too? What did it feel like? Who did you tell? Did you have anybody to talk to just to get it off your shoulders?"

These discussions lasted hours, ending only when Ramos, either out of genuine pain or wariness, would claim searing headaches and retreat to his bed. Fischer would wait to hear the snores, then he'd turn on his two-dollar commissary-issue Japanese lantern and start to transcribe.

"Ramos has taken me into his confidence," he wrote in the notes he was saving for GraBois. Fischer explained how he'd told Ramos that he needed to fill him in if he wanted help on the legal case. "He's starting to rely on me."

Putting it on the page made it real, but most of the time Fischer refused to be moved by what he was hearing. Feelings were just too complicated, especially in this cell. He was playing a part, and like any good actor, he needed to just *be* the part and not overanalyze. Otherwise, he feared, Ramos wouldn't respond, and he himself might falter. Any combination of fear, disgust, even self-loathing both for getting drawn into Ramos's scheming and for the massive deception he was perpetrating—all those feelings would only jeopardize the work.

Fischer knew that his own moral compass often skewed wildly off course—he'd enjoyed a long career of bald deception and criminal acts. But now somewhere, in the hours either spent feigning his sympathy or in writing it all down, he could feel a shift. At some point during the feverish incantations of violence and the chilling admissions of child abuse, a line had been crossed, and Fischer's motivations were now both self-serving and selfless.

He tried not to dwell on his own vulnerability. The indirect threats were constant. If I ever found a snitch, Ramos often said, I would kill him without hesitation, and Fischer knew that Ramos could, even in a bare cell. A sharpened pencil, a broomstick, those utilitarian toilets—four inches of water could drown a man whose head was lodged in one.

Fischer worked to banish such outcomes from his mind; he focused instead on advancing to second base. His own obsession ran to the Mets, and now he tried to see himself as just a player in the game. Daylight helped him maintain the illusion, so at moments like this, he would order himself to sleep. In a caged space that small, sleep was the only escape.

The first real mention of Etan himself, perhaps understandably, came not during a therapy session, but in the ongoing Patz case legal discussions, while the two were "working" on Ramos's various briefs. In a recurrent thread, Fischer was attempting to ingratiate himself by mapping out a plan to remove GraBois from the case. He'd quickly learned that invoking Gra-Bois's name would make Ramos more volatile, and thus more loose-lipped.

"You've got a good case for prosecutorial misconduct," Fischer would say, and they'd plot that for a while. Sometimes he'd instruct Ramos to lay out the facts of the Patz case, working GraBois's name into the conversation as often as possible. Fischer tried never to ask a direct question, putting them instead in terms of GraBois.

"GraBois thinks this, GraBois knows that," he'd say.

"GraBois doesn't have a shred of evidence," Ramos would retort, "except what I told him. He doesn't know shit."

Then, with any luck, Ramos would show how the prosecutor was all wrong by telling Fischer what was *right*. How ironic, Fischer thought, that I'm working for GraBois, and he's working for me.

"You told GraBois yourself you picked the boy up in Washington Square Park," Fischer now tried. "The newspapers even say that."

"And that's wrong, too. I didn't pick him up there. It was blocks away."

It was the sound of wood connecting with the ball. Fischer headed to second. "I need to see it on paper, Jose, otherwise the words just go into the air. If you want me to help you, I have to see it to understand, just like I need case law to write a brief. Something I can stare at over and over 'til it makes sense; that's the only way we'll figure out how to recant what you told Gra-Bois." Fischer found a piece of paper and prodded Ramos to draw it all out, just like he'd done for Jon Morgan some two weeks earlier. Ramos sketched in the X on the makeshift map where, he said, he'd picked Etan up. It was a spot on Prince Street, a block from the Patz apartment.

"Then what?" Fischer pushed a bit.

"Then we went back to my apartment. But I never forced him."

"Why would he ever go with you?"

"I just walked up to him on the street and said, 'Hi, remember me? I'm Sandy's friend.'"

"Ramos didn't meet him at random, he was very forceful about this point," Fischer later reported to GraBois. "He didn't elaborate as to whether he'd met Etan before. I think it mattered to him that I didn't think he had just 'picked him up.' That's it so far as direct Patz involvement goes. If anything's going to happen, it'll come soon."

It wasn't long in coming. Once Etan's name had been broached in the legal discussions, it was easier to bring it up in the therapy sessions. Fischer believed that Ramos actually yearned to talk about what had happened back in 1979. At the end of previous confessional moments, he had always appeared relieved, drained, as though he felt expiated of his sins.

Within a few days, an opportunity presented itself. Ramos had already mentioned other boys by then; visitors to the drainpipe, a young teen in Greenwich Village, and the boy in Ohio, whom Ramos called Peter James. Once again, as he often did, Ramos distinguished between his "relationships" and abuse. Fischer egged him on—in the absence of force, he concurred, Ramos was guilty of a societal rather than a legal crime. "These young lovers of yours." Fischer tried to appear curious about the technicalities. "What constituted sex with them?"

Ramos took the bait. He matter-of-factly described rubbing up against them from behind, sometimes taking them orally or having the boys fellate him. Penetration was difficult, he explained.

"Is that what you did to the Patz boy?" Fischer kept his voice very neutral.

"Yes, before I sent him home." Ramos was still hedging his bets, but Fischer had just hit a double, and he had to go on playing his part for the team.

Ramos seemed completely at ease, and Fischer affected a casual air as he pushed for more detail, mixing in Etan's name with the others he'd heard. This felt like the culmination of everything he had been working toward.

He was trying to commit the words to memory, so that later he could write them all down faithfully. When he got the chance he would relay to GraBois how Ramos was clear and graphic about the sexual acts he'd committed, both orally and anally, on the boy. How Ramos acknowledged that Etan had been fearful and unwilling but that Ramos had reassured him that he wasn't doing anything wrong.

"I honor him every day," Ramos said.

Now as the session swung back and forth between conversational and confessional, Ramos's mood was alternately calm and overwrought. Sometimes, discussing the sex acts, his eyes would glaze over and he'd rock back and forth.

"You'll never be whole until you get it out, Jose," Fischer urged him on. "Redeem yourself." This was a common tack. Fischer often encouraged Ramos to separate himself from his acts, so that he could purge those acts; the only way to heal, he told Ramos. Now Fischer wanted to hear Ramos finally say in no uncertain terms that he'd killed his victim. He knew Gra-Bois needed that in order to clinch the case, as well as what Ramos had done with the body.

But the moment never came. Instead, Fischer later told the Feds, both men were jolted out of their session as the door banged open and guards announced they were searching the cell. Fischer never knew why, but the two men were separated long enough for the intensity of the moment and the mood to pass. Now he could only sort through all he'd heard, while he waited until it was safe to put it on paper. He knew from experience that Ramos would need a break before the next foray, so for a few days he made notes when he could and looked for his next chance to play therapist. But at night, as he relived the exchanges and wrote them down, he began to hope the chance wouldn't come again. He couldn't deny that playing the game was a kick; his senses were alert in ways he'd almost forgotten since he'd gone back inside. He wanted to get the job done, for Ramos's victims now as well as his own agenda. But even the heartless character Fischer was playing during the day was starting to feel things, things that made him feel awful. And he was starting to feel he'd had enough.

CHAPTER 24

Double Play

Jeremy Fischer: Ramos said he knew Etan from Sandy. Ramos said, "I
honor his memory." ... "GraBois knows I did it—I'll take him [GraBois]
to the grave with me and Etan." ... I asked, "Is he dead?" Ramos said,
"What the fuck do you think? Of course he's dead. ..." He said, "... They'll
never, ever convict me because they'll never, ever have a body."
  —*Jeremy Fischer phone conversation with Stuart GraBois,*
    April 19, 1991

The phone rang midmorning on Friday, April 19. It was more than
ten days since Stuart GraBois had last spoken with Jeremy Fischer.
During that whole time Fischer had been unable to get word to GraBois.

"I'm here in the city, at MCC," Fischer said. "I've been writing down as
much as I can. I have a lot to tell you."

Fischer quickly listed the most incriminating of Ramos's admissions, up
to and including the sexual assault of Etan Patz.

"He definitely admitted to molesting Etan Patz, as well as the others. He
said, 'I did it, and it's killing GraBois that he can't get it out of me' a bunch
of times in a bunch of different ways. He didn't tell me what I know you
want to hear from him—the words 'I killed him.' But I'm going to get it."

"This is great news. You're almost there." GraBois didn't want Fischer to
lose his enthusiasm over one setback.

"We were so close," Fischer bemoaned. "Those morons interrupted us at
the worst possible time. I haven't had another chance yet to go back at our
guy, but it's looking very promising. I want to hear him say what he did with
the body. Then we'll have him. If I can hold out that long. I gotta tell you,

this is not what I thought it was going to be." Fischer stopped—he knew it was pointless to tell GraBois about the psychic wear and tear.

"You're within reach of the home run," GraBois encouraged.

In her office on the other side of the building, Mary Galligan got the next call from Fischer, with the same hurried headlines. "The kid is dead," she scribbled on a scrap of paper. "'I honor Etan's memory'...he was Sandy's boyfriend...had sex with Etan, not a random act...he penetrated but not all the way...'I didn't use force...they'll never have a body.'"

Galligan had a different reaction to this breakthrough. She'd never been Fischer's biggest fan, and now in one brief phone conversation, without any context, he was offering up untold treasures. She was skeptical about anything this character said, let alone such shockingly incriminating statements. But still, this was huge. If it was true.

"It's a confession. It's not perfect, and we're not done, but this is great." GraBois was exuberant when he talked to Galligan a few minutes later. He had sweated blood to keep this investigation going, and now he had just heard vindication. For the first time since the "90 percent confession" in his office, the Etan Patz case had, he thought, clearly been advanced.

"We have to be careful not to put all our eggs in one basket," Galligan cautioned. "I want to sit this guy down face-to-face and ask him about a million questions, see his body language, and try to shoot holes in his story."

"And you will. But we have to give him another chance to pull more out of Ramos. If Fischer leaves the cell now, we jeopardize getting everything. We need to leave him in there as long as we possibly can."

They considered other options. A wire was the logical next step. In the movies, that was so simple—in one quick scene, a dark figure slips into the room, rummages around off camera; cut to men in a truck outside with headphones eating cold take-out as they monitor reel-to-reels. But in reality, undercover recordings were a nightmare. In New York State, it was illegal to tape a conversation unless one participant consented. If Fischer were that one person, what would happen if he fell asleep and Ramos said something to an unsuspecting guard or another inmate? Or to himself—Ramos was known to talk out loud. There were so many privacy issues that could demand a judge's ruling, not to mention the myriad logistical issues, especially in a jail cell. And this wasn't any ordinary cell. This was seg, where the inmates never left their little boxes. The stakes were high. Any slip-up could get someone killed. Fischer had just told Galligan he'd consent to being recorded, but she'd never have him wear the wire himself—too dangerous. They'd have to figure out somewhere to plant a bug in the tiny, nearly bare room. Even if they did that successfully, she knew there might be technology glitches. There were so many moving, breakable parts that these things worked only a fraction of the time. But it was worth a try.

The two also talked about Jeremy Fischer's potential for burnout. He sounded like he was nearing his sell-by date. If they pushed him too far, the whole thing could blow up. Not only that, if they couldn't get the wire in, they needed another plan to back up Jeremy Fischer's information. Either way, it would be great to open another witness and have him ready to go, the way Fischer was when Morgan came out. But the chances of another informant coming forward, as Fischer and Morgan had, were slim to none. As it turned out, that wasn't necessary.

Two days after Fischer's bombshell phone call from MCC, while he was still waiting to be returned to Otisville segregation from New York City, Morgan beat him back there. Morgan got into what he saw as a bullshit argument with his unit manager and what the other man saw as a failure to obey orders. Within hours he was in the hole again, hungry and outraged. He angrily rubbed the black-and-blue mark on his arm left by the unit manager, who'd thrown him out of his office.

Morgan spent the next several hours waiting around for the write-up, the medical exam, and the Polaroid photos documenting his bruises. Now he had a two-week hold in seg before a disciplinary hearing would adjudicate. His old cellmate Jose Ramos was the last thing on his mind. But the next morning, he realized Ramos was in another interior cell not far away, one flight up and across a small courtyard created by the L-shaped tier. Morgan was surprised to hear Ramos call out a greeting, then to invite him back to share his cell. Their last round together hadn't ended on the best of terms, but apparently now that was all forgotten. Out of courtesy, Morgan sent a note to GraBois to tell him what had happened.

"I am back in seg temporarily," Morgan wrote that first day. He told GraBois Ramos wanted him back for a roommate, but that he'd declined, needing to focus instead on the many court papers he had yet to file. Morgan knew he would never get his own work done with Ramos as a distraction. But even on a different floor, Ramos still managed to distract. Just hours later Morgan suddenly heard a commotion from somewhere on the tier above. Shrill screams that he recognized as Ramos's signaled Jeremy

Fischer's return from New York City, and Ramos was less than happy to see him.

During the four days that Fischer was in Manhattan, Ramos had been assigned another cellmate. When Fischer was brought back to segregation, the other man was abruptly ushered out and Fischer was put back in. This was highly unusual, evidently setting off alarm bells in Ramos's paranoid brain. He'd already begun to question Fischer's trip to MCC, a place that put Fischer, along with some very damning revelations, in suspiciously close proximity to Stuart GraBois. Now Ramos erupted, banging wildly on the walls and screaming.

"Get him out! Get him out right now. I don't want him back in here." When the guards seemed indifferent, Ramos did the one thing that guaranteed they'd be separated.

"I'm going to hang myself if he stays," Ramos bellowed. He pulled a sheet off his bed and started to drape it over the top bunk. Suicide threats were taken very seriously at Otisville, and were cause for immediate action. Inmates in seg often talked about "suicide vacations," where they'd be moved to the nearby prison infirmary and kept under constant surveillance. The "vacations" never lasted long, usually a few days, but they were coveted, especially since the infirmary had television.

"Are you okay, Fischer?" someone called.

"Yeah, fine. Everything's fine."

"He's a liar," Ramos yelled back, and the screaming ramped up again before the two were separated and Ramos, as he'd intended, went off to the infirmary.

After a few days in suicide watch, where someone kept an eye on Ramos round the clock through one side of the observation window, the guards brought him back to Jeremy Fischer's cell. Briefly Fischer's soothing words seemed to calm him down, but Ramos was flipping back and forth daily.

He demanded to be moved, and told prison authorities Fischer's health would be jeopardized if that didn't happen. Finally Fischer was removed from the cell again, and the two men placed in separation. When inmates are so volatile, "separation" is the official designation that keeps them apart, sometimes so far apart that the hallway is cleared of one before the other moves through it. Once again Ramos was alone, and more paranoid than ever, as he stared furiously across the courtyard into Fischer's new cell. The inmates on that interior side would listen to him vent.

"Jeremy, you motherfucker," Ramos would scream. "You rat son of a bitch."

"Ramos, you're crazy." Every time Fischer would call Ramos crazy, it would make Ramos crazier. It was the worst thing Fischer could come back with, and he knew it.

"I have to talk to you," Ramos implored with a desperate air, once he'd discovered Jon Morgan was just a few doors away. "You gotta meet me in the library." Ramos was clearly agitated about something and he told Morgan repeatedly, as well as anyone else who couldn't help but hear through their own windows, that he wanted him back.

Morgan said little and made notes for GraBois, not particularly anxious to be more than a bystander, until about a week later, when he was ordered to the lieutenant's office. The officer dialed the number for the assistant U.S. attorney, and even though the man then walked out discreetly, Morgan knew this was highly irregular and potentially compromising. He and GraBois spoke tersely, mindful of who else might be listening in.

"I don't know what happened exactly," Morgan said, "but our man is going crazy. He's talking to me every day, and he really wants me in there."

"I know, I know. Listen we're working on some things. We might need you to go back in, and I might not get a chance to talk to you again if the right moment comes. I have to warn you that Jeremy's been helping us too, and Ramos may have figured things out. If so, it's a riskier proposition and possibly more dangerous," GraBois said. "But we're at a very critical stage, and we need more. Can you do it?"

While Morgan hadn't planned to volunteer, he had to admit he wanted to get to the end of this himself. As long as he was in seg, he'd help out any way that he could, and since Ramos was asking for him, he was the only logical choice.

"In the meantime, even if you don't end up in with him," GraBois instructed, "any chance you talk to him, push the concurrent time angle. Tell him there's no way that he could get additional time if he were smart about making a deal on the Patz case. Tell him he could negotiate for ten to fifteen, and he'd serve it at the same time as what he's doing now on the Pennsylvania charge. That means no additional time for him, and we'd probably be willing to buy it because it finishes things for the family. I've said this to him, but it would sound better coming from you. Try that, and let me know."

"Here's another possible bargaining chip," Morgan responded. "He's terrified that when he goes back to Pennsylvania they'll send him to Graterford or Western." Located outside big cities at opposite ends of the state, Graterford and Western were maximum-security prisons, and Graterford, the largest in the state, was especially daunting. Unlike medium-security Rockview, Graterford housed the most hardened, violent criminals, numbering among them the Philly gang bangers. Rockview was like summer camp in comparison.

"We'll add it into the mix," said GraBois.

———

Maybe Jon Morgan didn't want to get involved, but he couldn't seem to help himself. A few days later, as happens constantly, the seg inmates rotated cells. Morgan was moved into the one previously occupied by Ramos, where he found something interesting his former roommate had left behind. He wrote GraBois to tell him he was holding on to a book about "sex therapy," annotated and underlined in places. He also told the prosecutor that Ramos was now in another cell around the corner from Jeremy Fischer and the two weren't speaking to each other. That could change, he wrote, since he knew from his own experience how unpredictable Ramos was.

Within days, Jeremy Fischer went back down to New York City for a court date. When he returned to Otisville segregation it was agreed they'd take advantage of the move and try once more to put the two men back together. So far, Fischer was still their best shot, and as Morgan had said in his letter, Ramos was unpredictable. On more than one occasion Fischer had been able to soothe the savage beast, and they wanted to give him every opportunity to finish what he'd started.

"I don't want that asshole in here. I won't room with him." Ramos was already screaming before Fischer walked in, but now he hurled the worst epithet you can use in prison. In a place where obscenities laced every sentence, this word could get you killed.

"Get him out of the cell. He's a goddamn snitch."

The guards looked uneasy. This was not going to work, but they had their orders.

"If I'm a snitch," Fischer returned, "then you'd better watch out. If I want to get you, I have enough on you to turn you in for murder."

Ramos was stopped cold. His mouth opened and closed again. Without saying another word, he picked up his cereal bowl and threw it at Fischer's head. Then he moved toward the other man and tried to throw a punch, but Fischer easily moved out of the way. As Ramos pursued and swung again fruitlessly a second, then a third time, the guards moved in between the two. The operation had clearly been compromised.

———

Fuck Fischer! Fuck GraBois!" Jon Morgan could hear Ramos starting up again after Fischer had been moved out, and he braced himself for what was to come. Ramos was alone in an already overcrowded unit, and if no one had wanted to share a cell with him before, he was even more persona non grata now that he was acting so out of control. Ramos himself would only consider one possible roommate, and the guards were anxious to shut him up. After Ramos's outbursts echoed on the tier all morning, Morgan's door opened at midday to reunite him with his old cellmate. But one month later, he was hardly the same man.

It wasn't so much his physical appearance—he had the same matted beard and hair, the same freakishly long fingernails. But now Morgan was aware of a persistent, noticeable twitch. The morning's events had completely unhinged Ramos—he was unsteady on his feet, and his eyes moved around the room even more erratically than usual. Although he seemed happy to see Morgan, his mood shifted in an instant. Morgan risked a few benign inquiries, and he watched Ramos's hand shake as he held it out to brandish a freshly sharpened pencil stub.

"Don't push me, buddy, or I'll use this."

Morgan knew people who'd been badly hurt by a three-inch pencil, even one who'd lost an eye. At five foot ten and 180 pounds, he was stronger than Ramos, and he didn't take the threat too seriously. Still, he knew from the start that he was going to have to tread more lightly than the last time. He couldn't imagine any further casual discussions of the Patz case.

From that moment on, Morgan sat back and let Ramos do all the talking. It didn't seem to calm him down, though. Morgan soon began to feel as if he'd been caged with a junkie going through withdrawal. Ramos feverishly continued to plan his escape and asked Morgan to get him New York City street maps. He still targeted GraBois, but now Jeremy Fischer had joined the prosecutor in the crosshairs. He asked Morgan to find him antitank rockets, grenades, and M-16 rifles.

"Well, obviously there's nothing I can do while I'm in here," Morgan would hedge, "but when I get out, sure, Jose, I'll look into it." Ramos knew Morgan had actually done some arms dealing before his current round of troubles, so this wasn't a totally outlandish request, but Morgan recognized one thing—Ramos himself was an unlit fuse, just one spark away from blowing up the whole cell.

Morgan tried vainly to determine just what had happened on Jeremy Fischer's watch to cause this heightened level of fire-breathing paranoia. It wasn't until a few days in, on a chilly predawn morning, that he began to piece it together. Climbing down from his bunk to relieve himself, he realized Ramos was also awake, with the light on. It looked like he'd been up all night, and unless he turned off his lamp, Morgan would be up now too.

"Jose, put it out and go to sleep."

Ramos mumbled unintelligibly, but Morgan assumed it was the usual fuck off. Ramos then edged farther away on the bed, obscuring a small object he held possessively.

"What is that?" Morgan could tell by the way Ramos shielded his hands that it was contraband. He climbed back up on the top and leaned over until he could make out two rolls of what looked like tape. No, he realized, it was a typewriter ribbon.

"What are you doing, you reading the ribbon?"

A hint of a grin came over Ramos's face. It was the first time Morgan had seen him smile since he'd been in there. The look was part sheepish, part triumphant, and he held two little attached spools up high, like a trophy.

"Jeremy is a rat. And this is the proof."

The law library typewriter had run out of its carbon ribbon. Normally, to get a new ribbon you had to turn in the used cartridge, but this one had simply been thrown away. The ribbon was supposed to be reversible, so even if potentially sensitive words were typed in one direction, they'd be rendered indecipherable by another layer of typeface going in the opposite direction. But someone had mistakenly ordered single-strike ribbon, which meant every letter typed on that typewriter was in essence copied in reverse typeface, white letters on black ribbon, then rolled up in a tidy spool inside a plastic cartridge. If you were extremely patient, or obsessive, or you had a lot of free time, you could read every piece of correspondence written there, word after tortuously unrolled word. Ramos had salvaged the discarded ribbon from the law library trash can, and that's exactly what he'd been doing.

Ramos had already discarded the bulky cartridge and was methodically unwinding one spool and then winding the other, reading carefully as he went. Morgan had no way to know how long it had been in his possession, but it was clear Ramos had already made a damning discovery. For all the precautions Jeremy Fischer had taken, scrawling secret passages after lights-out and hiding them down in his pants, he had written a letter to his lawyer on the law library typewriter, in which he couldn't help boasting of his success. It was a cryptic note, but all Ramos needed to see were the words "GraBois says I'm on second base" to know that his friend, his only confidant, his onetime savior, was a traitor.

Morgan frantically searched his memory. Had *he* written anything incriminating on that typewriter? There were recent letters to GraBois, but most of what he'd written had been by hand and he didn't know if the ones he'd typed were on this ribbon. As Ramos ramped up his threats against "that rat snitch Fischer," Morgan tried not think about what would happen if he were discovered too. Fischer was safely out of the cell; Morgan was locked in.

All through the following day he watched Ramos try to decipher more of the ribbon and grow increasingly more agitated. It was a weekend and Morgan couldn't reach GraBois; he didn't know what good that would do him anyway. The next night he was awakened again, deliberately this time by Ramos, who was shaking him urgently. Ramos was talking, saying the same words over and over, but it took a groggy minute to register.

"There's no body."

Morgan was half asleep, and he was pissed. "That's why you woke me up, Jose? To tell me there's no body? Jesus. Go to sleep." He rolled over and drifted off himself, a fitful, restless sleep this time. He dreamt he was sleeping with one eye open.

"He found out that Jeremy was working for you." When Morgan finally got GraBois on the phone, he was desperate to let him know what had happened.

"You need to get the warden to change the ribbon in the law library right away. Who knows what else was written on the new one! If he gets his hands on it I could be busted any minute. Tell the warden to get cloth ribbons, you can't read those."

"I'll call him right now. Did Jose say anything else?"

"Yeah," Morgan said. "You'll like this—he woke me up the other night to tell me there's no body."

The ribbon in the law library typewriter was replaced immediately. But the one Ramos kept twisting and turning in his hand was driving Morgan to distraction. Whenever Ramos read from it, he'd ratchet up a notch, and like a chain reaction, Morgan could feel his nerves fray a little more each time. Ramos even cycled through painstakingly to find Jeremy Fischer's letter again and made Morgan read it himself.

An incident at the shower area across the hall finally forced Morgan into action. As he had been doing without a fuss three times weekly for months now, Ramos left their shared cell for the shower "cage." The guard would typically lock down the inmate before unlocking the cuffs so he could freely soap and rinse. Before the clothes and cuffs went back on, the guard would have the inmate open the curtain to confirm he hadn't used shower time to remove a hidden weapon from a body cavity. It had been known to happen.

Ramos had never raised an objection before. But this time, when he was told to draw the curtain back, he refused, and then got into it with the guard.

"Don't look at me," he shrieked. Inmates were lining up at their doors to watch the show. "Don't touch me. You faggot, what's wrong with you!?!" Ramos was coiled and poised to strike, like a vicious dog, teeth bared to expose his fangs. It was one thing to lose it with your cellmate, Morgan thought, quite another to go off on a cop. Morgan caught a glimpse of inner venom that he hadn't seen before, despite all the rantings in the cell they shared.

"You've got to get rid of that ribbon," Morgan told him later. Maybe if it were gone, Ramos wouldn't have the constant stimulus to incite him.

"If you get caught with that ribbon in the cell, there's no telling what the guards will do. They'll ban you from the law library—is that what you want? Flush it down the toilet before it gets both of us in trouble." Morgan watched with relief as Ramos unspooled the tape and it went down. Maybe now he'd get some peace.

He was wrong. When Ramos found out soon afterwards that Jeremy Fischer had been pulled from segregation altogether, he told Morgan in a panicked voice that could only mean one thing—Fischer was being called before a grand jury in New York to testify against him. Listening to him rail, at times Morgan thought Ramos hated Jeremy Fischer even more than GraBois. Fischer had betrayed Ramos in a way that GraBois had not, and now Ramos believed the betrayal continued, this time under oath. Ramos began strategizing what he was convinced was his own impending grand jury appearance, swinging wildly between moments of despair and a cocky sense of denial.

"I'll just say I can't remember anything," he'd mutter, pacing back and forth in the tiny cell. Or he would sit on the bed for hours, staring up at the top bunk, and only occasionally make notes for his legal defense. "They have no body," he wrote at one point, echoing his midnight ravings, but Morgan was afraid to ask what that meant. Ramos talked about needing another "suicide vacation," and Morgan silently agreed. He actually thought Ramos was in shock. Aloud, he offered to recommend a few attorneys.

Ramos shook his head. "No attorney will ever represent me. It's too horrible. I'll have to represent myself."

"What are you talking about, Jose? That's ridiculous."

"No, I know. Any lawyer I could find would sell me out."

"Like how bad?" Morgan tried. "What'd you do, kill the kid and put the body in the wood chipper, like the guy in Connecticut?" Two years earlier, a Connecticut man had gotten fifty years for murdering his wife and disposing of her in a wood chipper. They'd convicted him without a body on the basis of stray hair, teeth, and five drops of her blood.

Ramos said nothing, just stared morosely at Morgan, who didn't have hopes of getting much more. In fact, soon afterwards, Ramos stopped talking altogether.

He began passing Morgan notes and demanding written responses only, claiming first that the cell was bugged, then that the whole tier was wired. Next he complained he couldn't read Morgan's handwriting, so Morgan was forced to type his notes on that same law library typewriter. On the one hand, Morgan was relieved to no longer hear Ramos running his mouth, but on the other hand this new system didn't help him do his job. He knew there were plans to wire the cell—he'd agreed to be recorded just a few days before—but never knew what might happen or when. As it turned out, even though Ramos was right to be suspicious, a combination of impenetrable cinderblock walls and the constraints of early-'90s technology protected him from incriminating himself when the bug yielded nothing.

By the end of their second week together, Morgan was counting the handful of days left before the hearing that would determine whether or not he'd be punished in the disciplinary section of seg or released back into general population. In any case, he was looking forward to getting away from Jose

Ramos. He'd decided he would stick it out in the cell until then, but by this point Ramos seemed to have written him off anyway, and the threat of violence was rapidly outweighing the benefit of working the case. When Ramos talked again of going to suicide watch, Morgan encouraged him.

"If you are sure that this cell is bugged," Morgan wrote him in one of the many messages they were now passing back and forth, "go to the hospital, and then when you come back you'll be in another room."

When he wasn't pacing the cell, Ramos spent hours taking notes from his cherished Stephen King novels, studying deranged kidnapper Annie Wilkes in King's *Misery* to perfect his act for an insanity defense. Morgan promised to send him more books after his release, knowing that any offer of help would in turn ensure his own safety. He hoped that despite Ramos's suspicions, he still needed Morgan too much to turn on him.

"Any minute now," Ramos wrote in his notes to Morgan, "I'll be called down to testify. They've got you in here 'til then, to monitor our conversations."

"He is bugging out," Morgan wrote in his own notes on his last day, the ones he carefully kept hidden. He noted how upset Ramos seemed to be, both at the thought that his cellmate was leaving and in reaction to any of Morgan's final questions. Ramos wasn't sleeping most nights, Morgan wrote, which meant he wasn't either.

On those nights, Morgan lay in bed with visions of Ramos choking him as he slept. If he stayed awake, at least there would an instant of warning. He began to imagine a scenario where he'd be forced to kill Ramos in self-defense. He hoped it wouldn't come to that. He'd incapacitate Ramos if he could and mentally rehearsed a one-two combination: full-on kick to the groin, followed by a hard blow to the Adam's apple. He regretted he hadn't been able to steer Ramos to a confession, but Morgan was now convinced Ramos had killed Etan Patz. And while he felt sadness at this conclusion, in practical terms, if true, that meant Ramos was capable of murder. Specifically, he thought, Ramos is capable of murdering me.

> Annie was writhing and moaning. A lick of flame shot up through the gap between her left arm and the side of her body. She screamed. Paul could smell frying skin, burning fat.
> —*excerpt from* Misery *by Stephen King, the book Jose Ramos read in segregation*

Morgan was vaguely aware of his mattress rising and falling. In his stupor he thought he was riding a gentle wave until he shook himself awake and realized Ramos was banging on the underside of his bunk. How had he fallen asleep? He remembered then that Ramos himself had finally dropped off, giving Morgan blessed relief and license to do the same.

"Wake up, wake up. Talk to me."

Ramos must have been so overwrought that he'd forgotten about the self-imposed ban on words, and now they were pouring out. He'd had a nightmare, he said. Morgan noted the worn copy of *Misery* that had probably first put Ramos to sleep but then had woken him up. His cellmate wasn't very coherent, but Morgan put it together. Ramos had dozed off while reading a particularly vivid scene about burning bodies in the Stephen King book, probably the brutally violent ending, and now he wanted Morgan to help calm him down.

Ramos lay in his bed, shivering. The passages had brought him back, he told Morgan, to the work he'd done for the super at his Lower East Side apartment. The basement boiler had a large fire box, large enough to accommodate a grown man's body. Ramos talked of unscrewing the front of the box and crawling inside to clean it out.

His story brought Morgan wide awake. If Ramos had killed Etan Patz, this would be the most logical explanation for how he'd disposed of the body. For a second, he considered voicing his thoughts, but he didn't dare. He made a mental note instead to pass the information on to GraBois. Morgan couldn't understand why Ramos was telling him this, and he never would. They would never speak of it again. In a matter of days, Morgan was relieved to say his goodbyes. His disciplinary charge had been dismissed, his hearing canceled, and he was going back to general population.

"Good luck with everything," he told Jose Ramos. He shook his hand, then turned to let the guards cuff him.

"Hey, Jon," Ramos called, as Morgan was led out. "Next time you're at MCC, will you send me a bunch of magazines? Especially the fashion magazines." What a nutcase, Morgan thought, as the door closed behind him.

As soon as Morgan got back to the compound, he would take a long shower to wash off the dirt of the cell, and the stench of his cellmate. But first he called Stuart GraBois. Then after his shower he called him again, just because he could.

CHAPTER 25

⌒

Debrief

Mr. Fischer is a New York State parolee who has been charged with violation of the terms and conditions of his parole release....

The Division of Parole has scheduled a final parole revocation hearing for him. It will be held at the Metropolitan Correctional Center at 10:00 am on Tuesday, May 14, 1991....Under the circumstances I am asking that you appear at his scheduled hearing so as to alert the parole authorities to the fact of and value of Fischer's assistance to your office.

—*letter from Jeremy Fischer's attorney to Stuart GraBois, May 13, 1991*

I'm telling you, if I had to go back in there, I'd hang myself." Jeremy Fischer was one month away from being a free man, with a lot to say about the price he'd paid for it. He was sitting in one of the drab, institutional interview rooms in the MCC that reeked of ammonia, with FBI special agent Mary Galligan and another agent who was present as a corroborating witness. Two weeks had gone by since his last contact with Ramos, but Fischer looked like he continued to feel the effects. Although he still sported the ponytail, he was thinner than the first time Galligan had met him before he'd gone to Otisville, and paler, from the weeks in sunless segregation. There was a weakness about him now, and there was something about his eyes. They were duller. The cocky air he'd radiated that first time was dimmer, dialed back to just above zero.

Galligan was finally getting her chance to sit face-to-face with Fischer, to get her own read on whether or not he was full of shit, and so far he wasn't winning her over. She already knew that Fischer had been busted by Ramos—two weeks earlier they'd heard from Jon Morgan about the letter

Fischer had written and Ramos had then found in the law library. It sounded like something from *The Gang That Couldn't Shoot Straight*.

To hear Fischer tell it now, he had barely escaped mortal injury while locked in the cell with Ramos. Galligan recognized he'd been in danger, but she didn't believe it was more than any con faced in prison. Prison was a dangerous place. Either Fischer was bragging or vying for extra brownie points to bolster his chances that the parole violation would be dropped. Blah, blah, blah, she thought. Let's get to the reason we're here. She wanted to understand the context of all these damaging admissions Ramos had supposedly made to Fischer.

Special Agent Jim Fitzgerald was the second agent in the interview. He was also from the Bank Robbery Squad, but his eventual goal was the special profiler team down at the FBI Academy in Quantico, the Behavior Analysis Unit. Fitzgerald had little previous knowledge of the case, but he'd been tasked with a very specific job.

"I want you to go in there without knowing everything and just assume he's lying through his teeth," Galligan instructed him. "Watch him, listen, and see if he can convince you that he's not."

Jeremy Fischer had handed over pages of scribbled and tattered notes when he'd arrived; she'd read through some of them and would examine them more closely later; they'd be important for double-checking consistency. But of course the most helpful factor on that score would be Jon Morgan's account. He had just gotten out of seg with Ramos, and she was hoping to get him down here the following week. She wanted to match up the two stories and see where the holes were, if any. She knew that GraBois believed Fischer was telling the truth, but she needed to be convinced too. Her ass was also on the line if Fischer proved to be lying about every single thing he'd said, as he'd often done in the past. Besides, GraBois had been on the case three years longer than she had, and he'd lived it and breathed it. He'd already come to the conclusion that Ramos was guilty. She, on the other hand, wasn't yet certain about Ramos *or* Jeremy Fischer.

Describing the sexual offender workbook Ramos had been working on, Fischer said this had been his "in." He explained how the book was a key part of the course Ramos had to take to qualify for parole, and how it created the therapist-patient dynamic.

"He had to do these exercises," Fischer said. "And here I was, someone he knew from before, a fellow Jew, so to speak, who was willing to help. I have a background in psychology. I knew the buzz words. It didn't take long before I was pushing all the right buttons. And as he grew to trust me, more and more spilled out." Fischer knew the agents were interested in Ramos's different admissions, so he skipped over most of the histrionics as he told them what he learned in the most incriminating "therapy" session.

Until now Galligan had only heard this story in a truncated form that had sounded bombastic and incredible, during the terse, time-limited phone conversation from MCC. Now the details were vivid and expansive, and came from a man directly in front of her, his eyes never wavering, his manner straightforward. Retold in context, they rang truer than before.

Fischer had no hesitation about offering up the most graphic material, as he talked about how Ramos remembered "the taste of the boy's penis." Galligan wrote it down as a lurid but telling detail. She didn't think a heterosexual nonpedophile male would come up with that on his own, no matter how long he spent scheming in his cell. If he were fabricating this, she thought, he might say something like "the kid was hot" or he "was turned on" by the child's hairless body, something in his own realm of experience.

"And he said he remembered the breadth of his penis," Fischer continued. "I remember that clearly because at first I thought he said 'breath,' and I was confused. It wasn't until a few minutes later that I realized what he meant."

She wrote it down in quotes, again, struck by the clear language and the way Fischer was so matter-of-fact as he detailed the story. Breadth, she thought, caught off guard for a second. This is a little kid, for God's sakes. She tried to stay mechanical, even as Fischer told them Ramos admitted to penetrating Etan.

"I asked him," Fischer said, "'Can you penetrate a child?' because I couldn't imagine such a thing, and Ramos said, 'Yes, but not too far,' and then he said the most awful thing. 'That's what separates the men from the boys.' I'll never forget that, because I couldn't believe he would make such a sick, disgusting joke."

Most of what Fischer was telling them now echoed his written notes, including that anecdote. It didn't prove he was telling the truth, but at least he was consistent. Galligan would never forget the next thing Fischer then told *her*. When Etan protested, Ramos said, he told the boy it was okay, lots of people did these things. And Etan had countered that if it was nice and okay, then his mommy and daddy would have told him about it.

"Ramos was quick to add that he didn't molest Etan," Fischer went on, "because he didn't use any force. So in his mind he justified it. It was all right if the boy ultimately let him do it. That's the way he saw things. And that's what he said about all the boys. That he never forced anyone. And there I was, agreeing with him. The whole thing made me feel pretty slimy." Fischer squirmed involuntarily in his seat, as though shaking off the memory.

"Hey, you're talking about one of the most horrific things an adult can do to a child; don't start questioning your own morality," Galligan said. "Look what happened. You asked him and you got an answer you didn't expect. Now we have another piece of information. Often we have to say things that make us sick to our stomach when we're talking to a subject."

Fischer described Ramos's account of having seen Etan before, with Sandy, so that when Ramos introduced himself that day as "Sandy's friend," the boy came with him willingly.

"He was very smug about how the papers got it wrong that he'd picked up Etan at Washington Square Park." Fischer handed over the map that Ramos had drawn, explaining that at first Ramos had penciled a sketchier version.

"I told him it was garbage, so he started over. He very carefully drew a map of the whole Washington Square area. It took him at least forty-five minutes to make it look this neat and intricate, and he talked me through it afterward."

Galligan was looking at a detailed map of Prince Street and the surrounding area, encompassing Washington Square Park to the north, and Avenue B to the east, near where Ramos had lived in 1979. The tidy lines denoting the street blocks suggested Ramos had used a straight edge to draw it, and they'd all been correctly labeled. She'd have it checked out, but it looked like Ramos's handwriting. She remembered Morgan had mentioned Ramos drew him a map too, and wondered if he did it often.

Galligan made note of the X marked on Prince Street, showing where the Patzes lived, the X showing where Ramos told Fischer he'd picked Etan up near the bus stop a block and a half from home, and the X at the location of Ramos's own apartment on East Fourth Street, several blocks away.

"What else did he say about Etan?" Galligan asked.

"He said that he honored him every day, whatever that means." Fischer shrugged. Then he told her about the other children Ramos said he'd "never forced."

"He talked about a kid named Peter James," Fischer told the agents. "I'm not sure where he was, either Atlanta or Ohio. He talked a lot about Sandy's son Bennett."

When Galligan heard these names, she recognized insider information. No one had ever publicized the existence of P.J. or Bennett, and Fischer had Ramos referring to them extensively.

"Ramos said Sandy didn't know he was molesting Bennett before he took his European trip; that she's nothing but a drunk. He used to take him to the movies, to dinner and the Empire State Building. He told me he had sex with Bennett a lot."

The rest of the list included a boy in Pennsylvania, one boy in New York named Ron who'd be sixteen or seventeen now, and some mentally retarded children Ramos had preyed on when he'd lived close to a hospital in New Orleans.

It was Galligan's turn to recoil, but she was careful to show no visible signs of a reaction.

"But the one he loved to talk about was P.J., because he got such a kick out of GraBois thinking P.J. might be Etan Patz. Ramos said he knew P.J. wasn't Etan. Said he'd known P.J. since he was a little boy."

Each piece of information that Fischer couldn't have gotten from anyone except Ramos added up, each a drop in the bucket until it finally spilled over. Okay, Galligan finally thought, this man is not lying to me.

"When I get out, he wants me to send him some watch that costs thirty dollars and has a compass in it," Fischer added. "He's going to use it when he's sent back to Rockview, 'cause he's going to escape. He told me his whole plan—how he's going to cut a hole in the fence, then use the compass watch to find his way away from the prison. He says he's already got maps of Pennsylvania squirreled away somehow back in his prison cell. Then he says he's going to go to Venezuela and no one will be able to find him. That's after he comes to New York to kill Stuart GraBois."

Fischer gave a sample of the threats his cellmate had made against the assistant U.S. attorney. "He's got a different plan every day," Fischer said. "No one will ever find GraBois when he's done with him—he'll be in little pieces spread all over. He wants to know where he lives, so he can go after him. He hates the man completely and absolutely. I used that hatred against him. I would prod him with all the things GraBois has on him, and he'd come back with, 'GraBois doesn't know anything that I haven't told him,' and eventually he said, 'GraBois knows I did it, and it's killing him because he can't get it out of me.'"

At various points, Jim Fitzgerald asked Fischer questions designed to get a sense of both Ramos's mental state and Fischer's: questions about Ramos's demeanor and his hand movements, the way he talked. Might Ramos have been acting? Fitzgerald was also interested in Fischer's own mind-set, asking questions about his motivation.

Fischer was clear. "Obviously, my own self-interest got me into this. But at a certain point it was more. I know there are lots of people in the world who do bad things, and I'm the first to admit, I've been one of them. But what he did is awful. It's sick."

What Fischer didn't tell the agents was that by the time he'd gotten out of the cell, his own part in this morality play had begun to sicken him as well: the trickery, the deceit, the betrayal, even of such a beast as Jose. As Fischer described to the Feds the admissions Ramos had made in the false therapy, he also remembered the occasional remorse in Ramos's voice, and the shred of humanity that he thought he'd glimpsed at those moments, in such tight quarters. And while Fischer still blanched at the memory of his time in seg with Jose Ramos, it wasn't because of the threat to his physical safety—Mary Galligan had been right to think he was laying it on thick in advance of his appearance before the judge. His own deception, and the depravity that had rubbed off of Ramos, had left a residue he still felt. He might have done some good with this particular con game, but he did it with his bad side, and it felt pretty crappy. He suspected it would take a long time for the feeling to go away.

———

There is so much here, I don't even know where to begin," Galligan said as soon as the two agents had quit the interview room. She was talking very fast, the adrenaline kicking in as she finally dispensed with the reserve she'd maintained throughout the last few hours.

"When he said the part about Peter James, I almost fell off the chair."

Fitzgerald looked at her blankly. Galligan had forgotten he had no prior knowledge of the case, and no idea who P.J. Fox was.

"But based on what I do know," Fitzgerald told Galligan, "I think he's telling the truth."

———

Stu, did you ever tell Jeremy Fischer about P.J.?" The following Monday Galligan was in GraBois's office.

"Of course not; you know I would never do that," GraBois said.

"I didn't think so, but I had to ask. Who knows, you could have said something like, 'If he talks about a kid named P.J., it's really important to pursue that.' I mean, it was wild to hear him say the name—and not just the initials—he knew what they stood for. I checked the records and he had it right."

Galligan had dictated her notes to the steno pool the day after Fischer's interview, and now she'd walked the written report over to GraBois, but he preferred to hear her tell it, especially the next thought.

"I gotta say, Stu, what I heard last Thursday is starting to make a believer out of me." In fact, Mary Galligan's earnest delivery made GraBois smile—not in an "I told you so way," but as an expression of satisfaction that his judgment was being confirmed.

"I'm glad to see you get to this point," he said. "Especially since you got there on your own, with the facts."

He put up his hand before she could state the obvious. "I mean, look, is Fischer a con man? Absolutely. But he's come up with some good information." He held up the map she'd given him with the report. "This didn't just come from Fischer's devious mind."

"All the same, I'm going to have the guards search Ramos's cell." Galligan stood up to leave. "There better be a map of Pennsylvania in there, or Jeremy Fischer's going to have some explaining to do."

"And once you hear from Morgan tomorrow," GraBois said, "I think you'll find some of the things he says back Fischer up too."

The next day would mark Jon Morgan's second debrief with Galligan. Back in April, when Morgan had left segregation the first time and they'd all thought he was finished with Ramos for good, he'd sat down with Galligan and walked her through his stint. Since he'd gone back in a second time, both GraBois and Galligan had received sporadic phone updates from him. The "sex therapy" book Morgan had retrieved from Ramos's cell was a particularly important find. With such a blueprint to work with, it helped explain why Fischer had extracted more of the sexual admissions out of Ramos than Morgan. But still, the bottom line was that only Fischer claimed to have heard these most damning admissions, not Morgan. Galligan would be looking for anything Morgan could offer that would give Fischer's account the verification it needed.

———

You see, Ramos got his hands on this typewriter ribbon from the law library. I think he fished it out of the trash can, but I was never sure."

Jon Morgan was sitting in Stuart GraBois's office. He'd been out of seg now for almost a week. He was giving GraBois and Galligan a much clearer account of how Ramos had discovered he had a snitch in his cell.

"I don't know how he got it past the guard, but when he came back into the cell with me, he must have had this little bundle hidden on him." Morgan was warming to the topic. "You should never put a single-strike cartridge in a prison typewriter. This typewriter, I think it was a Royal, with a daisy wheel, and it was supposed to use a multistrike ribbon so the words get covered over, but maybe someone was cutting costs. They're a lot more expensive than single-strike. Or they should have used a cloth ribbon, at least it's better than those single-strike carbon ribbons. You try reading a cloth ribbon, it's next to impossible."

Morgan certainly knew an awful lot about the most esoteric of topics, and Galligan couldn't help thinking he'd make a good *Jeopardy!* contestant. Someday.

Morgan described the very noticeable difference in his cellmate the second time around.

"He was bugging out," Morgan kept saying. "He's always been nuts, but he kept it in check before. Now he was like a wild man, he was so upset, like terrified. And he was pissed at Jeremy Fischer."

"Why do you say that?"

"He was going on and on about what he told Jeremy," Morgan continued. "That he never admitted he had sex with Etan Patz. He said he told Jeremy he was with a boy, and that he had sex with this boy but that he never said that it was Patz. Now, I could never tell if Ramos was making that up to cover something."

Galligan very deliberately didn't make eye contact with Stuart Gra-Bois. In her recent conversation with Jeremy he'd graphically contradicted Ramos's denials about sex with Etan. Sounds like a man in a panic, trying to backtrack and lay groundwork for claiming Jeremy Fischer's a liar, she thought.

Morgan told Galligan and GraBois about Ramos's near breakdown and how the overwrought man had been convinced Fischer was talking to authorities. Morgan repeated Ramos's mantra about how no one could touch him because "there's no body." And he recounted the dream about burning bodies that had woken Ramos one night, and the revelations about the boiler.

Galligan had already heard about Ramos's nightmare from Morgan's notes smuggled out of the cell. GraBois had mentioned it too, less interested in the psychology of Ramos's nightmare than what it had led the man to reveal. If Ramos so intimately knew the internal workings of an oversized boiler in his own building, it might indeed explain what had happened to Etan's body, a mystery that had dogged every investigator over the last twelve years. In New York City, there were only a few places you could successfully hide a body without someone finding it. Even in the East River, which had always been a favorite theory, bodies eventually surface.

Now, as GraBois sat across the room and let Morgan tell it, Galligan was intrigued too. While it wasn't proof of anything, she thought, it just made sense. With access to the basement boiler, Ramos would never have had to leave his building with the evidence. It would just go up in smoke. And with no physical trace of a body, no matter what else happened in this case, there would forever be room for doubt.

Mary Galligan recalled the day she'd met Stan and Julie Patz when she oversaw their blood being drawn so their DNA could be compared to P.J. Fox's.

"I just want to bury my son," Julie had said to her that day. Listening to Jon Morgan repeat Ramos's description of unscrewing the burn box, removing it, and crawling inside to clean it, Mary considered that there might never be anything for the Patzes to bury.

She forced her mind back to the business at hand, but Morgan was off topic.

"At one point Ramos said he knew the Zodiac killer." Name dropper, Galligan thought scornfully.

"And he was absolutely obsessed with the book *The Silence of the Lambs.* He wanted to see Jodie Foster in the movie. And he said he thought the Buffalo Bill character was very unprofessional."

"Did he say anything else specifically about Etan Patz?" she asked Morgan, trying to get him back on track.

Morgan looked at his notes, which he later gave to Galligan.

"He asked me about that statute of limitations question again. He was always wanting me to explain to him the statute of limitations for kidnapping. Oh yeah, I forgot, he did say at one point that in his mind, the Patz kid was the kid he took on May 25."

Galligan's cynical side didn't put much stock in that revelation. Morgan would have known they'd want to hear that and could have easily come up with it himself.

"But then he said he never told Jeremy that the kid was Etan, and he'd go on and on about how Jeremy was a snitch. I don't know what he told Jeremy, but whatever it was it seemed to scare the crap out of him. When he saw the name GraBois on that typewriter ribbon, he was convinced you"—he nodded toward the prosecutor—"were behind the whole thing. He kept saying GraBois was going to pay for it. By the time I got out of there he was convinced the room was bugged, that Jeremy was already in a grand jury, and that I would be called in next. I'm telling you, I never met anyone as paranoid as Ramos."

It reminded her of that old expression, Galligan thought, as she cuffed Morgan to take him back to the marshals. Just because you're paranoid doesn't mean they're not out to get you.

CHAPTER 26

Nothing to Lose

"Do your job, just don't ever forget what he is."

"And what's that? Do you know?"

"I know he's a monster. Beyond that, nobody can say for sure. Maybe you'll find out."

—*Jack Crawford assigns Clarice Starling to interview Hannibal Lecter,*
Thomas Harris's The Silence of the Lambs

Whether or not there was enough to convict him, the evidence was mounting that Jose Ramos had killed Etan Patz. But neither informant had gotten Ramos to make a full confession or say what he'd done with the body, and Morgan and Fischer had gone as far as they could. The next step, GraBois and Galligan ultimately agreed, was to confront Ramos and hope for him to do the unexpected. He'd done it before, especially when he was thrown off balance, like that day in GraBois's office, when he made the "90 percent confession." And according to Jon Morgan, Ramos was already teetering on the edge.

"The most important thing I heard from Morgan was that Ramos acted so crazed coming out of Fischer's cell," Galligan mused as she and GraBois reviewed her notes. "He sounded like he was falling apart. And the 'They can't get me—there's no body' line where Ramos kept having to be reassured he hadn't hung himself out to dry? Morgan may not have directly corroborated everything Fischer got, but it sounds like Ramos realized he'd just made serious admissions to someone working for the other side."

Now they had to decide the best way to get Ramos to make even more admissions. Should they bring him to New York? Double-team him? Play good cop/bad cop? The reality was, their options were limited. They didn't have much to offer him—neither carrot nor stick—that would pry out a confession, persuade him to admit he had killed a child. But you didn't *not* interview someone because you doubt he's going to confess.

"The odds that he'll give us everything are pretty low," GraBois acknowledged. "He has nothing to gain by confessing. But at this point, *we've* got nothing to lose by talking to him."

"A group of profilers are up in New York this week for meetings," Galligan said. "Let me pick their brains."

The FBI Behavior Analysis Unit was a legendary, elite group within the Bureau. Out of some thirteen thousand agents, fewer than forty were full-time profilers. Highly trained specialists in behavioral and forensic sciences, they studied violent crime cases and the psychopathology of the criminals who commit them. They didn't spend all their time in mindlock with serial killers, learning what made them tick so as to stop other serial killers, but that certainly was their public image, especially after the release of Jose Ramos's—and everyone else's—must-see film of that year, *The Silence of the Lambs.*

After hearing the case history, the profilers agreed an interview was the next step. But one thing was clear, they stressed. Stuart GraBois was toxic to Ramos, and he should have no part in the conversation. He can't be within miles of the place, one behaviorist told Galligan, or Ramos won't say a word.

"I understand," GraBois said when the agent relayed the consensus opinion. As much as he wanted to get his hands on Ramos again, if it was not what was best for the case, he had no problem stepping back.

It was Mary Galligan who looked pained, standing in front of his desk. "There's more."

"Yes?"

"Not only do they say you shouldn't be there, but we may be forced to disavow you if he starts railing, which of course you can count on. We might even have to rail a little with him."

"Mary, say whatever you have to," GraBois replied, a smile playing at the corners of his mouth. "I don't care what you have to tell Ramos about me. Because it's not going to be true."

Over the next week, Galligan talked often to the profilers, now back at Quantico. They put her on speakerphone and asked a million questions, then tag-teamed a practice session, role-playing Ramos to help her develop a series of themes that might draw Ramos out.

"Appeal to his religion..." or "Leverage a visit with his parents..." or "Ask him to give the Patz family the closure they deserve." If one doesn't work, they said, you'd better have a dozen others ready. She solicited suggestions from everyone in the squad and sat at her desk writing a packet of index cards.

Galligan would be the lead agent on this interview, but Special Agent John Winslow was chosen as her backup. A fifteen-year veteran, Winslow was the senior agent on the squad and the most seasoned agent Galligan had ever met. He was famous for a number of daring cases, including one of GraBois's, where he'd masqueraded as an IRA member—with a flawless Irish accent—pretending to buy plutonium from a Canadian mobster. Since he'd had no previous involvement in the Patz investigation, Winslow had Galligan sit in the bullpen area of the squad room, and he drilled her on the history of the case, to prepare them both. In the end, she boiled all her material down to a one-page cheat sheet, which she tucked into an innocuous manila folder to keep in her lap for reference, together with a five-by-seven color photograph of Etan Patz.

––––––

It was only a few hours' drive from her home to FCI Otisville, and Mary Galligan felt like she needed every second to strategize. She'd met up with John Winslow at a rest stop—he was coming from another direction—and they drove the rest of the way together. Since it was her case, it was understood she'd do most of the talking, unless for whatever reason Ramos seemed to respond better to Winslow.

Everyone at the office knew where she was going today, and not just the rest of her squad, but her family too, and some of her closest friends; she was at once excited and nervous, and felt the burden of the twelve years that previous investigators had spent to get her to this point. And after all those months of her own time investigating this man, today she was going to look in his eyes and make her own judgment.

A few miles away from the prison, they passed a work crew of inmates on horseback traveling down the side of the road. Galligan realized that other than New York City's MCC, this was her first federal prison. When the agents arrived at the Otisville front gate, Galligan could feel the anxiety jump-starting her nerves. For weeks in the back of her mind, she'd nurtured a wishful scene, a fantasy that had helped her through the late-night hours drilling on the case's facts and themes.

Blessed Mother, Mary Galligan silently prayed, the ingrained habits of a lifetime of Catholic school kicking in, help me get the confession so the Patz family can finally know what happened.

Winslow gave their names to the guard and the two waited to be cleared through. When the man came back, he shrugged indifferently.

"He doesn't want to see you," the guard said.

Galligan was enraged, both at Ramos and herself for being so naive. During all those weeks of preparation and endless mock conversations in her head, it somehow had never occurred to her he could just refuse to talk.

"I understand," Winslow said smoothly. "But we need to hear him tell us that himself. Have him brought down and we'll wait."

The agents busied themselves signing in, and when they were done they were led to a narrow cinderblock interview room. Through the chicken-wire-laced window of the door they could see it was bare except for three chairs, one already occupied by Jose Ramos. As Galligan and Winslow walked in, the smell of overripe, unwashed inmate assailed them. They sat down with their backs to the door as Ramos grunted, "I told them I didn't want to see you." He was uncuffed, his arms and legs crossed defiantly. His beard was a tangled mass, and his fingernails were startlingly long. A yarmulke perched on his long gray hair.

Galligan and Winslow stayed in their chairs, silent, acclimatizing themselves to the stench. A minute or two passed. Ramos sat there scowling but he didn't ask to be taken out. She noticed he was loaded down with a stack of documents, newspaper clips, and other papers, and eyed them conspicuously until Ramos followed her gaze.

"All right," he finally said. "I'll talk to you, but it's gonna be what I want to talk about and nothing else."

Winslow had advised Galligan on the drive up to listen for the cue to weave Miranda rights into the conversation, and now she jumped in.

"You know, I'm really glad you said that, because, you know, Jose, you don't have to talk to us if you don't want to, you understand that, right?"

Ramos nodded.

"And you know if you want to you can have an attorney, you understand that, right?" GraBois had counseled her to stop and confirm that Ramos understood her as she listed each one of the four lines of Miranda, so that no one later could claim he hadn't been aware of what she was saying. She made it through her spiel, proud of how conversational she'd played it, and nonetheless terrified he'd ask for a lawyer. If he did this whole trip was a waste. But Ramos waved his hand at her, as if to signal how transparent her careful efforts had been.

"Yeah, yeah, I know my rights." And that was that. He had no visitors and was still in lonely segregation, so he had plenty to say. Galligan began to calm down. She didn't think Ramos would be asking for a lawyer.

"Did Stuart GraBois send you here?" Ramos said the name like it was a curse.

"No." The behaviorists had been clear—whatever you do, don't lie, they'd said, it will only trip you up. Ramos wasn't stupid—he knew very well they were FBI agents and GraBois was an assistant U.S. attorney. But it was true that he hadn't sent them; they'd been planning this trip anyway.

"This isn't about Stuart GraBois. He didn't send us."

This seemed to work, since Ramos immediately launched into a diatribe about GraBois's persecution.

"What he's done to me is illegal…" The rest of it washed over Galligan as she reverted to the agreed-upon strategy: Act like you're bored, and steer him away when able. She was trying to figure out how to bring up the Patz case, when he beat her to it.

"I assume you're here to talk to me about Etan Patz. Tell me, have you seen this *Vanity Fair* article about the Patz case?" Ramos asked. The new issue of *Vanity Fair* magazine included a long feature on the Pennsylvania Rainbow molestations and their link to the New York investigation, and the profilers had predicted that he'd be dying to see the article. "Do you have a copy I can read?"

"No, I've heard about it, but I don't have a copy with me. I can try to get it for you, if you want," Galligan offered. Because she knew she had almost nothing to offer Ramos, the agent was listening for anything that might turn into leverage. If he wanted the article, she could certainly get it for him. But she'd have to get something in return.

"What makes you think we're here to talk about Etan Patz?" she ventured.

"Because everyone wants to talk to me about Etan Patz. People think I know something about the case."

And then before she could find out what, the moment was gone, and Ramos was off on a tear about many other things. He flitted from topic to topic, and Galligan was reminded of the headaches Jon Morgan said he'd suffered while he tried to keep track of his conversations with Ramos. She alternated between letting her subject ramble to relax him and attempting to corral him back with the themes from her memorized list. Nothing worked. Ramos didn't respond to the plea of closure for the Patz family, nor the idea of connecting him back with his own parents; that just got him going again about "Stu," as he referred to GraBois. "Stu" was baiting him by dangling his family in front of him. More persecution.

Then Galligan tried one theme inspired by Jeremy Fischer. He'd talked about the different Ramoses—today's good versus the bad, "other" Jose. Score more credibility points for Fischer—Ramos seized on it. The "other" Ramos had been a terrible person. Now a different man sat before the FBI agents, reborn, in a sense, and able to distance himself from his predecessor.

It was the other Jose, Ramos stressed, who had been near Washington Square Park the day Etan disappeared when he saw a young boy playing handball in the park. The boy said his name was Jimmy, but he didn't give his last name. This was new—she'd never heard the name "Jimmy" before. Was "Jimmy" really code for Etan? And if so could she get him to break the code? Galligan wrote down "Jimmy LNU," the designation for "last name unknown." The boy said he lived with his aunt in Washington Heights, at the northern tip of Manhattan.

"What did the boy look like?" Galligan asked him casually.

Ramos looked from one agent to the other. His response left Galligan nearly speechless.

"How tall was Etan Patz?"

"I, uh, we don't know offhand, Jose," Galligan replied.

The scathing look Ramos gave her in return said, "What kind of FBI agents are you?" Galligan didn't take it personally. She was happy to let him be smarter. She was willing to be the dumbest person in the room if necessary.

"Okay, well, the boy in Washington Square Park was about four feet tall," Ramos went on. "And he was definitely eight or nine years old. I remember reading that Etan Patz was seven."

Galligan recalled what the profilers had said, that often the subject would assume authorities have evidence against him and are trying to catch out a lie. So he will tailor his story to incorporate true details, omitting only the incriminating ones. Even if they are fabrications, the experts had said, listen carefully because there will be truth laced throughout it.

"Then I took the boy to my apartment," Ramos was saying.

"What happened when you got to your apartment?"

Ramos crossed his arms and again looked at her disdainfully. "I can't answer that question," he said, "because if I did, it would incriminate me."

"What do you mean, it would incriminate you? What is it that you did?"

"Well, you know, as the FBI, that I used to be a child molester."

Galligan took notes and waited. She'd been reluctant to put anything on paper for fear it would shut Ramos up, but he didn't seem to mind. Now she looked at the words she was writing as if to convince herself he'd just said them. As far as she was concerned, he *had* just incriminated himself. This was how she'd hoped the interview would go. Maybe in another hour he would give her another piece.

"It was the other Ramos who used to hurt children and abused them. I'm not that person anymore," Ramos went on. "Now I could be in a room filled with children and left alone. And I would never touch or abuse any of them."

But it was the old Ramos who'd brought Jimmy back to his apartment.

"The FBI," Ramos said, "could assume what the old Ramos did when he brought him to his apartment."

"We don't like to make assumptions because they can be incorrect." Galligan allowed herself a brief glance at Winslow, who nodded, and she finished. "We prefer that you tell us what happened."

Nothing.

"Look," Galligan tried, "we're not here to judge you. Different people will do different things to give themselves pleasure. Help us to understand."

"You can conclude what happened." Ramos wouldn't budge. "But after I finished with the child, I got into a cab with the child on Avenue A and Prince Street and we went to the subway stop."

Galligan was incredulous. "Finished?" she thought. Finished didn't mean giving the boy a glass of juice, as he'd previously told authorities. Finished meant something else entirely. It was a word adults used after sex. If there was any doubt about what Ramos was hinting at, that word dispelled it. It was clear that he had just said he molested "Jimmy."

Ramos described how he bought the boy a token from the token booth clerk, and then put him on the northbound subway to the aunt in Washington Heights. The mythical aunt in Washington Heights, Galligan and Winslow knew. This was the part of the story that matched the 90 percent confession, the part of the story the profilers had said was a typical response child molesters might have: They can get almost to the point of telling you that they harmed a child, but can't bring themselves to say it all, so their version has them veering off at the last moment to substitute another action in place of admitting to murder.

"Why would you let an eight- or nine-year-old boy take the subway by himself?" Galligan couldn't help but ask.

"Well you gotta understand something," Ramos responded, with an odd studied manner that sounded like a clinician interpreting someone else, which in his version of events he was. "I was nervous about being seen with the child and I wanted to get rid of the child as soon as possible."

Galligan had told herself over and over going into this interview that unless Jose Ramos was threatened with something much worse if he didn't admit to killing Etan Patz, there was no reason for him to fully confess. But at this moment, she had a flicker of hope. If they kept talking, if she could keep building a rapport, maybe they could get him to that point. They were already more than an hour into their interview, but the feeling bolstered her.

"Jose, I'm curious," Winslow asked, "you used the word 'child molester' when you talked about the 'old Jose.' What did you mean by that—were there other children that you molested?" Normally, an agent wouldn't use the term "molest," it sounded too harsh. Something like "you liked children" would elicit a better response. But Ramos had used the word himself. Now he gave them a list, shorter than the one they already had, but still surprising to hear him admit to. He told them matter-of-factly how the "old Jose" had sexually molested more than one retarded child in a New Orleans hospital.

"What hospital was it, Jose?" Galligan asked casually, putting the pen down as though this were idle chitchat. In truth, she was starting to feel physically ill.

Jeremy Fischer had told her about the retarded children, how Ramos, devoid of affect, had listed them among his conquests. Fischer had written about them too while still in the cell, particularly about one Down syndrome boy who was so damaged from the sexual abuse by his own family that he was—both mentally and physically—an even easier target for Ramos. "A wonderful little boy," Fischer had quoted Ramos.

"Do you remember the name of the hospital, or the names of any of these children?" The chances of being able to track one of these kids down was next to impossible, but Galligan had to ask.

"Don't remember, but I'm sure you could find out. And there was a boy in Ohio named P.J.," Ramos added, "but I never knew his last name." That was a lie, Galligan thought, picking up the pen and writing P.J. Fox's name.

"Let me ask you about this Jimmy some more. What did Jimmy look like?"

"Light hair, light eyes, like I told you, eight or nine years old."

"So you're in the park, or you're near the park on the same day that Etan disappears, and now you see this other kid playing handball. Isn't that a pretty big coincidence? Are you sure this kid couldn't have been Etan?"

"Okay," Ramos said. "It could have been Etan. But even if that child was Etan, I put him on the subway, and I have not seen that child since. You know what you need to do? You need to go to Washington Heights and ask people there if they saw a child getting off the subway the day Etan disappeared."

"Interesting idea. But you know if it *could* have been Etan that you took back to your apartment and you molested him, I mean, it's very hard to believe that there was another boy just out playing handball in Washington Square Park at that time on a school day, and that this boy is, as you said, eight or nine. You're a smart man, Jose, tell me, if you were me, do you think that would make sense? Where were his parents? Why was he in the park? Isn't it true that it was Etan?"

"I said it could have been," Ramos said in a hostile tone. "All I know is, he told me his name was Jimmy."

"Why do *you* think you abused kids at one time?" Galligan asked. "There's usually a reason."

"Because it happened to me. I was abused myself as a child."

"Well, if you knew personally how painful it was, why did the old Jose do it?"

"You can't stop yourself," Ramos said. "It's all you know."

That's as much as Ramos would say about his own experience, not about what happened to him, when, or by whom.

"So what you're saying then is when you had the boy in your apartment that you said might have been Etan, you couldn't help yourself. We could understand that. And he was such a good-looking child, Etan, with that beautiful blond hair and blue eyes. I can understand why you'd be attracted to him, or why the 'old Jose' would have been."

You have to play along, the profilers had said. Pretend you're talking about Mel Gibson or Robert Redford, not a child. That's how you might talk to a woman friend, and he has to think you're in this with him.

"And he had such soft skin, too," Galligan continued, hoping for anything that would click. "I mean, I have to say, I can understand how a person could find little boys attractive." Ramos's body seemed to relax, as though he accepted her empathy, but he didn't say anything—he didn't agree, but he didn't correct her by saying it was Jimmy, not Etan.

"So this was a very attractive little boy, Jose, and of course Etan was also a very smart boy, and he knew who you were." Galligan tried to give him a justification to cling to. "I'm sure that he probably said to you, 'I'm going to tell my parents.' And I could see how you got angry and maybe you just shook him so he'd be quiet. You didn't mean to do it, it was an accident. It was just an accident. And then you got scared. Isn't that what happened?"

Ramos didn't go for it. "I'm getting out in 2014. I can do that," he said, and that was it. If he said anything more, the implication was, he'd be in a lot longer.

"You think this boy could have been Etan," Winslow said, pushing him now. "So it seems to me that it was Etan."

Ramos slumped down in his chair. They'd gone round and round. Galligan wondered, were they wearing him down?

"Like I said"—he looked up at Winslow—"it could have been him." Then, as though he'd caught himself, he spoke in a rapid-fire burst, giving his rote speech about putting the boy on the train.

And then out came the papers, his religious drawings and poems about God, his testament to his faith, the draft of his request for representation to famed attorney Alan Dershowitz. Galligan tried to use that, and offered to approach Dershowitz on Ramos's behalf.

"But why would he come all the way here?" Galligan wondered. "He'd have to think you had something pretty big to draw his attention..."

Both agents worked hard to divert him back to 1979. But their forward movement was stalled, and Galligan could feel herself slipping back, like a mountaineer scaling a sheer rock face, except now she could find no cracks to dig into and secure her position.

They'd circled around several times and John Winslow's attention was drifting. He wondered how much longer it would be before they were sure there was nothing more to get from this guy.

"Hey, you!" Ramos's sharp bark invaded Winslow's reverie. "I'm over here." The inmate shook his head in high dudgeon. "If I'm going to take the time to talk to you, you should pay attention."

Winslow apologized.

Galligan was going to take a chance. She changed direction with a hard left. "Isn't it true, Jose, that you made comments to other inmates, including, 'You'll never find Patz's body' and 'There is no body'?"

Ramos paused and Galligan thought he was mentally sorting out what would sound the best.

"No, I didn't say that." He didn't ask who had said that or where she'd heard it—the kind of response Galligan would have expected if he were responding naturally, the kind of response the interviewing experts who'd trained her told her to look for.

"We have you on tape saying these things, Jose. We could play the tapes for you if you want. And then how will you explain those comments?" This was a huge bluff and she hoped he wouldn't call her on it.

But Ramos didn't challenge her. "If the FBI does have tapes of me saying those things, I don't remember ever making those comments," he said stonily. "And even if I heard them, it wouldn't help my memory."

The mention of tapes and the informants reminded Ramos of Stuart GraBois, and he was now back on a rant against GraBois's unjust vendetta.

"He's obsessed with this case." Ramos smiled. "I bet if I helped you and he wasn't in on it, he'd have a stroke."

Galligan lobbed another one of the themes. "So why don't you do it, then? If you helped us after stonewalling him all this time, he'd get none of the glory." This was an easy one, as she knew GraBois couldn't care less who got the credit. "Help the FBI and give Stuart GraBois a stroke. It would be the best payback for everything he's done to you."

"But I am going to get back at him. I'm going to tell the world about his tactics. I've been talking to Lisa Cohen from ABC *PrimeTime Live* who's been begging me for an interview, and I'm going to do it. I'll tell everyone how much he abused me."

"We don't want to abuse you, Jose," Winslow said. "We want to help you. The FBI can make your life easier. If you tell us what you know, if you tell us where the boy's body is and what really happened, we can arrange for another prosecutor to handle the case, not GraBois. We can set it up for you to do federal time too, not state."

"It would be safer for you, doing federal time," Galligan added. "And we might be able to get you into a prison in Florida, near your mother."

Ramos wasn't interested. "It's not so bad in Pennsylvania. I have more freedom at Rockview than I do here in the federal system."

"Yeah, well, here's the thing, Jose. When Pennsylvania takes you back, they're transferring you to Graterford, which isn't quite so free. I believe that's maximum-security, isn't it, Agent Galligan?"

"Yes, it is."

"You can't do that!" They were coming up on hour five, and all the niceties were out the window. They'd saved this theme for last.

"It's already done. But if you help us, Jose, we can get that changed."

"It's not possible." Ramos was clearly agitated. Gone was the chatty self-assurance. "You're wrong," he said through clenched teeth.

"It's going to happen, but we can control it. We are the FBI, and you keep telling us this was another boy that day, and it could have been Etan. C'mon, it was Etan, and you're not helping us. Just help us here, so we can help you."

Ramos was struggling to tamp down his fury. A full two minutes passed before he finally composed himself, gave a bizarre, fake-hearty smile, and signaled the end to the interview.

"Thank you very much for coming to see me," he said, as though he'd just hosted an intimate dinner party. "I'll think about it, and if there is anything more I can do to help you with the case, I will certainly let you know. But really, I'd suggest that the FBI do a better job of investigating the facts if you want to find Etan. This could all be over if you'd just do your job properly."

The two agents walked out of the room, leaving Jose Ramos sitting there with his arms full of the paperwork he'd refused to hand over, waiting for the guard to cuff him and take him back to the cell. Neither Galligan nor Winslow spoke as they made their way down the prison hallways and out into what remained of the daylight. It was muggy and gray, which matched Mary Galligan's mood. There had been no food breaks, no bathroom breaks, no mental health breaks. It felt as though their visit with Ramos had lasted for days. She was bone-weary exhausted. She was also nauseated.

They walked through the parking lot, still in silence, until Galligan couldn't go any farther. She stopped between two cars, doubled over, steadying herself with a hand on each vehicle. She was going to throw up.

She never got sick like this, let alone on the job. Despite her short time at the Bureau, she'd witnessed some gruesome sights. She'd never cried in front of another agent, and she'd never gotten sick. But now she didn't think she could stop herself. It was mortifying that John Winslow, the most senior, most revered agent on her squad, a man she wanted to model more than anyone else, was standing there to watch her do it.

"You have to give me a minute," she called to Winslow. "Go ahead. I'll be right there."

She tried to distract herself by taking stock of the last five hours. Yes, Ramos had said more here than he had in the past—they had taken the case a little further. It was clear to her that he had sexually molested a boy on that day. But Ramos had not admitted to anything more. She had failed in her appointed task. She was angry, frustrated, and self-recriminating. Now she had to drive for hours, before calling GraBois and telling him she didn't have what she'd come for. She was not Clarice Starling and Jose Ramos was not the likable, if murderous, psychopath Hannibal Lecter. This was real life, and it sucked.

As much as she'd envisioned the triumphant Hollywood-ending phone call to the Patzes, she'd have nothing for them today. But that's not what made her sick to her stomach, it just made her heartsick. No, her insides were churning after spending the last several hours locked in a small room with that man. Now she understood why Stuart GraBois was so firm in his convictions. He'd been in that room too, more than once. She was certain now that Jose Ramos had taken six-year-old Etan Patz and done things to him that no human being should have to suffer, let alone a child. Then he had killed him. She was sure of it. And she had practically held his hand in there and told him it was all right. She knew she'd had to do it, but it was the most sickening experience she'd ever had in her life.

CHAPTER 27

⌒

Prime Suspect

Jay Schadler: . . . Were these boys that you had molested?
Jose Ramos: See, if I answer that and tell you that, you know, there's a
    possibility I could be charged with a crime, you understand?
Jay Schadler: These were other kids, though, that you had molested?
Jose Ramos: I'm not about to commit perjury on national TV.
    —*interview with Jose Ramos, ABC News* PrimeTime Live, *conducted
    June 20, 1991, aired August 15, 1991*

Leaning over in the parking lot of FCI Otisville, Mary Galligan
swallowed hard several times, breathing the mist in deeply to expel
the toxic air of that small, fetid space. She felt the gorge settle back down
into her stomach, and walked toward Winslow's car. Luckily, the ride home
was a smooth one, and her insides gradually calmed, despite one lingering
image she couldn't shake. It wasn't so much the graphic sexual nature of
his exploits in New Orleans, but the idea that Ramos's targets were mentally disabled. Children were vulnerable enough victims, but obviously they
weren't vulnerable enough for Jose Ramos. When Jeremy Fischer had first
raised it in his interview, she'd almost hoped he was lying, but now Ramos
had inadvertently corroborated one more of the informant's claims.

When the agents got to the rest stop where they'd left Galligan's car,
they found a pay phone and reported in to GraBois.

"I think he's your man," Winslow told him, before putting Galligan on.

"He did it, Stu," Galligan agreed. "I've never been more sure of anything.
I'm just sorry I can't say he told me himself." Then she filled him in.

"You did great," GraBois told her. "You got new information, you corroborated the informants, and we all knew that he wasn't going to hand you a confession. Go home, take the weekend, and we'll just have to see what happens Monday. At this point I don't see why you shouldn't be there with me."

On Monday, Ramos would be transported from Otisville to New York where GraBois was going to meet with him a final time in a conference room off the third-floor U.S. Marshals' holding area.

Three years earlier, GraBois had met Jose Ramos in the same exact place and had seen firsthand that when the inmate became highly emotional, he dropped his guard. Now, apparently, just the sound of the prosecutor's name made Ramos foam at the mouth. Maybe GraBois could use that blind hatred to his advantage. Who knows what would happen if I were actually in the room with him, he had wondered to Galligan. If Ramos went 90 percent of the way last time, maybe he could be provoked into giving up the final 10 percent.

Both GraBois and Galligan believed that Ramos would act consistently with his past behavior in Pennsylvania, when he'd resisted pleading guilty right up until the very moment of trial. The only way he'd make a deal in exchange for a confession was if he truly thought he'd be indicted and go away for life otherwise.

But even if Ramos didn't confess, and went after GraBois as he'd threatened in the past, GraBois would just use that to his advantage. Assaulting a federal prosecutor could keep Ramos in prison five more years.

Over the weekend, Galligan gave one of her profiler contacts a full account of the Friday session. While he marveled at how close she'd gotten, he felt Ramos had behaved exactly as predicted. In the agent's opinion, Ramos had skated to the edge of admission, and then each time substituted the words "I put him on the subway" for "I killed him." Ramos's explanation that he "wanted to get rid of him as quickly as possible" was also significant because it was the way someone would talk about a body. Galligan explained the plan for Monday and wondered what would happen when Ramos saw her in obvious cahoots with GraBois.

"He's going to be angry," the man said, "but he's going to focus all his emotions on GraBois. If you can, just try to use that too, like you did before."

Monday morning, Mary Galligan and Tom Moore, another young agent in her squad, arrived outside the U.S. Marshals' holding area. They checked their 9mm semiautomatic pistols and went in to collect Ramos. Galligan always felt extra cautious in those moments when she went through the doors without her weapons for protection; some of these men were desperate and capable of deadly violence. But the last thing you want is for a motivated prisoner to get hold of your gun and demonstrate his capabilities. She looked Ramos over, as she and Moore prepared to move him outside the marshals' confines. He was not a large man, but he wasn't slight either, just an inch or so shorter than Moore. When Galligan had debriefed Jeremy Fischer two weeks earlier, she'd pooh-poohed his fears, thinking the pedophile was dangerous only to children. But since then, she'd spent several hours with him and personally heard him spew his hatred for Stuart GraBois. It was not, she now recognized, just your typical prison bravado.

Galligan had heard back from Otisville, where they'd searched Ramos's cell and had, in fact, turned up a topographical map of the area around Rockview prison. There was also a crude diagram in Ramos's hand of several connected boxes, including three that seemed to be marked as Rockview, Otisville, and New York. Next to the box labeled "NY" was an equal sign and the word "Liberty." Both informants had reported that Ramos talked incessantly of his escape plans, including the New York detour to kill Stuart GraBois. Galligan knew that the more specifically conceived a plan was—cutting holes in a fence, using compasses and maps—the more credible. Jose Ramos was proving himself one motivated son of a bitch.

Leaving the holding cell, the two agents retrieved their guns and brought their charge into a nearby unused office where Stuart GraBois had just taken a seat behind a wooden table. As soon as Ramos saw him, the profilers were once again proved right. It suddenly didn't matter what Galligan had said about her connection to the prosecutor. No one else in the room existed for Ramos except GraBois.

"I want to go back. You can't make me stay here. Get me out of here." Ramos stood immobile, glowering, until the agents led him to an office chair on one side of the conference table.

"Ramos, sit down," Galligan said. "All you have to do is hear what this man has to say. The sooner you do that, the sooner we all get out of here."

When he sat, she uncuffed one hand and relocked the cuff onto the arm of his chair. Tom Moore sat down next to him. Galligan took the chair across the table from GraBois, flanking Ramos on the right. GraBois stood up, arms folded as he glared back at his subject. Once again, and for the last time, he began to advise him of his rights.

"I don't need an attorney, 'cause I'm not going to say anything." Ramos almost seemed insulted, as though he felt he could fend for himself just fine. After all, he'd been a jailhouse lawyer now for years.

GraBois put his hands on the table and leaned toward the man who had vowed to blow him into a million pieces.

"I want to give you one last chance."

Ramos barely looked at the prosecutor.

"You think you're through with me. Well, you're not. You think we don't have enough on you, but you're wrong. Let me lay it out. I want you to understand exactly what's in store for you."

"Go ahead, indict me," Ramos scornfully threw at GraBois. "If you're gonna do it, then do it."

"You have a pattern of molesting young boys—so many boys, Jose, I'm sure we don't know half of them. But we know about a boy in New York; there's the Erie boy and Bennett Harmon and a number of people whose names *you* don't even know; and of course Joey Taylor on that bus in Pennsylvania. We've got a pattern of violence; the voices who tell you to hurt people—the ones you reported during your Bellevue stint in 1982. Then there's the time you spent in Jacobi Hospital; it's in the records—you were in danger of hurting yourself and others.

"We've got a motive—Etan said what you were doing to him wasn't good, or else his mother and father would have said it was okay. You were afraid he was going to tell on you. You couldn't afford that, so you had to stop him, didn't you, Jose?

"Come on, Jose, this is your one chance to make amends and do something to benefit society," GraBois urged. "Don't throw it away. Do the right thing."

"Just indict me," Ramos repeated.

GraBois spoke in a calm but more disgusted tone. "You think you're some kind of hero, that you're such a big man? You're not. The only thing you're bigger than is a helpless child, because anyone else would beat the crap out of you. But I'm not one of those little kids you abused, Jose—"

It happened so fast that later no one could say exactly what triggered Ramos's move, but suddenly he was up and out of his seat, straining toward GraBois and pulling the heavy leather and wood chair into the air by his handcuff. He swung out at GraBois with his free hand, but didn't connect, and in the same instant the two agents were out of their own seats. Galligan

pushed Ramos down with full force into the chair, which was propelled
back to the ground with a loud crash. As she noted the strength behind the
man's fury, Moore restrained him in a headlock.

"Ramos," Galligan said as he continued to struggle, planting herself in
front of the inmate to make him meet her eyes, "you're going to make this
worse. You touch anyone in this room, you're going to be in jail a lot longer."
At her words, Ramos went slack. There was a brief silence, broken finally by
Moore, looking down at his prisoner.

"Man," he said admiringly, a trace of humor in his voice. "The stuff they
teach you in Quantico really works."

Ramos was unrelenting; he wanted to go back to his cell and he wanted
an attorney now. The meeting—which had lasted all of ten minutes—was
over anyway, and the agents led him away. He wouldn't be returned to Otisville, though; from MCC he was heading to his old cell at Rockview, in
Pennsylvania. Once Galligan had handed him back to the marshals that
morning, she sent Ramos an assignment of counsel form. Then she and
GraBois put in a call to Jack Allar, the superintendent's assistant at Rockview, to tell him what had just happened and relay the evidence of Ramos's
planned jailbreak. Allar promised them Rockview would take steps to deal
with what they also perceived as a viable threat.

———

Go ahead, indict me," Ramos had said. The "I dare you" was silent, but
clearly implied. Despite what GraBois had said, that wasn't going to be so
easy. Although it was still possible Ramos had crossed state lines with either
Etan or his body, which would constitute federal kidnapping, they had nothing to support that. Indeed, every piece of evidence authorities had amassed,
especially in the last six months, pointed gruesomely in the opposite direction, toward an apartment, and a boiler, in lower Manhattan. At this point,
there were no federal grounds to charge him. Murder was a state crime.

Over the next weeks, as they'd done since they'd begun working together,
GraBois and Galligan sought a creative way to pursue federal charges, and
came up blank. GraBois was disappointed when his superiors shot down
charging Ramos with attempted assault of a federal officer. He knew there
were some people who thought he was overinvolved, but he didn't care. They
didn't know the case like he did, nor had they grown to know and respect
the family the way he had. A few weeks earlier, he'd been interviewed by

ABC News *PrimeTime Live* for the same story Ramos had boasted about to Mary Galligan. The correspondent, Jay Schadler, had waited until almost the end of the conversation before asking GraBois the inevitable.

"The plain and simple truth," Schadler had said, "is a lot of people think that you're obsessed with this case."

"I understand that some people have said that." GraBois had suspected the question would come up, but the answer wasn't difficult for him. "I define obsession as an abnormal feeling. I personally do not think it's abnormal to feel for the Patz family, nor is it abnormal to try to find out what happened to their son."

One month later, Schadler asked Jose Ramos the same question, in the only television interview Ramos had ever granted.

"Is Stuart GraBois obsessed with you?" They were sitting in a visiting room at Rockview prison. Ramos had been back at the Pennsylvania prison for three weeks, since his last confrontation with the prosecutor in New York.

"If he's obsessed, that's his problem," said Ramos.

"Well, perhaps, but it's also your problem," Schadler countered, "because he's the man who put you in jail here."

As the producer of this story, I was sitting in the room too, off camera and equidistant to the two men. I'd tried for several months to "book" Ramos for an interview, knowing nothing of what was happening behind the scenes in segregation. After several letters and phone calls, he'd remained reluctant but had never said no. I'd figured he was going to string me along until airtime just to keep me off balance, and was shocked one day at the end of May when he said yes.

He told me he'd been craving a New York hero sandwich since he'd been in prison and if I brought him one, he'd agree to talk. I was doubtful, fearing this was yet another game he was playing.

"All right, I'll bring you your sandwich," I said, "but let me make this clear. Several people have to travel hundreds of miles to the prison for this interview, as many as six, including myself, two camera crews, and Jay. If we get there and you've changed your mind..." I had no idea what to say next, since nothing would happen if he said no. "...It will be a very bad thing."

"No, no, I agreed. I keep my word."

On the day of the interview, he shuffled into the visiting room impeded by leg irons and dressed in his prison browns. His cotton workshirt was open at the neck to reveal a white T-shirt bearing the mysterious handwritten letter M probably the M in Ramos. His hair was tidily trimmed, beardless, with just the full mustache. Despite being handcuffed, he was laden with paperwork. Occasionally during the next several hours, he presented an odd picture as he peered at documents through broken brown plastic aviator-style reading glasses, masking-taped at the temples and attached to a dirty string he wore slung over the back of his head. He had deep, dark circles under his eyes, which roved around the room. Schadler couldn't hold his gaze through any exchange.

As it turned out, the sandwich with which I'd kept *my* word was deemed contraband and stayed in the car, but the guards allowed Ramos soda from the visiting room vending machine, which he threw back, one can after the next. He seemed more pathetic than scary, and right from the start he rambled disjointedly, sometimes incoherently, although he was often perfectly intelligible. He immediately made such disparaging remarks about the story on the Patz case in *Vanity Fair*'s June issue that I quickly understood the reason we were there. He was outraged at how easily Stuart GraBois had been able to publicly make his case in that article while he, Ramos, hadn't. This was his chance to set the record straight.

But he didn't do a stellar job defending himself, other than to deny he'd ever met or known what had happened to Etan Patz. He said he'd been sleeping in his apartment at 8:00 a.m., when Etan Patz set off for the bus stop. As for the child in his apartment that day, Ramos stuck to his story that "Jimmy" had been older than Etan.

"I would put him between eight and nine," he told us, "and he was a very, very open person." Despite that "openness," Ramos maintained, the boy did not respond to his sexual advances.

"I tried, you know," he said. "The child refused to have sex with me, okay, and so I took the child and put him on the subway."

He talked about the "old Jose," long gone, who harmed children; the Jose sitting in front of us had been healed. He made the point forcefully when Schadler leaned over to ask another question. The two men were sitting facing each other, close enough to touch.

"Don't put your hands on me!" Ramos barked. "Don't put your hands on me, now, because I have my own energy. And don't take your energy off of me." He pulled back in his chair, wild-eyed and wary.

"I'm curious that you're so appalled at the possibility of me touching you," Schadler pursued, "which of course I'm not interested in doing. *You're* the man who molested children."

"I don't do that anymore," Ramos said, raising his voice as he motioned with his own hands as much as the limited range his handcuffs would allow, "and I don't want you to put your hands on me because that's where it starts, okay? Now, you get that straight."

"That's how you started?"

"That's how I started and I don't want that anymore, okay?"

"By putting your hands on children?"

"Right! Right."

Even though he'd just admitted to putting his hands on children, he also claimed he'd never been a child molester, which he defined as "someone who does it continuously to one person." Nor, he said, was he a "total pedophile."

Schadler raised his eyebrows. "Isn't that like saying, 'I'm just a little bit pregnant'? Either you're a pedophile or you're not a pedophile, which is it?"

"If they put a label on me to say that I'm a pedophile," Ramos reasoned, his gaze flickering to the intrigued Schadler, then down to his lap, "that's the label *they* want to put on me. I'm putting a label on me saying that I was"—he searched for the right words—"a little mentally unstable."

At one point Schadler, annoyed with being run in circles, asked Ramos to simply "tell me what you feel about all this."

"No, you don't want me to do that." Ramos's voice went even lower.

"Why?" Schadler looked like it was one of the first genuine-sounding responses he'd heard.

" 'Cause then I'd pick up this chair, smash it against the wall, smash those cans. Smash everything, you understand? And I don't." Ramos appeared suddenly aware of his tone and brought it back down. "I'm not violent. I don't want to be violent."

At this point he seemed less pathetic and more alarming, and I was grateful for the cuffs and the burly guards nearby. I knew nothing of the threats the informants had reported, or even the very existence of informants. Nor was I aware of the recent attempted assault on GraBois, although Ramos himself hinted at it.

"If Stu is watching tonight"—he looked straight into the camera—"I apologize for my actions, Mr. GraBois. I know I got out of hand with you and I should have been a little bit more professional."

On June 26, less than a week after the *PrimeTime* interview, Jose Ramos was transferred to Pennsylvania's largest maximum-security facility, Graterford Prison, just outside Philadelphia. The authorities at Rockview felt that his risk of escape required the higher security. GraBois had marked the date on his calendar, so that he would remember to call the warden and give him some background on his new inmate.

Within days, a copy of the *Vanity Fair* article was making its rounds of the Graterford guards and inmates, and Ramos was soon placed in protective segregation after he received death threats. He wrote to the Warren County judge who had presided over his case, begging to be transferred back to that area. He complained that he couldn't be considered for parole if he didn't attend counseling, but he couldn't attend counseling while in protective custody. And he couldn't leave protective custody because he feared for his life.

The day after Ramos wrote those words, Jeremy Fischer, who was now a free man, put on one of the many blue Brooks Brothers suits preserved from his previous life, carefully adjusted the red tie over his freshly ironed white shirt, and brushed his newly shorn hair before walking into the U.S. District Courthouse to appear in front of a federal grand jury. This wasn't the first time he'd testified at such a proceeding, but he was still awed by the majesty of the building's marble-lined halls. He couldn't help but contrast the bright, high-ceilinged surroundings with the dark, close hole of a cell that had brought him here today.

GraBois had explained that this wasn't a grand jury convened to indict Ramos; Fischer's sole purpose for being here was to preserve his testimony for possible future use. Fischer didn't blame Stuart GraBois for assuming he might be hard to find up the road. He didn't plan to continue with his checkered past, but, well, better for GraBois to cover his bases.

In the jury room, Fischer took an oath swearing to tell the truth and answered every question GraBois asked, recounting his interactions in segregation with Jose Ramos. He tried to describe the tawdry details with as little hesitation as possible, although he could sense that some of the jurors flinched as he listed them. Afterwards, before Fischer left to meet up with his wife, GraBois told him he'd been highly believable.

But despite the informant's grand jury testimony and GraBois's creative brainstorming, the federal role in the Etan Patz case was coming to an end. It was clear that the jurisdictional issue could not be overcome. Four weeks after Fischer testified, GraBois and Galligan met with the U.S. attorney, Otto Obermaier, and his senior staffers to make a final presentation of their evidence. If their conclusions were correct, and Jose Ramos had raped and killed Etan Patz in New York City, then it was a prosecution for the Manhattan district attorney, Robert Morgenthau, to pursue. They would approach Morgenthau's office in the coming weeks and present their case. Finally, even though GraBois had been unofficially keeping Stan Patz abreast of events, the FBI also planned to bring in both parents and give them the official results of its six-year investigation. Everyone in the room agreed that they had a right to know.

GraBois and Galligan called Stan Patz the next day.

"We'd like to sit down and bring you up to speed on the progress of the case," GraBois said. "There are some things you already know, but a lot you don't."

"Give it a little thought," Galligan added. "If you have a question and we know the answer, we'll tell you."

Stan considered this, in his measured way.

"Let me discuss it with Julie. I don't know if she'll want to come. But I will. I'd like to hear your information." Over the years Stan had always looked forward to these offers, rare as they were, of an official progress report. They made him feel there had in fact been progress on the case. After twelve years, he was encouraged that anyone was still paying enough attention to give him an accounting. This time he would urge Julie to come too. Stan had been in much closer contact with GraBois since the Pennsylvania case, and he'd gotten phone updates from time to time. Julie didn't hear any of this, so it was always his task to pass it along, or decide not to. Often he didn't, but when he did, he recognized that the secondhand information lacked the legitimacy that came from direct contact with authorities.

That night Stan got a preview of where the case stood—and some of the reasons authorities considered Ramos the prime suspect—when the *Prime-Time Live* piece aired. Watching it alone, he also saw for the first time what Ramos had to say. GraBois too watched the segment at home with his wife. In the television report, he had the last word.

"Is this case closed now?" Jay Schadler asked him.

"Closed? For as long as I'm in this office, absolutely not," GraBois replied, his voice firm with conviction. "What do you tell the Patz family, 'Sorry, your son is gone and there's nothing anyone can do about it anymore'? You can't just say, 'Forget about it. It's over.' Because it's not over."

In his den, GraBois listened to the words come out of his mouth on the screen, and hoped that Jose Ramos was hearing them too, because they were a direct promise. Jon Morgan had told GraBois that Ramos believed he would be left alone once GraBois had moved on from the case; that no one who came after him would care about it the way GraBois did. All Ramos had to do was ride out "the temporary storm," he'd told Morgan, "and the rain would stop."

Ramos was wrong. GraBois and the Patzes had had a rough start, but over time he and Stan had developed a truce that had grown into respect. GraBois had meant it when he'd said he owed it to the Patz family. Their feelings were never far from his mind as he had worked this case. That was one of the things that had kept him going.

While he could never imagine the pain they'd experienced, he had gotten a small taste of it two months earlier, a few days before the twelfth anniversary of Etan's disappearance. GraBois and his son had gone to a nearby department store to buy a Mother's Day present for his wife. The two were in the electronics department, and his son was watching TV while GraBois talked to a salesclerk. When he turned back, Andrew was nowhere in sight. He'd sat down near a television set, immersed in a baseball game, oblivious to the search around him. GraBois would never forget what those few moments felt like, and he just couldn't imagine living with that feeling.

This case might be moving to another venue, but that didn't mean he wasn't going to pursue it. He'd figure out a way; he was very creative. Prosecuting Ramos in Pennsylvania had proved that.

———

The meeting with Stan and Julie Patz was scheduled for a Monday in late August, the week leading into Labor Day weekend. Both GraBois and Galligan approached it with some trepidation. They knew the details would be unimaginably painful to hear. Should we really be doing this to them? Galligan wondered, changing her mind a dozen times. GraBois reflected on the rare occasions he'd told other parents their child had been molested. Even if they already suspected, there was always that moment before the words were said when the knowledge was just floating in the air, and then the endless moment after, when you could never take them back. He realized today would be the first time for him that those irrevocable words would be "Your child is dead."

Julie Patz came to the meeting with her husband after all, the two looking strained and subdued. They expected to see Mary Galligan and Stuart GraBois when they walked into the FBI's twenty-ninth-floor conference room, but they were also introduced to John Winslow, to Galligan's boss and her boss's boss, who as the highest rank would open the meeting. With all these layers of authority, the room had the solemn feel of a formal proceeding. Stan and Julie sat close to each other across the long rectangular table from the others.

GraBois took the lead and Galligan followed up with some of the details. Starting from the beginning they outlined what the federal government had learned during their nine-year investigation. The evidence, they said, clearly pointed to Jose Antonio Ramos as the prime suspect.

"I will tell you, I've only been on this case for two years," Galligan added, "but I know the scope of what's been done, and in order to conclude Ramos did it, we've had to rule out a host of leads. Agents have traveled around this country and even across the world in that capacity." Stan asked and Galligan answered several follow-up questions—about the unsubstantiated NAMBLA connection, the "Bubble Man," and other theories he'd been privy to in the past.

GraBois confirmed previous accounts that Ramos had already admitted taking a young boy he thought was Etan to his apartment that day. Galligan then gave the FBI consensus—it was their view that Ramos had molested Etan, and killed him.

"We believe Etan is dead, and that his body may never be found."

The Patzes said nothing in response, but silent tears wet Julie's face, and Stan struggled to hold his in. The words were not earth-shattering; they weren't saying anything that twelve years into the case both parents didn't already know. But now for the first time law enforcement was sitting across the table, telling them that the weight of evidence supported their worst fears. Stan reached over to soothe his wife, gently placing his hand on her shoulder.

There were credible informants, GraBois went on, who'd heard Ramos incriminate himself. In addition, both he and Galligan had heard much of this from Ramos's own mouth.

"And so with this conclusion," Galligan said, "the FBI has gone as far we can go in our investigation at this time. We are ending the active investigation. The next step would be an indictment and a prosecution."

"The thing is," GraBois added, "our conclusion means that, as much as we want to, the U.S. Attorney's Office can't do that. We just don't have jurisdiction.

"But it's not the end of the road," he hastened to say. "It's true Ramos didn't confess, but there is strong, convincing, circumstantial evidence against him. Now what happens is that we take this case to the New York County district attorney, who *can* prosecute it. Agent Galligan and I will personally present our case to the DA in the next few weeks. We'll hand over everything we've got, share all our evidence, and go from there."

As difficult as the meeting was, Stan Patz was relieved. When he'd heard Galligan say the FBI was "ending the active investigation," the words had tapped into the disquieting concern always lurking in the back of his mind that someday one or another of these agencies was going to say, Sorry, we didn't find anything, and it's over. Goodbye. But as he listened further, he felt hopeful that it wasn't over, just moving to the next step—one step closer. "Thank you," he said. He knew that they had all worked so hard, and he felt as though he couldn't adequately convey his appreciation. "Thank you for everything you've done. You can't know how much it means to us."

Julie echoed her husband's words, saying, "We're grateful that you brought us here today." She looked at the woman directly across from her, as though she'd sensed Galligan's apprehension. "As hard as it is to hear this, it's better than what my mind can, and has, imagined."

"I want you to know this doesn't mean we're giving up on this case," Galligan replied. "If and when there is more that we can do, we absolutely will."

"And even though we may not be *actively* involved, you can bet we'll be involved," GraBois concluded the meeting. "We've gotten too close, and the stakes are too high."

CHAPTER 28

Civil Action

ETAN PATZ'S FATE STILL A MYSTERY AFTER 20 YEARS

...Etan Patz vanished from a SoHo street 20 years ago today, launching one of the city's greatest unsolved mysteries and galvanizing public awareness of missing kids.

...A former federal prosecutor who spent eight years investigating the case believes the prime suspect is Jose Ramos, 54, who is serving 20 years in a Pennsylvania prison for sexually abusing a young boy....

Despite strong circumstantial evidence against him, Ramos has never been charged in the Patz case. He is eligible for parole in Pennsylvania next year.

—New York Post, *May 25, 1999*

S tan Patz sat in front of his office computer in the spacious sun-drenched front room that formed his workshop/photo studio, taking a break from his latest assignment. He had spent the morning at his second computer, laboring over a project, deftly adjusting hues and softening shadows, retouching the image with Adobe Photoshop. In the past he would have handed off a finished project by relinquishing the original film; now he delivered the photos to his clients on a disc. He hadn't used his darkroom to print out actual paper pictures in almost two years.

He'd grown more solid over the years, still trim, but no longer slight. These days his professional dress tended to collared cotton knit shirts and khakis, to match his closely cropped graying beard and neatly combed thinning brown hair. The especially strident howl of a power tool many years earlier had saddled him with tinnitus, which he masked by filling his studio with an ever-present low background noise of classical music.

In the eight years since federal authorities had taken their case to the Manhattan district attorney, much had changed. The missing children's movement had continued to grow; in fact, the National Center for Missing and Exploited Children was in the midst of a move to spacious new head-quarters outside D.C., equipped with state-of-the-art computer systems that linked directly to the FBI, Customs, and the U.S. Postal Service through the burgeoning World Wide Web. The previous year the center had inaugu-rated its CyberTipline, allowing anyone with access to a computer to file tips about child exploitation online, and had already received over ten thousand submissions. Since it was founded in 1984, NCMEC had reported work-ing with federal authorities on over sixty-six thousand cases, in which some forty-seven thousand youngsters had been found.

Sadly, tragedies still occurred, and out of them had come other innova-tions. In 1993, twelve-year-old Polly Klaas was murdered, which pushed California to pass strict laws requiring sex offenders to register their where-abouts and be monitored by authorities. A year later, seven-year-old Megan Kanka was kidnapped, raped, and murdered by a New Jersey neighbor who was a convicted sex offender, and two years after that, President Bill Clinton signed Megan's Law, asking state law enforcement to release sex offender data to the public. And in 1996 Amber Hagerman's abduction led to AMBER Alerts, a partnership between law enforcement and broadcasters to rapidly send out the word as soon as a child went missing.

But in New York City, one thing had not changed. The Etan Patz case, along with all of the background information and the Feds' offers of help, was sitting somewhere in the DA's files. Officially, it remained an ongoing case, but that was all anyone would say. In the first months after the case had been presented, there'd been some positive signs, and a series of meetings between GraBois and various Manhattan assistant DAs. But as time passed, it became clear the case wasn't moving forward. They say they need more evidence, GraBois reported back to Stan, and they're looking for a smoking gun. GraBois disagreed and he told them so, but it wasn't his case anymore.

At first Stan had held out hope this phase would be just like all the other incarnations. GraBois's efforts had taken years to pay off. But gradually, when no one except a frustrated Stuart GraBois called to check in, Stan Patz knew he was being told by the DA's Office "we're done, goodbye." In 1993, Stan had begun a twice-yearly ritual to signal that while the authori-ties might be done, he wasn't.

Stan called up the Word document he'd been looking for, a single sentence on the stark white screen. He walked through the small "computer room" that had been Shira's bedroom before she'd moved to Brooklyn, and stepped into the adjacent darkroom. He had to yank hard on a heavy back drawer before it crankily responded. Stan thumbed through, then carefully removed one 8½-by-11-inch sheet from the stack of posters he kept tucked in the rear of the drawer. These days he visited this particular file only twice a year, once on Etan's birthday and again a few days before the May 25 anniversary.

The poster he chose was the one most people would remember, with two pictures of Etan, artfully rendered with professional lighting, designed to highlight the playful glint in his eyes. There was no shyness, no awkward formality in his expression—he was sitting for his own father. One of the pictures had the Future Flight Captain hat transplanted onto his head. The other photo came from the shirtless series, the one that had raised such eyebrows, but the likeness was so true that Stan preferred using it, so he had cropped it to show Etan from the neck and shoulders only.

Stan could see the posters were yellowing as he gently smoothed the faint wrinkles from the one in his hands. But there were more than enough left to last until 2014, when Jose Ramos would walk out of prison a free man.

When Stan had left the meeting with the FBI and GraBois in 1991, he'd thought long and hard about what they'd said. There were subsequent conversations with both GraBois and Galligan to fill in details, and to Stan the pieces fit together. Finally, after all the years facing an agonizing void, there was a completed picture, and he wanted to assure Ramos that the crime he'd committed was not part of a long-forgotten past.

He returned to the computer and fitted the missing poster backward into the printer. He scrolled down on his screen to change the date to the current May 25, 1999, and clicked the "print" icon. The paper ran through the printer in an instant, and came out with just one sentence on the back, in a typewriter-like Courier font.

```
May 25, 1999
What did you do to my little boy?
```

Stan had chosen that typeface to be consistent; he had still been using a typewriter when he'd started sending this message to Jose Ramos.

Back then, he'd thought he'd react differently when it became clear the prosecution was permanently stalled. He'd expected to mourn all over again and then move on. And it wasn't as though he did nothing but stew on the case. Yes, he could honestly say that twenty years later Etan still came into his thoughts at least once every single day. But he *had* moved on—he'd raised his other two children, supported his family, puttered with his myriad hobbies, railed about politics with his friends. In high school, a precocious teenage Stan had settled on three life goals—the right job, the right place to live, and the right companion. He had accomplished those goals. After almost thirty-five years, he loved his wife, he got to play with all of his toys—the gadgets and technology that surrounded him in his very comfortable home. He viewed his life as privileged, except for one thing.

And he couldn't just forget about it. He agreed with Stuart GraBois—it wasn't over. He'd waited all this time, watching as the case moved forward in tiny increments, stood still interminably, moved a bit, stopped cold, and on and on. There had to be more. He'd wait a lot longer if he had to.

From his computer database Stan pulled up Ramos's name and printed out an envelope with the address: State Correctional Institution at Frackville, a maximum-security prison in eastern Pennsylvania. Ramos had been moved five times since 1991, and Stan had found him each time. After methodically folding the customized but unsigned poster in thirds, Stan slid it into the envelope and sealed it.

He was alone in the apartment. Julie would return midafternoon, like most days, from her job at a local middle school. With Shira out of the house, that left only twenty-two-year-old Ari living at home. After high school, some college, and world travel, he had settled back down in his old bedroom as he taught some photography classes and figured out what to do next. Currently a longtime girlfriend was living there too, the daughter of an old family friend they'd all known for years. It was an unconventional arrangement, but they were both such likable kids, and Ari was very helpful setting up and maintaining Stan's new computer systems. Besides, both Stan and Julie couldn't help guarding their time with Ari possessively. The boy, now a handsome young man, had grown up with two very attentive parents. He was always the first to say that he didn't feel smothered, but his mom had been a presence in nearly every school he'd attended and he'd certainly played a lot of ball with his dad. Ari was playing for two, Stan sometimes thought.

Stan left the apartment and turned toward the SoHo post office half a block away. He skirted the colorful, mawkish jumble of sidewalk vendors that he liked to gripe were turning SoHo into one giant flea market. The storefronts he passed were less obstructive but just as disagreeable to the pioneer sensibilities of those who'd lived in the neighborhood as long as the Patzes. The sweatshops and hardware stores had been gradually replaced with Chanel and Louis Vuitton, and the bodegas were now tony sushi bars. Stan often wondered how many customers were needed to support the lingerie shops that seemed to be on every corner, selling $100 underwear. Even the post office he now entered was rumored to be clearing out soon and moving to an annex in the rear of its 1920s landmark building, to make way for some fancy top-secret retailer.

Stan took out the letter, along with a second one he sent annually to Sandy Harmon, begging her to come forward with any information to advance the case. He put hers in the local slot, and dropped the envelope addressed to Ramos in the one marked "out of town."

Back in the apartment, Stan listened to the answering machine. A *New York Post* reporter wanted a quote for his retrospective, pegged to the twentieth anniversary. Out of habit, Stan marked it down in the spiral logbook, but he wouldn't be returning the call. These largely ignored requests were few and far between nowadays, although the tradition of the logs remained. By 1999, one notebook lasted much longer than in the past, a year or two per book, and the entries were more along the lines of a family message board.

"9:20am, Gary, borrow a ladder?"
"18:52 Ben for Ari. Game?"
"Happy 35th Anniversary."

But every once in a while, there would be a reminder of why the logbooks were there in the first place. This twentieth year saw a few more hangups than there usually were around the actual day.

And there was this call, an invitation to lunch.

"11:10 Stu G.—Tuta Pasta on Carmine South Side @13:00 Stu's office."

On the designated day a few weeks later, Stan Patz walked ten blocks due west to GraBois's Hudson Street office. Entering the lobby of the stately building, he admired, as he always did, the gleaming, ornately inlaid cherrywood paneling. The custom-crafted workmanship was a fitting showcase for the New York District Council of Carpenters Union, the headquarters for the area's union carpenters. Stan walked to the elevator and passed an imposing three-and-a-half-foot-square sign with raised lettering that read "New York District Council of Carpenters, Carpenters Benefit Funds, Stuart R. GraBois, Director."

In 1993, after over eleven years as an assistant U.S. attorney and more than twenty-one with the Justice Department, GraBois had left to oversee a staff of some two-hundred employees—money managers, accountants, attorneys, and assorted others needed to grow the multibillion-dollar funds. At the time, the union itself was under scrutiny from the federal government amid corruption allegations. The U.S. Attorney's Office had filed a civil racketeering suit against the Carpenters Union in 1990, and just months after GraBois started his new position, the union submitted to court-appointed oversight. GraBois's presence as a scrupulously honest and tough but fair manager of the union's benefit fund was a step in the right direction.

He had loved being a federal prosecutor, but this was a great opportunity—a real change and the kind of challenge he thrived on. GraBois was reluctant to leave the Patz case unresolved, even though he'd officially handed it off years earlier. Ultimately, he'd decided that with his long history at the U.S. Attorney's Office, and the inside contacts he'd maintain after he was gone, his voice would still be strong working the case from the outside. When GraBois had called Stan Patz about his plans, he'd told Stan he'd continue to give him legal counsel; support him in any way he could.

Whenever Stan came to the West Side for these occasional meetings, he enjoyed the panoramic views overlooking the Hudson River that took up one whole wall in GraBois's spacious new quarters. The other three walls were filled with memories: photos of the old office softball team, framed commendations, the U.S. attorney's edict that recalled GraBois's grandfather's words about justice. GraBois's souvenir mesh cap collection adorned the top of a wall-length filing cabinet, hats cadged over the years from every branch of the government—NYPD, FBI, the Postal Inspectors, U.S. Customs—each one a souvenir of a case he'd worked. There was even one from the Pennsylvania State Police. Above the display hung a large framed courtroom artist's sketch of the 1990 sentencing hearing in Warren County, catching GraBois mid-argument, his hand raised toward the judge while Ramos, in his bright orange prison jumpsuit, slouched dejectedly next to him.

Before he'd left the U.S. Attorney's Office, GraBois had written to the

Pennsylvania Parole Board and requested an advisory in advance of Jose Ramos's first parole date. Over the years he'd stayed in touch and had marked his calendar so he couldn't forget—September 13, 2000.

Now at lunch a year ahead of time, Stan Patz and Stuart GraBois strategized about how to ensure the 2000 parole date would come and go, leaving Ramos right where he was. During GraBois's civilian years, it was GraBois who tracked Ramos's moves to different state facilities and listened for any news to pass along. Out of their shared frustration, he and Stan had formed a bond, vigilantly looking for opportunities to keep the case alive. Keeping Ramos in prison was ancillary, but it was also a goal in and of itself.

"We'll need press to do this, to get the word out," GraBois cautioned Stan. "If the parole board is going to vote no, they have to understand who this character is, and they have to know the public is very aware of him, too."

Stan looked doubtful but he didn't immediately object.

"Will you talk to the press? I know it's been a while, but I think it's important."

This was the part Stan hated more than anything else. He'd had cameras trained on him many times, and it always made him feel like he was trapped between layers of glass under a microscope lens, midway through a dissection. Besides, people got interviewed for all kinds of reasons, usually because of some impressive accomplishment. In his case, it was always as a victim. Early on he'd been relieved whenever Julie would get out in front. But Julie wasn't going to be involved in this campaign. He knew without asking she'd be unwilling to thrust herself back in the limelight. He was on his own now.

GraBois was promising to be at his side in whatever he chose to do. The former prosecutor had a lot of contacts and a few ideas of his own. If they did this right, it could mean extensive, targeted exposure with very few actual interviews. As usual, Stan Patz agreed to think about it. Months later, GraBois called Stan to tell him I was now a *60 Minutes II* producer, interested in reporting on Ramos's impending parole. But that update alone wouldn't sustain a lengthy network news story.

"Would you go on camera and make the case against him?" GraBois asked Stan.

So with some trepidation, in April 2000 Stan Patz sat down in front of a camera for the first time in over a decade to warn the public about Jose Ramos.

"He's a predator," Stan said angrily, "and he should never be allowed to be near children again. He should be kept behind bars until he's too old to walk." As much as he hated public speaking, he'd foregone his usual ritual of writing out talking points in advance and simply spoke from the heart.

"I would appeal to anyone who could possibly keep him in jail—this is the time to come forward."

The reporter facing him, Vicki Mabrey, wondered at his motivation. "Is it enough that he is in prison now, even on an unrelated charge?" she asked.

"For me, it *is* enough that he's behind bars." He stopped himself midthought. "Well, no, it isn't," he said, pausing briefly as he changed his mind. "I—I really do want him to admit it."

The story gave an overview of the case, including a mention of the two informants' claims. "Over the years," Stan said, "he's made certain incriminating statements to the effect that Etan's dead and that no one's ever going to find anything."

Breaking down in public was anathema to him, but he knew it was red meat to most journalists. When the interview ended, he worried the piece would highlight his tears, rather than what he hoped had been the persuasive argument of a father fighting for his son's case to be heard.

Julie went to bed every night no later than 8 p.m., so Stan occasionally watched evening television with a neighbor from the building. But the night the broadcast aired, he called his friend and asked her not to come over. He didn't want her to witness him losing his composure again, as he'd done at that one point during the interview. So he watched alone and cried again, when the moment came.

"I believe this man stalked my son," he said to Mabrey. "I believe he lured him back to his apartment. I think he used him like toilet paper, and I think he threw him away." His voice quivered, full of emotion, and then he looked down.

Watching this, Stan was relieved to see the camera cut away quickly to another shot, and gratified that he'd accomplished what he'd set out to do, without looking like the pathetic victim he'd feared appearing. I can do this, he thought, thankful for Stuart GraBois, the cool hand behind the curtain, moving him into position, if not pulling the strings.

The next day, GraBois had an early morning meeting in his office with the benefit fund's outside counsel. Brian O'Dwyer was senior partner in O'Dwyer and Bernstien, founded in 1935 by his late father Paul, such a legendary New York political figure that the firm's address, amid the stately downtown courthouses, was Paul O'Dwyer Way. The elder O'Dwyer, a vocal civil rights supporter and champion of the underdog, was the quintessential liberal Democrat of an era. His son, also a noted attorney and New York Democratic Party stalwart, had the classic, silver-haired, ruddy-faced, genial look of a true son of Ireland.

Like GraBois, O'Dwyer had watched the broadcast the night before, and the former prosecutor was now giving him more background on the case as he described the scene portrayed in the court sketch on his wall.

"Have you ever thought about filing a civil suit against this guy?" O'Dwyer asked, almost thinking aloud. "I ask because I've done a few like this myself, where there was clear guilt, but for whatever reason the criminal case wasn't going to proceed." Winning a civil case, O'Dwyer reminded his friend, only required a preponderance of evidence rather than the "beyond a reasonable doubt" standard of a criminal prosecution.

GraBois was interested. "Tell me more."

"It can make a practical difference in certain cases. I had one recently where a man was killed by his jealous wife, who caught him in flagrante. She was found civilly responsible for his death, which kept her from inheriting his big insurance payout."

"It's an interesting idea," GraBois said. "Ramos has no money, but he's been talking forever about making big bucks in a tell-all book, and that would be just unacceptable." The "Son of Sam Law," passed in New York and adopted by many other states, prohibited a criminal from making money off his crime—any profits would go to the victims. But Ramos had never been convicted for this crime; he'd never even been charged.

More importantly, Ramos had been sitting in prison for fourteen years. Who knew how good his defenses were now? During the process of a civil suit, he might incriminate himself in a deposition, or even confess. And at the end of it, he might be judged responsible for Etan's death—a finding that could push the DA to action.

"We need some legal research done, though," GraBois said. "Would we be on firm legal ground? How viable is our case?"

O'Dwyer offered to have his office look into it, and they agreed Stan would have to be brought in very early to give his blessing. He was the one, after all, who'd have to file the suit. GraBois took it as a good omen when independently reporter John Miller, now a network correspondent on ABC's

20/20, came to him with a news story he'd recently aired of a similar Long Island lawsuit.

"It's an incredibly valuable tool," Miller pressed him. "How many times as a reporter have I wished I could just slap a subpoena on someone and make them answer my questions when they said 'no comment'? It's like deputizing Stan to do some of the things the cops or FBI could do."

When O'Dwyer came back to say the initial findings were encouraging, GraBois thought another Carmine Street lunch was called for, this one featuring guest speaker Brian O'Dwyer.

O'Dwyer had grown up in New York City, in a sprawling apartment on the Upper West Side. As a boy of eight or nine in the mid-fifties, he'd walked to school and hung out in Central Park with friends until dinnertime. In late 1978, after a ten-year-long effort, he and his wife had finally adopted their son, and he was still an infant when Etan disappeared. O'Dwyer had passed the posters every day when he went to work in downtown Manhattan, and read in the newspapers about every parent's worst nightmare. His family lived in the tame suburbs now, but Brendan O'Dwyer was never out of his parents' sight. His father walked his young son to school; his mother or babysitter picked him up. They knew where he was at all times. If the boy didn't have an adult to go with him, he didn't go out. Brian O'Dwyer was one of those parents for whom everything changed after Etan disappeared.

O'Dwyer had never met Stan Patz, and once the three were seated at a quiet table in Marinella's, GraBois's favorite Italian restaurant, he was immediately impressed by Stan's educated air, and his soft-spoken but articulate demeanor. GraBois had already outlined the idea of the civil suit over the phone, but after two decades of shaky proposals and wild goose chases, Stan was clearly cautious. Over seafood and salad, the three talked through the details.

"You have to be very comfortable with this idea," O'Dwyer started carefully. "It's an unusual approach. We could launch the suit, and then Ramos could easily torpedo it."

O'Dwyer explained that once the lawsuit was filed, Ramos would have thirty days to respond. If he didn't, the Patzes would win by default—meaning that Ramos wouldn't be able to keep any blood money should he ever sell his story. It would also be seen by the Pennsylvania Parole Board as another good reason to keep Ramos in prison for his full sentence.

"But if that happened, we wouldn't get the chance to depose him," the lawyer said.

O'Dywer turned to GraBois sitting beside him. "Now, Stu hopes Ramos won't be able to resist filing a response, that he always engages with Stu given the chance. This is a guy who has very little to keep himself occupied and fancies himself a jailhouse lawyer. I'd love for Stu to get his wish, but frankly we'd both be surprised. There's nothing in it for Ramos."

Stan asked the first of several questions. "What exactly is the point of all this? He doesn't get punished; he has no money, and I don't *want* his money. If I ever got any, it would go to charity. Worst of all, he's still not convicted of anything."

GraBois and O'Dwyer explained that more than anything else, the lawsuit would be a chance to wrest some control back from the district attorney. In a civil case, the defendant is under oath during his deposition, but it's not cops or DAs asking the questions, it's the plaintiff's own lawyer. "The DA says he needs more evidence, so why not try to get him some?" O'Dwyer said.

"The U.S. Attorney's Office has advised me that while representing your family is a conflict of interest," GraBois added, "I can be your unofficial, unpaid adviser and work with Brian to fill in any aspect of the case."

"Do you honestly think Ramos would talk to you?" Stan asked. "He has a long history of successfully avoiding that."

"He'd be required to answer the questions or he'd lose his case," O'Dwyer replied. "He may not bite, but again, we think there's a chance he will. In a best-case scenario, this is an open court case, and we add to new evidence that prompts a criminal trial. Middle ground—we win a civil suit and get a judicial judgment that Jose Ramos is responsible for the death of your son."

"And the worst-case scenario?"

"He doesn't respond and it all fizzles, which still has the advantage that he loses by default. Or, worse, we have the ugly full court scene, a tabloid spectacle, and everyone gets to see us lose. There's a whole matrix of outcomes." Both GraBois and O'Dwyer were clear—this had to be a decision made with eyes wide open.

"So I guess this is how they got O.J.," Stan said after digesting for a moment.

"O.J.'s the most prominent example, but it's a growing trend." O'Dwyer told of his own experiences. "There are two big advantages to a civil suit. When you go into the criminal system the family has no influence. You're basically waiting on the authorities. Here, the family runs the case. You make the decisions about where you want to go and how, and I would consult with you at every step."

As ideas went, this one landed square in Stan's ambivalence column. He liked the prospect of ensuring Ramos would never make money from his family's tragedy, and any such award would go straight to charity. And he agreed that a judgment against Ramos would influence the parole board favorably. That was a huge plus. But he doubted the two other men's hope that the DA would be moved by their efforts. Plus there would be the resurgence of unwanted publicity. He'd done his dance on national television, and had hoped he was off the stage. A full-blown court trial, civil or otherwise, guaranteed a media circus à la JonBenét Ramsey that would be hard on his family. And then what if they lost?

"This is always the issue," GraBois agreed. "The publicity is a constant source of aggravation. But it's what we need to keep Ramos in prison."

O'Dwyer had yet to tell him the biggest obstacle to overcome. In order to file a wrongful death suit, the lawyer explained, the Patzes would have to go to court and have Etan declared legally dead.

"There's no way we could proceed without it. It's a legal prerequisite."

Stan looked bleak. "That would be very difficult," he said.

"I understand." O'Dwyer handed Stan a memo outlining the research his office had done on the law. Stan scanned the page, then put it away for careful perusal at home.

"This is all very interesting and I appreciate the time you've put into it, but a lawsuit would no doubt be prohibitively costly."

"Stan, Brian has offered his firm's services pro bono," GraBois said.

Stan turned to his new acquaintance with a quizzical look, but O'Dwyer had a ready explanation.

"My father's philosophy at the firm had always been that at the end of every year, when we look back, if the only thing we did was make money, then the year was a failure. We've always had a tradition to take a certain number of cases pro bono, to give back. And frankly, so much of the work I do can't give me the kind of personal satisfaction your case would."

Stan perked up at the mention of Paul O'Dwyer. He'd heard the pro bono explanation before and didn't always buy it, cynically seeing it as nothing more than a soul-saving device for wealthy but guilt-ridden corporate lawyers. In this case, though, he believed the idealism behind the words.

As far as he was concerned, Paul O'Dwyer had walked on water. He would have voted for him no matter what the office. His admiration for the man was part of the reason Stan had agreed to this lunch, despite his apprehension. From what he could see, Brian O'Dwyer was cut from the same cloth as his father.

Then the attorney explained how he'd been so personally affected by the case. He was well aware from GraBois that Stan had been victimized often in the past by people "trying to help," and wanted to reassure the man his motives were pure. "I have a son too," O'Dwyer said. "I can't possibly know what you've been through but I can empathize, and so I want to do whatever I can."

These were the moments that spurred Stan Patz to see this case through. People like Stu and Brian made an effort not just because it was their job but because they had felt touched by the crime itself.

"Obviously, it's a decision you have to think on long and hard," O'Dwyer said. "The way I look at it, a civil case may have a great deal of value. It may have some value. But it won't have no value."

Stan walked back home after lunch, reflecting on what he'd heard.

He believed that people like Jose Ramos shouldn't go unpunished, and in that sense, it had almost nothing to do with Etan. Someone who commits these kinds of crimes shouldn't be ignored. He should be held accountable, yes, to prevent him from doing it again, but also to let him—and everyone—know that it's not acceptable behavior to molest and murder children. This was the equivalent of society shaking its collective finger to say, You simply can't do this. That's what justice was for. Justice wasn't some vague concept etched in stone on a courthouse wall. It was how society was supposed to keep itself from falling apart.

Stan could feel mercy toward robbers and burglars, but crimes against children were almost inexplicable, and they were certainly unforgivable. If he didn't seek justice—if he simply shut the door and tried to forget—wasn't that wrong too? Especially when so many had worked hard to track this villain for over a decade. Yes, Ramos was in prison, but someday he'd get out if no one tried to stop him.

By the time Stan got home, before he even broached the subject to Julie, he knew what his answer to the lawyers would be. But he could guess how Julie would react. She'd have the same concerns he did with none of the incentive or the same conviction of Ramos's guilt.

This was their fork in the road. When she'd left the FBI office after that last meeting all those years ago, there'd been an unspoken understanding that they weren't to talk of it again. She had no interest in learning further details of the case against Ramos, no interest in making up her mind one way or the other. Any mention of the case or what might have happened to Etan was simply a razor to her heart, ripping and shredding at the layers of scars that protected her. Stan loved his wife and never wanted to add to her pain, so he'd always been complicit in her disengagement. Now he was going to have to wield the blade.

Julie's divergent path took her into a very different world than her husband's. By nature a much more social person, she didn't work in the cocoon of a home office, where Stan conducted business largely by phone, fax, and Internet. She left the loft every morning and caught the uptown subway to a bustling, overinhabited public school. Out of their home, she was much more exposed to the raw elements. Sometimes, even now, she'd be recognized on the train.

"I know you," strangers would say. No you don't, she'd think, as she smiled and nodded and wished them away. She was the one, not Stan, who had to deal with random, well-intended, but heartstopping comments from people who thought they'd seen Etan once, back in 1982, or 1993, or yesterday. Thank you, she'd say politely, although it was ridiculous to think it helpful now. At school, the staff, the parents, and by some point every year many of the students knew who she was and what she had suffered. Her experience, working at a place as transient as a school, was like being in the movie *Groundhog Day*. Every year, a fresh crop of kids would discover the tragedy all over again and the stares would begin, sympathetic, suspicious, pitying—that special, urgent anguish adolescents feel so acutely. Then she'd be the one to comfort some poor thirteen-year-old crying on her shoulder after a night spent online researching twenty years of Julie's life. It never stopped.

Fortunately, it was easy to distract herself with the hectic workload, and she often felt that as crazy as it was, the work kept her sane. Julie's official title was supervisory school aide. She'd come to the Manhattan middle school in the late eighties, when Ari was starting sixth grade there. Though she was no longer an unpaid volunteer, the modest salary only jumped her a narrow step up the ladder, and she worked exhaustedly for it. Crammed into the top floor of a building that housed a bigger elementary school below it, the school wasn't for the faint of heart. On fire drill days especially, the hundreds of steps to go down and then back up wreaked havoc on the knees, not so much for the young and agile students but for the staff. Other than teachers, staff consisted for many years of the principal…and Julie. The two shared an office and Julie was the de facto secretary, nurse, school aide, handyperson, lunchroom monitor, assistant principal, and disciplinarian. Every day she performed triage, racing the halls, ponytail flying, or her neat bun adorned with extra pens and pencils, dispensable to needy, forgetful young teens. She was the one called to fix the copy machine, even as Stan teased her about any home repair attempts in her actual home. She wrapped students shivering with fever in a blanket and held them while they waited for a parent to come, and she held them tighter after they learned the parent wasn't coming. She matter-of-factly explained the basics to the girls who got their periods for the first time—in school—and were too embarrassed to tell anyone else, not even their own mothers. She awarded detention to the student she caught in the bathroom, pants off, leg in the sink, frantically wielding a razor as the first class bell rang.

"I didn't have time to shave my legs at home this morning," the girl said plaintively. "I'm sorry, Miss Julie."

Julie loved it. She was a mother; that's what she knew how to do well, and she found her efforts here every bit as meaningful as the speeches she'd given in Washington advocating new missing children laws. She even found herself reprising some of her earlier words. The middle school allowed its eleven- to fourteen-year-old students to leave the building for lunch, in one of the pizza joints or delis within a several-block radius. Every year a few parents balked at giving the necessary permission, branding their fledgling teens with an irredeemable stigma. Julie would intervene occasionally to plead a student's case.

"They have to grow and gain confidence in themselves," she'd say to a reluctant mother, reassuring her of the proximity of the school's security guards. "You can't lock them in the house or in class. They'll never learn how to fend for themselves." Some parents were ignorant of Julie's history, but others knew, and they were the ones more likely to listen.

"Walk with them," she'd counsel. "Teach them *how* to protect themselves. Give them a life."

She advocated for her young charges in other ways too. One year she fast-talked first the principal into ceding a small room and then the PTA out of a few dollars for books.

"We need a library," she told them. "Some of these kids don't even know their alphabet. I'll be the librarian, too."

She begged, borrowed, and hustled books, then spent her own money in the hidden recesses of secondhand bargain bookstores. She recruited a volunteer student corps, taught them how to sign out books, and how to reshelve—which required a thorough knowledge of the alphabet. At first, her little room remained empty save for delinquents kicked out of class and banished to the only available space. Julie probed them for their closely held passions, then enticed them with customized books.

"I like weapons," a boy might confide, and days later a World War II memorabilia book would magically appear. Julie would first tear off the cover that revealed its fourth-grade reading level, then cajole her new disciple into taking a look. Gradually, the library developed a following, and Julie knew the exhilaration of matching a book to a student, then watching a resistant mind open, if just a crack.

"Oh, Miss Julie," a normally mute young teen would say, "that was so wonderful. Do you have any more like that?"

"It's what makes me jump out of bed in the morning and race to work," Julie would tell Stan. And Stan, whose mother had been a librarian, was so proud.

Julie cried on the first day of school the year she came in to find the principal had reappropriated his room. But she never stopped working with the students, learning their names and interests, engaging them in the smallest and largest of ways. And always, she would talk to them about the books she loved and encourage them to love books too. What she gave to "her kids" was perhaps the deepest possible expression of love for the son she had lost. Whether she acknowledged it consciously or not, hers was a very personal way to honor his memory. It was different than Stan's more direct approach—to seek justice—but no less heartfelt or valid.

When Julie reached home from school and Stan met her with news of the proposed civil suit, as he'd expected, her reaction was immediate, spare, and unreceptive. She didn't see the point. Any new jolt in the press would raise her profile yet again, and even if it were Stan's turn now to face the incoming fire, she wouldn't be able to escape the fallout. She'd spent over a third of her life in this hell, and she wanted it to be over.

"It won't bring Etan back," she said aloud to her husband. Stan acknowledged that truth, then quietly went on to outline the lawsuit's first step. Even though they both knew Etan was gone, the thought of making it official was just too painful for Julie to even consider.

"You do what you have to do," is how she finally left it, "but I can't have any part of it."

———

Only the weekend kept Stan from letting GraBois know he was ready to move ahead. On Monday morning Stan was told the lawyers would prepare the case, and he'd get word when the documents were ready to be faxed over. There'd be no court appearance, just his name on a piece of paper.

When Ramos was denied parole the next week, Stan felt some satisfaction. But he knew the inmate would be eligible again in two years. By the end of the summer the lawsuit was announced, and on November 15, 2000, Stan presented himself to Brian O'Dwyer's office to finish off the paperwork that would ask a judge to rule Etan was dead. All that was required of him was a simple rote signature. He would tell reporters gathered afterwards in the conference room that he felt like he'd just signed his son's death certificate, although in the moment he sensed no more than his pen moving across the paper.

But in truth there was a well of emotion behind that gesture. Stan believed he had failed his son. Probably many times, when he was too busy working to look at Etan's artwork or play ball; but one time when it was irrevocable. He had failed to protect him, which was his job, his duty, the biggest responsibility he'd ever been given. He'd always told himself it wasn't anyone's fault—not Julie's, not his. There was evil in this world and there was bad luck. The two had collided that morning, and no one could have done a damn thing about it. But now there was something he could do. He'd never been able to get Robert Morgenthau to make this case, and he knew the lawsuit might not sway the DA either. But for more than twenty years, he'd been forced to sit back and helplessly watch the cops and the task forces and the prosecutors and the FBI do their best. Now for the first time he had the opportunity to take a step on his own, and he couldn't just stand still. He had to do what he could to further his own cause, to get justice for Etan.

CHAPTER 29

The True Story

...To Stanley Kenneth Patz send greetings:

Whereas, Etan Kalil Patz died intestate on May 25, 1979 and whereas the decree of this court made July 17 2001 directed the issuance to you of LETTERS OF ADMINISTRATION....

...NOW THEREFORE, KNOW YE that you are hereby authorized to administer the estate of the said deceased subject.
　　—death certificate of Etan Patz, granted by Judge Eve Preminger,
　　　July 17, 2001

Twenty-two years after the moment had passed, Manhattan Surrogate Court judge Eve Preminger declared it so.

Once Stan had set the legal wheels in motion by signing his name, they'd moved excruciatingly slowly. Because Julie Patz had refused to sign the documents, a seven-month waiting period was required by law, in case she decided to file an objection to Stan's request. She did not, and on a fresh, balmy June day in 2001, Brian O'Dwyer and Stuart GraBois were in court to accept the decree. Neither Stan nor Julie needed to be there, and they weren't. On any regular business day, the exquisite Beaux-Arts, landmark Surrogate Court, with its ornate carved woodwork, elaborate façade, and twin marble fireplaces drew tourists along with New Yorkers finalizing adoptions or authenticating a loved one's will. Often a backdrop for television shows like *Law and Order*, the Surrogate Court was packed with press on July 17 to hear the judge announce Etan Patz's death. It was the last place Etan's aggrieved parents would want to be.

Afterwards, in an informal Q&A outside the courtroom, one of the younger reporters asked the Patzes' lawyers how any parent could have let their child walk the city streets alone at such a young age.

"It was a different time," Brian O'Dwyer replied, speaking for himself as much as the zeitgeist. "For many parents, May 25, 1979, was the end of innocence."

Even as the civil case received a green light, the NYPD was making its own revived push for a *criminal* prosecution. Over the last few years, the Missing Persons Unit had revisited the case, and in particular 234 East Fourth Street, where Jose Ramos had lived in 1979, and where some investigators now believed Etan Patz may have died. This new round of detectives tackled the same scattered paperwork and discovered that back when Ramos had first become a suspect—after the 1982 drainpipe arrest—very few people had been canvassed in his old building. By then three years had already passed since Etan's disappearance, and 234 East Fourth was a transient, crime-ridden quasi–shooting gallery in the drug-infested "Alphabet City" neighborhood. The names on the mailboxes were perpetually outdated, a procession of tough characters or struggling artists, including, in her salad days, Madonna. In the early eighties she'd lived briefly in the apartment directly below the one where Ramos had once brought his young victims. Many of the elusive tenants were junkies who scored their dope in the conveniently located heroin spot on the first floor, welfare scammers, and poor, mistrustful immigrants, all unlikely to answer the door to a police knock. But flash forward to the late nineties and that earlier level of crime in the building became a helpful investigative tool to Missing Persons detective Frank Saez. He was able to pore over the faded DD5 police reports of robberies, drug deals gone bad, and shots fired that in 1979 had constantly brought squad cars streaming to 234 East Fourth Street. There were so many incidents, Saez was able to piece together a fairly complete list of the building's inhabitants in the years around Etan's disappearance.

Jose Ramos himself had filed complaints against one of his neighbors, and Saez tried to track the man down. When the detective called a contact number, explained he was from Missing Persons and was looking for Jose Lopez, Lopez's widow assumed the detective was looking for her son, Jose Jr., now a cop himself. She passed along the message, and the young Detective Lopez, a burly, genial man in his late twenties, appeared in person one day at the MPU to ask who was looking for him. When the mistake was cleared up, Lopez Jr. explained that his father, a renowned drug dealer and

heroin addict, had died of AIDS several years earlier. But the son was happy
to help, and was handed a mug shot of Ramos.

"That's 'Hippie,'" he immediately said, using a nickname the cops had
heard before. Lopez knew Ramos by sight if not by name, as the man folks
in the building stayed away from. He was weird, Lopez told the other detectives, and went after the little kids. Then he told a chilling story.

As a chubby seven-year-old with a *Saturday Night Fever* hairdo, Lopez
was playing with his sister one morning in their bedroom when he happened to glance out the window to see a row of toy soldiers and an old Barbie
doll magically appear. He drew closer and realized they were dangling from
above, suspended by clear fishing wire. Curious, he opened the window and
reached toward one of the toys. But before he could touch it, the line was
yanked upward a few inches. He tried again, and again the toy jumped up.
Lopez craned his neck out the window, looking up to find the source of this
manna from heaven. Sitting one flight above on the fire escape that led to
his upstairs apartment, "Hippie" grinned at him widely. Seeing Jose Ramos
gesture for him to climb the rusty metal stairs, the boy slammed the window shut. He told his sister not to say a word to anyone about the man who
was literally fishing for his prey.

Ramos's now grown would-be victim was transferred to Missing Persons
and given a long lead with which to pursue his old neighbors. A detailed,
painstaking search eventually turned up former tenants who remembered
Ramos accompanying children up to his apartment. One even told detectives Ramos was spotted in their building with a young blond child around
the day Etan disappeared. When this person asked Ramos who the "white
kid" was, Ramos replied that his girlfriend took care of the boy.

It was a twenty-year-old memory at this point, but the new leads, added
to the story Ramos had once told Jon Morgan about his work in the boiler,
led Missing Persons to take another look at 234's basement. Back in the
'90s GraBois and NYPD detectives had already sifted through the space
for bone fragments and other evidence, before they'd eventually learned the
boiler's lining had long since been replaced. But by the summer of 2000,
cops wanted to try updated DNA methods, so they hauled away barrels of
ash and dirt from the basement floor there, and even brought in a cadaver
dog. Ultimately they found nothing new, but Stan Patz was heartened by all
the activity, and the new eyewitness reports.

When he heard that the district attorney remained unmoved to take action, Stan wanted to hear the reason why from Robert Morgenthau personally. A week after Etan was declared dead, Stan sent a letter to Morgenthau requesting a meeting. He'd been told by both federal and local investigators knowledgeable about the case, he wrote, that there was enough evidence to go after Ramos. He wondered if politics were playing a part in the DA's inaction. He soon heard back from the assistant DA handling the case, Armand Durastanti, who offered to set up a meeting with Morgenthau's number two. Stan demurred. After waiting ten years to learn anything from that office, he was looking for a dialogue, a real conversation to inform him of the hurdles and then give him the chance to clear them away. He wanted to make his case directly to the district attorney himself. Anyone below that, he felt, would simply parrot the party line.

At the end of the summer, Brian O'Dwyer was ready to file the lawsuit and serve Ramos. Then September 11 threw his time line into disarray. There were months of delay as the lower Manhattan office of O'Dwyer and Bernstien was shuttered and its staff dispersed. For six weeks, O'Dwyer operated out of a conference room in GraBois's Benefit Funds offices. By the time the suit was once again ready to go, Stan had already mailed Ramos his October biannual reminder, the missing poster with Stan's question on the back. For the first time in eight years, Ramos replied—in a jumble of semi-legalese—demanding Stan desist his "criminal harassment by mail." Harassment, Stan thought; you ain't seen nothin' yet. But he used the opportunity to prod the inmate into responding to the upcoming lawsuit.

"I see you fancy yourself a legal expert," he wrote back, a few weeks before Ramos was served. "Okay, prepare yourself, because I will be seeing you in court. What will you say then? Are you going to come to tell the truth or spout more weasel words?"

Stan was referencing a Web page he'd discovered earlier in the year, entitled "To Tell the Truth," which he'd been amazed, then outraged, to find was posted by Jose Ramos himself. A desultory essay that included yet another version of the "Jimmy" story, it offered the promise of more, upon demand. "As to what actually happened to Etan Patz," Ramos had posted, "if any freedom-loving American wants the true story, I kindly ask that you send $2 to my snail-mail address." Stan might have been willing to pay the two dollars, but he wanted the "true story" to be told under oath.

Jim Nauwens, the investigator who'd once chased Rainbows in Woodstock for GraBois, had long since retired from the U.S. Attorney's Office.

But when GraBois called his friend for help, Nauwens didn't hesitate, even though it meant a three-hour drive on a holiday week. This time it wasn't a trip to Woodstock, but to SCI Dallas, near Scranton, Pennsylvania. A few days before Christmas 2001, while the Patzes were on their annual New England family trip, Ramos was called to the inmate interview room, where Nauwens, with GraBois at his side, formally served Ramos notice of the civil suit, then turned around and drove back to New York. Ramos had thirty days to respond or he'd lose the case by default, and the team waited to see if he would take the bait. All through the holidays, GraBois checked in with O'Dwyer.

"No mail yet, Stu," O'Dwyer began to respond every time he picked up the phone. But with only a few days left before the deadline, a package of legal documents arrived from SCI Dallas. Thanks to Ramos, who had denied each cause for action included in the civil argument, the case could go forward.

Stan was gratified by the progress, but he was willing to make a trade-off. In a second letter he sent in early 2002 to the Manhattan DA he wrote, "I do not want the civil action to hinder your investigation, or cause problems for your department. I would appreciate a response and would make myself available for a meeting at any time." In other words, bring a criminal indictment and I'll happily drop the suit.

By this point, Stan Patz had heard plenty of speculation from other, third parties—friends, cops, or reporters—who could rattle off a list of reasons why the DA might balk at an indictment. He knew the difficulties of prosecuting a case with no body; but both he and Stuart GraBois had been encouraged by the DA's recent conviction of Sante Kimes and her son, two grifters who'd killed an elderly New York woman and disposed of her body to appropriate her home. Stan also understood all too well how old the case was, and that Jose Ramos was already locked up for more than twenty years. Why put all those resources into a case that might result in a concurrent sentence or, worse, an impolitic acquittal? Stan knew how long the odds were, but they'd always been long. He still wanted to talk about it, strategize, understand. Besides, Stuart GraBois had also faced such odds, and that hadn't stopped him from pushing the case as far as he could.

A meeting with Morgenthau's chief assistant was again offered up, and this time Stan went to see what he would say. But James Kindler only sat impassively while Stan made the points he'd spent hours preparing, listing the evidence he felt was substantive enough to indict and hopefully convict Jose Ramos. When he finished talking, Stan waited for Kindler to engage his arguments. But he heard nothing more than a terse acknowledgment that the District Attorney's Office would not be proceeding. Stan was caught off guard. He'd expected at the very least a show of sympathy, a wish that more could be done, but there was nothing. He had the sense that he faced a stone idol who gazed back at him with unseeing eyes. Flooded by a mix of fury and frustration, he felt the tears leak out despite his best efforts to will them away.

"I just want to get the bastard who fucked over my son!"

The shocking words broke from him before he could rein them in. He struggled to hold his composure, calling on almost sixty years of innate passivity and his cherished sense of propriety. But he was overtaken by a surge of emotion. It recalled the sense of helplessness and failure he'd felt that first night, pacing the sidewalk outside his Prince Street loft in the rain. At least that night, hundreds of other people had swarmed around him, mobilizing the search, desperate to help. Now, ADA Durastanti politely saw him out and murmured mildly hopeful words. But Stan knew that as long as Robert Morgenthau was in office, the Manhattan district attorney would never prosecute this case.

With no apparent chance for a criminal prosecution, Stan Patz was left to fashion whatever justice he could from the civil case. But the wheels of justice move even slower when obstacles are hurled under them. Over the next two years, Ramos ducked and weaved as Stan's legal team tried to force the true story from him. In Brian O'Dwyer's first attempt to depose him, he and GraBois arrived at the prison only to hear that Ramos refused to answer any questions without a lawyer of his own, even though, unlike criminal cases, the plaintiff in a civil suit doesn't have the right to counsel. Ramos could have lost the case on those grounds alone, but Judge Barbara Kapnick gave him another chance, warning him that if he continued to refuse to cooperate, she'd rule for the Patzes. Once again, GraBois and O'Dwyer made the three-hour trip to Dallas, Pennsylvania, GraBois driving and prepping O'Dwyer with mock scenarios. At the prison, they joined a stenographer in the small room provided to visiting attorneys and waited for Jose Ramos. His appearance had changed little in the twelve years since GraBois had watched FBI agents restrain him in his chair. The hair under his yarmulke was longer and grayer, the beard snow white.

Both men took pains to present a solicitous front when Ramos arrived. They couldn't risk giving him grounds for a harassment claim. GraBois even remained silent throughout, mutely passing O'Dwyer the occasional note to add a point of information. And while at first Ramos angrily objected to the former prosecutor's presence, he ultimately acceded.

It was immediately clear, however, that Ramos's cooperation was a sham. He denied every accusation, and then minutes later would say he couldn't recall the same incident. He refused to answer many of the questions, pleading his Fifth Amendment rights, even after O'Dwyer explained several times that the Fifth Amendment wasn't applicable in civil cases. Amid his various obfuscations, Ramos defaulted to the Jimmy story.

In the past dozen years since Ramos had begun telling this tale to authorities and the press, it had changed several times. In this latest incarnation, the Jimmy story had become not just a convenient way to explain away his appearance with a young boy that day. Now it was his alibi, backed up by no less than the NYPD. The new version put Ramos, as always, with a boy named "Jimmy" in Washington Square Park the day Etan disappeared. There, Ramos told O'Dwyer, a patrol car from the Sixth Precinct approached the two, and the cops compared Jimmy to a photo, quickly concluding he wasn't Etan Patz.

"They showed me the photograph," Ramos said to O'Dwyer. "'We're looking for this boy, have you seen him?' And I told him, no sir. Then they left, and I took Jimmy to my place." Like the Seventh Avenue subway clerk from Ramos's 1991 account to FBI agent Mary Galligan, the canvassing officers of the Sixth Precinct would clearly be able to exonerate him.

"I don't know who they were," Ramos told O'Dwyer, "but I'm sure you could find that record."

Ramos's alibi, however, was less than airtight. He put the time of this encounter at late morning, "between 11:15 and 11:30," several hours before Etan was even discovered to be missing, long before any patrol cars were on the streets looking for him.

After reading the deposition transcript, the judge agreed with Brian O'Dwyer's motion that Ramos didn't get to pick and choose the questions he would answer. His refusal to comply with Judge Kapnick's previous order prompted her to strike his entire testimony, and in late April 2004 the judge ruled on the case in a summary judgment that found Jose Ramos legally responsible for the death of Etan Patz.

When Stuart GraBois got word, he immediately called Stan.

"It's good news, thanks," Stan said, brightening first, before his customary caution returned. "I guess we won the consolation prize." Now Ramos would never be able to help someone write the Pulitzer Prize–winning book he'd once boasted about, and any chance of him getting out before 2014 was next to impossible. But in practical terms, Stan wondered what they had really gained.

"In practical terms," GraBois replied firmly, "Jose Ramos is sitting in prison for more than twenty years, and he won't go anywhere else before then. If you're Jose, and you're in a cell the size of a bathroom twenty-three hours a day, that is your number one most practical consideration. And in practical terms, this case is what put him there."

"I do get satisfaction out of that," Stan said. "But you know I was hoping for more; that this would move us closer to a criminal conviction."

"There may never be a criminal trial, and sometimes that really disappoints me. But I want you to hear me on this, Stan. When I told the judge in 1990 this guy was a monster, it was the most accurate word I could come up with. And because of Etan, this monster hasn't been near a child since he was arrested almost twenty years ago. A whole generation of victims were spared. That's Etan's legacy.

"Now we're doing everything we can to make sure he's locked away as long as possible. And in very practical terms—it's something to feel good about."

———

Stanley Patz took his obligations seriously. It went along with his sense of propriety and his natural self-effacement. The specific obligation he felt toward Etan was enormous, but it wasn't his only one. Stan was a very conscientious man, and ever since the loss of his son, a sense of debt had been slowly piling up. And it wasn't just the gratitude he owed Stu GraBois and Brian O'Dwyer now, or to the men and women who'd spent twenty-five years searching for Etan, first to try to get him back, and eventually to answer the question Stan had written on the back of his annual posters to Jose Ramos. All those people had tried so hard, with nothing to show for it. Many still bore the burden of those failed efforts, some long after they'd turned in their badges and guns, and some never even got the chance, like Detective Bill Butler, who'd smiled reassuringly while he walked the streets for years, foraging unsuccessfully for clues. In 1986, two years after he'd been transferred off the Patz case for good, Butler had been found by his daughter on the floor of the family kitchen, where he'd shot and killed himself with his own service revolver. Neither the family nor the NYPD, citing "personal problems," ever mentioned the Patz case as a factor, but Stan and Julie remained unconvinced. They'd witnessed and been the beneficiary of his personal attachment to their son and seen his despondency as the investigation had languished.

After all these years, Stan felt an obligation to Butler, and to all the others in between, the cops like Bobby Shaw and Owen Byrne, the FBI agents like Ken Ruffo and Mary Galligan. For years after the Feds had stepped back, Galligan had made a special request, despite several career moves, to keep the Patz case among her files. When she was promoted to supervisor in 2001 she'd called Stan and told him she was finally being ordered to officially hand off the case.

"Don't worry," she told him, "it's being reassigned to another agent. And I'll always keep an eye on it." Just months later she was sent to Washington to head up PENTTBOM, the FBI's 9/11 investigation. In her improvised basement office in the J. Edgar Hoover Building, she propped one of Etan's original missing posters on top of her bookcase.

But the searchers and seekers who'd given their time and their sweat were just the most visible links in the chain that tied so many more to this case. For twenty-five years, people had been moved to action by the sad story: the friends and neighbors, some he barely knew or could remember, the ones who'd brought the casseroles, and cared for Etan's brother and sister; who with great trepidation had scoured the darkened basements and abandoned elevator shafts of SoHo. All the strangers over the years who'd written him unanswered letters, who'd whispered unanswered prayers, lighting their candles in church sanctuaries around the country, around the world. All those people had given their time and gotten nothing back and Stan believed Jose Ramos should be held responsible for that too. In the meantime, Stan himself felt responsible for coming up with an answer.

———

Almost seven months later, Etan's father sat on the witness stand and looked down at the sketch artist in the front row of the lower Manhattan courtroom. From upside down, it was hard to tell if she was drawing a good likeness. He tried to twist his neck around without revealing his wandering eye. Checking himself out on the page was a welcome distraction from the attack of nerves—or was it vertigo he felt, sitting up high in the chair with everyone looking at him? Fortunately, the courtroom was smaller than he'd expected, and the turnout was even smaller. Judge Kapnick looked comforting yet businesslike in her brown bangs and pearls, sitting even higher than Stan.

Today, November 22, 2004, for the first time ever, Stan Patz was in court for Etan, in the damages phase of the civil suit. This morning Stan's testimony would help the judge put a dollar figure to the family's pain and suffering over the past two and a half decades, if such a thing were even remotely possible. It struck him as obscene, but Stan couldn't tolerate the even more obscene thought that Jose Ramos might profit from Etan's death, so money damages had to be assigned. Stan struggled to pull his gaze away from the artist's broad pencil strokes as she filled in his navy jacket and matching tie. Putting on the tie that morning had helped the day's importance sink in, maybe even more than the hours of preparation at the lawyer's office; more than the *New York Daily News* headline—"Finally, Etan's Family Gets a Day in Court"; more than fielding the phone calls such headlines had inevitably prompted. For Stan, a tie meant serious business: weddings, funerals, and now court appearances.

Stuart GraBois sat a few seats down the row from the sketch artist and watched Stan easily answer preliminaries—name, address, profession. Then, as O'Dwyer prepared to ask the next question, GraBois leaned closer to hear Stan's answer and caught his eye, nodding in encouragement. The two men had spent a few hours together that morning while Stan had one last chance to practice what he'd say, and GraBois knew that talking about Etan in open court was going to deplete his inner resources. He had faith in Stan, though, because he'd come to recognize his quiet strength.

From their first hostile days, through the gradual thaw, then hours of tactical meetings, the two had forged a friendship out of mutual admiration and respect. When GraBois had the Carpenters Union give office space to the New York chapter of the National Center for Missing and Exploited Children, he'd also arranged for Stan to sit with him on their New York advisory board. At their infrequent lunches the two fathers talked about other subjects besides the legal intricacies of the case. Ari Patz, now living in Hawaii near his girlfriend's family, gave his father tales to tell of his exotic new life. Andrew GraBois was a recent third-generation law school grad, an associate at O'Dwyer and Bernstien. The baby who'd helped spark his father's interest in the case was now helping prepare the briefs for this damages phase.

Today the elder GraBois was sitting in the courtroom, as at all such appearances, for moral support. Up on the witness stand, Stan felt especially thankful for his friend's presence. As usual, Julie had left for school long before Stan was even awake that morning. Had she been there, she might not have been talking to him anyway. They rarely fought, but there were those long periods of silence, and he knew how she felt about what he was doing today, just as she in turn felt his disapproval for shunning the lawsuit.

"Mr. Patz, could you describe Etan prior to his disappearance?"

The question seemed to hang in the air, as Stan's breath had hung in the chill fall morning when he'd walked over to the courthouse earlier and had struggled with what he would say on the stand. He knew he should deliver pathos, an image of Etan powerful enough to fly like an arrow to pierce the judge's heart. Stan wanted to make the strongest case possible.

"I thought Etan was a wonderful child," Stan answered. "He was as nice a little boy as there ever could be." Afterwards, he couldn't remember what else he said; just one more sentence, short, and filled with positive adjectives—happy, outgoing, beautiful. There should be more, Stan worried, but that was it. He had safely navigated the emotional precipice; no repeat of his outburst in the DA's Office, and the moment had passed.

In the end, though, it really didn't matter. His lawyer had already introduced into evidence a series of photos Stan had taken: his son's birth announcement, with Etan lying in Julie's arms, her eyes closed. His birthday party—the six-year-old smiling widely, hugging his mother tight. The last photo Stan had taken of Etan, looking serious and thoughtful. These were some of the same masterful photos handed out back in 1979, the ones that had made everyone care. They said more about Etan and what his family had lost than words ever could.

Afterwards, Stan and his attorneys walked out of the majestic New York Supreme Court building through the central front door, passing between the Roman columns and under George Washington's words engraved into the granite façade: "The true administration of justice is the firmest pillar of good government."

The three men started down the expanse of the hundred-foot-wide steps, en route back to Brian O'Dwyer's office. But Sheryl Crow was in court that day as well, testifying against an alleged stalker, and photographers were out in full force. When they saw Stan, they peeled off from their rock star stakeout to join the reporters already covering the inquest. It wasn't a full-on press swarm, more an organic gathering, as one after the other reporters and photographers joined the migration, sprinting up the steps to meet Stan and his legal team halfway.

"This represents to the family very incomplete justice," Brian O'Dwyer told reporters, as Stan stood quietly next to him.

It was something, Stan reminded himself. Something was more than the nothing of the last twenty-five years. It would sustain him until the next little something. And as he took questions, Stan felt resignation, but not despair.

Hands stretched out, extending tape recorders, pens jotted his words into spiral reporters' notebooks. Stan, out of empathy for the line of photographers, varied the angle of his face, as once again he chose his words carefully. Even though he was no longer making his case in court, he knew that at this stage the court of public opinion weighed more heavily than any other. He told reporters he was grateful that Ramos would never be able to profit from Etan's death, and called on the District Attorney's Office to mount a criminal prosecution. This wasn't about closure, he said. That would never happen, and he didn't harbor such false hopes.

"But now I know what this man did," he told a reporter, "and he should not be allowed to get away with it."

———

When Stuart GraBois dropped Stan off at the loft later, Julie was already home, and he was happy to see that she was talking to him, with no sign of rancor over the day's events. She was too excited about another news item that day. An article in the *New York Daily News*, "From Under the Bridge to On Top of the World," was about two brand-new Rhodes Scholars, New Yorkers who had overcome all odds as Russian immigrants. One boy had for a time even been homeless. But there were "guardian angels" over the years, Lev Sviridov told the reporter, people without whom he would surely not have made his way off the streets. He cited one, the woman who ran his middle school office.

Lev and his mother, Alexandra Sviridova, a prominent investigative journalist, had arrived in New York from Moscow in April 1993 on a visitor's visa. Lev's mother spoke at universities in both the United States and Canada, and planned to return to Russia in the fall. But Boris Yeltsin made that impossible when in October, on the very day the Sviridovs were booked to fly home, the Russian president sent tanks into the Moscow streets to fire on the parliament building and beat back public protests. In the weeks of ensuing chaos, Lev and his mother were stranded, their visas expired, their passports useless. They were suddenly illegal immigrants, staying with friends and on some nights homeless. For the rest of the year, Lev watched other children go to school, while he and his mother walked the streets, desperately trying to sort out their identity crisis. Alexandra Sviridova appealed to office after office where bureaucrats shuffled their now invalid papers around. At one point, an official shook his head at Lev.

"In America, kids his age have to be in school. You can't keep him with you all day," he told Sviridova. She was in a panic. What if on top of losing her home, her livelihood, and her identity, she lost her son too? She couldn't bear the thought. She heard about a middle school that might take Lev even though he'd already missed half the year and struggled to speak English. Armed only with a testimonial letter from an NYU contact, the first day after the Christmas break the two went to meet with the school's principal. Both Lev and his mother felt terrified and out of their element, when a small woman with a warm smile came toward them to say hello.

But Alexandra Sviridova didn't notice the smile on Julie Patz's lips as much as the expression in her eyes. She'd seen such eyes in Russia all the time, but never in the United States. In Russia, she would tell Lev, the people have no life but they have a history. Here they have lives, but no history. Americans were happier, maybe, but their eyes were blank.

Not this woman, she thought. Her eyes had layers, thick and deep, as if they had been painted by Sviridova's favorite artist, Titian, with fine, almost transparent brushstrokes, one on top of the other. She didn't know who this woman was, or her history, but she knew there was one. Sviridova was overwhelmed by her frustration and fear, and she could barely speak. In Russian, she directed Lev to ask for help with the letter that she now held out for Julie.

"Can your mother speak any English?" Julie asked Lev, then turned to Sviridova. "What's your name?"

Alexandra fumbled for words, wishing her English wasn't so limited.

"Please," she begged. "I am nobody. I have no name, no profession, nothing. I am just mama now. I am garbage from street. But I want my son to go to school. Can you help us?"

Tears welled in Julie's eyes, as she went to the earnest-looking eleven-year-old and hugged him. She continued speaking to him but looked back at Alexandra. "Tell your mother that she's not a nobody. She's an immigrant in a country filled with immigrants who came here with nothing, just like her. She'll be somebody very soon, and even now she's not a nobody. She's a mother."

Now Alexandra Sviridova was weeping openly. The two women stood with the boy between them. He could understand that something important was happening, even if he didn't know quite what.

Julie took the piece of paper from Sviridova's hand and examined it.

"This isn't going to help you," she said authoritatively. "You'll need to get approval from the Board of Ed." Lev translated as Julie started to explain what to do. They followed her instructions and went immediately to an office some blocks away, where a stern-looking functionary finally signed the necessary paperwork that would require the school to accept Lev. Then the two hurried back, where Julie looked through everything and pronounced them successful, hugging Lev again.

Until then, Sviridova had despaired for Lev's safety in this city, in a whole new reality where they suddenly had so little and were constantly forced to depend on near strangers. But looking at Julie, with her arms wrapped protectively around Lev, Sviridova thought: He is safe with her. She is the first person in this country to whom I can give my baby.

When Julie learned how little they had at home, she convinced Sviridova to let Lev stay at school long after hours, eating an extra meal there, doing his homework, meeting new friends at afterschool activities, until his mother could come collect him. When Julie cobbled together her improvised library, Lev was her first librarian, a proud member of the "library squad" who posed with her in the yearbook picture. She was the same height as everyone else in the photo.

Many years later, after Lev won a Rhodes Scholarship, Alexandra Sviridova listened in when the reporter called to interview him. She was outraged to hear her son completely skip over his early immigrant days. He'd been the proud son of a distinguished journalist back in Russia, and he was embarrassed by the rough times that had followed. She broke into the conversation, yelling at him in shrill Russian.

"Liova, you have to talk about the worst days," she scolded him, as he held the receiver close to his chest to mute her words. "If you don't, no one will know about all the people who helped you out of such troubles. That's important. And say their names." She wagged her finger. "You have to make it about real people." So Lev sheepishly did as his mother told him and talked about washing up some mornings in the bus station bathroom under the George Washington Bridge. And he gave the reporter Julie Patz's name. When Sviridova saw Lev's story in the same paper that carried news of Stan Patz's day in court she was stunned. She wasn't particularly religious, but she saw it as a sign that God was watching over them all. For their part, the Patzes savored the family name in print for once in a story about triumph, not tragedy. But Julie was baffled.

"Guardian angel?" She turned to Stan as they scanned the article again. "I just don't get it—all I did was my job. Her English wasn't great, and so I spent a lot of time with them; calmed them down. And treated them the way I was raised to treat people. It was no big deal."

And even though Stan knew what a big deal it really was, he also knew that Julie was telling her true story. Yes, it was also the truth that in one tragic day a pall of grief had descended over both of them, a cloud that could never fully dissipate. Such an event sends some people into a cold, bitter place forever, and there had certainly been frigid days for both Stan and Julie. But Stan always liked to say that in the end, he hadn't changed much from the person he was before Etan's disappearance, that he and Julie were still who they'd been raised to be.

In the years after Etan was lost to them, Stan had witnessed so much proof of the good in man. The accumulation of all those smaller acts of kindness over time had muted Stan and Julie's enormous sense of loss, like the sweet strains of Mozart and J. S. Bach that obscured the ringing in Stan's ears as he worked. He took his small comfort from finally knowing the fate of the child lost to them, always the cruelest part of this long story. But he took much greater comfort in what he had held on to. He thought of Lev Sviridov heading off to Oxford, and the labor-of-love library that had opened so many little minds, and the stories Julie would regale him with of "her kids." Jose Ramos may have tested Stan's faith in humanity, but he hadn't destroyed it. The best and most obvious example was the woman sitting next to him.

He read Lev's section of the article one more time, and the pleasure Julie took from it he felt too, as his own. That was the way of it. Their next anniversary would mark forty years together, and they were still and always partners, who'd looked out for each other in the worst of times and cheered each other on in better. Not that they didn't disagree. Today's court appearance proved that. But the trick, those four decades and the tough moments had taught them, was *tolerating* each other's differences. It had worked up until now, which was good, because Stan wasn't done.

Stu GraBois had already talked to him about a new path to try. A year from now, New York district attorney Robert Morgenthau would sit for reelection, and for the first time in his three-decade reign, he faced a real challenger—a former assistant DA from his own office, who was also a former judge and now partner in a powerful Manhattan law practice. GraBois had known Leslie Crocker Snyder for many years, and at Stan's request he'd arranged for the two of them to meet with her a few weeks from now. If she was willing to study the case and agreed it was worth pursuing, then Stan was willing to study her candidacy and might support her publicly. And if she didn't, well, they'd try something else. The FBI had also told GraBois that they planned to take a fresh look at the case, and Stan knew he'd help in any way he could.

Both men agreed—they had no choice. There was just no way they could stand by as the years passed, until September 2014. When Jose Ramos was released from prison, unless there was a way to stop him, he would slip away as he had done so many times, losing himself among the unguarded, to return to his old ways. Ramos would be seventy-one years old by then, but he had always preyed on the small and weak, who would be defenseless against anyone, no matter their age. It would be nice to think that the passage of time had healed his wounds as well, but in all the years Ramos had been in prison, he'd never completed the treatment that, above all, required he admit to and show remorse for his crimes.

Whatever the two men could do, they had to do it. It was the way they had both been raised.

Coda

Julie Patz gets up at her normal hour, sometime after 4:00 a.m. It is two hours before sunrise, but over the years she's gotten into the habit of savoring this early time to herself. She will trade it off at the other end of the day, sometimes asleep by seven, before the late spring sun has even set. Today, she pulls a short, lightweight shift over her still lithe form, in preparation for the sweltering heat of an un-air-conditioned public school, but adds a sweater in deference to the cool, drizzly night skies outside her window now. Then she ties her straight brown hair—liberally streaked with gray—into her usual tidy ponytail, leaves her husband sleeping, and heads into the kitchen to look over his lunch choices for the day.

Once every few weeks, Julie cooks up a big pot of beef stew, or a casserole of bacon-laced meatballs, or her specialty, adapted from an old recipe of Stan's mother's—steak in wine sauce. She herself eats at her desk most days, take-out from the local deli or fast-food Chinese. But it's a point of pride to Julie that Stan eats her home cooking. She freezes her dishes in separate single portions, then he picks one out every morning to defrost. Around four o'clock he will heat it up for the late afternoon lunch that has remained his custom. Often he waits for Julie to get home, and she serves it to him on the black matte stoneware that complements the larger white plate she might place underneath. Left alone, he'll just eat from the container, but Julie's careful presentation always adds to the dish and the accoutrements she brings with it—a side tray of olives swimming in their own oil, a row of small bowls filled with different-flavored coarsely ground salts. Sometimes she sits with Stan as he eats and shares her day.

This morning she gets to her desk near the principal's office at around six and settles in to another quiet hour or two of steady work, preparing for her day without distractions. No gum-popping thirteen-year-olds clamoring for late passes. No recalcitrant class-cutters serving penance on the chairs beside her.

When May 25 hits on a weekend, she and Stan usually spend it in solitude at a rustic church camp a few hours outside the city. This year it falls on a Wednesday, right in the middle of the school week. This year, the judge in the civil suit has ruled on the damages, awarding two million non-existent dollars to Etan's parents. All that means to Julie is more headlines, more gawking. This morning she braces herself for the inevitable—that some youngster will have spread the word about the anniversary, conjuring up the stares she'll have to ignore, or the tearful child she'll have to assuage. But otherwise she'll proceed like it's an average school day. Just like every year.

————

Stan hears her slide back the heavy track-mounted front door to the loft that afternoon, just as he's breaking out the food she's left him for lunch. She's carrying a rolled up tubelike sheaf of art posters, and she is beaming. She unrolls the heavy papers and spreads them on the worn maple planks of Stan's studio space. "Look what my kids did!" she tells him. She is practically breathless with glee. She recounts to Stan how two twelve-year-old girls had read about Etan online, then Googled the details. One student told a few of her friends. But instead of the sorrowfully averted gazes that always made Julie feel so uncomfortable, the girls wheedled time from their teachers, and everyone in school spent a class constructing two-foot greeting cards.

And that's how 250 or so inner-city kids have made Julie a new kind of poster, filling all the white space with their love for her.

Stan Patz struggles to make out the slanted, adolescent handwriting:

"Thanks for making us feel so safe."

"Thanks for being so patient when I lose my metrocard."

Julie circles the posters, nudging them with her stocking feet, pushing them apart to reveal more words. "These," she says in wonder, "are the perks."

She reads out loud to her husband. Her eyes are shiny, but there are no tears.

"You always make me feel good when I'm feeling bad."

"Thank you for covering my back all those times I did stupid shit."

"You are the mother of the school."

Finally her face gets damp. She holds up a poster for Stan to get a closer look at one particular message:

"You've been nice to me since the first day of school. How come? No one likes me."

Julie shakes her head. "I can't even think who this kid is." She gives a small laugh. "But he's my next project."

Acknowledgments

Over the last five years and, really, much earlier than that, a lot of people have given me a hand...or a push...or a boot, advancing me along on my maiden voyage. There are far too many to name here, but I'm going to try.

First and foremost, my undying gratitude goes to Stuart GraBois; my collaborator, my consultant, my cheerleader, and my inspiration. He always kept going, and he inspired me to do the same.

And to Stan Patz, invaluable for everything from information and insight, from fact checking to photography, from encouragement to empathy on any given day. To Julie Patz, who is such a hero of mine, and Mary Galligan, who embodies girl power in this story. Thanks to Ari Patz, Lisa Helms, Kitty Brown, Bill Sillery, Denise Cealie, and so many others who lived through this and gave their time and thoughts. As I struggled to sift through thirty years of memories, I want to thank all those who added research and legal background; journalists like John Miller, Joanne Wasserman, Anna Quindlen, Richard Rein, David Blum, and Jerry Schmetterer; legal and investigative experts like Brian O'Dwyer, Jim Nauwens, Frank Carroll, Alicia Tejada, Patrick Eanniello, Owen Carrugher, Ian Weinstein, and Ken Javerbaum. My gratitude to the many folks at the New York FBI public information office who helped facilitate interviews: Jim Margolin, Christine Monaco, and Monica McLean. Thanks to Jack Allar, Paul Ott, Marylou Barton, Joe Massa, Gene Casasanta, Blaine Kuhn, Tim Reitz, Chris Braun, John Bowler, Carla Breen, Amazing Dave, Garrick Beck, and Joanee Freedom for adding to my reporting on events that took place out of New York City. Thanks to Bonnie GraBois for everything.

I'm grateful to those who put the broadcast stories on the air that led to this book, both at ABC and CBS News. From ABC days, thanks to Rick Kaplan, Betsy West, Jay Schadler, Ray Lambiase, John Landi, Mark French, and Alison Hockenberry. At CBS, thanks to Jeff Fager, Patti Hassler, Mike Whitney, Vicki Mabrey, Rich Koppel, Elizabeth Pearson, and Sean Herbert. Thanks to Carole Cooper for her savvy and support.

I'm also grateful to those in the publishing world who led me along. At Grand Central Publishing, thanks to publisher Jamie Raab and to Amy Einhorn for having faith in a first-timer, Deb Futter, and my editor, Mitch Hoffman, whose guidance, encouragement, and calm voice were especially appreciated. Thanks to the gracious Jimmy Franco, publicist extraordinaire, to Joe Finnerty, and to the tireless Kim Hoffman. My thanks also to Deborah Brodie, who helped at a critical moment, with some well-placed words of wisdom. Special thanks to my favorite literary midwife, my agent, Alice Martell.

There were so many who weren't part of the case but instead part of a circle of unflagging friendship. The producergirrrls: Nicole, Molly, Sarah, Shelagh, and Jeanmarie. Thanks to Marjorie, Trish, Beth, Rita, Terri, Kim, Suzanne, Julie H., Karyn, Rob and Christine, Ben and Antonia, Gwyn and Les, Barbara, Nikki, Deloris, Tom, Debbie H., Ben S., Jillian, and Amanda, who pointed me to the invaluable peer support of a writer's workshop. With Charles in charge, along with the two other Lisas and the two Sallys; Vivian, Chaya, Ovie, Craig, Betty, Leslie, Paul, Margaret, Sharon, Marilyn, Patty, Kristine, Judy, Julie, Ellen, and Patricia—you gave me safe haven. Thanks to the Humanities Council at Princeton University and the Graduate School of Journalism at Columbia who offered me refuge. Thanks to chemo-babe Dee Dee, who both inspired me and gave extra-special support. Thanks to Gordon and Tania, who got me inside, and to Christine P., who got me online.

Thanks to my big brother, who's an expert in compassion. And my deepest gratitude to my parents, who always make me want to act the way I was raised.

Special thanks to my family, who were there all along the way, even though so much of the time I wasn't.

And finally, to Jeca Taudte, my reader, researcher, organizer, editor, muse, sympathetic ear, cajoler and caregiver, midnight oil-burner and shrink. Thank goodness. Thank you.

Index

(cont.)

(cont.)